MW01247471

My Way
of Looking
at It

An Autobiography

Second Edition:
Revised and Expanded

William Van Til

i

MY WAY OF LOOKING AT IT
AN AUTOBIOGRAPHY

Second Edition: Revised and Expanded

By William Van Til

Copyright 1996 by William Van Til

Second Edition: Revised and Expanded 1996
Published by Caddo Gap Press
   3145 Geary Boulevard, Suite 275
   San Francisco, California 94118

First Edition 1983
Published by Lake Lure Press

ISBN 1-880192-17-9

Price $29.95

Library of Congress Cataloging-in-Publication Data

Van Til, William.
    My way of looking at it : an autobiography / William Van Til. --
2nd ed., rev. and expanded.
        p.   cm.
    Includes bibliographical references and index.
    ISBN 1-880192-17-9
    1. Van Til, William. 2. Educators--United States--Biography.
I. Title.
LA2317.V36A3 1996
371.1'0092--dc20
[B]   96-24631
                                                              CIP

Dedicated to the human family in general
and to mine in particular.

BY WILLIAM VAN TIL

TRADE BOOKS
The Danube Flows Through Fascism
Foldboat Holidays (contributor)

TEXTBOOKS
Modern Education for the Junior High School Years (collaborator)
Education: A Beginning
Secondary Education: School and Community
Writing for Professional Publication

EL-HI BOOKS
Economic Roads for American Democracy
Time on Your Hands
Education in American Life (co-editor)

ANTHOLOGIES
The High School of the Future (contributor)
Curriculum: Quest for Relevance (editor and contributor)
Honor in Teaching: Reflections (contributor)
Teachers and Mentors (contributor)

UNITS/ MONOGRAPHS
Democracy Demands It (collaborator)
The Work of the Bureau for Intercultural Education
The Development of Education for Desegregation and Integration
Widening Cultural Horizons (collaborator)

BY WILLIAM VAN TIL (CONTINUED)

ENCYCLOPEDIA ENTRIES
Encyclopedia of Educational Research
American Educator

YEARBOOKS (EDITOR)
Democratic Human Relations
Intercultural Attitudes in the Making
Forces Affecting American Education
Issues in Secondary Education
(contributor to eight other yearbooks)

SELECTIONS
The Making of a Modern Educator
One Way of Looking at It
Another Way of Looking at It
Van Til on Education
Sketches

MEMOIRS
My Way of Looking at It: An Autobiography (first edition)
ASCD in Retrospect (editor and contributor)
The John Dewey Society: A Memoir of the Middle Years, 1947-1973

Plus various pamphlets, columns, magazine and journal articles,
and book reviews.

Top left: William Van Til as a child in New York. Middle row: William Van Til (left) and Beatrice Van Til (right) on the Danube, 1937; Bottom left: William Van Til at Ohio State University in the 1930s. Bottom right: William Van Til at Indiana State University in the 1970s.

TABLE OF CONTENTS

Contents (Continued)

Acknowledgments

I have quoted freely from several of my published works in telling this story of my life. I wish therefore to acknowledge again in this edition with thanks a number of permissions granted by copyright holders, as follows:

Charles Scribner's Sons, for several quotations from *The Danube Flows Through Fascism* (copyright 1938, Charles Scribner's Sons; copyright renewed 1966, William Van Til).

Indiana State University, for material taken from "To Walk with Others," *Contemporary Education*, December 1969, pp. 334 & 335. Also, the publishers of *Theory Into Practice*, in which the article appeared simultaneously.

Phi Delta Kappa, for my column "Calcutta: A Vision of the End of the World," *Phi Delta Kappan*, June 1974, pp. 699 & 700, and one portion of my column "Start Your Own Spring Conference," June 1975, p. 713.

Bobbs-Merrill Educational Publishing, for several portions of "We Went to Europe as a Family," from *The Making Of a Modern Educator*, 1961.

I have also included in this expanded edition excerpts from my more recent writing. I thank the following organizations and journals for their publication of my writing during the later 1980s and the 1990s from which I have used excerpts: the Association for Supervision and Curriculum Development (*ASCD in Retrospect*), *Educational Theory* ("The John Dewey Society: a Memoir of the Middle Years, 1947-1973"), *Teaching Education*

("Advice to Young Teacher Educators"), *Educational Forum* ("What I Have Learned"), National Association of Laboratory Schools (*Laboratory Schools and the National Reports*), Kappa Delta Pi (*Honor in Teaching: Reflections*). Thanks also to the gone but not forgotten *Saturday Review* for publishing my much anthologized 1962 article "Is Progressive Education Obsolete?"

Thanks especially to readers of the original manuscript at one or another of its stages of development: Milton Rugoff, Stanley M. Elam, Fred T. Wilhelms, Virgil A. Clift, Mary Anne Raywid, and Glen Hass. Thanks too to Sally Lifland of Lifland *et al* Bookmakers of Williamsport, Pennsylvania, for production of the first edition; to BookCrafters, Inc., of Chelsea, Michigan, for printing the first edition; to Stanley M. Elam for copyediting; and to Ruan Fougerousse for typing.

Thanks to Alan H. Jones of Caddo Gap Press for publishing the revised and expanded second edition. Thanks also to Darrell F. Swarens for technical assistance and Betty Drake for her capable and much appreciated typing.

And, of course, thanks to Bee. You'll see why when you read this book.

Chapter One

THE WORLD
I CAME INTO

William Howard Taft, all 300 plus pounds of him, was President of the United States. Nobody talked or wrote about World War I or World War II or shivered in anticipation of World War III, because up to the time I was born there hadn't ever been a world war. Little wars, yes: the Spanish-American War thirteen years before, the Russo-Japanese War seven years before, and the Turks and Italians were now gearing up for their war (surely everybody remembers that one). Every year revolutions took place in Latin America, crises sputtered in the Balkans, or little wars were fought here and there. But nobody paid much attention to them.

In 1910, the year before I was born, people paid more attention to the search for a Great White Hope, because a black man named Jack Johnson had just retained the heavyweight world championship by beating a white man, Jim Jeffries. Connie Mack's Philadelphia Athletics had beaten the Chicago Cubs in the World Series despite Tinker to Evers to Chance. Barney Oldfield drove like sixty along Daytona Beach.

An aviator had flown a flying machine 300 miles in little more than eight hours in 1910, and the year before that a French daredevil, Bleriot, had crossed the English Channel in one of the contraptions. In the three years since the first commercially made plane had been produced, five airplanes had been sold to individual buyers.

In the year that my mother was pregnant with me, former President Teddy Roosevelt returned from a trip to Africa and

1

was featured in all the newspapers in his hunting clothes. Leo Tolstoy, Mark Twain, Florence Nightingale, and Julia Ward Howe died. The Manhattan Bridge was completed and the tango became popular. Congress passed the Mann Act against the white-slave traffic and Boy Scouts of America was organized. Stravinsky's *Firebird* ballet shocked Paris and Victor Herbert's operetta *Naughty Marietta* opened in New York. John Galsworthy wrote a play and H. G. Wells wrote another novel. The first permanent waves were given to fashionable women by London hairdressers. In America, nickelodeons set up in empty stores showed moving pictures with piano accompaniment; admission was a nickel or a dime. Marie Curie published *Treatise on Radiography* and J. J. Thomson experimented with magnetic fields. Mad scientists—obviously nothing would come of that. So nobody paid much attention to them. Instead, people worried about whether Halley's Comet on its coming return in the spring of 1910 would destroy the world.

The year I was born they invented the self-starter. If it worked, people would no longer have to crank the motor to get their horseless carriages started. Meanwhile the 181,000 Americans who bought passenger cars and the 6,000 people who bought buses and trucks in 1910 continued to get cricks in their backs from cranking.

By 1911 they hadn't yet invented such creature comforts as air conditioning, instant cameras or instant coffee, cellophane, computers, push-button elevators, laundromats, loud speakers, movies with sound, nylon, radios, electric razors, long-playing records, stainless steel, television, transistors, automatic toasters. They traveled as passengers by railroad trains and trolley cars and ships rather than by airplanes, hydroplanes, helicopters, or rockets. They didn't know about neutrons and protons and isotopes and atomic numbers and spectroscopes and conditioned reflexes. Their scientists had not yet developed atom-smashing theory or cyclotrons or uranium fission or electroshock treatment, and people didn't have such doubtful blessings as depth bombs or military missiles or radar or nuclear weaponry or Geiger counters.

Yes, Virginia, by the time I was born they already **had** the cotton gin. Yes, Virginia, the spinning jenny too. The steamboat also, dear. Maybe more important, they already had birds and flowers and trees and songs and poetry and picnics and sleigh riding and backyards and friends and families.

I was born in 1911. According to the census of 1910, the population of the United States was 91,972,000. Since I was born on January 8, 1911, I may have swelled the population to precisely 92 million. However, I can't prove it. Nobody paid much attention to my arrival except my family. The Wise Men had come and gone. January 8 is not a very good day to be born. Not only is it cold, but after Christmas people don't have much money left for birthday presents. No frankincense or myrrh. Not even a partridge in a pear tree.

If I were Henry Adams, I'd now tell you all about my ancestors: President John Adams, my great-grandfather; President John Quincy Adams, my grandfather; Minister to Great Britain Charles Francis Adams, my father. And to avoid sexism I would throw in my lively great-grandmother, Abigail Adams. But I'm not writing one of the books that influenced me most in my youth, *The Education of Henry Adams*, and I know very little about my ancestors. That's partly because my father once told me, with a twinkle in his eye, that people who trace ancestry often stop when they encounter sheep stealers and horse thieves in the family lineage.

Since my name is Van Til ("You're Dutch, aren't you?" "Not really," I explain), I will begin with Jacob Van Til, my grandfather, and I'll often use words such as "probably." One reason I don't know more about him is my family's Wars over Religion, which I will come to later. Also, old Jacob didn't talk very much.

Jacob Van Til was born somewhere in Holland sometime near the midpoint of the nineteenth century. What do people do in Holland? Among other things, they grow tulips and other flowers. So when Jacob came to New York City as a young man, he settled "out the Island" (a New York City provincialism for Long Island, the huge fish-shaped island that nibbles at Manhattan). He acquired a tract of land, built a greenhouse and, naturally, started a florist business. He built a small, square, two-story frame house and planted lilac trees at the boundaries of his property. I can still smell the perfume of the lilacs as well as the sharp acrid odors of the greenhouses and the funereal smell of the surrounding shrubs and bushes.

Jacob was no John Jacob Astor, but he prospered through hard gardening that rounded his shoulders and stooped his figure. Or maybe it was arthritis, which we then generically called rheumatism. My visual recollection is of a bent-over old man who muttered hybrid Dutch-English through his large and droopy gray-black mustache. He was a kindly though gruff-sounding man. He puttered and repaired about our property and drank coffee in our kitchen even during our Wars over Religion. In his prime, he brought his flowers to "the city" for distribution.

Jacob was tight with money. All the stereotypes applied, including squeezing the nickel until the buffalo bellowed. There's a family legend, probably apocryphal (and I have no intention of trying to authenticate it), that he was a member of what he called "the schul board" and consistently voted against all proposals for spending on schools.

In the New York City area of my childhood, you lived either in what the residents called "the city" or "the country." "The city" was of course Manhattan and it spilled north into the Bronx. "The city" was also the thickly settled part of Brooklyn nearest to Manhattan. "The country" was "up the River" (the Hudson), beyond the Jersey meadows (Indian country?), and "out the Island," which included much of Brooklyn and all of what in time became the counties of Queens, Nassau, and Suffolk. Many people who lived in "the country" did not farm, though they did have vegetable gardens. Some of the people who lived in "the country" went "into the city" to earn their living or to shop at the big stores such as Bloomingdale's and Macy's and Wanamaker's. You didn't "commute," for nobody knew the word; you "went into the city."

When Jacob came to Corona in the Queens area of Long Island, he lived in "the country" about six miles from Manhattan as the crow flies. People aren't crows, however. For their trips into the city, local families walked to the Corona station of the Long Island Railroad about two miles from Jacob's property, then took the train, which made frequent stops, then boarded a ferry at Hunter's Point to cross the East River into Manhattan.

Well along in Jacob's lifetime, which stretched from the 1850s to the 1930s, "the city" took over his "country." In 1909, two years before I was born, a splendid bridge, the Queensboro, crossed the East River and linked Long Island to Manhattan. In 1910, the Long Island Railroad burrowed under the East River. Trolley cars ran along Jackson Avenue, later to be renamed Northern Boulevard, one block north of Jacob's property, then bobbed on across the wonderful bridge to the city. People began buying automobiles. The New York City subway system was extended to Corona. So canny Jacob began to sell pieces of his property in the teens and twenties of the century. The fragrant lilac trees went down and two-story frame houses went up. The greenhouses vanished, but the little square house and a small garden persisted. He lived in it until he died in 1935.

In the New World, during the 1870s, Jacob had married an Irish girl. Her first name was Maria, pronounced in the Irish way (Muh-*rye*-a), not Spanish, and her last name was Mitchell. When she came to America and how they met I don't know. Maria had worked as a servant before she married Jacob.

Jacob and Maria lived a block and a half from the house in which I was born and brought up, the house from which I went to elementary school, high school, and college. In the approximately twenty years that stretched between my birth and the death of my grandmother, I visited her in her home around the corner no more than twenty times, probably fewer. To the best of my knowledge, she never entered my house except at the time of my father's death.

Maria Mitchell was a devout Irish Catholic. She would not compromise on the doctrinal observances of Catholic orthodoxy. Jacob Van Til practiced a Dutch variety of Protestantism. To marry Maria, Jacob became a Catholic. He embraced his new faith zealously. Maria and Jacob went to church regularly. They had three Catholic children, Loretta, William Joseph (my father), and Ida.

As an adult, Will (my father's nickname) fell away from the Catholic Church. I don't know why—you didn't talk about such things in those days. You just felt. He remained nominally a Catholic, but he did not attend Mass. He fell in love with my mother, who was non-Catholic. She came from a Presbyterian background and, as an adult, was not a churchgoer. My father and mother were married in a Protestant church.

My Irish grandmother refused to go to her son's wedding. She refused to recognize his wife. She refused to recognize his two children. To attend their Protestant christenings was out of the question. To her, Will's wife and children did not exist. She maintained this position for more than a decade. During that period my sister Florence Josephine was born and, six years later, I was born.

My father sometimes walked around the corner to see his parents. I have no idea what they talked about, for he always went alone. I don't know what conflicts accompanied the visits.

After some years, he achieved an unsatisfactory, half-hearted family reconciliation. When I was a little child, I was dressed in formal clothes by my mother and walked with her around the corner to visit my grandmother. My grandmother sat in her parlor. The conversation between mother-in-law and daughter-in-law was stiff and awkward. I escaped from the parlor as soon as I could and hung around with my grandfather in the greenhouses and the garden. My mother cried when we got home, and not because I got dirty. Then she talked a little. I took her side; it was the only side I knew. When, as a child, I wanted to show my mother some temporary hostility I would say that I was really Irish. I never mentioned my Irish grandmother. But my mother understood what I implied.

As I grew toward adulthood and as my grandmother grew much older, I visited her a few times, largely at my mother's urging. We tried to communicate, despite the gap of age differences, the Wars over Religion, and decades of separation. We succeeded only partially. When she died, I didn't go to her funeral.

Old wounds sometimes can't heal. Better than most people, I can understand today's troubles in Ireland.

The nearest I can come to a distinguished ancestor is my great-grandfather on my mother's side of the family. I owe my knowledge of him to my cultured cousins, the MacLeans, who took family trees seriously, unlike my father, who welcomed any bawdy reference MacLean research might uncover. My father particularly enjoyed learning that my distinguished ancestor lived in Ramsbottom.

The Reverend Andrew McLean—for so his biographer spelled

the family name—was moderator of the Lancashire Scottish Church Presbytery in Dundee, Scotland, in 1833; moderator of the Presbytery of Lancashire in 1858; and moderator of the 27th Synod of the Presbyterian Church in England in 1863. The red granite obelisk in Old Dundee Churchyard bears the following inscription: "Andrew McLean, D. D., 40 years minister of the Presbyterian Congregation, Ramsbottom. Born at Glasgow, 1st January, 1799. Died at Barwood Mount, October 22, 1869. 'I have lived in the faith of the Gospel.' 'Precious in the sight of the Lord is the death of His saints.'"

The Rev. Andrew was the son of Malcolm MacLean, a prosperous cloth lapper. Andrew was educated at a parochial school—not Roman Catholic, you can be sure—and matriculated at the University of Glasgow "at the absurdly early age of 13 years, taking his degree when 19 years old. He was already attending the Divinity Classes and was a Prizeman in Hebrew." Apparently young Andy was a prodigy. He became a Sabbath School instructor in the Glasgow School of Industry, an institution for girls. At age 31 he became minister of the Dundee Chapel, Ramsbottom.

A prosperous elder of his congregation, William Grant, Justice of the Peace, promptly built a new church for the communicants. (Grant was reported to be one of the Cheeryble brothers of Charles Dickens's 1839 novel *Nicholas Nickleby*.) When he was 38 the Rev. Andrew McLean married Grant's niece, Elizabeth Grant, my great-grandmother, thus knitting "more closely the relations between the two families." "A man of cultivated tastes, especially in natural history, his [Andrew's] collections relating to the antiquities, geology and fauna of the locality grew to such proportions that the Grant family gave him the use for the rest of his life of the spacious Barwood House, where he had ample room to accommodate them." The house became "the centre of culture and improvement of the Ramsbottom people." He became a recognized leader of the Scottish Presbytery of Lancashire and in the English Synod.

During eleven years of marriage to Rev. McLean, my great-grandmother bore him three children, including my grandfather. Then she "died on April 16, 1848, age 39 years, and with her still-born child was interred." Twelve years later, in 1860, the

7

Rev. Andrew McLean remarried. In 1866, when she was 45 and he was 67, his wife Jane presented him with a son.

When Dr. McLean was in is early sixties he was required by "the Episcopalian heir of the Grant Estates to quit the house that had been his home since 1837, when he married William Grant's niece, and when it had been given to them for life." The Rev. McLean "suffered much mental distress." He broke up his natural history collection. "The only house he could secure was a small damp house at the gable end of a mill two miles away....The climax came in August 1869, when Dr. McLean and his people were given notice to quit their Church, their persecutor having discovered that his uncle had neglected to complete his gift by vesting it in trustees." During the proceedings that ensued, Dr. Grant was "struck down with fatal results." He died at age 70. My family's Wars over Religion were foreshadowed.

Though he may have been loved and honored by the villagers, the Rev. Andrew McLean seems to have encountered problems in his role as a father. The dourness of the surroundings, the harsh Scottish climate, the limited social life of Ramsbottom, and the splendid natural history collection apparently held few charms for his children. The oldest, Jean, married the Rev. Dr. William McClure, went to live with him in Nassau in the West Indies, and eventually became a nurse in Bellevue Hospital and nurse to a member of the Rockefeller family in New York. The nextborn, William, "went to New Zealand and was lost sight of," as *The Journal of the Presbyterian Historical Society of England*, May 1938, from which all of these quotes are taken, quaintly puts it. The third-born, my grandfather, named Daniel Grant in honor no doubt both of Rev. Andrew McLean's wife and his Grant family benefactor, became a medical student in Glasgow. Daniel fell in love and married Susannah Rex Perry, my grandmother, who was born in Yarmouth, England. The couple migrated to Canada. Even the child of Rev. McLean's second marriage, born three years before Rev. McLean's death at 70, went to America and became a journalist in Brooklyn.

So let us follow the lives of Daniel Grant MacLean—for so he spelled it—and Susannah Rex Perry, my mother's parents and my grandparents, who married young (he was 23, she was 21) while Daniel was preparing to be a doctor of medicine. It takes little imagination to envision the probable displeasure and distress of father Andrew, the successful Presbyterian cleric, over this impediment to his son's completion of studies for an honorable medical career. Voices must have been raised. The upshot was that the young couple left the British Isles for Canada, where Daniel Grant MacLean followed his next best alternative and became a veterinary surgeon in the Canadian militia. They lived in a little town in Ontario called Gananoque opposite the Thousand Islands of the St. Lawrence River. The marriage was fruitful; within a twelve-year period six children were born to Susannah, in 1871 (this child died before its first birthday), 1873, 1876, 1878, 1880, and 1883—two boys and four girls.

Less than two years after the birth of the last child, tragedy struck. Daniel Grant MacLean, 39 and now well established as a veterinarian, died. As a child I was always embarrassed and ashamed when my mother mentioned how her father died. I had not yet learned that only suicides can determine the way in which they will die and that few people ever die gloriously. Daniel Grant died from the effects of a kick from a horse he was attempting to help back to health. Susannah was left with five little children. At 37, Susannah, homemaker, had no vocation and no income. Relief programs were nonexistent in the 1880s. Family savings must have been minimal. She was an ocean away from her relatives in the land of her birth.

So she gave her one-year-old, christened Violet Elizabeth and called Elsa, to sister-in-law Jean McClure. Nurse Jean welcomed Elsa, for her own only child by Dr. McClure had died in infancy. My mother, Florence Alberta, then age five, was now again the youngest MacLean. A long odyssey of wandering now began for Susannah and her brood: Andrew, 11; Eveline, nine; Edith, six; and little Florence, five. They crossed the border into the United States and moved from town to town through New York and New Jersey. Their stops included Watertown, Elizabeth, Rahway—the names sound like the chant of a train caller. Susannah did whatever work she could. She worked as a "practical nurse." She tried to start a small dry goods store. It failed. The children shifted from school to school. Andrew went to work as soon as anyone would employ a boy so young. The girls went to work as soon as they were old enough.

Somehow they survived.

The three girls got married within eight months of each other in 1902 and 1903. I hope Susannah, a true Mother Courage, danced at the weddings. The last wedding was that of my mother, on August 7, 1903. But Susannah may not have danced. Susannah Rex Perry MacLean died of cancer two and a half years later, which was almost five years before I was born. Rex is a name used by royalty. It fits Susannah.

Chapter Two

THE HOUSE
I LIVED IN

I was born in the front bedroom of the house in which I would live until a year after my college graduation. In the early twentieth century you didn't go to hospitals to be born; you went unwillingly to hospitals to die. When you were born, the doctor came to your house; in this case the doctor was a general practitioner who lived "down in the village" about a mile away. "Down" indicated southward, for when we went swimming we went "up" to Flushing Bay, a mile to the north. The doctor was called Dr. Dowdy by everybody, though I suspect his name was written Daugherty. In my family we **called** things, we didn't **write** them. Of course the doctor made house calls. All doctors did, except for fancy specialists in the city on fashionable Park Avenue. There was a "nurse" too (probably a midwife) named Mrs. Danker, of German background. She came around for a while after my birth, for I was a big baby and, while aborning, gave my 30-year-old mother some trouble.

Mrs. Danker was responsible for my nickname, "Umpy." When I became an adolescent, I managed by insistence and repetition to transfer the nickname back to my mother, who became lovingly known to my own wife and children as Umpy. It's particularly useful to your recently acquired spouse to have a nickname for the in-laws, because it avoids the necessity of the father-in-law and mother-in-law going nameless or being addressed as "Uh..." prior to being called Grandma or Grandpa.

One of the many reasons why I never became President of the United States is that I was not born in a politically fashionable log cabin as was my presidential idol, Honest Abe. My house in Corona Long Island—we usually spoke of Corona that way without recourse to a comma—was a two-story frame house topped by a blessed attic under a peaked roof. Incidentally, one explanation of why some young people don't amount to much these days is that modern houses don't have big attics for children to retreat to for total privacy, particularly attics sealed off from the world by a second-floor trap door and reachable only by a ladder generally avoided by adults.

Our house was important to my mother and father. To my mother, Florence Alberta MacLean, newly become Florence A. Van Til, it symbolized the end of wandering through the dreary low-income neighborhoods of upstate and Jersey towns. The Susannah MacLean clan eventually had reached the New York City area. They lived in Brooklyn during the Great Blizzard of 1888, and my mother remembers how her brother Andrew, at age 14, went out into the storm to bring food home for the family. The MacLeans also lived on Mott Avenue (not Mott Street, my mother explained to me, since Mott Street was in Chinatown where they had opium dens, white slaves, and tong wars, and the family hadn't come to **that**!). At 16, she left school and went to work. A sixteenth birthday had great meaning in low-income families of the late nineteenth century, a child could then be legally employed and no longer had to lie about age to the boss. Florence worked at whatever minor clerical and shipping jobs were open to an unskilled worker.

Formal studio pictures taken before her marriage show that my mother had fair skin, good features and complexion, an attractive full body, and masses of hair which she wore piled high on her head. She was a popular young woman who had many dates and escorts. Her suitors gave her rings and pins, including a gold ring with a small diamond that she proudly kept till her death at 93. When, at 23, she married my father on August 7, 1903, the young couple lived in a small apartment on Thirty-Seventh Street near but definitely not **on** Fifth Avenue in Manhattan. My sister Flo was born a year and a half later. When the baby was six weeks old the family moved to the Corona house, which had been built during the year 1904. They occupied their house in late January 1905, just before my mother's twenty-fifth birthday. Home at last. An end to wandering. She lived in her house for fifty-seven years until, at age 82, she couldn't get about independently anymore. Then after having fought the move every step of the way, she came to live with my family.

The house was important to my father too. It symbolized that he was getting somewhere in life on his own. William Joseph Van Til was born on May 23, 1878, almost two years before my mother. He had lived most of his life in the home of Dutch Jacob and Irish Maria, had attended elementary school in Queens, and had gone to work young. Though Jacob was frugal—perhaps **because** Jacob was frugal—Will always knew where his next meal was coming from, as the colloquialism of the time put it. Jacob's life-style and the expectations of the times did not include a high school education for the children. Yet, unlike my mother, who read little, my father read some of the classics. As a child, I found such authors as Thoreau and Emerson in the attic along with some histories. Will grew to be almost a six-footer, tall for his generation. He was thin, sharp-featured, and quite handsome, though he made fun of his own looks. He was humorous, generous, and loving.

During the years when he met and courted my mother, my father worked as a shipping clerk and as a timekeeper for a popular humor magazine, *Judge*. My mother worked in the Judge Building too, and so they met. Up in our attic, I found complete files of *Judge* and *Leslie's Weekly*, the *Time/Newsweek* of the turn of the century. As a child, I pored over their magnificent cartoons and drawings of the Spanish-American War and the early Progressive Era. With despair, I must report that after I left home my mother and my sister threw junk out of the attic, and it included stacks of these precious—even priceless—magazines, all in mint condition.

My mother was quiet and even-tempered. She accepted people as they were. A kind woman, she almost never spoke harshly to or of anybody. For wisdom, she relied on proverbs that reflected her work ethic world view: "Waste not, want not." "A stitch in time saves nine." "Never put off till tomorrow what you can do today." To ease my childhood worries about tests and teachers, bullies and baseball, she told me over and over the tale of the old lady who constantly worried before coming to the

13

bridge. The old lady was sure it would be down. Of course upon her arrival she found it in place, so "Don't cross the bridge till you come to it." Yet I would come home at the end of a school year, full of dread of the future, and announce, "I've got Miss Peterson next year," as though this were a case of terminal smallpox. When I contracted actual childhood diseases—measles, mumps, chicken pox, and a bout with scarlet fever that left me with a weak left eye—she patiently nursed me through. She lived for her family; no alternative life-style ever seemed to cross her mind. Will and Flo and Billy, who could do no wrong, plus a few tradesmen, relatives, and neighbors, constituted her universe. At the center was her cherished Corona home.

Soon after his marriage, my father became a steamfitter and worked for a construction company that built skyscrapers. To become a union man in the building trades, a member of the American Federation of Labor; to regularly work for a major construction firm, the Thompson-Starrett Company; to put in the heating system in one building and then be assigned to another site were for him distinct steps up in the world, both socially and financially. Consequently, a year after his marriage he began to build the Corona house in the middle of two lots so that he would always have space around the residence.

He supervised the building of the house every step of the way, and on weekends he himself worked on the construction. He and his father could certify to the qualifications of every man who worked on the house. He also had the help of his new friends in the building trades. So the lumber for siding and the shingles for the roof and the flooring for the rooms were carefully selected. The best 1904 had to offer went into the fixtures, including gas lamps in the upper hall and the two bedrooms, copper leaders and gutters to carry off rains, a kitchen with running water, and a bathroom with an authentic flush toilet. No outhouse for Will's house; in the attic the water in the little box filled with Rube Goldberg gadgets regularly rose and fell at the bidding of any chainpuller in the bathroom below. "Don't pull it too hard, Billy." The big stove in the cellar had a wide door into which my family shoveled rock-size hard coal from the coal bin. The radiators that emitted steam heat throughout the house were, needless to say, classics. In winter when my father came shivering in after a day on the job and a walk through the snow, the first place he would head toward was a radiator. There the master steamfitter sat like a king on his throne until he thawed.

The house contained five rooms and bath, though it seemed larger to me than William Randolph Hearst's San Simeon. You went up a front stoop of five steps to a porch that ran along the front of the house. Through a heavy wooden door, you entered a small hall with a forest of hangers awaiting your outdoor clothes. Then, with the aid of a banister, you could climb a straight flight of stairs to the two bedrooms and bath. You could slide down the banister impeded only by the large ball polished by many hands at the end of the balustrade or by your parent's strong vocal disapproval. Or you could proceed along the hall straight ahead into the dining room, with its heavy round table into which an incredible number of boards could be fitted when relatives came for dinner.

In theory it was possible to open the door off the hall to the right and enter the parlor. In practice you never did this, for the parlor was not a living room. In fact, the parlor was not a room for living—the parlor was for company only. The door from the hall remained shut, as did the two doors that slid along on runners and separated the parlor from the dining room. In the parlor stood the best furniture: a couch, a massive sideboard, a side table, uncomfortable upholstered chairs, and a large painting of Paul and Virginia fleeing through a storm. Virginia was clad in what appeared to me to be gauze; she must have been engaged in some nocturnal activity when rudely surprised by the storm. I don't remember what Paul wore, because I looked mostly at Virginia.

The house was built in open fields. There were daisies on one side and buttercups on the other side. My grandparents' home was about a tenth of a mile away, one of the two or three houses on a large oblong block of land. Jacob had not yet begun to sell off lots to other than family members, Will and his sister Ida.

A rutted dirt road ran in front of our house; to hoots of "get a horse," automobiles were pulled out of the mud by reliable quadrupeds. This excuse for a road was grandiloquently called Prometcha Avenue. When I rode my tricycle in front of the house, going back and forth on the little sidewalk that went nowhere and connected with nothing, I always thought Prometcha was the name of a beautiful Indian maiden—however, don't count on it. As the years went by, my father made improvements in the house. First, the front porch was enclosed, and a seasonal ritual took place that any ancient Druid might have envied for its regularity. Each fall my father took down the screen frames and replaced them with seven heavy slabs of glass and wood; each spring these windows were taken down in turn and replaced by the screens.

The house itself grew larger. A large kitchen, containing a gas stove, a kitchen sink with a wash tub, closet space, and a kitchen table, took the place of the original small kitchen. The new kitchen and the expanded dining room were our center of family living, though the parlor gradually evolved toward becoming a true living room. On the second floor atop the new kitchen, a bedroom of her own rewarded my sister for becoming adolescent and emancipated her from sharing a bedroom with a brother six years younger; I became the lord and master of my own bedroom at the top of the staircase. The motor age arrived and a wooden garage was built, complete even to a hoop for shooting baskets.

As I grew up in my house, "the city" remorselessly moved in on "the country." The open fields of daisies and buttercups were replaced by two-story frame and brick houses, cheek by jowl on single lots. We acquired next-door neighbors, the Romars and the Dowells and the Dotschers. Sewers replaced cesspools; sidewalks were laid; roads were paved; even the mysteriously named Prometcha Avenue became Fillmore Avenue in honor of one of our least distinguished presidents. During my youth, the ultimate in urban depersonalization blighted our address, when Forty-Four Fillmore (which at least had the virtue of doggerel poesy) became 100-11 Thirty-Fifth Avenue; Millard no doubt turned over in his forgotten grave.

In the 1920s our urbanization was crowned by the razing of the old Campbell house at the eastern edge of our property and the construction of a massive five-story apartment. Its rump, pimply with fire escapes, loomed over our land, cut off our sunlight, and bathed us in the sounds of discordant radios and family quarrels. Our house, now dwarfed and hemmed in, looked for all the world like the stage set of Arthur Miller's *Death of a Salesman*.

As the city steadily encroached, our house feebly adapted to urbanization. The hedges, which formerly served as handsome property boundaries, were replaced by ugly wire fences to discourage vandalism and keep out discarded newspapers blowing in the wind. The heavy porch windows stayed in place both summer and winter. Bolts, chains, and heavy spring locks appeared on our doors. A two-car metal garage was built for rental to apartment dwellers; the tinny structure covered much of the former vegetable patch.

My father would have resisted these desecrations of the house of which he was so proud. But he died when I was 15. His property began its downhill slide. Still, each spring the forsythia flamed and the magnolia tree he had planted became briefly a mass of pink and white defying urbanization. He would have liked that. One spring, almost a half century after his death, each mourner dropped magnolias in full flower onto my mother's coffin. Whenever I see magnolias, I think of both of them and of their love for each other and for Flo and me.

Chapter Three

GROWING UP
IN CORONA

T here is a kind of autobiographer whom I admire but cannot emulate: the autobiographer with total recall. Bright childhood sayings are remembered; names come trippingly to tongue; conversations are recorded verbatim; details are meticulously rendered. Such a biographer, blessed or cursed with camera-ready memory, I am not. Years telescope. Things blur. I am an unreliable witness—so be forewarned. Yet who can contradict me, particularly when I write of my childhood? As Longfellow put it in "Paul Revere's Ride," "Hardly a man is now alive who remembers that famous day and year."

In her old age, my mother reported that as a baby and a child I was "good as gold" and that she "never lost a single night's sleep with me," a judgment that draws derisive hoots and groans from my children. I tell them that I attribute their disbelief to envy of a perfection they did not inherit. Grudgingly, I will admit that in her later years my mother's memory may have declined.

The old photograph albums testify that I was a healthy-looking baby with golden curls and a ready smile. They usually show me clutching my sister's hand across the six-year age gap between us or perched on my mother's lap, the beginning of a dependence on women that has accompanied me throughout life. The albums picture me as a child dressed in baggy rompers or in droopy, blousey shirts that reached well below my behind. My garb frequently reflected the times. At age two I wore Rough Rider clothes while Teddy himself was running as the Bull Moose Party candidate, bent on returning to the White House. At six I was photographed in a khaki army uniform with a flag upon my shoulder, apparently testifying to my undying opposition to Kaiser Wilhelm and the hated Huns. At seven I was decked out in an Indian suit, including headband with feathers, and carried a warlike *papier-mâché* hatchet. The costume was an outgrowth of seeing William S. Hart and his horse Paint in Westerns at the local movie house. My parents seemed remarkably able to buy clothes for their children. My sister Flo constantly sported new dresses in her photographs and wore velvet coats with giant buttons and floppy face-shading hats.

The building construction industry prospered in the World War I era and steamfitter Will prospered with it. Figuratively and literally, he reached the heights in 1913 when he worked as steamfitter foreman on the tallest building in the world, the Woolworth Building. When I was a child he took me once to the top floor of the building he was working on (the Municipal Building, I think) and pointed out the Woolworth Tower. He said to me with pride, "Billy, your father put the heating system into that building."

World War I meant regular employment for the building trades worker, supplemented by substantial overtime at time-and-a-half or double-time. My father became a steamfitter foreman in the early teens of the century, thereby leaving the working class for the lower middle class. But he never forsook his loyalty to the steamfitters' union and the Democratic Party. His pay envelope, which he brought home regularly each week (Will was a steady man), grew plumper. After the war he bought an automobile, a fine old Buick with giant wheels, a vertical windshield, and no side windows whatsoever. I frequently posed in my best Sunday suit behind the high steering wheel.

I must have been happy as a child; I was frequently pictured smiling. But I had unphotographed moments of terror too. My parents bought me the customary childhood gadgets, and some of them stand out in my memory because they were related to dramatic, even traumatic, events in my young life. I remember my roly-poly, a clown figure that rocked on its weighted round bottom. One day in the dead of winter when I was three, I used it to break the dining room window, climb out, and slide down the cellar door amid shattered glass and several inches of snow so that, clutching the roly-poly, I could flee in my bare feet through the high snow to our neighbor's house. My mother had left me alone in our house because of some household emergency or essential purchase. Amid the eerie emptiness, I had panicked. She came home to a vacant house, a missing child, a broken window, and a trail through the snow that led her to the Dowells' house. She never left me alone again.

I remember too my first three-wheeler. I recall my first ride even more vividly than my later joys of racing along the sidewalk, which now stretched from our house to the corner. On that first ride the Dowells' big, savage-barking dog pursued me as I pedaled madly to escape. I can still hear his ferocious barking and feel the fear. He wasn't a good dog like our mongrel Prince or airedale Boy or poodle Henry (named after Flo's piano teacher).

Naturally, there are unblemished memories too, like the wind-up trains from Santa Claus, with tracks and cars and stations; the absolute necessity that the Xmas tree, whether it stood in the dining room, parlor, or porch, precisely touch the ceiling; the beloved series of Oz books acquired regularly, thanks to the fertility of author L. Frank Baum. I have many pleasant memories of playing in the yard and in the wonderful dark places in my tent, in the attic, and in the musty-smelling space under our front porch.

One sport of my youth seems to have vanished from the face of the earth. In the stage of life between tricycles and grown-up two-wheelers, kids of my time rolled automobile tires down the streets and bumped them over the curbs. A boy rolling his tire was apparently regarded as a pedestrian, for we used the sidewalks in our pristine version of jogging. Once I trotted alongside my tire all of the way to Woodside, miles away, and boasted of the feat for days.

With wheels, my play horizons widened to include all of Corona and eventually aristocratic Jackson Heights with its new garden apartment buildings and wealthy East Elmhurst with its fine old houses facing Flushing Bay. These seemed very grand neighborhoods to me; actually, they were upper-middle-class areas.

Once, in the late fall, I biked all the way to North Beach, an amusement park that was eventually razed and replaced, first

by North Beach Airport and then by the sprawling LaGuardia
Airport. The North Beach Amusement Park was completely
deserted and deliciously spooky. I wandered for hours in the
shadow of the looming, spectral skeletons of scenic railways, as
roller coasters were then called. I inspected frozen merry-go-
round horses, the Tunnel of Love (through which no water
gurgled), the Whip poised to descend, the boarded-up booths
where wheels of fortune once spun and nauseous pink cotton
candy was once sold. All life was immobilized and suspended. I
shivered with delight.

Before adults acquired their own wheels, as the automobile
made its way downward into the lower strata of society, the
major family excursions of my youth were via public transportation. What an unglamorous name that is for the joy of climbing
aboard a trolley car with open windows and clanking and
clanging through Long Island communities and crossing the
spidery new Queensboro Bridge as the awesome city with its
probing towers came into view! At the end of the bridge the
trolleys dived into a noisome dark hole, then disembarked
passengers who climbed stairs and emerged into the big city at
59th Street. The passengers would disperse and my mother and
I would head for the department store, Bloomingdale's, where
both cheap and costly treasures were on display. Occasionally we
would take the Third Avenue L downtown and walk across to
Macy's, way down at 34th Street, or venture even further south
to Wanamaker's or Hearns'. Then we returned to the lair where
the trolleys reversed direction and regrouped for homeward
trips, to the accompaniment of deliciously clanging bells and
flying sparks.

A couple of times each summer we went to Rockaway Beach
via the Long Island Railroad. Today's children, accustomed to
popping into a car, cannot conceive of the preparations for such
a safari, the packing of bathing suits and of lunches and dinners,
the days of anticipation. Then the first smell of salt water inter-
laced with brackishness—let us not inquire too closely into other
smells—as the train clacked daringly along long trestles over the
bays. Then the sight of the promised land on the horizon, complete with the Thunderbolt scenic railway—or was it the Cyclone?—and the giant Ferris wheels. Then the waves, the sand

in the bathing suit, the agonizing sunburn, the happy total exhaustion.

Still more rare was the trip to Coney Island, which offered a choice between Luna Park and Steeplechase. True, Luna Park had the shoot-the-chutes and the tunnel-of-love and the fantastic lights shaped like crescents. But Steeplechase with its giant slides was our own true love. In its great enclosed domed building, prophetic of superdomes to come, the slides drew us like magnets. We climbed endless stairs to the top, hesitated at the dizzying crest, finally swallowed hard, folded arms, and launched our bodies into space. The steep slide was punctured with delicious bumps, and we scrambled to our feet at the bottom and rushed again for the stairs. I know that Steeplechase had a myriad of other attractions, such as the spinning disc that whirled faster and faster until centrifugal force prevailed and even the lucky few who had clambered to the apex were dislodged and spun off. I admit that Steeplechase also had a mammoth merry-go-round that dwarfed all other merry-go-rounds and offered flying chairs on which you revolved above the heads of your doting parents. But Steeplechase to me will always be the towering slides.

At Steeplechase you paid a fixed admission charge, and a blue paper disc was attached by string to your strongest shirt button; only extravagant people rented colored coveralls. The disc wore the magic name George C. Tilyou's Steeplechase and a grinning face similar to the countenance of Alfred E. Neuman, familiar to later generations who read *Mad*, all encircled by magic numbers. These were punched by surly, tired, and uniformed old men at the entrance to each attraction. It was a point of honor for me to use up not only my own disc but that of my parents.

"The horses" were the *pièce de résistance* of the day. I always saved them for the last. Regardless of the hour, people filled the cattle chutes that serpentined toward the entrance to the horses. The eager riders shuffled forward a foot at a time, waited, and shuffled again. At the boarding platform six fierce-looking wooden horses awaited, each astride its own single rail. You climbed on and clung for dear life as the rail-riding horses took off, climbed a hill in roller coaster fashion, and raced downhill onto straightaways, around perilous curves, down stretches through the fun house and the outdoor areas of Steeplechase Park. I never learned how many riders were thrown; people didn't seem to be much concerned about safety in those days. Full speed ahead and damn the torpedoes—I ached to come in first.

After you dismounted, the departure ordeal followed. The only exit from the horses was across the stage of a theater presided over by a dwarf clown who brandished a noisy slapstick and a rod with a mild electric charge. He herded people across the stage through revolving barrels or across platforms that vibrated. He ignored most men and children unless they were dilatory or otherwise pesty. But any good-looking girl or fat woman was his prey. His confederates operated controls atop a mechanical elephant that overlooked the stage. Innocent females would come down the chute from the horses and hesitate, aghast. Sometimes they would turn back. But there was no exit; they eventually must cross the stage. The audience laughed in happy anticipation. With rod and slapstick, the clown herded them into position—and whoosh, a jet of air would blow their skirts head high while they vainly clutched and loudly shrieked. The audience would roar. The complexities of ladies' undergarments were revealed to me as never before or since.

But Rockaway Beach and Coney Island visits were rarities, whereas visits with relatives and friends were frequent. My mother and father were host-types and dearly loved to entertain. My mother, a very good cook, would toil endlessly in advance in the kitchen, readying the turkey or chicken or roast beef or lamb, plus the mashed potatoes and a variety of vegetables. On the appointed day, usually a Saturday or Sunday, the leaves would be fitted into the table and the groaning board would stretch across the dining room. The guests were usually the families of my mother's sisters and brother, Aunt Edith, Aunt Eveline, and Uncle Andrew. Interspersed were an odd assortment of friends of the family: Billy Housel, a prissy bachelor left over from my parents' pinochle days; Steve Mitchell, a witty and intellectual lawyer; and Jack McDonald, a burly prize-fighter.

Dinner was served at noon. Throughout the afternoon the children would play and the adults would talk. By four or five in the afternoon it would have become obvious that no one had any intention of going home early, so I would be dispatched to the corner delicatessen run by Mr. Cohen. I would bring home an assortment of "cold cuts"—swiss cheese, thin-sliced ham, bologna, liverwurst, and salami, all crowned with buckets of potato salad. The feasting would be renewed until, sated, the relatives and friends would vanish into the evening and the massive clean-up would begin.

We visited the relatives too, though less frequently, since our home was admittedly Mecca. Sometimes the long subway ride was to the Bronx where my Aunt Edith lived in a flat opposite a factory that manufactured pianos. Aunt Edith was an affectionate person who faithfully read the Sunday "funny papers" to me so that I might learn of the doings of Buster Brown, Boob McNutt, Krazy Kat, Barney Google, the Katzenjammer Kids, and other worthies of early twentieth century comic strips. Carriages and cars crawled by four floors below on Southern Boulevard, today part of the devastation of the South Bronx. Meanwhile, Aunt Edith's balding husband Gus, who was much older than she, sat silently in a Morris chair and exuded the smell of stale pipe tobacco. He was a night watchman. During our visits, Eddie, Uncle Gus's son by his first marriage, came and went. He had fought in what was then called the Great War and had been "shell-shocked," a blanket term covering a myriad of war-related psychological disturbances. Cousin Edith, a "poor relation" from England, also lived with Aunt Edith's family. She did fine needlework at home and worked as a chambermaid in luxury hotels like the old Waldorf. After eating, she would always fall asleep in her chair and, on awaking, explain that she was merely resting her eyes. When awake, she talked in a little bird-like voice with a cockney accent. She was good to me too, a classification I used for differentiating among relatives. I usually played with Miriam, born to Aunt Edith and Uncle Gus late in their marriage and a few years younger than I. On a scale from one to ten, I would rank visits to Aunt Edith's flat at about five.

Yet it was far better than visits to Aunt Eveline and her family, who lived in a railroad flat in the Bronx. The windows looked out across areaways at other railroad flats; I recall no other view. You entered through a long, dark, narrow hallway and were promptly hit with the smells of near poverty from an unreliable toilet and the cooking of cabbage. Aunt Eveline was meek, mouse-like, and kind. Uncle Johnny alternated between unemployment and irregular work as a custodian in low-income tenements. Mustached, red-headed Uncle Johnny, handsome when young, was mercurial, amiable with relatives in the first glow of drinking, withdrawn and nasty when sodden. There were five children underfoot in the railroad flat; they were good kids who did the best they could, given their environment. All grew into middle-class lives, except for one who as a young man plunged from a roof top. The cause of death was never established. On a scale from one to ten, I would rank visits to Aunt Eveline's railroad flat as low, below one.

Visiting my Uncle Andrew's family was another matter; these excursions rated eight or nine and sometimes even ten. As a youth, Uncle Andrew had studied art at Cooper Union, one of New York City's fabulous free institutions, and throughout his life he painted as a skillful amateur. His was the hand that reproduced the romantic painting of Paul and Virginia that dominated our parlor. The Protestant ethic, symbolized by trudging to work in the Blizzard of 1888, must have shaped Uncle Andrew's character; as a career, he adopted house painting and eventually became a painting contractor with a company of his own.

On the surface, Uncle Andrew was a successful entrepreneur; underneath, he was a lifetime American Socialist, and he argued amiably with my father about politics and over societal developments. My father sometimes heckled him from the point of view of a trade unionist and Democrat. "Andy," my father would say, "how can you be a Socialist and a friend of the working man when you yourself hire non-union men?" Andy would deny any inconsistency. He contended that Samuel Gompers had led workers down a primrose capitalist path and asserted that after a peaceful Socialist takeover he, Andy, would serve the state as a Socialist manager. However, for the time being he must live under the iron laws of capitalism and play society's games. "After the revolution, Will, ..." Neither ever converted the other. Consistent or not, Uncle Andrew was a delightful and humorous man, an artist and an intellectual, a foe of the status quo, a cynic and a questioner, and thus a tonic for me in a world where we took things as they were for granted.

Uncle Andrew, Aunt Clara, and their five children lived in a big house on Ogden Avenue in a prosperous area of the Bronx and summered at a bungalow at Edgewater Beach on Pelham Bay. For me, a trip to Edgewater Camp meant swimming, canoeing, sunning, playing, and new ideas. Cousin Dorothy became my sister Flo's bosom companion and cousin Beatie my companion in games and giggling. Carlton was the oldest of my cousins; he served in the Great War, which Andy, despite his socialism, apparently supported, if a patriotic photo of Carlton and three of his sisters, each elaborately uniformed, is to be trusted.

Perhaps Dorothy, Florence, and Eleanor wore Girl Scout uniforms; if so, I can understand better my father's condemnation of the scouting movement as military-oriented and his refusal to allow me to join the Boy Scouts. My father may have been peace-oriented; I never really knew. The only conversation about the war that I can recall came one night in 1917 when my father, on coming home, said grimly to my mother, "Wilson has declared war." With panic in her voice, my mother said, "Oh Will, would you have to go?" My father said, "Not yet; they'll take the young unmarried men first." I began to cry and they stopped talking.

The MacLean family not only swam and boated and enjoyed Edgewater Camp; they also read books, visited museums, had hobbies, and conversed about ideas. In my family we talked family matters at the table; discussion of ideas and events was foreign to us. The MacLean children took for granted that they would go through high school and could even attend college, an assumption I couldn't make. Returning home from a visit, my family sometimes mocked the MacLeans as "snooty" and "high hat," harsh words derived from our plain-folks environment. Yet the older I grew and the more I sensed the intellectual sterility of my own environment and that of other relatives, the more I secretly envied and admired the Andrew MacLean family.

Chapter Four

A SHORT
ATHLETIC CAREER

I began to acquire athletic equipment at a tender age. In retrospect, I now suspect that my father feared that my gentle mother might rear that abhorrent monster, a sissy. Curls were clipped and later my Buster Brown haircut vanished, to my mother's regret. Basketballs, footballs, soccer balls, golf balls, tennis balls, rubber balls, and, eventually, boxing gloves appeared.

I never became much of an athlete, but it was not for lack of trying by my father and by me. He put up a basketball backboard on our garage, converted the grassy yard into a miniature golf course, sanctioned endless hitting of tennis balls against the house, taught me to catch and hit and field.

I played madly after school and throughout weekends, organizing bicycle races along several blocks of rutted roads from my house to Junction Boulevard, setting up golf tournaments in my yard, playing stickball in the street and on the P.S. 92 playground, playing baseball in the weedy vacant lots with neighborhood kids, playing boxball on the street. Yet in the races, their lightweight bikes always won over my heavier Ranger. They drubbed me in golf and outdribbled me in basketball; they hit the hard rubber ball atop the school roof and I never could; they pitched and played the infield while I was relegated to the outer garden, since, as we all know, anyone can play right field; they rounded the bases in boxball while I was lucky to get to first. Apparently I was too frail or unmuscular; maybe I lacked the killer instinct. Of course, I had no professional instruction—but

27

then nobody of my acquaintance ever had lessons in sports during that era of learn-it-yourself. The one exception was my boxing lessons.

My father had a friend who had been a heavyweight boxer. Jack McDonald was fondly described by my parents as a "good-natured slob." The label didn't impugn his hygiene; so far as I know he bathed regularly. "Good-natured slob" meant that he was a soft touch, a pushover for every pal who needed money and for every bartender who stayed open late. After acquiring cauli-flower ears and a bruised face, Jack had taken to the bottle. My father did not drink either beer or liquor; I don't know the origin of his decision. Yet he had a peculiar affinity for friends who did drink. Many times he steered them home late at night and en-dured the abuse of their spouses.

My father took charge of Jack. As a foreman, Will got him into the steamfitters' union, no easy task given the steamfitters' creed that new union members should be close relatives of exist-ing steamfitters. He took charge of Jack's finances and saw to it that money was regularly banked from Jack's pay envelope. Jack was eternally grateful and became a frequent guest at our home.

Jack taught me to box when I was about eight. I learned the left jab, the right cross, footwork, and how to keep up my guard. Since I was peaceable—or to put it more plainly, cowardly—I seldom found occasion to use the lessons in the streets or in the school yards.

To further encourage my development in the manly art of self-defense my father often took me with him when he and his building construction buddies went to boxing matches at the small fight clubs then popular in New York City. I remember vividly going to fights on Saturday nights at the Commonwealth Club in black Harlem. My favorite boxer was a lightweight named Spencer Gardner. Gardner, a white, frequently fought blacks, since the Commonwealth Club scheduled interracial matches. One Saturday night when I was about 12, I had my first lesson in race relations. From ringside—my father and his friends always bought the best available seats—I was rooting strenuously for my beloved Spencer Gardner by calling out, "Kill the nigger! Hit him again! Pound the nigger!" Some of my black neighbors must have reacted, for my father leaned over to me and said, "Billy, don't call him 'nigger'; they don't like to be called that." I was amazed. I knew that was their name. By now Corona included, in addition to micks, heinies, and squareheads, a new migration of niggers, polacks, and ginnywops, sometimes called dagos. So niggers had other names? I asked my father, "Can I call him colored guy?" My father said maybe. "But it's better to call him by his name, or just call him 'him.'" So for the rest of the match I rooted, "Hit Jackson again! Pound him! Kill that colored guy!" My black neighbors seemed appeased.

Once on our way home through the streets of Harlem, I lagged a few steps behind the men, and a small nigger—no, a colored kid—asked me to tie a bloody bandage that had come loose on his hand. But the night was dark and the streets were dark and the kid was dark. So I brushed by him and caught up hurriedly with my father and the men. Then I was haunted for weeks afterward by guilt that I hadn't helped. I knew that you should help people when they needed help, and the little nigger—no, the little colored kid—had needed help. But I hadn't stopped to help him. I never told anybody about this.

About that time a disturbing thing happened in our WASP and white Catholic neighborhood. Some colored people—by now I had mastered the new vocabulary—moved into the house on the next block. Everybody knew that if you let one in, the whole block would soon become a colored neighborhood. It was bad enough already, since a polack family now lived at our corner and the old Polish man kept balls that were hit into his garden unless we got over the fence fast and retrieved them.

By day, people gathered across the street from the colored people's house. They just watched. By night, windows were broken by the big kids. The colored people soon moved out. "Keep away from all that, Billy," I was told by my family. And I did. I don't know what my parents really thought of the situation; my guess is that they were ambivalent. They didn't like what they thought might happen to the neighborhood if "the colored" moved in. Yet they certainly didn't approve of violent measures.

Despite my boxing lessons and my frantic participation in neighborhood games, I never became an athlete. I settled for being a fan. What sport? Football was for Yalies; tennis was for snobs; golf was for people who wore bloomer-like knickers;

opportunities to swim at Wenzel's bathhouse were infrequent, for Flushing Bay was becoming increasingly polluted; basketball was two-hand set shots against a backboard on a garage. But baseball was The American Game. On summer Sundays, with my father and his friends or alone, I watched the semi-pro Corona Caseys play such rivals as the House of David, a bearded traveling team reputed to occasionally lose the ball in their whiskers, or take on such ancient local enemies as the Springfields or College Point. The center fielder for the Caseys was Bunny Dwyer. One Sunday I asked my pop if he was the son of Father Dwyer, the priest at Our Lady of Sorrows. My father and his friends rocked the grandstands with their laughter as I sat mute and embarrassed.

I became a rabid New York Giants fan, and my scrapbooks grew fat with the doings of such Giants as George Kelly, first base; Frank Frisch, second base; Davey Bancroft, shortstop; Heinie Groh, third base; and later the kid Freddy Lindstrom breaking in at third. What an era to be a Giants fan! Babe Ruth had come to the Yankees from the Boston Red Sox in 1920. Yet in the World Series of 1921, when I was 10, the Giants beat the Yanks four games to three, beat them again in 1922 in four straight, and then lost (a fluke, no doubt) the next subway series, four games to two.

On especially blessed summer days I went to the Polo Grounds to see John McGraw's Giants or to Yankee Stadium for Miller Huggins's Yankees. What ecstasy to see the Fordham Flash initiate a double play or the Babe belt one! First I went to the major league games with my father or my mother. But soon I was traveling alone by subway from Corona into Manhattan and transferring to an uptown subway line for the Polo Grounds or a different subway line for Yankee Stadium. In that age of innocence, no one seemed unduly concerned about perverts, child molesters, or muggers. My sole sex education preliminary to these pilgrimages to my baseball shrines was, "Billy, never go off with a stranger who offers you ice cream or candy." I always wondered why hot dogs were never mentioned and were apparently acceptable. But no one even offered me a hot dog. I stretched out each happy day by a long walk across the Harlem River from the game at the Polo Grounds to the empty Yankee

A Short Athletic Career

Stadium, where I took the subway or, vice versa, from a game at the Yankee Stadium to the empty Polo Grounds, from which I caught the subway downtown.

My passion for baseball was enhanced by my Uncle Tom. He had married my father's sister Ida, a happy and mirthful woman who bore him a son, Griff, nicknamed Red Mike, and a daughter, Alida, nicknamed Sisco. Tom Clarke and Ida and their children lived in a big house next to my grandparents. I was as happy in the joyous atmosphere of their home as I was unhappy in the glum atmosphere next door.

Tom was a major league baseball player and thus the leading Corona celebrity in the years of my infancy and childhood. He was catcher for the Cincinnati Reds, 1909-1917, and the Chicago Cubs, 1918. The baseball record books report that he was a good catcher and a middling hitter, with a .265 lifetime average. What they do not report is his later baseball career as a New York Giants coach under manager Bill Terry and then as a coach for Newark, an International League farm club.

Tom was an amiable and popular man who was adept at spinning baseball yarns. He affected jaunty porkpie hats and a devil-may-care look. In any social circle he was the center of a group of admiring listeners. In those days baseball players did not earn the salaries they command today. So, in the off season, Tom supplemented his ballplayer's salary. My father, ever helpful, brought him into the steamfitters' union. As a member of my father's construction crew, he regaled his fellow steamfitters with his anecdotes. That may have slowed down construction by his co-workers but must have been good for morale. My father, who highly enjoyed Tom, fondly called him by a nickname, "Privy." I was an adult before I caught all of the implications of the nickname. Tom hit more solidly in saloons and around the wintertime fires built by construction workers on emerging skyscrapers than at the plate, and, on occasion, he was known to stretch the truth.

As I was completing my first decade on the planet, Tom Clarke in his thirties was descending the baseball ladder into coaching in the minors. So Red Mike and I sometimes occupied the best box seats at Newark games in the New Jersey wilderness. Red Mike, a baseball sophisticate, bored readily and spent

31

much of his time traveling back and forth to the refreshment stand. Once, when we penetrated the clubhouse, my man-of-the-baseball-world cousin told player Lew Fonseca, who had hit four for four at the plate that day, "You had a pretty good day." Pretty good? Perfect!

Yet despite regular contact with my Uncle Tom and all of the tips and lore, I never made it in the athletic world of sweat and jockstraps and rowdy locker rooms. That I was always a year or two younger than my classmates no doubt contributed to my abortive athletic career. Although I haven't mentioned it, I did go to school. The teachers "skipped me," so that I entered Flushing High School at 12. The scars still show. But they don't derive from the spiked shoes of baseball players as I would have preferred.

Chapter Five

School Days

U p to this point I have said nothing of my intellectual development. That's because there is little to report. There were no preschools or kindergartens when I was growing up in Corona. To the best of my recollection, I didn't learn to read until I went to school. My mother and sister read aloud to me: fairy tales, the Bobbsey Twins, and the Oz books. When I was six, the bells tolled and I went to school.

The first sentence I learned to read was "Run with me to the tree." It appeared on a faded brown placard over my teacher's desk in P.S. 15. I mastered it quickly. From then on, school was a cinch. They put things on the board or read things to you. Then, if they asked you, you told them what they had written or said. That's all there was to it. They rewarded you with gold stars and A's. B. F. Skinner would have been pleased with my education at P.S. 15, though I am sure John Dewey would have clucked disapprovingly.

P.S. 15 was a weathered gray wooden building that sat on a rise at the corner of Junction Avenue and Hayes Avenue a third of a mile from my house. One wall of the two-story building looked out at the big hill of the Leverich estate where we went sleigh riding every winter. Don't look for the hill now; they leveled it long ago for apartments.

P.S. 15 housed grades one through six in twelve classrooms. There was also a principal's office that you avoided being sent to for misbehavior, and an ungraded class attended by "mongolian idiots" whom the normal children avoided. At recess time all of us except the idiots went out into the schoolyard, where we screamed and chased each other for as long as the teachers would allow. Then we went back and sat at our assigned seats in the fixed rows and told the teachers what they had told us.

I liked school. I gave back what the teachers had said, though some others couldn't. So the teachers liked me. They had me pass out the pencils and pens and collect the papers and erase the blackboards. They sent me with mysterious messages and forms to the principal. They called on me for the answers after other children had failed miserably. They patted me on the head. Willyum was a good boy. As Willyum's literacy developed, his papers were posted at the front of the room and his compositions were read aloud to the class. Willyum also read *Pinocchio* and other stories to the class. When teacher left the room, Willyum was appointed as monitor; on teacher's return, he "reported" those who talked.

Consequently, my fellow pupils learned early to loathe me. In the chaos of the schoolyard they shoved me, tripped me up, and poked me in the general neighborhood of my genitals. My name became Will-*Yum*, pronounced with offensive deliberation and saccharine sweetness, or Kaiser Wilhelm, enunciated with the hissing malice of 1917 and 1918. Or they called me their worst name of all: sissy. Even those inferior creatures, girls, were mean to me. I liked school but I didn't like recess. I often tried to hide. But in the prison-like atmosphere of fenced-in school yards, there are no places to hide.

My teachers continued to demonstrate how much they liked the good boy. Notes went home to my parents explaining that I was too bright for my class and that I should be "skipped." In P.S. 15 we were promoted twice a year, once during the winter and again at school's close in the spring, as pupils moved from 1A to 1B, 1B to 2A, 2A to 2B, 2B to 3A, etc. I was skipped four times during the first six grades of schooling. So I spent only four years at P.S. 15. My parents were pleased that I was so bright. And who could doubt the wisdom of teachers? I think I skipped during the second, third, fifth, and sixth grades. Why they overlooked the fourth grade I'll never know.

No one except me seemed to notice that, as the years went by, I grew younger and my classmates older. In the first grade we were all six. In the fourth grade I was nine and they were 10. In the sixth grade I was 10 and they were 12, and there were some big dummoxes of 13 to 15. My social and physical lag behind my classmates increased annually. No one except me seemed to notice that skipping militated against my making school friends, though new classfuls of loathers were all too readily acquired.

No one—not even I—seemed to notice that though my proficiency stayed high in reading, writing, spelling, history, and geography, my knowledge of mathematics skidded with each skipping. My report cards still recorded with machine-like monotony A for effort, A for schoolwork, and A for deportment. Years later I read Lewis M. Terman's glowing affirmations of the fine social adjustment that accompanies acceleration—and I mentally filed my dissent.

My major rebellion against being a good boy was brief but savage. Once, in the fifth grade, I was walking the aisles to pass out test papers the teacher had marked. Big kids tugged at me to pass back their tests. I complied. When Adolf Suchay also tugged at me, I stabbed his hand with a pen I was carrying. He screamed. The class was delighted. For Adolf Suchay was not only a sissy, he also spoke with a foreign accent, Hungarian I think, had a stupid name, and wore good clothes to school. At recess they surrounded Adolf and me and pushed us into each other till we struggled briefly in a combination of wrestling and boxing. Remembering Jack McDonald's tutelage, I emerged victorious in this battle of the sissies. I was a hero for fully fifteen minutes. Thank God for Adolf Suchay!

Thank God too for summer vacations and play in my neighborhood with kids of my own age or younger. I made up in effort for what I lacked in athletic skills, and I was well accepted by such friends as Whitey, so-called because he was an albino, and his brother Pimp. When my father suspiciously inquired whence this latter name, I explained that he was small and his full name was "Pimple," and so naturally he was "Pimp" for short. I had good times with Buddy, who lived across the street, and Hawky, a large, powerful lad who once unintentionally pushed me through a plate glass window of the corner delicatessen when I was making a brilliant run in touch football. Away from school, life was good.

I am confident my teachers meant well. They soon had a kid on their hands who read omnivorously and indiscriminately. Sometimes in bed I would burrow under a blanket and read by flashlight till my mother detected a crevice of light under the door and exercised her veto power.

Some people read books; I read series. In elementary school I consumed literary junk food ranging from Laura Lee Hope's volumes on the Bobbsey Twins through Percy K. Fitzhugh's books on the doings of Boy Scouts named Roy Blakely and Pee-wee Harris. I read the Tom Swift and the Rover Boys series. I began with the Baseball Joe series and went on to the baseball books of Burt L. Standish, and I can still people a diamond with the mythical Lefty Locke, pitcher; Brick King, backstop; and Courtney of the center garden. I began haunting a stationery store to await the delivery of the latest Nick Carter mysteries or the doings of Frank Merriwell and his younger brother Dick. Undiluted literary garbage—and I wallowed in it joyously.

My favorite subject was geography. To my teachers and to me, geography was place names, not "the study of the earth and its features and the distribution on the earth of life, including human life and the effects of human activities." I pored over the maps in the geography books and atlases, and I memorized as many place names of countries and cities and rivers and moun-tains as my mind could possibly store. Though during my ele-mentary school years I had never been north of the Bronx, south of New Jersey's Atlantic Highlands, east of Long Island's Montauk Point, or west of Newark, I knew the day would come when I would see such exotica as Tahiti, Samoa, Fiji, New Zealand, Australia, Bali, Bangkok, and Calcutta. It came—about a half century after my elementary school years.

I wrote too. Nothing has come down to posterity. But my teachers called my stories creative writing and encouraged me. The principal, Miss Emily Curry, acquainted with me through my role as courier, took a personal interest in me. One day, dur-ing a faculty meeting in the sanctuary of her office, she called me in to read one of my "stories" to the teachers. On other occasions she asked my teachers to show her my writing and she talked to me about my compositions.

One red-letter day, Miss Curry invited my mother "up to

school." My mother was naturally alarmed, since at P.S. 15 only the parents of ginnywops and micks who had been kicked out of Our Lady of Sorrows were ever called to the principal's office. Miss Curry told my mother that "some day Willyum will make his mark in the literary world." My mother jubilantly brought the message home and she never forgot the predestination. My father paid me his highest compliment, "That boy is **there.**" I never knew where "there" was, but knew it to be a desirable place. So the oracle had spoken and my destiny was determined and my fate fixed.

I owe Emily Curry a substantial debt. She almost made up for the horrors of recess. She contributed much to the love aspect of my love-hate experience in P.S. 15.

When I was 10 years old and in the sixth grade, my P.S. 15 teachers provided their final service/disservice to me. The junior high school in America was then new, born like me in 1911, and they suggested that I go to a junior high school a considerable distance from my home. My parents rejected the idea. So I went for my seventh and eighth grades to a large local neighborhood school, P.S. 92, across from my grandfather's home and two blocks from my house

I went and I got almost straight A's. But there was no question of a love/hate relationship with P.S. 92. Without any qualifications, I hated it. The teachers were aloof and indifferent, or so it seemed to me. They expected me to climb rope ladders in the gym and I couldn't get off the ground. They expected me to build things in manual arts and my lifelong antipathy to tools began.

My most vivid memory is forgetting the lines of poetry I had to recite during an assembly program. The principal, Miss Agnes G. Cording, an angular and homely woman, handed me the poetry book and said, "Here, little boy, take the book. Read the lines." Little boy! Kaiser Wilhelm—even sissy—was preferable! I can't recall ever hating anybody more than I hated Agnes G. Cording at that moment.

My disillusionment with schooling became total during my graduation exercises at P.S. 92. I had won the prize for being the best speller in my class. Miss Cording presented me with a *Webster's Elementary School Dictionary*. On the flyleaf she had written "Spelling Prize 8B Grade P.S. 92 June 26,1923," plus my name. But she spelled my name wrong. She wrote it "Wm. Van Tyl."

At age 12 I went to high school. My mother would say, "Fountain pen, pencil, glasses, money, gym key." Slapping at the appropriate pockets, I would repeat, "Fountain pen, pencil, glasses, money, gym key." Then I would pick up my bookstuffed briefcase and head toward the trolley car that carried me to high school. For four years the ritual never differed, the repetition never varied.

P.S. 92 graduates bound for high school went either to Flushing or to Newtown High School. Corona could boast of no high school; Corona, alas, was better known as the home of the Corona dumps, immortalized in F. Scott Fitzgerald's *The Great Gatsby*. "Life is unfair," Jimmy Carter once said; as evidence of this I cite the fact that the area called the Corona dumps became known as Flushing Meadows when a World's Fair was erected on the land.

Corona was the working-class/lower-middle-class community that lay between fashionable Flushing and comfortable Newtown/Elmhurst. My mother had an innocently snobbish explanation of why I went to Flushing rather than Newtown High School. "We thought a better class of children went there." Flushing High drew from prosperous and established Flushing and new upper-income Bayside and Douglaston, as well as from poor relation Corona. Many P.S. 92 graduates did not go to high school (too dumb, everyone agreed). Most of those who did enter high school went to Newtown.

So the little band from Corona and East Elmhurst who boarded the trolley cars along Jackson Avenue drew together for mutual reinforcement. Bobby Crockard, Eddie Keliher, Randy Hansen, Sidney Goldberg, Joey Carter, and I were a motley group. Bobby, my best friend in high school, was of Scotch ancestry and from an engineering family in comfortable middle-class East Elmhurst. His neighbor Eddie, of English background, handsome, a success with the girls, was from a prosperous family. Randy was of Swedish background, a deadpan comedian from a humble Corona home. Sidney was Jewish, a gifted, creative artist; he lived above his parents' small hardware store. My friend Joey was colored, and he was a deft cartoonist; though he was my seatmate for a while in a crowded sixth grade at P.S.

15, I have no idea where he lived, for you didn't visit colored people's homes and you didn't invite a black kid to your own home for fear of what the neighbors would think.

On the trolley car we sat separately wherever a seat happened to be available, did our homework and reviewed for tests, or looked vacantly out the window at Flushing Bay in the near distance and thought of girls. After the street car bumped over Flushing Creek Bridge and the tracks ended, those of the six of us who had caught that particular trolley gathered together and walked a half mile past the RKO Flushing Theater and the business district to Flushing High School. At school we helped each other over academic hurdles, sat together at lunch, shared jokes, and eyed girls.

Some buildings look better in nostalgic retrospect than in actuality. Magisterial Flushing High School, built of light-colored stone, was handsome in both recollection and reality. The central building rose five stories, was topped by crenelated, fortress-like openings in the wall, and was crowned with four graceful spires. Three-story classroom wings joined the tower. A gracious auditorium with cathedral windows, crenelations, and stone statues was frequently pictured in architectural magazines; the building would have fitted well into the Gothic structures of an Eastern college.

I was overpowered by Flushing High School, yet proud to go there. I went to all of the Red Devils games that I could, whether baseball or football at Memorial Field or basketball in the school gym. I was proud to attend the same classes as a freshman named Harry Taylor, who caught for the varsity and who even talked to me. But I was in awe of the Flushing and Douglaston kids, who seemed so confident and assured, and of the teachers, most of whom seemed so remote.

As early as the first month of my freshman year, the chickens of skipping grades came home to roost. I found algebra incomprehensible, and I didn't speak up in my other classes. From my first period report card, my parents learned that A-A-A Willyum of P.S. 15 and 92 had become an unknown mediocre William Andrew Van Til struggling to make B's. My mother went "up to school" to talk to the teachers, a brave act for her. The school saw little need for parent conferences; you either succeeded by the school's standards or you failed. But somehow she got a conference with several teachers. They told her they didn't remember who I was. I should contribute more often in class. They said I should raise my hand frequently. I did, and things improved somewhat, except in math. I squeaked through algebra and then flunked both geometry and intermediate algebra. After a while my ability to memorize, my insatiable reading, and my writing began to pay off. In the upper years of high school, when my schedule did not include math, I made the honor roll.

A few teachers stand out: a Mr. Grosfeld, a New York Jew uncomfortable in his first year as an English teacher, who encouraged me to write; Miss Green, a motherly, generous lady who displayed to her students the souvenirs of her memorable trip to Spain. And a history teacher whose name I have forgotten, teaching about the French Revolution, made me suddenly aware that Danton, Marat, Robespierre, and the greedy and stupid kings named Louis were flesh and blood, real human beings, not just words on a page. Also, there was kindly Mr. Townsend, another history teacher, who took three of his best students, including me, all the way to the Sesquicentennial of 1926 in Philadelphia, where we even stayed overnight at a hotel! I was 15, and it was my first night away from home; my mother sewed some emergency money into my pocket. But I didn't lose my wallet.

As for the other teachers, I jumped through the hoops they set before me, except for math, where I sprawled. In biology I cut up things and made drawings of frogs. In chemistry I memorized the valence table and learned that if you put liquids in a test tube and held it over a Bunsen burner the liquid changed color. In music we sang discordantly in chorus, then listened to incomprehensible classics by composers whose names always seemed to start with B. In English literature we studied *Silas Marner, As You Like It, Macbeth*, and *A Tale of Two Cities* (of these I liked only the last-named). Out of class I read *Street and Smith Detective Story Magazine, Amazing Stories* (an early version of Sci Fi) and Sax Rohmer's novels about FuManchu.

Flushing High rote taught me. School was a place where you gave them back the facts they told you. School had nothing to do with living, thinking, feeling.

What little education I received during my high school years I owed more to libraries than to schools. P.S. 15, of course, had no library, and if P.S. 92 had one I never visited it. But there was a branch library in a former candy store across from P.S. 92 and a larger library "down in the village." I carried on my hungry, undiscriminating reading through these libraries. While at P.S. 92 I mingled *Treasure Island* and *Tom Sawyer* with Gene Stratton-Porter's *Girl of the Limberlost* and *Freckles* and with George Henty's romances, and I seasoned all with continued reading about the endless doings of various valiant members of the Merriwell, Rover, Carter, and Swift families. In the manner of other autobiographers, I would like to describe how the better literature took over and shaped my mind, but this is an honest memoir—at least so far. So I read Huck Finn as an adventure story, with no foreknowledge of Hemingway's coming dictum, in *Green Hills of Africa*, "All modern American literature comes from one book by Mark Twain called *Huckleberry Finn.*"

While in high school I added the Flushing Public Library to my sources. So Edgar Allan Poe and A. Conan Doyle joined with Sax Rohmer and Philo Vance in my detective story stage. I edged over from the children and youth sections into the adult stacks, to the distress of librarians who were either overly conscientious or prissy. They eventually got used to me. Still, they raised eyebrows when I withdrew authors I had heard were dirty, such as D. H. Lawrence—what literate 15 year-old could resist a title like *Sons and Lovers?*—or deMaupassant—French, and you know what **they** write—and they firmly vetoed Boccaccio's *Decameron* and Rabelais's *Gargantua and Pantagruel.*

By my high school years, sex had raised its reputedly ugly head. How else could you learn about sex than through reading? Girls in my classes were too old and inaccessible; the existence of sex was not publicly admitted by my parents. I couldn't ask Flo—she was too grown up. Being a Peeping Tom or playing doctor on a dark stairway, roles occasionally assayed, contributed little to carnal knowledge. Street wisdom was too stark, oversimplified, and inaccurate.

When, as a child, I had asked my mother where babies came from, she had fallen back on the stork and the doctor's black bag. I threatened to ask Franky, a Boy Scout on the next block, since

Boy Scouts knew everything. Franky had bandaged my arm when Congo Pinkel pushed me through our cellar window onto a lawn mower blade. You may say, "Congo Pinkel? I thought this was to be a truthful memoir. Now when you come to sex, you begin lying." But his name really was Congo Pinkel, and he had a sister, Dorothy, with whom I was romantically in love. Romantic love, however, is different from sex. Romantic love meant rescuing girls from burning buildings, snatching maidens from villains, being worshiped for one's athletic triumphs. Not like sex which means—well, you know.

When my mother wouldn't tell me and forbade me to discuss the matter with Franky, I had recourse to a massive "doctor book" in our attic. It had many illustrations and plates, and I came to the conclusion that the manufacture of babies was a remarkably peculiar process and that people were put together in awkward ways indeed. I was glad all this had nothing to do with my romantic love, at age nine for Dorothy Pinkel, at 10 for Dorothy West, at 11 for Agnes Windel, and in my early teens for several unattainable high school goddesses.

So during my high school years, books—especially fiction— became the source of my early sex education. They didn't have R and X rated movies then. So I read like mad.

Chapter Six

A QUIET RIVER
AND THE WIDER WORLD

L ife in my family ran along like a quiet river during my childhood and early adolescence. The twentieth was a century of mobility, but we stayed in our Corona house. The war to make the world safe for democracy was fought in the trenches of France, but my father didn't have to go. Prohibition became the law of the land in 1919, but my father didn't drink. Woman's suffrage was achieved in 1920, but my mother didn't care to vote, apparently thinking that it only encouraged them. A worldwide influenza epidemic struck in 1918, but I didn't get sick—due, no doubt, to the bag of asafetida I wore around my neck.

There was a post-war depression, but my father kept on working. During the post-war period there were many strikes, but my father's union struck only once and then briefly. In 1923 inflation destroyed the German middle class, but we experienced only "the high cost of living." Calvin Coolidge was elected president in 1924, but—as I said, life in my family ran along quietly during my childhood and adolescence.

Not that we didn't have our family crises. After the war the Jazz Age began and my sister bobbed her hair and smoked cigarettes. This was hard on my parents, but not as bad as Flo's belated discovery at age 18, after graduation from Jamaica Training School for Teachers, that she hated teaching. She desperately wanted to quit and get another job, any other job, though preferably as a singer. Her true love was music; she sang with strength and quality and played the piano and accordion skillfully. My parents envisioned disreputable, smoke-hazy night clubs, and my father bought her off with a present, a fine fur coat. Her compromise was to become a gifted musical amateur, the "life of the party," while continuing in the profession she disliked. Friends did the polka to the fast tempo of her accordion and gathered round the piano to join her in song; her school days were relieved only by directing musically talented kids in assembly programs. She became a nine-to-three, "let's get away fast," TGIF teacher, except when coaching assembly programs. (When she was 45 she cracked up, quit teaching at P.S. 143, and retired on a disability pension. Hindsight tells us that my father was wrong in his insistence that she remain in teaching; as we all learn, parenting is a losing game and the road to hell is paved with good intentions.)

Even that early in the twentieth century the memorable occasions stirring the placid stream of our life were media events. They date from that night in 1921 when my father beckoned me over to our kitchen table, which was strewn with tools and radio parts. He placed earphones on my head and bade me listen to the crystal set he had been assembling. Plain as could be, the announcer said, "KDKA, Pittsburgh, Pennsylvania." KDKA was the first station to transmit regular radio programs in the United States. We had gotten KDKA way out in Pittsburgh!

The crystal set was soon supplanted by a commercial model. The outside world, formerly limited to the yellow journalism of Joseph Pulitzer's *New York World* and William Randolph Hearst's *New York Journal*, flooded in on radio waves. Graham McNamee brought my beloved Giants from the Polo Grounds into my house via WJZ, Newark, New Jersey. We huddled around our set to learn about Jack Dempsey's triumph over the Frog, Georges Carpentier, and of Big Bill Tilden's and Little Bill Johnston's and poker-faced Helen Wills's conquests of the tennis world. We heard about the Finn, Paavo Nurmi, running the mile in an incredible four minutes and 10.4 seconds. With most of the two million other radio owners, we were glued to the set during the blow-by-blow account of the 1923 Jack Dempsey fight with Luis Firpo, the wild bull of the pampas. We chuckled at Will Rogers and were shocked by the Loeb and Leopold murder of 12-year-old Bobby Franks. We rooted for the English Channel conqueror,

Gertrude Ederle, a girl from Astoria, a Long Island town that was much like Corona.

We adored the little tramp, Charlie Chaplin, in *The Kid* and *The Gold Rush*, and America's sweetheart, Mary Pickford, in *Pollyanna*, and Lillian and Dorothy Gish in *The Orphans of the Storm*, and the agile Douglas Fairbanks in *Robin Hood* and *The Thief of Bagdad*. I pilgrimaged every Saturday to the Palace Theater on Jackson Avenue to see Westerns with such stars as William S. Hart, Tom Mix, and Hoot Gibson. Before "the big picture," I roared at the Keystone Kops pursuing the Mack Sennett bathing beauties and shivered deliciously as heroes and heroines of the serials were left dangling from a cliff or strapped down in the path of an approaching buzz saw till next week's episode.

Sometime in the early 1920s the even tempo of our family life was interrupted by a meteoric visitation from the wider world. Jacqueline van Til, a relative from my father's family who spelled her name in the old Dutch manner, became a frequent visitor. Jackie was a heroine of the late Great War. A celebrity in my house!

A young Dutch girl in 1910, Jacqueline had gone to Brussels to be a "pupil nurse on probation" in the training clinic headed by Edith Cavell. She remained with the clinic and associated hospitals through late 1915, while Edith Cavell became a leader in the Belgian underground resistance movement, a world-famous martyr, and a symbol for British war recruiting propaganda. The *Columbia Encyclopedia* summarizes Edith Cavell's story:

> 1865-1915, English nurse. When World War I broke out, she was head of the nursing staff of the Berkendael Medical Institute in Brussels. In 1915 she was arrested by the German occupation authorities and pleaded guilty to a charge of harboring and aiding Allied prisoners and assisting some 130 to cross the Dutch frontier. She was shot Oct. 11, 1915, despite the efforts of Brand Whitlock, U. S. minister to Belgium, to secure a reprieve.

In 1922 Jacqueline van Til, then living in America, published *With Edith Cavell in Belgium* (H. W. Bridges, NY.), an account of her experiences. Jacqueline's chapters dealt with the period before the war, the outbreak of the war, the first refugees, Christmas 1914 at the clinic, and Miss Cavell's arrest and execution. The book is moving and dramatic. It tells of the young nurse's initial awe of the tall, distinguished, and discipline-conscious Edith Cavell; of personal care by Miss Cavell during the young nurse's illness in 1912, followed by Jacqueline's recuperation in England with Miss Cavell's sister; of the declaration of war by Germany in early August, 1914, followed a few days afterward by the entry of the Boches into Brussels; of the taking in and hiding of wounded British soldiers on September 27, 1914, after the Battle of Mons; of the visit by a woman of the underground movement to the clinic on October 6, 1914; of the hundreds of Tommies and Poilus whom Edith Cavell concealed in the clinic, then smuggled into neutral Holland; of the drunken carelessness of Irish refugee soldiers who stupidly sang *Tipperary* while en route back to the hospital from a visit to a bar; of the infiltration of the clinic by German spies; of the eventual arrest, trial, and execution of head nurse Edith Cavell.

After the Great War, Jacqueline came to America and lived in White Plains, a small city north of New York City. After her book was published in 1922, she initiated friendship with our family. A 1924 picture of her with my family shows her as a tall, angular, attractive young woman somewhere in her thirties. Her hair was heavy, unbobbed, and coiled on her head and across her forehead; her cheekbones were high and her eyes bright. I remember mostly her theatrical presence, her flood of conversation in charmingly accented English rather than the Dutch, Belgian, and French more familiar to her, and her restless movements touched by nervousness. She was a demanding person accustomed to "being waited on," as my mother phrased it; even during the occupation by the Germans, the servants, rather than the nurses, did the menial work at the clinic and Jackie didn't learn to make her own bed till 1915.

On her frequent visits to our house, she required that my father call for her and deliver her back home—and perhaps she should have, as a foreign young woman living in a strange land. Yet it was a considerable expedition in the Buick from Corona to White Plains in that era before bridges crossed Long Island Sound. However, my father obliged with alacrity. Apparently he was taken and even possibly smitten with "cousin Jackie." Though I was only entering into adolescence in those days, I suspected that my mother was somewhat wary of Jackie, even though Will was "a steady man." But if you think that Jacqueline and steady Will had an affair, prepare for a disappointment. My best retrospective judgment is that Will found this volatile celebrity an unusual, refreshing, and diverting current in the quiet flow of the river of our lives. She brought the wider world into our home, then in 1926 vanished from our ken as suddenly as she had appeared. Our life went on as before.

Chapter Seven

A DEATH
IN THE FAMILY

On radio, Gracie Allen had a pleasantly silly poem that she annually read to George Burns. Its opening lines were, "Labor Day, oh Labor Day, it comes but once a year." True to her prediction, Labor Day came again in 1926. To New Yorkers, Labor Day meant that summer was over, despite the calendar's denial. No true New Yorker swims after Labor Day. Back-to-school Tuesday remorselessly followed Labor Day Monday. Oh blue, blue Tuesday! From Labor Day onward the leaves would fall, the days would grow short, the pennant races would end, and dispiriting work or study would jail all who had earlier luxuriated in summer's freedom.

For me, Labor Day of 1926 meant that I would return to Flushing High School as a senior. Seniors are supposed to look forward to lording it over mere sophomores and unspeakable freshmen and to enjoying the tribal rites of seniors: proms, dates, the yearbook, class rings, senior privileges, and inquiry into what they were going to do after high school. But I was an immature 15, not a child, not yet a youth. The term "adolescence" was unknown to us; in my environment I was simply regarded as "a boy."

The summer of 1926 had been like other summers. My father had gone to work daily and my mother had grown plumper, yet otherwise her loving self. My sister had "gone around" with her boy friend, Gus, and her training school "gang," Helen and Muriel and Ella and Etta. The family had entertained relatives, gone to Edgewater Camp, and traveled "out the Island" to the beach at Miller Place with the Romar family, who drove a lumbering Packard that looked like a wartime tank.

I had played baseball, shot baskets, and banged tennis balls against the house with neighborhood kids such as muscular Hawky, who hit long balls onto the school roof at the P.S. 92 playground. My heavy Ranger bike, with its handsome tool chest slung along the bar between the handles and the seat and with its clipped-on battery-powered flashlight, was my companion on cruises through neighboring communities. Sometimes I read, usually magazines on college life or junk mysteries or "good books" encountered by happenstance.

As blue Tuesday approached, I made my usual beginning of school resolutions. "Pep up! Belong! Join!" If I continued as in the past, what would I list under activities in the school yearbook? The conventional wisdom had already told me that in the world of jobs—dare I think about the alternative, going to college?—activities were more important than grades. All I could record was membership in the Spanish Club and Drama Group plus membership in the Service League, a group of smart kids with special privileges as their reward for making the honor roll. The Spanish Club and Drama Group were plums, but the Service League was the same old P.S. 15 monitor game, a goodie for the goodies. However, its advantage this year was that, as a member of the Traffic Squad, I could legitimately leave classes two minutes early and come in two minutes late. I was aware that the other seniors were racking up baseball, football, basketball, and track letters, along with editorships, presidencies, vice-presidencies, and secretaryships of a variety of clubs—French, Biology, Civics, Swimming, Rifle, Hi-Y, Sketch, ad infinitum—plus such committee honors as Class Prophecy, Pin, Ballot, and who knows what all. So I decided to be a new person. This year I would be a leader!

This year I would even ask a girl for a date! I would be witty and charming and sophisticated and the girls would swarm around me like flies! I would begin by talking to small and demure Mildred Miller, who regularly took the trolley car for Flushing from the same corner that I did. For three years I had said "hello" and she had said "hello" and that was all. But now my new personality would launch a casual and suave conversation that would sweep the girl off her feet. I would scintillate like a *College Humor* frat man who attended one of the Ivy League schools whose pennants decorated one of my bedroom walls. Full of resolutions, I recited to my mother on that first blue Tuesday, "fountain pen, pencil, glasses, money" (not "gym key," for that would be issued today), and strolled to my assignation at the corner. Mildred was already waiting for the trolley car. I said "hello." She said "hello." That was all. At school they scheduled me for English IV, American History II, Spanish III, lunch, Advanced Chemistry, study hall—and in gym for those damned ropes, parallel bars, and horses.

Summing up, at 15 I was still a boy who had not yet become a youth, schooled rather than educated, bright but not brilliant, sensitive and self-centered rather than aware of the feelings of others, groping into books for models for a life-style, talking things over with myself through my compositions, dimly aching for wider experiences yet unable to find the entrances.

Just at that point in my evolution my father died, September 20, 1926. He was 48.

My father, like all fathers, had seemed to me eternal. He was part of an unchanging universe. But, without warning, he and my universe crumpled. The doctors mumbled about pneumonia, followed by kidney failure. For a few days he had lain ill in his bedroom; then the ambulance men had carried him down the steep staircase. At the bottom he had reached for my mother's hand and said, "Don't worry, Tom, I'll be all right." Tom was one of his pet names for her; in later years my mother couldn't recall the derivation. But my mother and Flo and I standing in the hallway knew that he wouldn't be all right, for he was going to a hospital in Manhattan, not to a local hospital, and when you went to a Manhattan hospital you were dying.

The hospital was big and ugly and old. I was standing on a balcony and looking at the frightening city when someone came out and told me that my father was dead. I hated life for taking away my loving, concerned, and kindly father, who had been so good to me. I hated the hospital and the doctors and the city. I hated the world.

My father's corpse was brought to our parlor for services prior to the funeral and our War over Religion flared again. The battle this time was over my father's body.

My mother wanted him to be buried in a cemetery where she could eventually lie by his side. That they be together in death as they had been in life was of surpassing importance to her. My father's parents wanted him to be buried in holy Catholic ground. Yet if he were buried in a Catholic cemetery, my mother could never be interred with him.

So hour after hour the living waged a battle while my father lay dead in the next room.

Brought up a Catholic, Will in his youth had given up church attendance. He had often expressed his contempt for the hypocrites who behaved badly, received absolution in the confessional, and immediately behaved badly again. Throughout his adult life his position on the hereafter had been that of the skeptic. His attitude toward organized religion—and the Roman Catholic Church in particular—was negative. His parents' refusal to attend his wedding in a Protestant church or his children's christenings had hardened his position.

The target of the Catholic attack in the battle for my father's body was my shattered mother. My mother believed in God and assumed that people who lived well, as she and Will were doing, would go to Heaven. Her policy was not to trouble the Lord with prayers or ceremonials; she took for granted that, in turn, the Lord had more important things to do than make trouble for her. She wasn't concerned about denominational distinctions—to her, Protestants were Protestants—so in our childhood she had sent Flo and me to the nearby Grace Episcopal Church rather than to the Presbyterian Church of her forefathers. My father raised no objection to her choice.

The battle for my father's body first involved only my mother and my Irish grandmother. The struggle was quickly joined on the Catholic side by my grandfather, long converted from his original Protestantism, and my father's oldest sister Loretta, a pious widow who lived in my grandparents' house. My sister Flo supported the Protestant side, as did my Uncle Andrew. Neighbors and visitors who had come to see the body also took sides.

For my mother, the decision on the burial place was deeply tied to her simple and loving philosophy of life. To my grandmother, this was a battle for her son's soul, for without Roman

Catholic services and proper burial, her son's soul would burn in Hell throughout eternity.

In the battle, the Catholics brought up their biggest guns, the priesthood. In their black robes, local priests from Our Lady of Sorrows Roman Catholic Church shuttled between planning conferences at my grandparents' house and argumentation against the Protestants in our home. Compromises were proposed. For instance, the Protestant side proposed Catholic services held either in our home or at the church, followed by burial not in Protestant soil but instead in a nonsectarian cemetery. But Catholic dogma called for Catholic services and Catholic burial on consecrated Catholic soil. Would the priests consecrate the nonsectarian soil? Not possible. On the Catholic side, the question was raised as to whether my mother might convert to Catholicism and thus be enabled to lie side by side with her beloved husband. Not immediately of course, but after the grief in the years ahead? Unthinkable—the decision against conversion had been made in the earlier battle more than two decades ago.

While they argued in our dining room, the sliding doors to the adjoining parlor where my father's body lay were shut. Warfare, however savage, must be conducted with decorum. We must show our respect for the dead.

I was barred from participation in the war, for I was too young. Occasionally a participant or a camp follower, fresh from kneeling beside the coffin, would come upon me disconsolate on the front stoop and offer sympathy. I never knew what to say in response, so l would simply nod. Mostly I sat on the steps, alone, bereft, lost, aching for my father's presence, wondering what would happen to our family, what we would do without our anchor, what they were saying in the living room, what awful things I had done to bring life down in ruins about my head.

On the beautiful early autumn afternoon before my father was buried, I was suffering alone on the porch when I heard the rhythmic steps of marching men. Startled, I looked up. Coming toward me from a block away were scores of steamfitters and carpenters and electricians and bricklayers and laborers and foremen and superintendents with whom my father had worked for decades. They had gathered together at electrician foreman

Jim Marshall's house, a quarter of a mile away, and were now marching under the overarching linden trees of Fillmore Avenue as a body to pay their last respects to their friend. The silent group reached our house and filed in. They filled the parlor and the scene of the war, the dining room. Their leaders said a few humble, inarticulate things to my mother, and some of the men knelt at the coffin. Then, still silent, they filed out, reassembled, and marched back the several blocks to their point of assembly.

Soon afterwards, I was told that the undertaker was about ready to close the coffin and that I should say goodby to my father. My family and some of my relatives were standing in the parlor. I went in and had my last look at my father. I was stunned by my love for him and by our loss. I knelt at the coffin rail. Suddenly I was agonizingly aware that I had a hole in my shoe and a rip in my stocking that everybody could see. Then I was overwhelmed with guilt, because I realized that, even at the final moment, instead of thinking of my father I had thought of myself. Maybe that's why I went back on to the steps and cried in pain and confusion while the undertaker closed the coffin.

They buried my father in nonsectarian Mount Olivet Cemetery, where, almost a half century later, my mother was put to rest at his side. The Protestants had prevailed in a battle in our insane, unending War over Religion in which nobody was a winner and everybody a loser.

Chapter Eight

THE MAN
OF THE FAMILY

As soon as she could gather strength to listen to me, I told my mother that I was leaving school and going to work. A city government agency was charged with the issuance of working papers to boys and girls under 16 who went to work out of necessity; I proposed to apply next Monday. As to schooling, I would take night classes at Bryant High School in Long Island City.

My mother immediately said "no." My mother had two kinds of nos, one that was subject to negotiation and thus open to persuasion, and one that was as immovable as the Rock of Gibraltar. As in the battle for my father's body, she exercised the latter type of no on my proposal. I was to finish high school, take a summer vacation, then go to work. Though my mother was soft, gentle, and even timid at times, I knew that I couldn't argue against her immovable no. If social characteristics are inheritable, I owe my own stubbornness to my mother. Neither heaven nor earth could move either of us on some decisions.

The family had some insurance and savings, she explained, not a great deal but enough for awhile. She was not specific as to the amount. Flo would contribute to the support of the family through her salary as a teacher. (So Flo at 21 found herself locked into teaching.) I would contribute to the family income when I went to work; the mores of our milieu took for granted that children contributed to family support.

Thus, after my father's death back I went to Flushing High School so that I might receive a high school diploma. I wore a wide black band on the sleeve of my coat (in those days, kids wore jackets to class) to remind the world that I was in mourning. The custom was for people who had suffered a death in the family to wear these bands for months and to avoid frivolities. I remember slinking into the Corona Theater one winter day while still wearing the band. I hoped no one would see me and report my disloyalty to my mother. Though the movie was innocuous, I sidled in as though I were going to a burlesque show.

Though I never felt that I truly "belonged" at Flushing High, my senior year was better than the earlier three. Freed of the incubus of required mathematics, I got high grades and again made the honor roll. The Spanish Club elected me vice-president, a nothing office with no responsibility, yet the first elected office of my life. I owed this dubious honor to my friends: black Joey Carter, Jewish Sidney Goldberg, Scotch Bobby Crockard, and Swedish Randy Hansen, fellow travelers in three years of Spanish. I patrolled the halls with the Traffic Squad selected from the smarties of the Service League and strolled proudly into my classes a few minutes late after seeing that students went down the down stairway, up the up stairway, and kept to the right while passing between classes.

Despite my P.S. 15 literary predestination and my emerging ambition to be a journalist, I did not join the Literary Club or the *Folio* magazine staff, which were dominated by the socially arrived who were headed for Wellesley, Barnard, Vassar, Columbia, Haverford, Alfred, and N.Y.U. No staff member of indifferent-to-guidance Flushing High School suggested that I should try these clubs.

However, I stayed with the Drama Group and mustered all of my available courage to try out for the senior play, George Kelly's *The Show-Off*, a popular Broadway comedy that has often been revived. The central character of *The Show-Off* was the boastful, arrogant, yet appealing Aubrey Piper. Heywood Broun, one of my idols in American journalism, had said of *The Show-Off*: "I might as well begin boldly and say that *The Show-Off* is the best comedy which has yet been written by an American."

I played Joe Fisher, a gifted young inventor who tinkered mechanically—it should be quite obvious to anyone who knows me that the director was not casting to type, for my mechanical background was limited to holding a flashlight for my father. Rehearsals during the spring were a delight to me, and the cast was congenial. I acquitted myself well and felt good about my performance, except for that moment on opening night when I rushed on stage with the big news of acceptance of my invention and flung my overcoat on a pole used for hanging clothes. The clothes hanger collapsed and the audience roared with laughter. I didn't have the presence of mind to pick up the clothes, so I went right on with my lines. The director later sent Aubrey on to *ad lib* and gather up the garments, which he did after some excellent feigning of surprise. The second night we played, the prop man saw to it that a stronger coat hanger was on stage.

I continued to adore girls from afar and occasionally managed to converse with them without catastrophic damage to my self-image. Yet I couldn't bring myself to invite one of the breed to the senior prom, nor could the quaintly titled "Coupling Committee" persuade me to do so. The responsibility of the socially adept students who constituted this committee was to bring together the shy boys and the wallflower girls. I was arbitrarily assigned a girl named Jean as a prom date, and I responded with an indecision that Hamlet himself might have envied. A few days before the prom I phoned her that I was "unable to attend," which was close to the truth if interpreted as a description of my emotions. I suspect she felt like a rejected dog, and I know that I was miserable and shamefaced for days afterward. But what can you do at a prom when you're a 16-year-old boy and don't know how to dance? You don't go; you stay home and study for that invention of the devil, the Regents Examinations.

When the June 1927 issue of the *Folio* came out with a class ballot on two long pages that listed The Best _____, and The Most _____, and The Class _____, I achieved neither such complimentary designations as Class Sheik or Most Attractive Boy nor such insults as Class Bookworm or Class Woman Hater or Class Baby. I simply wasn't mentioned. However, I emerged from anonymity through the Class History and thus avoided that high school fate worse than death, having your picture and name appear in the yearbook followed by a complete blank. Of me, the Class History reported: "Spanish Club, '25, '26, '27: Vice-President, '27: Dramatic Club, '25, '26: Service League, '26, '27: Traffic

Squad, '27: Cast of Senior Play: Honor Group. Future intention—Business." Take note Business—the young man engaged in activities. And the *Folio* carried a picture of me in my role as Joe; no coat hanger was in the background.

As to scholarship, of the 160 seniors only Richard O'Keefe was listed in the commencement program as "average scholarship over 90%." Flushing High School was proud of its high standards and low grading. Twenty-seven of us achieved the dignity of "average scholarship over 80%." Among the grades that constituted my average were the flat F's in geometry and intermediate algebra; my English and social studies grades were high. As I said a while ago, "bright but not brilliant."

Now I was the man of the family, a high school graduate about to enter the world of employment. Last year I had been a boy; now at 16 I was a man. I had skipped my youth.

People at Thompson-Starrett Construction Company, the building construction firm for which my father had worked about twenty years, had been fond of him. He was remembered not only by his fellow skilled workers but also by top officials. Immediately after my father's death, A. E. Barlow, a vice-president of Thompson-Starrett, a gentle, thoughtful, and good man in a rough industry, had written my mother that there was a job with the company anytime waiting for Will Van Til's son. So I wrote him, and one summer day in 1927 when I was 16 ½, I received a letter from the company telling me to come to work at Thompson-Starrett, Equitable Trust Building, 15 Broad Street, New York City.

Broad Street is in the heart of the financial district and intersects with Wall Street. I wore my best suit, took the subway to the Wall Street station in the heart of the downtown skyscrapers, and began to look for the offices of Thompson-Starrett in the Equitable Trust Building at 15 Broad Street. But there was no skyscraper on Broad Street numbered 15 and there was no Equitable Trust Building. I looked at the long listings in the lobbies of skyscraper after skyscraper. No Thompson-Starrett. I began to panic. Finally, a kindly soul told me that 15 Broad Street was under construction. Across the street from where I stood worrying, a skeleton of steel beams was reaching for the skies. In the cavernous entrance from which trucks hauled rubble stood a wooden shanty with an inconspicuous sign, Thompson-Starrett.

Rising on the site was a proud skyscraper to be called the Equitable Trust Building. I had thought I was going to work in a fine office in a completed skyscraper. Instead, I had been assigned to the Equitable job. Of course!

Since I never liked being laughed at, I didn't explain to the roughhewn timekeeper and checkers in the construction shanty why I was late. The timekeeper talked to me briefly, filled out a form, and I was employed—an office boy on the Equitable Trust job, eight to five weekdays plus a half day on Saturday.

My work was largely carrying messages from the superintendent and the timekeeper to the various company foremen or the employees of subcontractors who worked somewhere throughout the building. As the structure grew, they moved from location to location, naturally without advising an office boy as to where they might be found. Some subcontractors, I learned, avoided messages they suspected would be unwelcome. So my work was to wander through the building in search of elusive people for whom messages were intended. The leaders of the goulashers were particularly evasive. Goulashers were the men who poured the great slimy grey piles that hardened into floors of reinforced concrete; goulashers got their name from the mess they poured and the fact that they were often Hungarians. I would sometimes prowl through the shanties, latrines, and work locations of the work gangs calling mournfully the name of the subcontractor "Kresse," following clues, asking "Where's the boss?" and eventually tracking down my prey.

I liked prowling through the emerging skyscraper. I enjoyed distributing the mail. My unfavorite hour came at noon when the regular telephone boy went out to lunch at the Exchange Buffet, where you stood at high tables to eat and reported on your consumption to the cashier, thus accounting for EB's nickname, "Eatem and Beatem." Though usually quiet at midday, the telephone switchboard occasionally lit up during lunch hour with flashing red and white lights while I frantically plugged lines into the wrong holes and pulled out lines while people were still talking. Meantime, busy people were instructing me to connect them with the main office or a subcontractor—or get another job.

Building construction workers have rich, profane, and obscene vocabularies; they always attach long, colorful strings of modifiers to their expletives. The language describing my ancestry and presumable habits was bad enough in normal social intercourse during my message deliveries; when people who phoned were cut off or delayed or irritated, the language was as luxuriant, rank, and foul as jungle vegetation. But I preferred even this to forbearing treatment by some who despaired of my potential. After all, a highly paid office boy who earned $15 a week and who cut off construction men working against time deserved being called a many modified son-of-a-bitch.

After a few months of the Equitable Trust job, I was promoted, due perhaps to the diligence with which I hunted Kresse and the other subcontractors, though certainly not because of my adeptness at the switchboard. In the Thompson-Starrett main office, I had new bosses. William Abramson was a middle-management man who supervised and hired and fired the timekeepers and checkers and watchmen on various Thompson-Starrett construction jobs. His junior partner was William Troast. They faced each other across their desks in a small office in the comfortable headquarters at 250 Park Avenue in the Grand Central area of Manhattan. Mr. Abramson (nobody called him Bill) was serious, poker-faced, reserved, and formidable looking. He had a nose for payroll padding or other hanky-panky committed by timekeepers and checkers. Out of his hearing, the men on the construction jobs called him "the Jew." Bill Troast (everybody except office boys called him Bill) was younger, more relaxed, humorous, and easy. They sometimes had to make hard joint decisions that were all the better because of the interplay of their differing personalities.

They needed an office boy, so they brought me in from the field to the main office, eight-thirty to five with Saturdays off. I learned. They marked job applications and I filed them in one of two categories. A fat file represented a limbo from which no application ever emerged. Only the thin file was referred to when an opening developed. Thompson-Starrett was paternal, else I never would have been employed; applications in the file frequently bore such annotations as "cousin of T-S V.P." or "recommended by Jersey City Treasurer." Yet if the prospective employees were not also capable and honest, the incorruptible Abramson would not hire them.

I became bonded, a distinct honor. Bonding meant that if I absconded to Patagonia with payrolls I carried to building construction jobs, the insurance company would lose, not Thompson-Starrett. So I picked up money at midtown banks, carefully counted it (Abramson trained me so well that even today bank tellers note, with eyebrows raised, that I recount bills they have carefully counted out before me), and brought the money to timekeepers on jobs too new for armored truck delivery. With small fortunes in my pocket, I rode the subways to shanties in holes in the ground that were to become New York's Paramount Theater, or the Brooklyn Paramount, or the Jamaica Paramount, or the Bank of this, that, or the other. While the timekeeper put the money into pay envelopes, I loafed briefly in the shacks. Friendly timekeepers and checkers tried to pump me for information about prospective hirings/firings and promotions contemplated in Abramson's office. But Abramson had taught me to keep my mouth shut.

Some members of building trades unions thought that occasional "liberation" of supplies and equipment was a fringe benefit owed them. So Abramson and staff checked materials. For a romantic like me, one of the high points of my job was the occasional surprise check on materials. Without advance notice, Abramson, Troast, and I would descend upon a construction site and measure the piles of hollow tiles and bricks and count the fixtures, the bags of cement, the two-by-fours, etc. These delightful raids took place at night when the buildings were silent as a grave. We climbed throughout the skeletons, flashlights in hand, recording what we found on the floors dimly lit by strings of electric bulbs. The moon and the stars looked down at the nocturnal prowlers in the abandoned city. The silence was delicious. In my mind I would write short stories.

Discrepancies had to be accounted for by the timekeepers and checkers. No wonder they tried to pump me. One of my favorite timekeepers was Tommy, an amiable and witty Irishman whose pumping was perceptive and deft. I enjoyed Tommy and wanted to be like him. One day Abramson looked blacker than usual. Tommy had been caught padding the payroll. Abramson fired him at once. I suffered for Tommy and grew years older in one day.

Chapter Nine

FRIENDSHIP, BEAUTIFUL FRIENDSHIP

Since I was 16 and a wage earner, I knew that I must put aside childish things and behave like a man. But how did men behave?

For one thing, they smoked. One day, soon after my father's death, I bought Old Golds, cigarettes that advertised "smoothness" and claimed "not a cough in a carload." I figured this would be a good beginning before going on to really wicked Turkish cigarettes like Melachrinos. After dinner I lit up, promptly wheezed, and lapsed into a fit of coughing. My sister, an experienced hand at smoking cigarettes, attempted to coach me. I am sure that my mother, who like my father had never smoked, disapproved of the whole proceeding. Yet she held to a policy that if people were going to misbehave, they should do so openly. My eyes ran. I wondered why I had to experience this rite of passage in order to become a man. However, I persisted and soon was handling and tapping cigarettes with what I callowly supposed to be the proper sophistication, a stage to which I desperately aspired.

Full-time employment meant that childhood games were out, save for infrequent weekend reversions to boyhood. Long working hours involved a rapid breakfast, faithfully prepared by my mother; a three-quarters of a mile walk to the subway, on which I read the tabloid *Daily News* (always beginning with the back pages and moving forward toward the front pages, a sequence often followed by *Daily News* readers who wanted sports news first, bad news later); a day on the job broken by midday freedom in a cafeteria; the subway return accompanied by

61

Hearst's *New York Journal* or a book; time for reading and radio at night. But weekends beckoned, and even office boys were entitled to two weeks of summer vacation. My mother was a homebody; my sister at 22 understandably went her own way in her quest for fun and a husband; my high school friends had vanished back into their own Jewish or black ethnic lower-middleclass or WASP upper-middle-class worlds and their college or "business" destinations; my neighborhood friends, with the exception of Hawky, were now too immature for an employed man. So I sought for friends elsewhere. Where? Three obvious locales: church, youth groups, work.

As a child I had been sent by my mother to Sunday School. Grouped by ages, we sat in circles in a large hall and recited lessons that we were supposed to study during the preceding week and hadn't. They were mostly about tedious Old Testament figures with unpronounceable names. (I always thought Isaiah was pronounced Isha.) Occasionally we encountered live wires like Daniel in the lion's den or my personal favorite, David, who slew Goliath and probably could have knocked off the bullies of P.S. 15 if he had felt like it. Sometimes the Sunday School put on a program for our proud parents. At one Christmas program I recited from memory a long poem called *Little Gottlieb's Christmas*, which began, "Across the German ocean in a country far from our own, lived a little boy named Gottlieb, lived with his mother alone." It ran on for stanza after stanza. I was fulsomely praised and my mother was proud of me.

I began attending church services as well as Sunday School. Church attendance raised some questions in my mind that my lay Sunday School teachers were unable to answer. So when I was 12 or 13, the teachers sent me to Reverend Arthur G. Roberts, the frail, quiet, kindly man who was our pastor. I talked with him in his dark parlor at the rectory. As an earnest student of geography, I asked him about the exact location of Heaven. As a student of Sunday School theology, I also asked him why so many bad things happened when God was supposed to be both all-powerful and good. I listened to his responses and then decided silently that he didn't know either. So I ceased going to church.

Going on 17, still suffering from the wounds inflicted by organized religion and having become a not especially reflective atheist, I went back to Grace Episcopal Church in search of friends, especially girl friends. Luckily, my church had a lively youth group, sententiously titled the Duwell Club. Though it was not quite clear what we were supposed to do well, the club held meetings and sponsored picnics, parties, dances, and that most licentious of events of adolescence—hay rides. The things one imagined that would go on deep in the hay! Sadly enough, they seldom did.

In the Duwell Club we never let our church relationship interfere with our real purpose, dating with new partners. So at parties and picnics and after dances we smooched and fumbled in cars or on beaches or on sofas or under the elms. As the argot of that era put it, we necked and petted. But we didn't go all the way, as we hushedly referred to it. Not that some males didn't make gallant tries; however, cooler female heads prevailed or the proximity of other couples interfered. Compared to the contemporary pattern, in which teenagers freely leap in and out of varied beds at the drop of a garment, we were positively antediluvian in our sexual behavior.

One thing that the Duwells did very well was putting on a play each year to raise money for the church. A veteran thespian after the two-night run of *The Show-Off*, I took to Duwell drama like the proverbial duck to water. I soon became the coach of the annual play, the club's play director.

I learned more from putting on the Duwell Club plays than I learned from all my classes in high school. Not that the plays were classics; they were trivial comedies with names like *Breaking Winnie* and *Cyclone Sally* and *Aaron Slick of Pumpkin Crick*, selected from Samuel French's catalogue with an eye to paying the minimum possible royalty to the copyright holder. But I learned how to work with distinct individuals, bringing out their abilities and assuaging their uneasinesses. I learned how to mount a production, sell advertising, handle box office receipts. I helped George, the club funny fellow, improve his timing; Florence, the ingenue, make more dramatic entrances; handsome Ray speak more forcefully. I nursed my good friend Harry through performances, despite his insistence that a few drinks before going on stage helped him be a brilliant actor. I had to work with adults as well as my contemporaries.

Through the job in Manhattan, I found a friend, an authentic buddy. Ben Sanders was an office boy at the main office of Thompson-Starrett at 250 Park Avenue before he went on to employment with an insurance company elaborately titled Royal London, Liverpool, and Globe. We met one day at lunch, enjoyed each other, and I found that he lived with his aunt and uncle in Jackson Heights relatively near my Corona home. His aunt and uncle were frequently away for weekends or vacations or trips, and they didn't object to parties in their absence, provided there would be no cigarette burns on the furniture. I frequently became Ben's party guest and he mine.

At parties at my home, my mother soon noticed that male guests would occasionally repair to cars in the driveway for a libation; she ruled that, if there were to be any drinking, bottles be placed in the open on her kitchen table. "No sneaking off to have a drink." Whether my father would have agreed I don't know, for I never had a drink during his lifetime—if you don't count the time when I was about 12 and the whimsical drunken Irish guests at a party celebrating my grandparents' wedding anniversary slipped me what they said was cider until I passed out under the grand piano at a local hall. My party guests admired my mother for her forthrightness and consumed less than had the drinking remained furtive. As to motherless Ben, he adored my mother; she immediately became "mom" to him.

Prohibition was the scoffed-at law of the land at the time, and vile-tasting liquor in the form of bathtub gin and other bootleg whiskey the fashion at parties and dances. To belong socially, you held your nose and gulped down the rotgut. To drink beer, you went to speakeasies.

Ben had access to one speakeasy in particular, the Economy on Roosevelt Avenue beside the elevated structure over which the trains rumbled. Ben would ring the doorbell and a suspicious eye would appear at the peephole. "You remember me," Ben would say. Usually the eye would disappear, the bolt would be drawn, and we would enter an old-fashioned saloon, drink pitchers of beer, consume pretzels or the free lunch, and fancy ourselves wicked and dashing fellows. Ben's friend Paul L., older than himself; Joe, a stolid soul who was the frequent butt of jokes; Harry, my friend from the Duwell Club; and I usually constituted a foursome. Age was not a factor in admission, since the whole operation was illegal; the speakeasy proprietor apparently followed the old Scottish proverb, "If you steal, you might as well be hung for a sheep as for a lamb."

One did not bring girls to such dives. Especially not my gorgeous red-haired girl Muriel, whose father was a police lieutenant. Her mother guarded Muriel like a veteran watchdog. When you could afford it, you brought girls to movies and parties and dances. Once, for a double date for a dance at the Saint George Hotel in Brooklyn (in the process of becoming a man, I had learned the two-step), I borrowed Flo's car with her permission. On the way home through Manhattan, my good friend Hawky was driving when we crashed into another car. His girl and my dark-haired Ruth suffered scalp wounds. Shaken, I accompanied the girls to the emergency room of a hospital while Hawky drove the wrecked car back home across Queensboro Bridge at five miles per hour. Fortunately, Hawky had been sober, our girls regarded their injuries as part of the risks of romance, and insurance took care of car repairs. Hawky and I couldn't possibly have paid for the hospital costs and automobile repair bills.

The largest part of my salary I turned over to my mother. Yet a few bills sometimes rubbed together in my pocket. So Ben and I amassed funds and bought ourselves an auto for $25. Cars were assumed to be of the female sex, so we named her Emma. Emma was an ancient Model T Ford. She ran bravely out the island to Port Washington and Miller Place, even climbing the massive Manhasset Hill, which lesser cars could not ascend. (Today the equivalent of Manhasset Hill would be regarded as a gentle grade that would require no warning road sign.) On such holidays as the Fourth of July and Labor Day, Emma steamed gallantly across Queensboro Bridge, threaded the complexities of Manhattan traffic, survived the Holland Tunnel, and carried us to Budd Lake in New Jersey, where Ben's aunt and uncle had a cottage. We respected Emma's age, polished her diligently, and I drove her with dubious legality on my learner's permit. Eventually she spluttered out and we gave her back to the original owner, for we still owed him a final payment on our $25 investment.

I found one additional source of friendship, the Order of

DeMolay. DeMolay was sometimes called the junior Masonic society; more precisely, it was under the guidance of Masonry and sponsored by men from the Masonic lodges. The order was named for Jacques DeMolay, the last grand master of the Knights Templar who fought the Saracens and was eventually executed in Paris by a French king jealous of the Templars' riches and fearful of their power.

The Order of the DeMolay had all the fraternal abracadabra that Americans, young and old, seem to love. My brothers, dressed in long, handsome robes, inducted the neophytes into the sacred ritual, which I swore never to divulge and won't reveal now, primarily because I have completely forgotten all except that I must "respect women," an echo that still lingers. We learned the grip, naturally to be used only on other brothers.

We had a host of lower officials such as the chaplain and the sergeant-at-arms. Lower officialdom was open to volunteers, who were then appointed by the councilors and advisors. My first office was almoner, visiting sick brothers.

DeMolay politics centered around the major elected office, the junior councilor. Candidates for junior councilor were usually age 17 or thereabouts. Though we were all loyal brothers, there were two major factions in our chapter, the Astoria crowd and the Elmhurst/Corona crowd. In our Nathan Hale chapter, Elmhurst/ Corona often ran against Astoria. Early on, I set my heart on becoming junior councilor, so I served loyally in the lower ranks, usually through appointment by my Elmhurst/ Corona friends. But early, and the hard way, I was to learn the machinations of practical politics.

It so happened that I had a close friend who had moved into a house two doors away from my home. Paul B. rode in Emma and shared parties and beach outings with me and my friends. Paul B. and I ran around with the girls next-door, Rita and Rose. He wanted to join DeMolay and I sponsored him. We were boon companions.

However, like Julius Caesar (and me), Paul B. was ambitious. As my time to run for junior councilor came around, Paul B. worked out an unprecedented deal with the cohorts of Astoria. He would throw to Astoria the support of those with whom he had influence in the Elmhurst/Corona faction. In return, Astoria would support his candidacy in the following year. It worked. Astoria beat me that year; Paul B. was elected easily in the following year.

I was sick at heart at my first experience with my pal Brutus. Paul B. no longer joined those of my Corona friends who remained loyal to me as we gathered after meetings at the local soda parlour, the Bellefair. Our friendship dwindled toward nothingness. I was glad when he moved away. I don't know where he went. He should have gone to Astoria. Trivial? Of course. But at 17 the trivial can be terrible. Or at 70.

Chapter Ten

DEAD ENDS

etween age 16 and 18 1 took some vocational wrong turns and sped down some dead-end streets. They showed my ignorance of a first law in philosophy, "know thyself."
My father had held to an ambition for me—engineering. Undoubtedly there was an element of projection in this aspiration, because, lacking a high school and college education, he had found himself blocked from rising beyond his foremanship in the building construction industry. He could not join the building construction aristocracy of executives, architects, estimators, and draftsmen in the main office or of superintendents and engineers on the building sites. His hope was that I would. He frequently told me, "Don't be a dirty neck like me, son." It wasn't that my father was contemptuous of those who worked with their hands; his comment conveyed the disillusionment of an able man whose potential was thwarted by a lack of educational credentials and who was thus barred from the fraternity of those who led. Yet he knew more about construction than many who were above him in the hierarchy. As I watched the nonchalant and relaxed engineers hanging around with superintendents and vice-presidents on the job sites to which I delivered money for payrolls, I could understand why he wanted me to be an engineer. What a good life they led!

Yet there was one insuperable block to his ambitions for me. I didn't speak mathematics. Out of a combination of ignorance and stubbornness, I wouldn't admit it. When night school at Bryant High School in Long Island City opened in autumn after

I went to work with Thompson-Starrett, I took a mathematics course three times a week. Long ago I forgot even its title; however, my archives reveal that it was trigonometry. I dimly remember that I just squeaked by.

Maybe, I thought, my entry into the Thompson-Starrett aristocracy would be through drafting. Consequently, in the spring I registered at CCNY for a course in blueprint reading. Though I got a passing grade, my major recollection of that course is my instructor's solemn explanation that wash basins are built waist-high so that males cannot piddle in the sink.

A slow learner, I began to reach the conclusion that I wasn't cut out to enter the Thompson-Starrett aristocracy via either engineering or drafting. My discouragement with myself was enhanced by my father's best friend, well-meaning Jim Marshall, the electrician foreman. Whenever I encountered Jim on a building construction job, he would tell me, "You'll never be half the man your father was." No doubt Jim hoped to inspire me to reach the heights; let's hope he was a better electrician than he was a psychologist. My self-image took a beating in the year I became 17. Yet I had read too many Horatio Alger books to quit. I not only read them; I believed them. With pluck—a key Alger concept— I could make something of myself. Onward and upward!

Perhaps Miss Curry was right and I was destined for leadership in the literary world! In the fall of 1928, I registered for a course in creative writing. My major opus was titled *Pop*. My story drew on my Thompson-Starrett experiences with my boss Mr. Abramson, Tommy the timekeeper, and the old men who slept through their hours as night watchmen. In my story, Pop is employed by Mr. Grimney as night watchman on the Presbyterian Hospital job. (His papers are filed by Mr. Grimney's office boy, "a bored young intellectual"—and this even before Hitchcock began to include himself in bit roles in his films!) Pop Poole reports to work under Jimmy Baron, the materials clerk, and comes to adore the personable Jimmy. Sam, Jimmy's co-worker, tells Pop that some plumbers' tools are being stolen from the job. Pop resolves to be vigilant, yet lapses into the customary night watchman's slumber.

> A noise from above roused Pop at 3 A.M. Quaking as though clutched by a palsied hand, the old man made his way

about the first floor. Just shadows, nothing to justify suspicions of human presences. Upward he climbed to the second floor. His flashlight gleamed on the metal stairs and seemed to radiate like an all-seeing eye. His footsteps sounded like the drums of doom to his tortured mind.

Far over at the opposite end of the building a fitful beam of light darted about piercing the gloom. It shifted rapidly along the ground as though the holder were familiar with the floor and needed light only to pick out gaping holes in the concrete. It came to the stairway farthest from Pop and went upward. Pop could hear the stairs creak under the weight of a heavy body.

To Pop it was no ghoul; it was a man and he knew who the man was. Frozen to the spot he could only stand and stare at the figure of Jimmy, **his** Jimmy outlined in the refracted glare of the flashlight. It was too unreal, too ghastly to be true. There was only one freckled face surmounted by a mop of tangled red hair, one such pair of aggressive shoulders in this world. It was Jimmy!

Then he saw Grimney. Forbidding of aspect as ever, Grimney was standing looking up the stairway Baron had ascended. In the uncertain glow emanating from the stairpit above, the man's natural resemblance to a bird of prey was increased tenfold. The vulture was poised for the inevitable swoop.

His single-track mind working to its limited capacity, Pop understood. Jimmy was the crook who had stolen the tools. Now he was on another marauding raid. Grimney had somehow suspected this and had either followed or lain in wait for him. And now Pop's Jimmy would be caught, eternally disgraced, jailed. Johnny Jenkins, the company president, would no longer seek his advice. Was there nothing that could avert such a catastrophe?

Pop hastened up another stairway, heading for the seventh floor where the plumbers' tools were stored. He must reach that shanty before Jimmy and warn him of Grimney's presence. The thought did not enter his mind that his warning's final effect would be almost negligible with Grimney only a few stories below. The fact that Jimmy was in danger and needed backing sufficed to send him stumbling and fumbling his way up the endless staircase.

He reached the fifth floor and seemed to be flying through a void, a vast awful blackness in which time or feeling did not exist. A sudden, heretofore unknown pain was tearing his heart into minute fragments and throwing the pieces about his body. Seventh floor at last, to him seventh heaven. He managed one hasty glance which showed him that he was first on the floor before he fell prostrate across the threshold of the plumbers' shanty.

He felt pain as he had never felt before. There was a demon inside him with a claw-hammer, pounding his side, trying to tear and crash a way to the outside. Even worse than the pain was the knowledge that he couldn't warn Jimmy. He could only part his lips a fraction of an inch. A gasp escaped his bursting lungs and he lay still. Nothingness. Lights. Voices floating across his consciousness. Grimney's rasping voice, "I must admit, Baron, that I thought you were pulling this stuff until we stumbled across the ungrateful old cur here. After all you'd done for him, too." An oddly weak, babyish "Yeah" from his Jimmy. A professional clearcut voice, "Old age and heart trouble, probably aggravated by fear of discovery." More gratings from Grimney on the ingratitude and perversity of human nature. As the last drops of resistance to death were ebbing, Pop heard the voice he longed to hear, the only voice worth hearing. "Pop, are you saint or devil?..."

"Do you want to put any remarks on this watchman Poole's card record, Mr. Grimney sir?" asked the office boy.

Grimney glanced up from his pile of routine work.

"Poole?" he said tentatively as though the name were new to him and unfamiliar.

"Yes sir, the watchman who died over on the Presbyterian Hospital."

"I remember now; let me have the card please."

So Pop Poole's only obituary was written on the records of the Jenkins Company, 'H. Poole Ngt Watch. Presb. Hosp. 7/4/28-12/9/28. Remarks: Died of heart failure due to discovery that he was stealing tools. LJ Grimney.'

But to Jimmy Baron he always remained a god.

The instructor penciled on the story a few lines: "You have a good theme here, but somehow the effect is unsatisfactory—an ending in such complete understanding all around leaves the reader with a sold feeling. He ought to have the feeling—at least we want it—that the sacrifice has won something of value, is worthwhile." The grade was C.

Years later when the editors of *Contemporary Authors* asked me for data for an entry in their guide to current authors and their work, I wrote in part, "After my high school graduation at sixteen,...I registered in hopeless night schools for hopeless courses taught by hopeless teachers to hopeless would-be writers. Naturally I wrote nothing publishable.... I began to dimly apprehend that to write well a person had to live. He had to know something and do something."

After writing *Pop*, it occurred to me that maybe I should **read** some short stories before I tried to write them. One of the Thompson-Starrett jobs was a building for NYU's downtown campus on Washington Square, so I knew about New York University offerings. In the spring of 1929 I registered in the NYU evening session for a course in short story writing. The book we used was the Dorothy Brewster anthology, *A Book of Modern Short Stories*. The authors included people named James Joyce, Anton Chekhov, Willa Cather, Stephen Crane, Joseph Conrad, Katherine Mansfield, and Henry James. But I particularly liked Ernest Hemingway's *The Killers*, Ring Lardner's *Haircut*, and a story by Anatole France. The only writer whose name I recognized in the anthology was Katharine Brush, who had written a story for *College Humor*, one of my bibles.

I "rose" at Thompson-Starrett. Now I was no longer an office boy; they called me a clerk, and my salary climbed to $25 a week. I banked some of it and by the summer of 1929, when I was 18, had accumulated $400. I still carried messages and money to the construction jobs and maintained the employment file.

One day I said to my mother, "My one disappointment in life so far is that I couldn't go to college." She never forgot my comment. Late in the summer of 1929 I vacationed for a week with Flo and her friends at Bay Shore, a sleepy little town on the South Shore of Long Island. I came home, expecting another year in the Thompson-Starrett dead end. My mother said, "You're going to go to college." "But the money?" I asked. "We'll use what you saved and you'll earn more in the summers. We'll manage somehow." My mother was like that.

I gave a week's notice to Abramson and Troast, said goodby to A. E. Barlow, who promised me employment during vacations (after all, Herbert Hoover had just been elected on the slogan "two chickens in every pot and two cars in every garage," and the economists were assuring us that we had reached "a permanent plateau of prosperity").

In those days you simply went to college. You didn't bother to apply. You got a transcript from your high school; during registration week you went to the college, transcript in hand. The college welcomed you. So I wrote off for the Columbia College catalog and, come registration week, took the subway up to Morningside Heights. I looked for the admissions office but couldn't find it. Shy, I couldn't bring myself to ask people for directions. After an hour of wandering around the Columbia campus, I took the subway down to New York University on Washington Square.

The people in charge asked me, "Which college?" There were different colleges? I said I didn't know; I just wanted to go to college. "What do you want to be?" they asked. "What do you want to work at when you graduate?" I gulped and made the same choice I had made for my entry in the *Folio* class history. "Business, I guess," I said.

New York University enrolled me as a freshman in the School of Commerce. I took marketing, introduction to business, economic geography, Spanish, and English composition. Each day I rode the subway to NYU, was crammed into the elevators in the School of Commerce building, ate in the same dingy commercial cafeteria, and promptly traveled home after classes.

Somehow this wasn't what I thought college was going to be. The School of Commerce at NYU was a far cry from the colleges I had read about in *College Humor*. My classmates seemed brassy and the co-eds weren't appetizing. The professors were businesslike and aloof. Of course, I enjoyed English and did well with an instructor who seemed lonely and who incessantly discussed, in class, movies he had recently seen. Another NYU instructor, Thomas Wolfe, was later to describe the atmosphere savagely in *Of Time and the River* as

> the brawling and ugly corridors of the university, which drown one, body and soul, with their swarming, shrieking, shouting tides of dark amber flesh.... As he hurried down the stairs on such an evening..., he hated the building more than he had ever hated any building before: it seemed to be soaked in all the memories of fruitless labor and harsh strife, of fear and hate and weariness, of ragged nerves and pounding heart and tired

flesh: the building brooded there, charged with its dreadful burden of human pain, unencumbered with its grief.

Christmas 1929 came and, true to his promise, A. E. Barlow, no doubt with the cooperation of Abramson, found me temporary work during the New York University winter vacation. For three weeks I became a checker on a Thompson-Starrett job; the Downtown Athletic Club was joining the cluster of skyscrapers at Manhattan's tip. Checkboard in hand, I recorded the presence of bricklayers, carpenters, and plumbers on the lower floors. "What's your number, please? Do you know where I'll find number 438, Joe Havorka?" Then I had to walk the eight-inch beams forty floors above the street to check the ironworkers. Ironworkers are deservedly among the highest paid of building trade workers. Many are of American Indian ancestry; all are rough, tough, proud to be ironworkers, well aware of where the last ironworker fell from a lofty perch, fully conscious of danger and yet scornful of risk. To reach them, I walked the beams that were sometimes icy during the New York winter. The ironworkers would lay genial bets. "Even money the kid falls off this time." "Give me some odds and I'll take it."

Nineteen-thirty was the first year of the Great Depression, which followed the stock market crash of October 1929. It was hard for Barlow and Abramson to find me summer work. Yet when the university academic year ended, they persuaded Gus, a Swedish carpenter of my father's vintage, to put me on the payroll as a carpenters' laborer, even though I held no union card. The hours were long. My family had rented a bungalow for the summer at Beacon Hill, a venerable colony of ramshackle cottages near Port Washington on the North Shore of Long Island. Each weekday morning at about six my sister drove me to the Port Washington station, where I took the Long Island Railroad to Penn Station in Manhattan.

I don't know which was harder that summer, the work or the waiting around. Before eight, I would change into work clothes and join Gus and his taciturn crew of carpenters, largely Swedish in background, and the dispirited miscellaneous carpenters' laborers. The work was hard enough, for when lumber arrived the laborers hoisted it to their shoulders and brought it to the carpenters. I can still feel the bite of heavy two-by-fours on my shoulder blades. Yet, in retrospect, the waiting now seems even harder. In my early weeks as a carpenters' laborer, I kept turning to the carpenters and to the foreman in the intervals between shipments of lumber with, "What do you want me to do now?" They responded, "You trying to get the job done in a day, kid? We got to stretch out this work." The Great Depression was abroad in the land; layoffs, the dread of the building construction worker, were in the offing. Building in New York City was dying; Thompson-Starrett had few jobs to which the carpenters and the laborers could shift after completion.

So there were endless times when the carpenters and their laborers had nothing to do, yet had to look busy. You couldn't sit down, because you don't look busy sitting down. Reading was out of the question. So we did idiot work, walking around picking up sticks and chips. Then a truck would arrive and the boards would gouge into my shoulders. After an hour or two of this, we would relapse into waiting. Sometimes my former bosses from the main offices would arrive and the word would be passed, "Look busy, kid," and the desultory pace of picking up chips would speed up.

When the five o'clock whistle delivered me from work and waiting, I would change clothes and, dirty and sweaty, head for the railroad station. At seven P. M. on Beacon Hill there was an opportunity for a swim and dinner before bed. I lived for the weekends of canoeing and for the parties Flo's crowd held on Saturday nights.

After a year in the School of Commerce dead end, I learned the magic words, "I want a broad liberal arts education." So in the fall following my New York University freshman year, I found the admissions office at Columbia University. They asked me what I wanted to be, and this time I said, "A journalist. But I want a broad liberal education first." I had little idea what that might be. They asked about a major and I responded "English." They credited me for courses in English and Spanish and gave me a few credits in economics for some of my business courses. The rest of my NYU courses were confederate money to them. They registered me in Columbia College as an English major. My education began.

What had shaped me to date? My mother and father. My varied relatives. Our War over Religion. Growing up in lower-middle-class Corona. Fact parroting in traditional schools. Being skipped into alien grades. Glimpses of a wider world. The trauma of my father's death. Dead-end building construction jobs. Miscellaneous reading. A few friends. Fooling around with girls. Higher education of the trade school variety. Vague aspiration to write something. Ambition to be somebody or something. But who? Or what?

Come now, young man. You're 19, weigh 170 pounds, and are 5 feet 11 ½ inches tall (though you claim you're 6 feet). The world is your oyster. Or is it?

Chapter Eleven

COLLEGE

C olumbia College looked and felt and smelled like a college. Unlike NYU, the separate schools of the university were scattered across a genuine campus. The old library overlooked a benign Alma Mater; she, in turn, looked down the steps at athletes trotting around an attractive athletic field. Though Columbia College students ranged freely across the entire Columbia University campus and occasionally took classes in the philosophy or science buildings, our college classes were usually held in our own building, Hamilton Hall, which adjoined our dormitories. Though I was a commuter, I thought of them fondly as "our" dormitories. We of the college had our own newspaper, *The Columbia Spectator*, our own dean, Herbert E. Hawkes, our own distinguished faculty. The campus was ours; the students in the professional schools such as law and engineering seemed to us transients. On autumnal Saturdays we bellowed "Roar lion roar" at Baker Field.

I was classified as a freshman, since half of my prior credits from NYU were counterfeit, and I wore my beanie on campus with pride. When I sat on the benches and ivied walls in front of Hamilton and the dorms, I felt that now I really belonged somewhere.

During that first year at Columbia I took both freshman and sophomore courses, a heavy load of nineteen points the first semester and eighteen points the second, including advanced composition, American literature, historical bases of English literature, psychology, and geology, along with lecture courses in philosophy and government and a daily course in contemporary civilization. American literature, as taught by the critic and poet Mark Van Doren, interrelated authors and their times; for the first time in my life I recognized that authors were men and women who were bringing the messages of their eras to me. Psychology was taught by Gardner Murphy, an eminent psychologist; I began to get some insights into what motivated and moved both me and other people. Geology involved field trips and even a visit with Armin K. Lobeck, our professor and the author of our textbook, in his home. But it was Contemporary Civilization 1, a course on the development of ideas throughout the history of civilization, that truly set me on fire. We read and discussed John Herman Randall's *The Making of the Modern Mind*. The history of mankind, which had previously been meaningless and routine, came alive and became relevant as past thinkers talked to me.

Roused by my program, I began to read hungrily yet selectively. I read on the subway, at lunch, in the cafeterias of Morningside Heights, in the Hamilton Hall library, and late into the night at home. I went beyond the laughing skeptics whom I had stumbled upon during my year at NYU and whom I had come to worship. In my pre-Columbia college year, I had found Sinclair Lewis, who took me to *Main Street* and introduced me to *Babbitt*. Through H. L. Mencken's iconoclastic *Prejudices*, I had explored the ineptitude of the booboisie. James Branch Cabell had introduced me to imaginary Poictesme through the sensual *Jurgen*. Dorothy Parker had contributed *Laments for the Living* in her stories of disillusioned sophisticates, and Ring Lardner had deglamorized baseball players in *You Know Me, Al*. Thorton Wilder had accompanied me across *The Bridge of San Luis Rey*. Several of the laughing skeptics had enhanced my anticlericalism, notably Anatole France through *The Revolt of the Angels* and *At the Sign of the Reine Pedauque*, Sinclair Lewis through *Elmer Gantry*, and H. L. Mencken through *Treatise on the Gods*.

Now, at Columbia, I met the lost generation as Ernest Hemingway's ambulance driver said *Farewell to Arms* and Lady Brett found no peace while *The Sun Also Rises*; as F. Scott Fitzgerald reported from *This Side of Paradise* on *The Jazz Age* and *The Beautiful and Damned* and as the green light at West Egg beckoned *The Great Gatsby*; as John Dos Passos recounted the disillusion of *Three Soldiers*; as Erich Maria Remarque lamented all wars in *All Quiet on the Western Front.*

I began to read plays: O'Neill's *The Emperor Jones* and *The Hairy Ape*, Maxwell Anderson's *What Price Glory?* with Laurence Stallings, Edmond Rostand's *Cyrano De Bergerac*, Hecht and MacArthur's *The Front Page.* Apparently there was more to the theater than the dramas I had seen in my teens at the Boulevard Theater in Jackson Heights: *The Cat and the Canary, Broadway, White Cargo* (ah, that Tondelayo!) and Mae West's *Pleasure Man.* I saw the latter stage production when I was about 14 and innocently reported to my parents that it seemed to be about men dancing with other men. They looked askance at each other. When *Pleasure Man* opened on Broadway after the Boulevard Theater tryout, the authorities closed it down. My opportunities to go to the Boulevard also came perilously close to being closed down. My first insight into homosexuality came during that first Columbia year through Radclyffe Hall's *The Well of Loneliness*, a pioneering account of lesbian experience.

Despite my early prejudice against poetry, developed by my inept English teachers and my immaturity, I began to find some lines in contemporary poetry that talked to me. I went about quoting Edward Arlington Robinson, who said, "It's all a world where bugs and emperors go singularly back to the same dust." I admired impartially both Carl Sandburg's *Chicago*, "Hog butcher for the world," and Edna St. Vincent Millay's *A Few Figs from Thistles*, "My candle burns at both ends; it will not last the night; but, ah, my foes, and, oh, my friends—it gives a lovely light."

Naturally, I missed many treats. Henry James and Edith Wharton were too "high society" for a lower-middle-class lad; George Bernard Shaw had to wait until my radicalization. Most Europeans were beyond me: Mann, Kafka, Pirandello, Conrad, Joyce, Proust, Woolf. But I did find Somerset Maugham and read still more of D. H. Lawrence.

At mid-term of the fall semester I drew three B's, two grades of B minus, and a C plus. At the end of the academic year I scored one A, one A minus, one B plus, and two B's. Two years later I graduated from Columbia College by dint of carrying twenty points each semester during my junior and senior years and I missed by a hair the chance to jingle a Phi Beta Kappa key. I always was a slow starter in life.

I didn't write much during that first year of Columbia—which I judge is just as well, when I look over what I wrote while at Thompson-Starrett and at NYU: football stories called *A Few Minutes with Spike* and *How to Play the Line; Haunted House* and *Little Guy* (about a sensitive shrimp); and *Making* and *From the Rumble*, explorations of the sexual mores of youth. Instead of writing, I read and learned.

By the end of that hybrid freshman-sophomore year at Columbia, I saw myself as an intellectual, though I was worlds away from being one; an agnostic, which seemed to me more sophisticated than being an atheist; an iconoclastic observer of the stupidity of what I had learned to call the bourgeoisie; an Ivy League campus man forced by humble circumstances to commute by subway. In short, I was well on my way to becoming a literary snob. My value words were "urbane, suave, unruffled." The aloof literary man or the dispassionate journalist—these were the roles I coveted.

The Great Depression saved me from becoming a phony. At first, I really hadn't paid much attention to the depression. Yes, the stock market crashed a few weeks after I registered at New York University, but my business-oriented NYU professors refused to acknowledge the existence of a depression; they never mentioned it. The Hoover administration maintained that prosperity was just around the corner, and the newspapers attempted to minimize the downturn.

During the summer of 1930, when I labored and pretended to labor on the crew of Gus, the carpenter foreman, the reality of the depression had come home to me. From my 1927-1929 days as an office boy and clerk for Thompson-Starrett, I had grown accustomed to a few men hanging around the shanties before eight A.M., hoping the foreman would put on some additional workers. In 1930, however, large groups of men surrounded the shanties. "Gus, anything today? How does it look? I haven't had anything since the Jamaica Theater job. I'm a good carpenter, Gus." In the 1927-1929 period, the men had drifted off when no work was forthcoming; now, in 1930, some stayed around all day, hungrily watching the employed and waiting for nothing. Family men eyed me, wondering what magic accounted for the employment of the tall, skinny, inept kid, and rightly concluding that it was pull with someone. Guiltily, I tried to avoid eye contact with them. As I traveled to and from work, the men sleeping in the subways and on the park benches and the men soberly and shamefacedly standing in the soup lines were inescapable. The system wasn't working.

During my summer as a laborer, a handsome and dapper friend of Flo's at Beacon Hill, Bill Charvat, a Washington Square College instructor in English, told me that I had a good mind but wasn't using it. He passed on to me his copies of *The Nation*, then as now an antagonist of the status quo and the establishment. I liked its liberal analysis, diagnosis, and prescription. Throughout that summer, on the long journeys to my labors, I began reading journals of opinion, including *Forbes, The Magazine of Wall Street*, and *Nation's Business* at one end of the spectrum and *The Nation, The New Republic*, and *The New Masses* at the other. I found the arguments of the left far more persuasive and more attuned to the contemporary reality I observed daily. Heywood Broun of the *New York World-Telegram* and Edmund Wilson of *The New Republic* made most sense of all to me.

I experienced the depression vicariously, through the mind rather than the belly. Our family hard times had begun years earlier with my father's death and the termination of his paychecks; we limped along in 1930 depression as we had in 1926 prosperity on part of Flo's salary and on painful withdrawals from meager family savings and insurance. But we were never hungry.

My doubts about the system returned stronger than ever during the bitter summer of 1931. By then even the establishment recognized that a major depression had arrived. Paternal Thompson-Starrett found me a job as a materials checker on the Waldorf-Astoria job. The luxurious new Waldorf-Astoria, a successor to its aristocratic predecessor, was rising on lordly Park Avenue. A few blocks south were the main offices of Thompson-Starrett beside the New York Central Building, from which an ironworker had hurtled to death during my time as an office boy.

What a study in contrasts during the summer of 1931 on the Waldorf job! The sleek limousines were lined up before the massive luxury apartments. The well-groomed residents punctuated their steps with flourishes of canes. The jobless workers grouped on Forty-ninth and Fiftieth streets; the police kept the unemployed off Park Avenue.

Inside the Waldorf we were creating a future promenade for wealthy strollers, Peacock Alley. We built huge high-ceilinged restaurants for gourmets, and at noon we played handball against walls that an artist was soon to decorate with stunning murals.

The building construction workers feared the completion of the Waldorf job. In 1931 it was as vestigial as the last dinosaur; few monuments to privilege were being built in America. Symbolically, my responsibility was to record the volume of rubble being carried away in tired, shabby dump trucks.

My radicalization began in my third college year, the second at Columbia. My heavy class schedule didn't reflect the shift; my program was dominated by literature: Shakespeare, Development of the English Novel, Masterpieces of Spanish Literature, and The Russian Novelists. I was required to take chemistry, taught by Harold C. Urey, a scientific giant who announced the isolation of heavy hydrogen that year and who became one of the fathers of the atomic bomb; he was a major scientist and an unimpressive teacher whose mind was obviously elsewhere. I also enrolled in a memorable project course in composition, in which I began to write a novel. The novel didn't reflect my shift either; it was too early in the game.

Quantitatively, my reading was heavier than in any other year in my life. It included the Russians—Tolstoy, Dostoyevsky, Turgenev, Chekhov, Gorky; the Spaniards—Cervantes, Lope de Vega, Blasco Ibanez; and especially the British—Samuel Richardson, Joseph Fielding, Jonathan Swift, Daniel Defoe, Tobias Smollett, Laurence Sterne, Horace Walpole, Ann Radcliffe, Jane Austen, Walter Scott, George Meredith, William Makepeace Thackeray, Emily and Charlotte Bronte, Anthony Trollope, Thomas Harding, Samuel Butler, George Gissing, Arnold Bennett, Max Beerbohm, Joseph Conrad, William Henry Hudson, Aldous Huxley—one major British novelist per week. Under gentle Mark Van Doren, who was devoid of pretension, I came to understand the language of Shakespeare's characters and read all of the plays and most of the poetry.

Qualitatively, my reading began to change. For instance, I

read Tolstoy to learn the reality of war and to envision his socialist society, Dostoyevsky and Gorky to understand the world of the dispossessed in which the revolutionaries lived, Turgenev and Chekhov to understand the lives of the hapless and hopeless middle-class intelligentsia. My experience broadened, too. Contemporary Civilization, having contributed to the making of our modern minds, now took up contemporary problems and required students to take field trips. We went to jails and mental institutions, to markets and ethnic communities. The misery of life in the city during a depression unrolled itself before our eyes.

In that junior year I occasionally attended sessions of Columbia's Institute of Arts and Sciences, a series of talks by leaders in the arts and culture of New York City, held on campus in the McMillan Auditorium. In search of light, I also went to radical meetings on campus. I looked in on the meetings of Yipsels (Young People's Socialist League) and the meetings of the left-wing forces contending for control of the League Against War and Fascism. But the campus radicals seemed dogmatic, doctrinaire, and humorless to me. I heard out the members of a variety of splinter groups. I especially disliked the adult Communists from Union Square. I listened to their speeches about bloody Harlan County and their pleas to students to join quixotic bus groups going to Kentucky to help the miners. I joined nothing. I remained an onlooker. I read about the depression rather than personally experienced its lash.

Yet I was moving toward a conclusion. It seemed to me that the best road for America would be the achievement of peaceful evolution to American socialism under the leadership of Norman Thomas.

But I tended to change slowly—certainly not overnight. My writing during my freshman/sophomore and junior years was romantic, primarily concerned with me and my problems rather than the social order and its problems. For instance, in an English Composition paper during my first year at Columbia, I wrestled with the conflicting character of Christ the man. I read the New Testament closely to check out the assertion in Sinclair Lewis's *Elmer Gantry* by a character who declared, "I'm appalled to see that I don't find Jesus an especially admirable character!"

I cited Jesus's occasional anger and pride. I concluded, "If Jesus was God, all that I have written is silly, as God may not be judged by men's standards. If he was human, he was just that—human."

When Mark Van Doren turned us loose in English Composition Two to develop our own project, our own piece of sustained writing, I reacted characteristically in two ways: Through shyness I did not take advantage of his invitation to confer with him in the office during the development of the paper (he held no formal classes whatsoever after the first sessions); and I chose a romantic, Edgar Allan Poe, and attempted to show the interrelationship between his imaginative writing and events within his actual life. The essay ran a substantial sixty-nine pages; of it Van Doren said generously that, if the validity of the theory of interrelationships were acknowledged, the product was highly creditable and readable.

Mark Van Doren emanated love of literature rather than dissected it. He became my advisor for my last two undergraduate years. Despite his kindness and accessibility, I would no sooner have brought my personal problems to this literary celebrity than to Jove. Appalled by the number of masterpieces I would never find time to read and the reams I would never write, I once asked him what he was going to do during the coming summer. Knowing that I was really asking what I should do, the quiet young literary eminence responded, "Just live." Van Doren, a poet, never wasted words. I got the message.

During the junior year my writing still focused upon me. Even my essay on Ivan Turgenev bore a characteristic self-perception in the subtitle, "Born Onlooker." Other essays dealt with the naysayers, H. L. Mencken and Theodore Dreiser. In my freer writing I did character sketches of my friends—Ben, Joe, Peg, Kido—and through writing of them, wrote of myself through a series of sketches with the omnibus title, *Saturday Night Party*.

My *pièce de résistance* of that junior year was a novel, *Loose*, embarked upon as I reached the age of 21. Professor Dick of the English faculty gathered together eight would-be writers and gave them free rein. He called the program "Project Course in Composition." Unlike Van Doren, he held several meetings weekly throughout the academic year so that the evolving manuscripts, largely plays and novels, might be regularly read aloud and criticized by the group. Inevitably, I chose to write an auto-biographical novel. The protagonists were James Roderick (my-self), his eccentric pal Ted (based on Freddy, a neurotic friend), whom James Roderick resolves to induct into life, a beautiful vision called Doris Flood and her battle-ax mother (based on red-headed Muriel's family), a grocery store owner named Mr. Schultz (based on Professor Dick), and an incredibly sensitive and perceptive dog, Daisy. In retrospect, Daisy was the best developed character. But let us see how James Roderick, also me, lived the literary life at 21.

He was writing with his usual desperation. The keys flew up and dropped back; the back spacer was called into use steadily, almost rhythmically, twice a line. The typewriter bell clanged timidly, as though afraid of offending this demon who was beating the machine from pillar to post, and occasionally, with cowardly slyness, did not clang. It was that kind of type-writer. Consequently, a long sentence heavily interlarded with semicolons and exclamation points, the writer's favorite marks of punctuation, would slide an inch past the margin of the yellow paper and come to rest in great perplexity on the metal clamp. A brief struggle would ensue and man would once more become master of his machine. The pecking would con-tinue while a cigarette burned itself out unnoticed, precari-ously leaning over the edge of the wooden table. What matter that the yellow paper wore a ragged and discouraged look? He was writing!

"And why shouldn't Dreiser be contemptuous of our weak, petty world? We do nothing to deserve the respect of God or man. We cheat, we steal, we snivel, we snarl;—and all for money, most miserable substance in the memory of living creatures! When we get it, we have nothing; happiness is unobtainable no matter what medium of exchange we offer. All we can live for, indeed all we can grasp, are those brief ephemeral snatches of beauty which at times Dreiser occasion-ally touches."

He leaned back for a second wind and nodded sagely to himself, "Good writing, son, good writing." "Brief ephemeral snatches." He rolled the words over his tongue, prolonging the beautiful emotions they had stirred in him. Mellowing wine and his writings had that same happy faculty of becoming more charming with age. And like wine, they had the same power to throw him off balance and detach him from the world.

It was most remarkable. At the supper table, with a truly noble effort at nonchalance, he would announce that tonight, after he finished his English Lit and Spanish, he intended to "dash off another little essay in the philosophy series." Along about the middle of the first page, sometimes even earlier while he was looking up a word in the English-Spanish dictionary, he would find himself drifting in rose-colored dreams, dreams which had little to do with the pains and practice of literature, but much to do with the rewards. They all had vaguely to do with James Roderick Kendall, artist among artists, cynic among cynics, man among women. In them, James Roderick always looked bored and nonchalant and slightly contemptuous while he flicked his ashes from his cigarette and uttered pronouncements that startled the literary world; truly an Olympian state.

"It is Dreiser and men like him who today are the only hopes to save America from her inevitable fall."

There was a world of power in feeling that he and Dreiser had ideas in common. A common disregard for money, a common distrust of the sincerity of women, a common contempt for pettiness!

"...her inevitable fall. Let those who must struggle futilely in the welter of their worlds..."

Hey, that was a good word, welter; he must remember it. But he'd better look it up before he used it, and not let anything happen like that other time when he had used something—what was it again? It hadn't detracted much from the essay though, even if Old Louie had picked it up and waxed sarcastic. That essay had been too doggone good to be spoiled by a trifle. Louie had waxed sarcastic just to keep in practice. A form of exercise. A nice duck in his way, Louie, but...w-e-l-l, kind of unappreciative. Stupid even. In fact, now that he thought of it, that was the trouble with most people. Well-intentioned, honest in money matters, kind, having all those middle class virtues—but stupid. Babbitty. Those first few pages of *Babbitt* though! Weren't they honest, swell? He'd never forget the time he read them. They were so powerful that he had stood on the elevated station after arriving at his stop and had watched several train-loads of people pile out. Ordinary, ignorant people carrying *Graphics* and Hearst papers and with never a thought in the world for the bigger things in life. He remembered how he had stood, his face half turned to them, a smile of cynicism wreathing his lips. And they, the fools, had seen nothing more than a tall young man leaning against a bill poster and smoking a cigarette. Then as a last cluster were going down the stairs from the platform, he had laughed, a bold, ringing laugh, and several of the sheep had turned and looked moonishly at him. He could still smile at the expression on their faces. Lewis would have enjoyed that scene. He really must read more of Lewis, more than just *Elmer Gantry* and the first fifty pages of *Babbitt.* It was a shame the darn book had come due at the library before he had time to read it. Dreiser too. It was all right to write an article on him from his present acquaintance; he thoroughly understood his philosophy; but for the pleasure attached he must read more than just "Free" and a few of the portraits in "A Gallery of Women."

Did he have any money in these clothes? He thought he'd stop awhile and go down the street and get some ice cream.

Eight chapters of the novel were completed under Professor Dick's ministrations and the group's criticisms. At the close of chapter eight, the dog Daisy is listening to a poet reciting his incoherent masterpiece in a living room.

Without warning, the gentleman began to declaim caressingly, in that tone characteristic of lovers, some types of feebleminded people, and authors reading from their own works. Daisy listened.

Then he heard the zither.
Wandering, turning,
Writhing pregnant for the twist,
It mourned...
Eerie, wailing goddess of the banshee...
Fighting with strife unalterable,
While she leaned to the right
And he watched;
While the horror of "No use, no use,"
Dire dooming legions stayed
Vapidly pale and beat against his breasts...
Eerie wailing goddess of the banshee...
To the windows of his soul it climbed and
Looked within.
A wasteland, parched and untillable.
Unholy mounds, dim veiled forms,
Knew the inexplicable, shouted the unsayable,
Left vacuum for the mind, yet said nothing.

How the wind is shrieking,
Tearing by the tombstones,
How the brow is wrinkled,
Waiting, waiting, waiting,
For the—
Eeeeerie, wailing goddess of the banshee...

The young man ended. His head drooped, and he gazed for another moment into the fire; then, like a maestro turning to his audience, he wheeled. He tossed his hair back from his forehead, and fixed his eyes on a spot far above the girl's head, while he registered manifestations of plucking himself back from Olympus. His lifted chin showed the delicate modeling of his throat; his hands were clenched. The girl sobbed and buried her head among the pillows. He came toward her, maintaining the same beautifully martyr-like attitude till he realized that she couldn't see him. Then he sank to his knees by her side and dislodged a key pillow. "Luke," she said, "Luke. God, it's wonderful; it's beautiful." Gracefully she lifted her slim, white arms, and drew him to her. He adjusted his body—one knee had been bearing all the weight—and kissed her again and again. "Love," he said, "love." They both believed it.

Daisy went away, meditating on the actors who tread the boards in the comedy, Life. She thought of the couple in the dining room, and growled, "Merely a matter of phraseology; ends and means are the same." But then it must be remembered that Daisy was a cynic. Worse, a sentimental cynic, a cynic by compulsion rather than predilection, in every new situation fresh, optimistic, yet—ever disappointed.

But the master, the young master, where was he during this desecration of the temple? She hastened to the living room, and in the doorway stopped, amazement written on every sensitive line of her face.

At this point the novel stops. What the dog Daisy saw will never be known.

Possibly Daisy saw economic reality. In the summer of 1932, prior to my senior year, I didn't even try to get a summer job with Thompson-Starrett. Largely, this was because of my newly found social conscience; I could no longer bear the thought of being favored with a job that rightfully belonged to a family man. Partially, it derived from the handwriting on the wall: The Great Depression was nearing its depth, and reached it in March 1933

College

when the banks failed in a society with sixteen million unemployed, one-third of the work force, and with industrial production at one-half of the 1929 level. That summer I tried to finish the novel and couldn't.

In this atmosphere, my words first appeared in print. My debut took the form of a letter to the *Columbia Spectator*, November 4, 1932. The letter criticized an earlier column in the *Spectator* defending Herbert Hoover:

> Stroller says, "It is time that someone realized that there was something to be said for Hoover," and he goes on to say something, namely, not swapping horses is not "a bad argument," and further even more recklessly, that "it happens to have some sense." With rapidly rising enthusiasm, he says that it is more meaningful than "Keep Kool with Kal"; we ourselves share this passion, as our imagination can conceive of nothing less meaningful than this latter unless it be Lewis Carroll on the Jabberwock and the Frumious Bandersnatch.

The letter went on to defend Norman Thomas and to advocate a vote for him. Franklin D. Roosevelt was elected in a landslide.

Just before the election of 1932, I tried my hand at prophecy. If you allow generously for youthful rhetoric, you may find that my crystal ball was not too badly cracked.

> Prophecy writ this twelfth year of the reign of God, the Republican Party, and Prosperity; 1932.
>
> Within ten years there will be another European war rivalling the earlier one in brutality, though not in duration due to the preponderance of power on one side and the relatively smooth crushing of the opposition.
>
> There will be no change in the government of the U.S.; it will neither be in the hands of big business frankly and undisguisedly as Aldous Huxley predicts, nor have become socialistic as the liberals hope. The workers will have been soothed by a concession from the bosses taking perhaps the form of some sort of social insurance, and by the return of inflation, known to Americans as Prosperity. Americans in their stupidity and complacency will relapse—as though they ever roused—into their normal state of political dormancy; the workers meanwhile will be bearing out the contention of Malthus, poor economist, but practical philosopher, that the wages of labor tend

89

to hover barely above the subsistence level. America won't worry—won't it still have the radio and movies—maybe even a job then?

The country will elect a Democratic President in 1932; Americans, with good native optimism, inherited we are told from our frontier ancestors, will think they have made a change and be quite proud of themselves.

Chapter Twelve

LOVE

S omething happened soon after I entered Columbia College: I met Bee and we fell in love.

The date we met was November 8, 1930. The place was the Jackson Heights Country Club where the De-Molays held a costume dance. Bee was charming in a crinoline dress with wide, flowing skirts. She came with Al, and I was with a date whose name has vanished into the fogs of memory. Al was a foul-mouthed toad whom everyone disliked. Bee was with him because, temporarily short of a date, she had resolved to say "yes" to the next invitation to a dance or party. Unfortunately for her—but luckily for me—it turned out to be Al. At some point in the evening Al and I switched dates and he went off with Nameless while Bee and I danced, then sat together for hours talking animatedly. Years later, Bee showed me her diary entry: "November 8th, 1930—What a nite! I'm not going out with Al again. Enjoyed the dance (old-fashioned costume at Jackson Heights Club). Talked with Bill Van Tyl for a long time on 'philosophies.' Home at four."

So I called her and we dated for tennis, for parties at Ben's and at my house, for dances sponsored by her Pal O Mine Club, a group of girls with whom Bee had gone through parochial school, and for long sessions of talk about the social scene, books, writing and, inevitably at 19, our "philosophies." I was accustomed to going out with girls who had bodies but no perceptible minds. Bee had both a body and a mind.

I soon learned of the origins of her way of looking at the

world. Beatrice Barbara Blaha was the youngest of seven children born to two Czech immigrants. Vaclav (Americanized to William) Blaha, deprived of any share of the family farm near Kocelovice by the primogeniture laws of the Austro-Hungarian Empire, turned to the New World alone in 1889, crossing the Atlantic at the age of 16. He became a skilled cabinetmaker. A quiet man, he seldom mentioned that he was an admirer of John Huss, the Bohemian religious reformer who opposed feudalism and the medieval church. Rose Vydra, with her parents and two sisters, made the stormy crossing of the ocean at age 9 to join three older sisters in the Bohemian section of Yorkville in New York City. Rose was a devout and unquestioning Roman Catholic; William, though nominally Catholic, attended church only until the day of his marriage. Rose married William when she was 20 and he was 26. Their first baby, born in 1900, died after a few days; their surviving children were born in 1901, 1902, 1905, 1907, 1909, and Bee was the last to arrive, 1911. Rose, a strong-minded woman, saw to it that all of the children went to Mass; if William objected, he kept it to himself. Both Rose and William were strong nationalists who loved Bohemia and the Czechoslovakia created after World War I, but they readily became American patriots; they named their first son George, for he was born on Washington's birthday.

In her Corona house about a mile away from where I lived, Bee grew up in a household with one older sister plus four older brothers who helped her become a competent athlete. Her father taught her to be amazingly competent with tools; she learned to repair anything. Since her mother's five sisters married and lived in the New York area, two of them in houses immediately next-door to Bee, she frequently saw and played with 29 cousins. She liked people and they liked her, and she willingly listened to their problems.

Bee took to schooling like the duck to water, became an elementary school teacher, and thirsted for still more education. She became an attractive and intelligent young woman. Soon after we met, friends would come upon us engrossed in talk with each other, divorced from the crowd at a party and dance, and would say, "It must be love." We would look up and say, "We don't know what it is, but it's something."

Love

Neither of us wanted it to be love. Our "philosophies" told us that we were too different. Bee was a faithful Roman Catholic who never missed Mass. I was still walking wounded from my family's War over Religion. She prayed to God and regularly confessed her supposed sins. I regarded God as an interesting myth and the confessional as mumbo-jumbo. Bee had been educated at Our Lady of Sorrows Elementary School and St. Bartholomew's High School, then two years at Newtown High School, followed by the highly vocationalized program of Jamaica Training School for Teachers. I had gone to public schools and was now in icon-smashing Columbia College.

Bee had begun teaching at the remarkably early age of 18, one year before we met. I had years to go before reentering the job market. She accepted conventions and I sneered at them. She was just beginning to think about politics and social developments and I was groping for radical political solutions. She was family-oriented and an adorer of children; I regarded family and child rearing as potential millstones around my neck. She was sentimental and I was trying to be hardboiled.

Yet we fell in love. We tried hard to escape. Perhaps the way out was to shun romancing and instead talk out our ideas, particularly the basic assumptions underlying our life-styles and behavior. Yet talk of our differences too often led to conflict and unhappiness. Perhaps a better way was to live and love and laugh and enjoy, and avoid worrying and all discussions "sicklied o'er with the pale cast of thought." Yet the underlying background differences always elbowed their way in.

We tried the contradictory approaches during the summer of 1931 when I worked on the Waldorf, a summer of weekend cruises with Bee in my blue canoe from my family's Beacon Hill bungalow to the solitary beaches of Hempstead Harbor, a summer of other weekends with my friends and Bee's friends at a big old house that the girls of Pal O Mine Club rented at Miller Place on Long Island's North Shore, a summer of meeting her family and nieces and nephews at her mother and father's bungalow at Lake Ronkonkoma farther out on Long Island.

Our friendship groups became acquainted. I attended dances and parties held by Bee's club, and Bee came to dances and parties and plays of the Duwell Club of Grace Episcopal Church and the Masonic-related DeMolay. Her "gang" became my friends and my "bunch" hers.

In Corona, Bee and I spent long hours on her darkened porch in talk of books and ideas, or in gossip on who was going with whom, before we fell silent in each other's arms. In the small hours of the morning, my head spinning with love, I would wend my way to my house a mile away. The only part of the walk I disliked was passing Our Lady of Sorrows Roman Catholic Church.

Weekdays we mostly went our separate ways, mine by subway to discover new ideas at Columbia, Bee by car to teach elementary school as a permanent substitute in College Point or Woodside or Jamaica or Corona or other communities in Queens. In the first year of the Great Depression, her reward for leading her 1930 Training School graduating class was to become number 2,225 on a formidable list of teachers awaiting permanent appointment to New York City schools. (Notification of her appointment came in 1948, eighteen years after her graduation, when she was the mother of three children; a brief letter instructed her to report to a school in Brooklyn. She didn't.)

They were hard times in the early 1930s; Bee answered the call of varied principals who needed a substitute teacher for a day, a week, or a month. One principal spent much of her day reading the *Daily News* camouflaged by an enveloping copy of the *New York Times*; others were active supervisors who observed and helped the able young woman. Some of her classes were delights; others were struggles. Once she was fired from a job teaching remedial reading in a Works Progress Administration program because a form she had filled out informed the bureaucracy that she had sinfully saved some of her earnings and established a bank account of $90. During dry periods when calls for substitutes were infrequent, she worked in Krug's Bakery or her brother Bill's construction company office.

While my eyes and mind were being opened at Columbia, Bee enrolled in the fall of 1931 in night school at Hunter College out of a combination of ambition, desire to be the best possible teacher, and hunger to learn more of her world. She knew that Jamaica Training School for Teachers had literally trained her, not educated her. So we had more and more to talk about—

authors such as Sinclair Lewis and Somerset Maugham, Dorothy Parker and Theodore Dreiser. We discovered the love poetry of Rupert Brooke and Kahlil Gibran. I shared with her my character sketches of people in her crowd, such as "The Wide-Eyed Child," a piece about her Pal O Mine friend Kido. She encouraged me, told me that I could write, that I'd be heard from some day. She wrote a short story about us, and I responded with a seven-page critical analysis drawing upon the rough treatment I had received in my night school short story writing class. If I had received such a reaction to my own writing I would have spit in the reviewer's eye and added him or her to my private hit list. But Bee said, "Gosh, you're great to spend so much time on a worthless would-be writer such as I am." I told you we had different personalities.

Some nights we met in Manhattan. We grew familiar with seats in the last row of the second balcony in many legitimate theaters on Broadway and the side streets. In those days you could attend performances of Shakespeare for a quarter. Our tastes were eclectic, but our accolades were usually reserved for the socially oriented playwrights such as Maxwell Anderson, Sidney Kingsley, and Elmer Rice. I exposed Bee to socialist thought; one night in 1932 we went to a Socialist Party rally at Madison Square Garden, heard Norman Thomas, Socialist candidate for president, and joined in singing lustily "'Tis the Final Struggle, 'Tis the Final Fight...." Bee exposed me to opera. It didn't take; I wrote a review of *Tannhaüser* in the scoffing, illiterate manner of a Ring Lardner character.

At the Institute of Arts and Sciences on the Columbia campus, we listened to lectures by such social commentators of the 1930s as Lewis Mumford, Joseph Wood Krutch, John Erskine, Fannie Hurst, H. A. Overstreet, L. T. Jacks, Frederic M. Thrasher, Gardner Murphy, Sherwood Anderson, Sir Norman Angell, and John Mason Brown. Traveling on to Corona as the subway clicked off the miles, we saw no fellow passengers as we talked over the ideas we had encountered. At home I inserted paper into typewriter and raced the clock as I did scathing or laudatory reviews of performances or speeches to meet my self-imposed deadline for an imaginary morning newspaper.

Most weeknights we studied hard and read widely. The

lights often burned late in our homes. One long weekend I wrote an entire 57-page term paper and submitted it on Monday; at that time I regarded rewriting as necessary only for lower mortals than me. Bee, open to new ideas, read classics and contemporary novels that sometimes startled her, and she struggled with leftist social thought. She studied history and literature happily and wrestled grimly with math as she worked toward her bachelor's degree.

Though we dated regularly over weekends and saw each other occasionally during the work week, we still found it necessary to bridge the long mile that separated our homes with letters. More than sixty years later, we still have our letters, now crumbling with age, in a box labeled "Love Letters." Bee's earliest were newsy and affectionate yet wary "Dear Bill" letters that helped her fight off jitters about us. My early ones were slapdash "Honey Bee" letters full of sophomoric humor, satire, and exaggeration that were intended to exhibit my sagacity but actually demonstrated only what a dolt a young man can be. When in the summer of 1932 Bee went off to Camp Maqua in Maine and I traveled with co-carousers Ben, Harry, and Paul L. to Ste. Agathe, Canada, to drink gallons of ale during the next-to-last summer of prohibition, the volume of our letters burdened the post office.

With time, the letters grew increasingly intense and personal. For instance, just before my twenty-first birthday I wrote Bee on a Sunday night from my home:

> Dear Honey Bee, I feel disjointed tonight, almost as though some essential part of me were missing, an arm or leg perhaps—and all because I haven't seen you today. It's funny what an inconsistent illogical animal man is; I've seen you, heard you, been with you, talked to you, and kissed you with short times out for sleep almost continually since Thursday—yet I miss you. I wish I wasn't so insatiable; it's uncomfortable. Right now (that's enough about you; before I lose the powerful, inflexible, dominant ancestral will and come dashing downstairs to call you in a minute!) I'm trying to write and as usual am feeling thoroughly—though I don't know exactly what—you might say tense.... As usual too, I can't write. I am honestly and unashamedly a dead duck. Write me from the office, will you, Bun? I need your tonic, often too, at least twice a day.

I don't think I'll read this or I mightn't send it.

As ever,
Ol' Split Personality

Despite our social consciences, even the surrounding travail in society could be banished from our ken. In early March, 1933, with American society in a catatonic state, the banks closed, and Franklin D. Roosevelt trying to reassure us that the only thing that we have to fear is fear itself, I wrote:

> I keep thinking of you, Honey Beetle, and I look right through books to your face. I keep feeling the joy of my arms around you—and I realize that now, for the very first time, I know what is meant by the language of love. How weak words are!
>
> I love you,
>
> Old it

At the same time, Bee wrote me:

> It seems so unimportant—the fact that banks are closed and that scrip will be issued when compared with the fact that we love each other. That's news and that's so important to us and it belongs so to us. Nothing can affect it. It remains intact no matter what goes on. How marvelous to have something real to hold on to, something constant, something not suscep-tible to any change whatsoever in this world of ours in which we are sure of nothing!...

We knew that we were in love. We also knew that our dif-ferences could not be reconciled. Bee reflected both our despair and joy three years after we first met:

> This typewriter is all dusty and stiff but I wouldn't feel right if I didn't type at least one letter. I hate this office. It's alive with all sorts of ghosts and not because it is Halloween either. This morning sitting here all alone with nothing that I had to do, I lived over a few of those terrible mornings—two years ago that was and it is just as vivid now. I thought I had lost you. What would I be like now if I had? I'm afraid to even think of it. Even at this moment when I let my mind travel back, I feel those same awful sensations and I want to run away. Memory is a strange thing—it can be so pleasant and so terrible. Just when one is sure that an episode is closed and forgotten, perhaps just the sight of one little thing will recall

97

all the details very vividly.

Darling, I don't know whom to thank for the three years of love and friendship that we have enjoyed. All I know is that we were mighty lucky to "come back." Two years ago I could not have said "I love you," yet I must have for no other feeling could have affected me so.

The telephone just rang and it awakened me from my not too pleasant reverie. I'm glad I can say "Honey, I love you."

Chapter Thirteen

CONCERNING
BREAD

Man doth not live by bread only." Note that the Old Testament writer carefully qualified the observation with "only." Bread too is needed. With my background, I required no reminder.

Whether through predestination by Miss Emily Curry or my dead-end jobs or my dedication to the written word, I came to recognize during my Columbia years that I must become a writer. But what kind? My ideal, of course, was the creative author—the novelist, essayist, short story writer, the free lance and free spirit writing as he pleased.

At 21, holed up for the summer of 1932 in my family bungalow at Beacon Hill, I gave creative writing a try. The novel would win a prize in a magazine contest; like F. Scott Fitzgerald's *This Side of Paradise*, my novel, *Loose*, would be my passport to the magic world of fiction. But that summer of 1932 on the shores of Long Island's Hempstead Harbor, my muse didn't respond. Daily the yellow paper in the typewriter stared back at me.

The alternative was journalism, an apprenticeship through writing at the behest of others—followed, to be sure, by realization of the dream. To become a cub reporter, then a Hildy Johnson of Hecht and MacArthur's *Front Page*, hat perched on the back of the head, glass at elbow, breaking the big story, off-hours writing the Great American Novel! Perhaps to be a foreign correspondent, filing stories for the *New York Times* or the *Chicago Daily News* or the Paris edition of the *Herald-Tribune*. Perhaps to write reports on the American scene for journals of opinion such as *The New Republic, a la* Edmund Wilson.

But the reality of the Great Depression, as I knew all too well, was unpropitious. Newspapers buckled and folded, magazines withered and collapsed, and even school of journalism graduates and experienced newspapermen fruitlessly made the rounds of the surviving media. I needed an option, some personal version of unemployment insurance to fall back upon. Teaching, possibly?

But I didn't want to become a teacher. The scars of P.S. 92 and Flushing High were too recent; the cuts still smarted. I knew from my own experience that high schools in New York State were Regents Examination factories. The liberal arts professors whose ideas I respected were cynical about the quality of public education and openly contemptuous of the caliber of education courses. And college teaching, necessitating a Ph.D. degree, was economically unfeasible.

Yet any port in a storm and beggars can't be choosers. To widen my options, I enrolled for some courses in education. During my senior year, tenderly holding my nose, I crossed what Columbia College derisively called the widest street in the world, 120th Street, which separates Teachers College from the rest of Columbia University. Most of my courses, however, were socially oriented liberal arts offerings on familiar 116th Street Columbia College turf.

I was prepared to appreciate my senior year encounter with the social sciences in Columbia College's Hamilton Hall, and I did. In the academic year that Franklin Delano Roosevelt was elected president and galvanized the nation with a flood of New Deal legislation, I studied economics with those of the Columbia economics faculty who did not join their chairman, Rexford G. Tugwell, in the Brain Trust in Washington. Liberal Robert Carey and Horace Taylor introduced me to a range of economic theorists, with a sustained stop along the right-left continuum at New Deal liberalism of the Keynesian and Tugwellian varieties. European Robert Valeur explored such international economic systems as those of Communist Russia, Fascist Italy, and imperialist Japan; his courses were neatly counterpointed by historian Carlton J. Hayes's *Imperialism and World Politics*. Conservative sociologist William Casey exposed me to William Graham Sumner's *Folkways* with its corroding pessimism as to the pos-

100

sibility of any reforms whatsoever, to the animal psychologists with their deterministic experiments, and to Walter Lippmann's *Public Opinion* with its documentation of how leaders manipulated the behavior of the common man through the use of words. With radical economist Addison T. Cutler, I examined the current spate of proposals for economic planning; they ranged from those of big business leaders like General Electric's Gerald Swope through the proposals of such liberals as Stuart Chase, Charles A. Beard, and George Soule, to the fully planned economies of the Socialists and Communists.

For me, all this was an intellectual feast. Paradoxically, I liked conservative Casey and radical Cutler best. My paper *Can Capitalism Plan?* (I argued that it couldn't) brought me to the attention of Professor Cutler, who introduced me to classic and current Marxism, including the masters Karl Marx and Friedrich Engels, the disciple Lenin, and the contemporary John Strachey of *The Coming Struggle for Power.* I stayed committed to gradualistic evolutionary socialism, the gospel according to Saint Norman Thomas.

My reading and play-going remained catholic (with a small "c"). I read widely in the social sciences and literature. My favorite autobiographies were *The Education of Henry Adams* ("a teacher affects eternity; he can never tell where his influence stops") and *The Autobiography of Lincoln Steffens* ("I have been over into the future [Russia], and it works"). The Broadway theater provided Bee and me a smorgasbord: Eugene O'Neill's comedy *Ah, Wilderness,* Jack Kirkland's adaptation of Erskine Caldwell's *Tobacco Road,* Elmer Rice's *We, The People,* etc. Odets was still to come.

From comments about education courses by my advisor, Mark Van Doren, I feared for the worst as I first crossed the wide street. Instead, despite my mindset, the venture into education was a revelation for me. Teachers College of 1932-33 was alive with feisty social consciousness. By sheer luck I encountered a teacher who really cared about people, Verna A. Carley. She believed in me. That was all I needed, a believer.

I breezed through my courses in educational psychology and history of education. In Verna Carley's program, High School Teaching, I was assigned to student teaching in the laboratory schools of Teachers College. At Lincoln School I worked in an integrated social science-English junior high school course under the direction of Frances Sweeney and Emily Barry, co-authors of a description of their teaching, *Western Youth Meets Eastern Culture.* At Horace Mann School, I took over the English work in a unit on the Middle Ages, and I also worked with tenth-graders on creative writing, literature, and the production of a play. I liked the progressive-oriented teachers and programs. I began to recognize that there might be hope for education.

For Miss Carley (and I literally mean **for**, since my reports were intended for her eyes only) I wrote sketches about each student. The first lesson I learned as to good teaching is that each student is an individual, to be respected and differentiated from every other individual. For a change, I learned fast.

Here, for instance, is Roger of Lincoln School:

> My first impression of Roger was that he would go Phi Beta Kappa at Yale, sell bonds, and become a junior partner. Now, after reading his attempt at poetry, a swash-buckling affair about a cavalier who remarks, "Be not wroth, you low-born sloth," discovering that his favorite character from the *Odyssey* is Circe, noting that his optional project is the Greek drama, hearing that he reads Euripides and Aristophanes so avidly that occasionally he neglects to prepare the assignment in Tappan's *Story of the Greek People,* watching him dream in class, only half-present unless a stray word or a rise above the usual class routine arouses him to sharp and brilliant thinking, voiced rapidly, clearly, incisively—to my great joy I can reject the first impression. He will only go Phi Beta Kappa by sheer power of intellect, if he does, for his keen intellect will not be concentrated on his studies but on that more important thing, education. He will be a junior partner only if beaten by old Necessity and thwarted in his natural desire and tendency to be a Ponzi, or an artist who occasionally misses a meal, or a social worker—in short, a dreaming, happy man.

I applied to my classes a social conscience, a sense of the dramatic, and a literary background. Thank you, both respectively and respectfully, Columbia College, the Duwell plays, and Mark Van Doren. Thank you, Verna, for your confidence.

Despite my deathbed conversion to teaching, I was still short on credentials for certification as an English teacher with a social studies minor. The day of my graduation from Columbia College neared. Tall, thin, thirtyish Verna, nearing her Teachers College doctorate, admitted no obstacles to her faith in me. She advised me to take teacher qualification examinations offered by New York State on education course content of which I was totally ignorant. "Read these books first," and she handed me books by George Counts, the social reformer, William Heard Kilpatrick, the philosopher of education, and others. "Write what comes into your head." I took the state examinations and New York soberly certified me for teaching.

I assembled a set of papers for filing with the Teachers College placement bureau and, knowing from Thompson-Starrett the fate of applications, fattened the dossier with recommendations from clergyman Arthur G. Roberts; vice president A. E. Barlow; bosses William Abramson and Bill Troast; professors Cutler, Van Doren, Dick, etc.; and my new friends Verna Carley and her associate, Harold Hand, a profane, blunt, and socially motivated 32-year-old aspirant for the doctorate who looked and sounded like a manual worker rather than an instructor. Typical Hand advice to me on teaching: "Keep the gaddamn pitch of your voice down." Typical Carley advice, "Whenever you don't feel confident, remember that they don't have as much on the ball as you think they have."

In May 1933, I contributed an article to the *Columbia Review*, edited by Milton Rugoff, for its symposium on the socialized state. I took my new interest, education, and linked it to my new social theory, socialism.

In the spring of 1933, at the low point of the depression, I graduated from Columbia College with a B.A. degree. I did not want to attend my own commencement, for I rejected ceremonials and was confident that the speeches made on the occasion would be reactionary, optimistic, and flatulent. They were. Yet I attended with my proud mother and Bee.

Come graduation, I applied for high school teaching through extended letters carefully designed not to be consigned to the limbo file. The Teachers College placement office and my former professors offered leads that I earnestly followed up. One was from a principal in a town up the Hudson River who wrote me that a Columbia source had told him that I too was interested in

"Eastern Europe," Aesopian language for the forbidden word, "Russia." But even this job with Lefty didn't materialize. I was unemployed. To my dismay, I had become one of the statistics. I wrote unpublishable stuff all summer.

There was no sense in applying for teaching jobs after the summer of 1933 was over; I reverted to journalism applications. Elaborate dossiers went to newspapers, magazines, and publishers. In October the *New York Times* said crisply, "I regret that there is no opportunity at present for employment on the City Staff of *The Times*." *The Herald Tribune* responded, "We shall file your application as you request, but fear that we cannot offer you any encouragement inasmuch as we have a long list of experienced newspapermen waiting for any opportunity that may arise." I got as far as an interview at the brand-new *Newsweek* and the very old *Brooklyn Citizen*. I unsuccessfully tried to sell the *Long Island Daily Star* on articles on the World Series (the New York Giants beat the Washington Senators) ghost written by me for my uncle Tom Clarke. I remained an unemployment statistic.

Late in October I tried free-lance academic slavery. Professor Cutler had some Contemporary Civilization papers for me to grade. Verna Carley, now at Fordham—luckily for me she hadn't moved a year earlier—wrote, "I was indeed disappointed to learn that you had no teaching position. I am even more determined to right the social order so that such talent shall not be wasted. What are you doing? If time is hanging heavily and you want to pick up some spending money, won't you come to see your old teacher who has a habit of trying to do more than time permits her to complete?" I did some research on workmen's compensation programs for a section of her doctoral dissertation.

November in New York City is cold, wet, and disheartening for an unemployed college graduate. Then a postcard came from the Teachers College placement bureau; Dr. John Herring, director of the education program of the Warwick Training School, wanted to see me. On a dreary Friday, November 3, I traveled by train to the New York State Training School for Boys at Warwick, New York, for an interview. I was immediately employed. Totally unprepared and abysmally ignorant of the situation, I reported for work on Monday. The bureaucratic prose of the State of New York Department of Civil Service, Albany, states: "This is to report that Wm. Van Til, 100-11 Thirty-fifth Avenue, Corona, N.Y., has been found qualified for appointment to the position of Housekeeper and Caretaker in the NYS Training School for Boys at salary of $840 and M, effective 11/6/33." "$840" translated to $70 a month and "M" meant food and lodging. "Housekeeper and Caretaker" meant custodial and teaching responsibilities in a reform school without walls located in the open farm area of Orange County in southern New York State near the New Jersey border. The nearest town was Warwick, some miles away, hence the shorthand for the school, "Warwick."

New York State Training School for Boys was a facility for teenage delinquent boys that had been open only a few months when I arrived. The school had no books, no paper, no pencils, no anything—except delinquents. The library contained only cast-off junk. The delinquents lived in cottages, low-lying buildings with dormitory facilities and a recreation room. After line-up on weekdays, the boys marched out in work gangs for a half-day of work in the fields and in the buildings and for another half-day of school in the Education Building. On weekends the staff supervised and patrolled their church attendance, recreation, and even sleeping hours.

The superintendent was a politician who usually remained invisible to both staff and delinquents. The assistant superintendent, the day-by-day boss, was a tough S.O.B. who administered corporal punishment to boys who tried to "breeze" (escape) or otherwise rebelled. The director of the education program was cultured, kind, and ineffectual.

Later I described my first day in a National Education Association pamphlet on discipline:

> When, in a barren classroom, I first faced teenage delinquents, I felt like a character in a Kafka nightmare. I saw before me boys who were sullen or mocking or hostile. As to discipline, the choice presented me seemed stark. Either I must put into these delinquents the fear of the master—namely me—through every scrap of authority I could muster, including a coercive curriculum, or I must jointly with them develop a curriculum somehow related to their lives. I gambled on the latter course.

Somehow I lived through those first two weeks. I got the boys to talk about how it happened that they had been sent to Warwick. Amazingly enough, all seemed to be innocent of the crimes for which they had been sentenced; they freely "snowed" the new teacher in hope of his support when they came before "The Committee" for consideration of possible probation. They talked about their lives in Harlem and Bedford Stuyvesant, their brothers' stays in jails, their favorite fighters, their experiences on the streets, what they hated most about school. Boasting and lies predominated. Yet I came to know them as individuals.

After an eternity, I was granted a weekend pass, a twice-a-month privilege. I went from local library to local library in Corona and Flushing and loaded up with library books on the elementary level that had anything to do with what the boys had talked about: crime, boxing, adventures, etc. Later I learned that such library exploitation was unethical. But at the time I was too young and desperate to have ethics. Flo supplied me with paper, pencils, and materials from her school, courtesy of the New York City school system; the statute of limitations has long since erased the crime, no doubt. The local butcher gave me sheets of wrapping paper for artwork by the boys. Bee got me a scrapbook for my "project," biographies of contemporary celebrities to be composed by my delinquents. Friend Ben and Bee drove me and my load back to Warwick.

Bored by the surrounding nothingness, some of the boys used some of the accessions, including free materials that Bee wangled from a variety of companies and groups. Some read simple books; few wrote anything at all. Some tried remedial work. One boy spent most of his school half-day drawing a frieze of boats, from Phoenician galleys to ocean liners. Some just sat and glowered; some picked fights.

Early in my stay I wrote to Verna Carley with news and for advice:

> I rose at 7:15 in the apartment on the second floor of a cottage in which the boys live—there are 16 such cottages—ran a block to the dining hall where the officers eat, breakfasted, then walked a few blocks down the road to the cottages where the boys who are in my first class live. The boys in my 8 o'clock class are first commitments, boys never having been

subjected to the brutalizing influence of the House of Refuge which, incidentally, must be literally (sic) hell. Here in this group of cottages I take the fourteen boys who make up my class from a lineup at 8:15. Together we walk up the road to the Educational Building, an impressive shell. In class and out I must check constantly to see that no one "breezes," "lams," "scrams," or otherwise leaves. My class is heterogeneous. One is here for breaking limbs from trees, another for stealing pipe for his hungry family, another for rape, another for six burglaries, another for running away from home, another for entering a store, calling "Mr. Greenberg," and no Mr. Greenberg appearing, robbing his till. I get on well with them all.

We talk in class of politics, of history, of current events. Today we finished a geology project, my first. Experiment has proven that projects cannot be individualized save in few cases and that the group approach is the only feasible one at least for the present. Tuesday we talked geology—formation of mountains, of earth, glaciation, etc. Wednesday we went on a Geology Walk through the grounds collecting fossils, specimen rocks. Today we drew diagrams of earth, folded mountains, and I showed pictures in college geology book and attempted to explain Evolution. With the 8-10 group it went well; with the 10-12 group it worked not so well because of the necessity of hounding one boy who had a terrific yen to smoke a picked up cigarette butt in class and another who had a movie magazine. Peaceable persuasion is usually effective. Discipline is a matter of interest—but how hard it is sometimes to arouse that interest! Between 12 and 1, I substituted in charge of a cottage for a cottage master who went to lunch. Five days a week, 1-5, I have free for preparation. At night from 6-8 I am in charge of a miserably small library. Some discipline trouble in cleaning up the place after using it.

Last night I went to Dr. Herring's home and talked and sang till midnight, then home, and up at 7.

Can you suggest possible projects? I can get material after some delay. Can you suggest several reading tests for dull eighth graders—my average student?

Dr. Herring gives me all possible breaks. I have selected my own groups from the new commitments—27 boys out of 64—I have in consequence a group with a high (!) I.Q., averaging about 88. I am the only man in the place with afternoons free to prepare. Herring and I are the only representatives of progressive education.

After a few more pilfering expeditions to New York City, I managed to initiate a mimeographed newspaper. *The State School News* was loaded with sports reporting and gossip; it also carried book reviews and creative writing. With the *News* as their outlet, some of the boys began to write. Our editor was Bryant, a bright black who was proud that he stole only Cadillacs, never lesser cars. Our biggest story was a visit to Warwick by Eleanor Roosevelt; Bryant interviewed her.

Though I fancied myself as a man of the world, life at Warwick opened my eyes. I grew familiar with the social structure of wolves (the sexually aggressive lords of the cottages) and punks (the sexually subservient slaves) and those who attempted, sometimes unsuccessfully, to join neither group. Years later I wrote a short story about sexual relationships at Warwick. It was never published.

There were few oases in Warwick life. One was the living room of Dr. John Herring and his wife, a comfortable room lined with books and mementos of trips, a room where the Herrings served tea and sherry, the kind of room that was as out of place in the Warwick atmosphere as were its gentle proprietors. Another oasis was Kelly's, the village bar against which Paul Mendenhall and I hunched as frequently as we could. Science teacher Paul was a cosmopolitan New Yorker who lived near Columbia. Paul knew everybody and was a frequent guest at Greenwich Village parties; those intellectuals whom he didn't know his older brother Jimmy did. Paul called the elite professors of Teachers College by their first names and knew precisely where each stood on radical politics. We talked endlessly and we drank too much too often.

My bare little room at Warwick, which I shared with fellow teachers Gochfeld and Greenfield, was no oasis, for the staff was always on call at night as well as day, and the boys sometimes breezed. For instance, on Christmas Eve, 1933, I was asleep when the siren screamed. I stumbled into clothes, reported in to the assistant superintendent at the Administration Building, and picked out a baseball bat from the rack. Tommy McCormick had been getting no mail from home for weeks, and on Christmas Eve he couldn't take it anymore. So he had breezed into the wide open country that surrounded the reform school without walls.

The assistant superintendent assigned us our posts; that bitter cold night they dropped me along the road to Sugarloaf Mountain. I waited with my bat for Tommy, one of my favorite students, and hoped against hope that he would somehow make it to New York. In the early hours of Christmas Day, the siren screamed again, telling us that McCormick had been hunted down and locked up. I returned to troubled sleep as the world celebrated the birthday of Jesus.

The letters Bee and I wrote to each other were full of news and the pain of separation. The week after I arrived in "jail," I wrote on a scrap of paper:

> Honey Bee,
> I just read your last letter, the one about your mom and your reading. I love you I love you I love you. I'm up in my classroom and it's getting dark and I'm I love you I love you I love you trying to prepare for tomorrow. So far I've had two I love you I love you I love you classes of four hours in length (no textbook). Yesterday we covered politics and election and today we worked I love you I love you I love you on war. Kids OK but hard as hell to keep homogenously interested. I love you I love you I love you. But the administration! X!—, !XZ*! I spent two hours today just trying to get into my I love you I love you I love you classroom.

I wrote her of the doings of delinquents with such implausible yet actual names as Judge Davis and Sinclair Lewis, of successes and failures in my teaching projects, of triumphs and disappointments with the boys, of long Saturdays and Sundays on duty, of boring supervision of recreation and cottage activities, of the superintendent fining me a half day of leave time for being a few hours late on return to the school after a weekend off, of breaking up fights, of being begged for the stubs of cigarettes called "dinchers," of roommate Gochfeld's comment "Van Til, don't you sometimes feel, after being up here, you can handle anything?" Bee wrote of her substitute teaching and college classes and friends and relatives and reading.

Sometimes we swapped anecdotes. Bee wrote of tucking her little niece into bed. Jeannie asked where God was. Bee told her, "Everywhere. Even in this room." Jeannie said, "Better tell him to go home and go to bed. It's late." I wrote an account of a

Christmas pageant put on by the delinquents:

> "The Problems of the Twentieth Century" stopped before the manger and had their burdens removed by "Angels." Jimmy White, a big baboon called King Kong by the boys, played an angel and had his robe spat upon by a spectator as Jimmy came down the aisle. The "Angel" is still looking for "That Guy." The humorous highlight of the show was that one "Angel" had a helluva time lifting the burden of Crime from the back of one "Problem."

Usually we wrote of our loneliness and self-doubts and love. During the fall and early winter I came home on two weekends each month to the abnormality of normal life. Bee told me that I looked haunted.

In February I enrolled at Teachers College for three courses on Friday night and Saturday mornings; the benevolent reform school administration allowed me each Saturday off in place of two weekends each month. One course was with Professor Donald Cottrell in higher education, one on teaching social studies with Frances Sweeney of Lincoln School, and one on philosophy of education with an old white-haired man who taught a class of hundreds of graduate students in the Horace Mann auditorium. I tried to relate the brute realities of teaching in the reform school to the shining ideals of teaching he espoused. They were far apart. On leaving each of his classes, I would mutter grimly to myself, "I'd like to see *him* try to teach that way at Warwick!" His name was William Heard Kilpatrick, and he was the great interpreter of John Dewey's progressive education philosophy.

My schedule that semester was insane. I traveled to New York with Paul Mendenhall late each Friday afternoon, nipped into a Friday evening class, slept at Paul's near Columbia, attended two Saturday classes, went home to Corona, dated with Bee Saturday evenings, got two hours sleep, returned to Columbia at 5:00 A.M., and drove with Paul to report for duty at 8:00 A.M. on Sunday mornings. From Sunday through Friday I worked for New York State Training School for Boys. In my "free time" I studied books and wrote papers for my Columbia courses.

How my relationship with Bee endured under such a regimen neither of us will ever know. Our snatched hours were precious to us and our correspondence helped.

Somehow I survived that year at Warwick and even scored small triumphs. For instance, I never physically struck a boy— which is just as well, for many of these veterans of street fighting could have easily thrashed or knifed me (in the school shops boys secretly made knives of any available metal). Nor was I ever struck or cut by a boy. Many of them came to recognize that I wanted to help them, and most at least recognized that I intended them no harm. When I left Warwick in June of 1934 for a summer of study at Columbia and an attempt to write at the Beacon Hill bungalow, the school newspaper bid me sadly adieu through a long story and a sentimental editorial.

I got good grades in my three Teachers College courses. Happily, my Columbia network, Miss Duggan and Clyde Miller of the Teachers College placement bureau and Miss Carley of the faculty, did not forget me.

Chapter Fourteen

DELIVERANCE

 ow I was delivered from bondage is lifted verbatim from an ancient collection of letters that I ironically labeled "Success Story." Warts and all, here are the letters. You may judge the actors in whatever way you wish.

December 7th, 1933.
State School
Warwick, N.Y.

Dear Miss Carley,

...Saturday afternoon, failing to find you in, I visited Miss Duggan, Teachers College Bureau of Educational Service.

...Monday I received a call from New York, Miss Duggan. She inquired whether I had my M.A. or many points toward it. I replied that I hadn't and she told me that a particular position she had in mind called for one. We expressed mutual regrets and terminated the call. But later she called again, said, in essence, "to heck with an M.A.; come in anyhow."

At four P.M. Tuesday I met in Miss Duggan's office a Mr. George Willard Frasier, President of Colorado State Teachers College, Greeley, Colorado, a bluff, hearty, positive man, certain of his institution and his own opinions. Herring was visiting Teachers College at the same time and the two, old classmates, met and exchanged greetings. Herring, who has a disease known as Carley's hallucination (namely, a belief that a Mr. Van Til is **good**), told Frasier kiddingly to keep away from me and rob his own cradles. Frasier told him that there wasn't much danger, that he needed an M.A. and at first wouldn't even consider the possibility of hiring a non-Master, that he consented to interview me only on Miss Duggan's urgent request. So we talked—or rather he talked a lot and I asked questions. He told me (paraphrasing and condensing), "If I offer you this position, you must study and prepare while at Warwick. You must take courses under Harold Clark, Harold Rugg, and George Counts at Teachers College during the summer to come. In the fall of '34 you will come to Colorado State, teach in our demonstration class in junior high school in a new integrated Social Studies. You will also teach in the college, **teaching teachers to teach Social Studies.**" (O Reverend Doctor Carley, only Mr. Van Til can appreciate the colossal irony of that!) "Your salary will probably be $150 per month. And maybe you can work on your M.A. here."...

Frasier and I left the conference room with our agreement tentative. He was to let me know his formal decision within two weeks. But on coming out, he remarked to Dr. Herring, "John, I'm going to take this boy away from you," and went on to say that he must consult his board. He added that they never refused him anything—which I can well believe.

So—unless he recovers from his Carley's hallucination, he will probably make me a formal offer within two weeks. It is here that I want your advice. Should I clinch it or request that he wait? The fall of '34 is a year away; whether I can do better rests on the lap of the gods. Yes, I know; I've asked the same question of Miss Duggan in yesterday's mail.

And here an itinerant ghost-writer, a young man greatly amazed to find himself in December, 1933, almost signed up for employment until June, 1935, will close, his mouth gaping wide open. He can no longer express adequately his thanks to you; let him say simply, "Yours for grander hallucinations."

Sincerely yours,
William A. Van Til

My advisor suggested that I clinch the agreement, and I did. There the matter rested till the spring. Then I wrote this letter to the Teachers College placement bureau:

New York State Training School
Warwick, N.Y.
May 13, 1934.

Dear Miss Duggan,

...I am the proverbial young man in search of advice, a role which I have assayed on your stage frequently enough....

With the dawn this morning (or, to be more exact, with ten

o'clock this morning) comes a call from Miss Carley in New York City. She told me that Lindquist of Ohio State was in town, that he was a valuable man to be acquainted with. Could I come to town; would I care to come to town? I said yes to both....

I arrived in New York after hitch-hiking in four automobiles, taking one train, one ferry, one trolley, and one cab and went to the Taft. There I met both Miss Carley and Dr. Lindquist.

Dr. Lindquist and I settled down to a prolonged and rambling talk which lasted from three-thirty, after a few words with Miss Carley, until six. We talked educational theory, my work at State School, his ideas and the experiences of his teachers at Ohio, my prospective job at Greeley. He knew, of course, of this latter from both Miss Carley and myself....

Dr. Lindquist and I hit it off splendidly. He explained his set-up with its lack of formalism or rigid curriculum. He told me of the three teachers who work together on the child, unrestricted by office requirements. He told me an amusing story of the social science class outfitting its room, painting its ceiling, and of the parents' protest that their children weren't getting "education"....

Toward the end of our conversation we talked ethics, for Lindquist offered me a position teaching Social Studies and English in his high school at a salary of $2000 for eight months. Here my need for advice especially enters. Ohio State, so far as we can visualize from verbalizations, has a better set-up for me than Colorado State. My work at Warwick with individual boys, with adjustment of the whole boy, with my own curriculum, seems a miniature of the work at Ohio State with added the blessings of materials, talented children, freedom to take trips, and a nonreactionary administration. Colorado State's position, and I think and certainly hope that I am doing the school and Dr. Frasier no injustice, seems essentially a job of teaching Rugg's books interestingly. Am I right on that?

In January, I accepted Dr. Frasier's offer to teach at Greeley. I will and would of course do nothing on the Ohio State proposition until I got more than Frasier's consent, namely, his approbation. This last sentence is a summary of the position Dr. Lindquist and I reached after our discussion of ethics. Violation of agreement we thought distinctly unethical. We could see nothing unethical in a request for release, concurred in by the employer, when release would result in a better job for the employee. What do you think?

I told Dr. Lindquist that I would do nothing on his

proposition until I played the role of Young Man Seeking Advice and Concerned About His Future....

How do you see this whole thing—Ohio State, Colorado State? I haven't written Frasier yet....

Those same personal regards,
William A. Van Til

Teachers College
Columbia University
New York
May 18, 1934

Dear Mr. Van Til:

...You like so many other human beings have reached the point where you must do one of the things that is always hard to do—and that is, to make decisions. I can well appreciate how much you enjoyed your conversation with Dr. Lindquist. We regard him as an unusually able administrator and a man under whom one would be more than fortunate to work. I am not surprised that he offered you a position in his high school.

I think right here that I must let you know the Bureau policy concerning contracts. We do not condone the breaking of contracts. When you registered with the Bureau, Mr. Miller and I were greatly interested in you and we still are because we believe that you have a definite contribution to make to education after you have had some good experience. In consequence, we exerted every effort to see to it that you would meet an administrator who had thus far shown by results that he could take young people, develop them, and because of his leadership help them to grow into professional life.....

Now I come to the point I made early in my letter. You are a free individual with the right to make whatever decisions you wish. If you decide that you desire to go to Ohio State, you should make your peace with Dr. Frasier, knowing definitely that a letter will go to Dr. Frasier from this Bureau stating definitely that we in no way condone the breaking of your contract.

Whatever you decide to do, you will be under an able man. Please let me know your final decision.

Sincerely yours,
Marie M. Duggan,
Assistant Director

I sought advice from Verna Carley. In late May she had visited Lindquist's school at Ohio State University.

Whitehall Apartment Hotel
754 N. Twelfth Street
Milwaukee, Wis.
June 5, 1934

Dear Conspirator,

...Running the risk of repeating what you already know, I shall state the situation as I found it. L. is still absolutely keen about you, and as I visited the school, I realized what a perfect place it was for you and your particular talents. You see, I'm crazy about the school—not that it's perfect, but because of what they are attempting and the experimental attitude they are taking. I think you could do a lot for them as well as they could for you. There is a problem of slow groups to be organized around activities, guidance of problem children, integrated programs, etc., to which you could contribute the best you have.... The young intellectuals gathered on that staff would be fine companions and RDL a sympathetic boss. So much for my impressions—whatever they are worth.....

Whatever happens, I am wishing for your success as you know. I feel justified in our activities as I have checked carefully with Fretwell, etc. who have concurred in our thinking. So I'm for you, no matter what you decide.

Best wishes. Keep me informed.

Cordially,
Verna A. Carley

State School
Warwick, New York
June 7th, 1934

Dr. George Frasier,
President,
Colorado State Teachers College,
Greeley, Colorado.

Dear Dr. Frasier:

This is the sort of letter which it is impossible to write in anything save a cards-upon-the-table manner. I think I know you well enough from our brief meeting to know that you will reply in this same blunt and honest spirit....

One thing prolonged our conversation greatly, the fact that I had agreed with you in December to come to Greeley next year to teach. Dr. Lindquist and I went carefully and as honestly as we could (for men are necessarily subjective) into the ethics of my asking you for a release from my agreement. We decided that it was not unethical for me to write you to request a release; we decided too that it would be emphatically unethical for me to persist in negotiating with Ohio State if your reply indicated that you were unwilling to allow me to break my contract. I have checked these conclusions with two fine people, Dr. John P. Herring and Miss Verna A. Carley, and they agree with me. Miss Carley has checked it with friends in academic circles and they too feel the same way. Miss Duggan and Mr. Miller, on the other hand, have told me that the Bureau of Appointments at Teachers College does not condone the breaking of contracts and that I should understand that if I accept the Ohio offer a letter will go to you from the Bureau stating unequivocally that they do not condone the breaking of contracts, that they do not condone any such action on my part.

I feel, Dr. Frasier, that with my particular training (English and Social Studies in college and high school teaching) and experience (at State School in individualized work) and philosophy derived from both experience and training that Ohio State is the position for which I am best suited.

To deny that the factor of salary enters at all into my decision to write you, after just this week Dr. Lindquist wired me an offer officially backed and approved by the University and conditional upon my release, would be hypocritical. Yet in my consideration, salary has always been properly subordinated to a secondary position, its only proper place. You may recall that you remarked in our conversation that I was remarkably disinterested (sic) in the question of salary. You have offered me $150 a month or $1350 for nine months. Ohio State has offered me $2400 for the school year of eight months. [A letter from Lindquist had upped the offer.]

Your position is a great stride beyond my present one for me; Ohio State's position is, I feel, a step for me beyond yours. I feel that I am best fitted for Ohio State; I feel that Ohio State offers to me the very best position and opportunity that I could be offered at present.

If in your reply you indicate that you do not see this matter as I do, I shall come to Greeley next fall prepared to do my very level best for you and your school. I hope I have not seemed unmindful of the value of the position which you have offered me. I have tried to be honest with us.

Sincerely yours,
William A. Van Til

Colorado State Teachers College
Greeley, Colorado
June 13, 1934

Mr. William Van Til
100-11 35th Avenue
Corona, New York
Dear Mr. Van Til:

Your letter of June 7 was on my desk when I returned from three days in the mountains. It is needless to tell you that I was much surprised and disappointed. I had never once thought that there would be any question about your being in Greeley this fall. But now the only thing I can do is to accept your resignation, because you would be of little value to me as a member of my staff here believing that you would be better off in Ohio State.

Dr. Lindquist is a very good friend of mine, and a wonderfully fine man. I don't know of a better man in America for a young man to work with than Lindquist. He is doing the same sort of experimental work in Ohio State that we are doing here, although they are not so far advanced with it. I think his school and our high school under Dr. Wrinkle are the only two real experimental high schools in America. You would have the same kind of work here under the same circumstances with the same sort of an adviser that you will have in Ohio State. You would have the association with the same type of faculty, and so far as the jobs and your educational growth are concerned, I think the situations are identical, and I know both of them very well indeed. It so happens that Lindquist has more money than I have right now; but as a permanent position, we have much more to offer you than they have.

Now that the thing is all over, I don't mind telling you what my plans were. Our college here is organized in seven departments. One of my largest departments is the one of social studies, which includes history, political economy, sociology, economics, geography, and business education. The man who is the head of this department will soon be retiring, and I am looking for a young man to bring up in the social studies who could take over those large responsibilities when my present man steps down. In you, I thought I had found exactly the young man I needed, and I had your future planned out to include in a few years a very important administrative position in a very important college. But now that's all over and I shall look for someone else.

118

May I add also that the next time I find a good man, I will say nothing about him. In Cleveland I was telling Lindquist about you and about the find I had made.

You may be surprised that I have not given you a lecture on the inadvisability of reneging on contracts before you have started on a job, but I have no intention of doing this because your educational life is for you to plan and not for me.

With very best wishes for your success, I am
Cordially yours,
G. W. Frasier

The Ohio State University
Columbus, Ohio
June 25, 1934

Mr. William A. Van Til
State Training School for Boys
Warwick, N. Y.
My dear Mr. Van Til:

My recommendation that you be appointed to the University School staff as Instructor at a salary of $2400.00, effective October 1, payable in twelve installments, will be acted upon by the Board of Trustees at their July meeting. A contract will then be forwarded to you. Please sign this and return it promptly.

There will be a faculty meeting at 9 A.M., Monday, September 24. School opens October 1.
Cordially yours,
Rudolph D. Lindquist
Director
The University School

Chapter Fifteen

UNIVERSITY SCHOOL WAS SPECIAL

Y ou have to understand the times to realize how special University School was.

During the 1920s Ohio State University gained national recognition as the home of one of America's outstanding colleges of education. OSU ranked with Teachers College of Columbia and the University of Chicago. National education names at the university included W. W. Charters in curriculum, Boyd H. Bode in philosophy of education, and Laura Zirbes in elementary education. Zirbes, physically hefty and equally weighty in campus influence, had developed a small, experimental elementary school; with many sympathetic colleagues, she campaigned vigorously for creation of an Ohio State University School. Dean Arps listened and acted, and a brand new University School was included in the blueprints of Ohio State University's ambitious building program. Even though the depression arrived in 1929, construction proceeded on the school during the early 1930s. Nationally, the progressive education movement was at its height. Many progressive educators advocated a child-centered school to meet the needs of young learners. Some believed that schooling should reconstruct the social order. Still others envisioned progressive education as a way of achieving democracy as a way of life. All recognized the inadequacy of traditional schooling.

The new Ohio State University School, kindergarten through high school, was created to be a truly experimental school, a testing ground for the ideas being advanced by the progressive

120

education movement. The College of Education faculty planned toward the newest and best school facilities and scoured the country for an outstanding director. Zirbes might have liked to be director herself, but local influentials have their adversaries, and she apparently settled for seeing that many of her Columbus staff members were included in the elementary school faculty. The OSU faculty found their director in a leading California administrator, Rudolph D. Lindquist, a tall, blue-eyed, pipe-smoking man of Scandinavian ancestry who was in his late forties. Lindquist was quiet, effective, and skillful in human relations. They gave him a good salary, a substantial budget for staffing, abundant funds for travel, and a free hand in hiring.

Rudy Lindquist followed an unique staffing policy: He employed promising individuals, each supportive of progressive education yet with a distinctive personality, set of experiences, and beliefs. He sought a balanced faculty. For instance, as one of his three high school social studies teachers he employed Arthur Henry Moehlman, son of a distinguished Michigan professor of educational administration. Moehlman was an ecologist and a scholar, cautiously experimental in education, relatively conservative on social issues. Lindquist also employed me, an untested unknown, literary in orientation, open to new ideas as to educational philosophy, to the left in the social arena. The third social studies staff member was Margaret Willis, a world traveler, an activity-oriented teacher, an unmarried woman whose whole life was given to her students, and a liberal in social persuasion. Thus, reasoned Lindquist, he would assure the school a balanced social studies staff that would use varied techniques and expose students to varied social views.

The school was not large; there was a single class for each elementary grade, kindergarten through sixth, and about fifty to sixty students for each of the six high school grades. The elementary grades were taught by a close-knit group, most of them Ohio women who were disciples of Zirbes, some of them teachers in her small school that antedated University School. Lindquist's first major responsibility was to staff the entire high school component from anywhere across the nation.[1]

---

[1] Perhaps the best testimony to Rudolph D. Lindquist's remarkable

121

What a training ground for educational leadership the University School proved to be! Lindquist discovered and recruited his high school staff (most of whom were unknowns) during the six years before he left Ohio State for leadership of Cranbrook School in the Detroit area. By the time I left the school in 1943, the new Alberty and Gilchrist administrations had brought additional future leaders to the staff to replace "old-timers" now in their thirties or forties who were leaving for new educational roles.

The school was in its third year of existence when I arrived. A standing faculty joke was that no matter how long I might teach at the school (actually I taught there almost a decade), I would never make up for having missed those first two years. Under the benign chairmanship of Lindquist, much preliminary curriculum skirmishing had already taken place, especially in

---

skill at recruiting is a factual review of the educational honors and posts eventually achieved by the twenty teachers who staffed University School's high school during the earliest years.

Of the social studies staff, Moehlman eventually became a professor of social foundations at the University of Texas and the president of a history of education society. Willis became the historian of the school and the author of *The Guinea Pigs After Twenty Years*, a follow-up on the University School class of 1938.

Of the science staff, Robert L. Havighurst became the University of Chicago's human development expert, creator of the developmental tasks concept and a founder of geriatric education. One of the nation's celebrated social researchers, he led the National Society for the Study of Education for decades. Oliver Loud worked on scientific projects and was a lifelong professor at Antioch College; at University School he teamed with Havighurst, who left for the General Education Board during the school's second year. Guy Cahoon and Harold Reynard became professors of science education at Ohio State University. Rose Lammel, a science teacher who made her specialty available to the students in both elementary and junior high school grades, became a professor of science education at Wayne State University.

Of the English staff, Lou LaBrant became a New York University professor of English education, then in her retirement a professor at Dillard, a black university in the New Orleans area; even into her eighties, she was a prolific contributor to scholarly journals. H. H. Giles of the English staff became chairman of the Bureau for Intercultural Education and was added by Dean Ernest Melby to the New York

the weeks that preceded the original opening of the school in 1932 and the early fall weeks of 1933. The faculty made and remade the schedule repeatedly. They achieved an enduring compromise between the faculty members who favored teaching through integrated problem-centered studies and those who favored teaching through separate subject fields. The former group was led by creative, brilliant, tough-minded Lou LaBrant, an experienced language arts teacher in her early forties who teamed with social scientist Margaret Willis and home economist Norma Albright, also veterans, in establishing the core program, a three-hour block of time on the junior high school level that absorbed English, social studies, and science and used the arts media in an integrated program. The latter group, less unified than the LaBrant bloc, was led by serious, logical, and

---

University education professoriate.

Of the mathematics staff, Harold Fawcett wrote a yearbook on the nature of proof for the National Council of Teachers of Mathematics and became a professor of mathematics education and administrator at Ohio State University. His colleague, Charles Weideman, was both a mathematician and an inventor of musical instruments, including a xylophone made of dinosaur bones; he became a national celebrity on radio shows. (Following a shipping mixup, he came to school one day mourning, "I've lost my bones!" Fortunately, they were found.)

Of the physical education staff members, Charles Cowell became an Ohio State professor of men's physical education and Virginia Blunt a major administrator in the Girl Scouts of America in New York City.

Of the foreign language staff, Paul Diederich became a leader for decades at the Education Testing Service in Princeton, New Jersey.

Of the arts staff, Beatrice Perham taught music education in California institutions of higher learning.

Some left teaching for marriage. Marguerite Richebourg, born in France, became the school's first French teacher, then married Art Moehlman. Her successor, Ann Vance, became the charming hostess of the University of Michigan campus at Ann Arbor as the wife of President Harlan Hatcher. Mary Albright married H. H. Giles, experimented in the varied arts, and became a professional creator of ceramlcs.

Norma Albright, home economist and a teacher of integrated studies, died early. In the industrial arts area, Warren Moore eventually moved on with Rudy to Cranbrook School.

likeable Harold Fawcett, a pioneering mathematician, and was supported by Moehlman and most of the scientists. They believed in progressive teaching of each separate subject, and they prevailed on the senior high school level. Apparently the humanistic and scientific wings of the school faculty saw the world differently. (Later, British writer C. P. Snow, in *The Two Cultures*, was to describe the prevalence of such quarrels between humanists and scientists.) The faculty compromised and, after exhaustive and exhausting discussion, established three-hour blocks of time plus separate classes in mathematics, physical education, and varied arts fields on the junior high school level. The compromise maintained the separate subjects on the senior high school level: social studies, language arts, science, mathematics, foreign language, physical education, and the varied arts taught as distinct fields of study.

I came on the scene as a neutral, largely through my ignorance of educational theory. I was willing to work under either the integrated or the separate fields approach. As to the separate fields, no one, including myself, was quite sure of whether I was a language arts or a social science teacher. So I taught them both. I also learned to teach in the integrated core, for part of my assignment was to become one of three staff members teaching in an eighth-grade core program.

My limited reputation as a reform school teacher had preceded me. Consequently, the faculty also included in my teaching schedule a strange assignment. On the basis of their experiences of the first years, they identified a dozen boys of the tenth and eleventh grades who were "having problems," which ranged from apathy to insubordination. They included a charming and personable boy with ideas that sounded totalitarian to me, a rebellious basketball player, a lad who had already had some scrapes with the law, a runaway from home, several unmotivated young men, and some who, though not retarded, were obviously below the usual intellectual level of the student body. Since the new teacher has a background in English and the social studies, the faculty reasoned, we'll ask him to teach both fields and see what Lindquist's young phenom from the reform school can do with our problem boys.

In those days I was a primitive progressive. I had gotten the message that you should begin with the expressed interests of the learners. Operationally, I knew little else. So when my problem dozen gathered in the round, heavily mirrored, and comfortably couched reception room for our daily two hours together, I simply did what came naturally. Recalling the early reform school hours, I had each boy introduce himself at length. My authoritarian-minded lad particularly enjoyed being the center of the stage as he explained why an elite would inherit the earth. The boys also listened with interest to my own autobiography, including some colorful tales out of Warwick. After our introductions, I pointed out that I hadn't asked to teach them and they hadn't asked for me as their teacher, but we were stuck with each other and might as well make the best of it. Then I asked them what they wanted to learn about. My question was put flatly; it was without elaboration or qualification.

There was a long silence. Then my young authoritarian signaled through body language that he was taking over and that the group should follow his lead. "We can study whatever we want, Mr. Van Til, right?"

"Right."

"Then I know what we'd like to learn about, Mr. Van Til. We'd like to learn about crooks. All about crooks. Is that okay with you, Mr. Van Til, for us to learn all about crooks?"

The basketball star added, "Yeah, Mr. Van Til, for some of these guys it would be like vocational education."

I was at a crossroads. I could either stand pat or scuttle by saying, "Well, you know what I meant. This program is primarily social studies plus language arts skills, so you can choose to study about Greece or Rome or the Middle Ages or a period in American history. But naturally not about crooks." Instead, I chose to remain with my primitive progressive approach. As Robert Frost put it, "Two roads diverged in a yellow wood and I—I took the one less traveled by and that has made all the difference."

So I gulped and said, "Okay. What do you want to know about crooks?"

They looked at each other—this joker was taking them seriously. So they would tell him. "Where do the crooks in Columbus live? Where do they commit the crimes? What kind of crimes? How often do they get caught? How much money do they make as crooks?"

We speculated on these abstruse matters and the morning crept to its close. Knowing that a good teacher makes an assignment, I told them to ask their parents where the crooks of Columbus lived.

The next morning they reported variously, dependent upon their cultural backgrounds: "My old man don't know where the crooks live," or "My father thinks they live in the slums." "Don't you know where they live, Mr. Van Til?" I explained that I was new in town.

Still testing, the class leader commanded silence. "I know who could tell us."

"Who?"

"The cops. Let's ask the cops."

We were nothing if not mobile. Several of the group had cars, so we piled in and went downtown to police headquarters. The stereotype Irish desk sergeant looked up expectantly at the dozen of us. "What can I do for you, boys?"

For the first time, my class showed deference to me. They waited for me to speak. I gestured that this trip was their baby. So one said, "Officer, we're a class from the progressive school up on the campus and we're studying all about crooks."

The Irish officer looked as though his worst suspicions of progressive education were confirmed. But he said, "Well boys, you've certainly come to the right place. What do you want to know about crooks?"

"Where do they live?"

"They're all over the place; the town is jumpin' with them. Let me show you the blotter." So he showed them the record of where crimes had recently been committed. Then he took them on a tour of the station house, including cells, and thus provided us with a dramatic morning.

The next day when we gathered back at the school, the boys said with a note of irritation, "That dumb cop didn't tell us where the crooks live. He just showed us where crimes were committed. Doesn't anyone in this hick town know where the crooks live, Mr. Van Til?"

By now I had found time for a bit of exploration, so I said, "There are sociologists who have studied local crimes, such as

Professor Reckless [his actual name] on campus."

"Let's ask him."

So we walked over to the sociology department, where Professor Reckless told us that one of his students had done a doctoral dissertation on crime in Columbus, and we could find it in the library stacks. We went to the library as a group, walked past the librarian's raised eyebrows, explored the stacks, found the dissertation, carefully blew the dust off it as a health precaution, and checked it out. The dissertation was replete with charts and maps on the incidence of crime, venereal diseases, illegitimacy, and other fascinating matters. We brought the dissertation to school and copied the maps.

The boys found what you and I already know, that multiple problem areas existed in Columbus as in other cities, and that if the maps were superimposed on each other the various social problems would overlap. High crime areas were also areas of high infant mortality, venereal disease, and poor health and housing conditions. But this generalization was new to the sophomores and juniors of my group.

Men of action, they were not content with the abstractions of map preparation. "Let's go see." So again we piled into cars and rode to inner city areas that proved, of course, to be slum regions. We moved about, talked to some residents, and came back to school for a discussion. Someone came up with a suggestion, "Let's tell the other kids what we saw." "How about through taking pictures?"

So we planned a picture-taking campaign in the slums. We shot garbage heaps, deteriorating buildings, bars, and shacks. We found that rats were reluctant to pose. Since the delinquents of the area seemed to be in school or otherwise engaged, my students willingly volunteered to be photographed in situations that dramatized delinquency. Once in a while I wondered what that dumb cop might think if he encountered our prowls during a patrol.

"You know how to develop photographs, Mr. Van Til?" No, but I knew someone who did, Hal Reynard, a science teacher. I urged him to teach some science in the process. "Do you know anything about lettering or assembling photographs or charts, Mr. Van Til?" No, but art teacher Mary Giles did, and I urged her to teach artistic composition in the process. "Do you know how to spell some words and improve some sentences?" Yes, I could help with that; let's get out the dictionaries and the grammars.

When the maps and charts and textual matter were ready, the question arose as to where to display them for the edification of the rest of the student body. Frieda Heller, the librarian, controlled strategic display cases in the hallways. When the boys went to her, requesting their loan, she told them that displays of books must accompany any library-related exhibit. "Now, if they would include books on crime and accompany each with a descriptive card..." The boys suspected me of dirty pool. Yet they got her help on how to use the Dewey decimal system, withdrew the relevant books on crime, read within the books, and prepared written summaries.

When the exhibits went up, the boys got some satisfying feedback from the rest of the school. I began to congratulate myself as I ticked off the social science concepts, the scientific generalizations, the art experiences, and the substantial reading and writing of the past few weeks. I contemplated the study that was emerging, an examination of what we could do about the conditions that we observed. (The crime study led into a study of housing, including the public vs. private housing controversy of the era. The housing study led into the study of race when one of our guides proved to be a highly educated black. "You know why he's so smart? Because he's got white blood. Isn't that how they get smart, Mr. Van Til?" "Let's look it up," I said.)

But pride goeth before a fall. One morning I was sitting in my office opposite one of the exhibit cases. Unaware of my presence, one of my boys was giving a lecture to a friend about the relationship of social problems to social class, as manifested by our charts. I was proud of him. Impressed, his auditor said, "You work on this with that new teacher?" "Yes." "Is he any good?" "Good?" said my boy contemptuously, "Good? He doesn't even have a book!"

In addition to my "problem group" and my participation in eighth-grade core, my third teaching assignment was to teach social studies to a terrific group of high school seniors, our first graduating class. They were motivated, brilliant, and socially committed. As a matter of fact, they had planned their senior social studies course late in their junior year prior to my employment; their only worry was that I would get in the way of their plans. They wanted to study competing economic systems proposed for the United States during the depression era: unrestricted laissez-faire, trust-busting, planning by business, governmentally planned economy, and socialism. The class members wanted to conduct individual studies, report on them to the group, organize panel discussions on social problems, go on trips within the community, and attend meetings of groups like the Foreign Policy Association. Would I be willing to read their papers and take part in their discussions?

Fortunately, I had sense enough to keep out of their way. They came to accept me and even included me in many of their social occasions—after all, I was only five years older than they were. They were a delight to work with, every teacher's dream. Years later I learned that the LaBrant bloc had planned to put me in charge, since her group differed with Moehlman's techniques of teaching. LaBrant's bloc had worked with the class the year before and Lindquist wouldn't sanction a repeat. So the new teacher got the plum. Never again was I to work with so brilliant and so motivated a group of students.

The Ohio State University School was special.

Chapter Sixteen

YOUNG MARRIEDS

I n 1935, after my first year at University School, I returned to Corona to be married. Finances were now no barrier; I was rich, for I earned $2,400 a year! By now, Bee and I had many interests in common: the enjoyment of friends, tennis, theater, books, etc. We opposed war, human exploitation, and racial discrimination. We shared many common values, though we reached them by quite different routes, Bee via Catholicism and liberalism and I via democratic humanism and socialism.

However, the differences that had characterized our relationship since Bee and I, at 19, had first met in 1930 still persisted. Bee was still and would always be a devout Catholic; I had only a tenuous play-coaching relationship to my Episcopal Church. Bee wanted children; I feared they would replace me in Bee's affections. Bee had been taught that birth control was sinful; I regarded it as sensible. Bee was home-oriented; I was travel-hungry. Bee was people-oriented; I preferred humankind in the abstract.

But we loved each other and had learned that we would love no one else. During my year away, Bee had traveled to Columbus for a football weekend and I had returned home for Christmas and spring vacation with her. In the intervals, we wrote letters to each other, full of the excitement of discoveries and the despair of separation. The year of separation taught me something that Bee had learned earlier. We wanted each other; we needed each other; we couldn't live without each other; we had to take a chance on each other. I had found that no substitute would do. In the spring and early summer of 1935 we came to terms. Taken for granted by both of us was that Bee would stay Catholic and that I would stay a skeptic—conversion of either of us was unthinkable. But we still had to reckon with Church policies. The Roman Catholic Church of the 1930s placed formidable obstacles in the way of mixed marriages, such as not allowing the marriage within the church walls and insisting that the non-Catholic partner agree to raise children in the Roman Catholic faith. The first obstacle was hardest on Bee; the second was hardest on me.

Our compromise was that we would be married in the rectory, the priests' residence, and that any children would be reared in the Catholic faith but attend non-Catholic schools. We would have children—but later. Bee would have to struggle with the Church's opposition to birth control; I would have to struggle with children growing up in a faith I couldn't accept. This was our uneasy peace settlement in the War over Religion that had haunted my family and my early years.

True to the great tradition of romantic love, I proposed to Bee and she accepted me in a little summerhouse in a wooded area. The summerhouse was a little open shell that had often been our sanctuary from the prying world. The spot overlooked the waters of Hempstead Harbor, the bay on which we so often canoed.

In the tradition inherited from Europe, I must ask permission from her father for his daughter's hand in marriage. Despite her parents' awareness of many of our differences, the ceremonial request went well. In retrospect, several factors must have helped. Bee's mother, a strong woman and a devoutly orthodox Catholic, knew that her daughter was in love with me. Bee's father, a quiet and kindly man, must have remembered his own repudiation of orthodoxy, his sympathy with the followers of John Huss, his courtship and marriage of Rose within the Church and its rules, and his subsequent firm refusal to go to Mass. Yet the love of Rose and William had survived these conflicts. Despite their unspoken doubts, they accepted the inevitability of our marriage with grace. Bee and I planned to be married on August 24, 1935, the day after Bee's twenty-fourth birthday.

Summer became a whirl of preparation, including the customary round of parties and showers. Bee finished Hunter College courses and acquired a bachelor's degree along with her early teacher training school certificate. I completed work for the master's degree in civic education at Teachers College, begun on weekends during the year I taught at Warwick and continued during the summer of 1934. Despite ownership of Emma, I had neglected to obtain a driver's license. So Bee taught me to drive a modern car, a Chevy, and I obtained my license a few days after we were married.

Decades before the concept of generation gap was popularized, our wedding plans reflected a recognition of the existence of different patterns for different ages. Only our closest relatives gathered in the dim-lit room in the priests' house, but our young friends pelted us with rice on our emergence from the rectory of Our Lady of Sorrows. Older generation members of both families gathered for an elaborate ceremonial dinner, replete with toasts, at the Amber Lantern Restaurant in Flushing. Later, at Bee's family bungalow near the shores of Lake Ronkonkoma, our age group gathered for a free-flowing party uninhibited by elders. For Bee's Pal O Mine Club, created by eight girls in the elementary grades of Our Lady of Sorrows, and my Duwell Club of companions and thespians, the wedding party was also a farewell; in a few days Bee and I were to leave for a honeymoon in the South and permanent residence in Columbus, Ohio. Our last guest, Paul Mendenhall, was ejected over his blurry protestation in the early hours of the morning. All too soon afterward we were having breakfast with the loyal Pal O Mine club who stayed in a cottage a mile away.

Where would we spend our honeymoon? Serious-minded children of the depression that we were, we went South to see for ourselves the social problems of American society, such as Scottsboro, Alabama, the scene of the infamous trial of the Scottsboro boys, blacks accused of raping white women who were alleged prostitutes. We saw the shacks and shanties of Franklin Delano Roosevelt's famous one-third of the American population "ill-fed, ill-clad, ill-housed." We toured extensively that beacon of promise, the Tennessee Valley Authority. We observed conditions and we even interviewed people. Then we headed north.

In an unfashionable area of Columbus we found and rented the second floor of a wonderful old house with a circular bedroom topped by a cupola. The newly marrieds now had an address, 464-1/2 Vermont Place, misinterpreted by Bee's father, who labeled and shipped a trunk to us at "Vermon Place." Rather than verminous, to us our house was paradise.

From my first year in Columbus, we had a good start on a friendship group. Closest to us was English teacher H. H. Giles, who repudiated Harry Herman and was called Mike. Mike was then a creative artist with a twinkling eye and irresistible charm; he was a bohemian who wore his moth-eaten fur coat in completely inappropriate social milieus. Close too was Mary, his wife, a skillful fine arts practitioner, a smiling and relaxed person, and an inept housekeeper. Rose Lammel, the "floating" science teacher, was blonde, taller even than I, a committed single, and a good companion. Another regular was Paul Diederich, a genuine intellectual yet an unworldly innocent; Paul taught an obsolescent subject, Latin, that was amusedly tolerated by the faculty in deference to parental wishes.

In the year that Bee first came to Columbus, Art Moehlman went on leave for a special project in ecology. Our serendipity brought to campus as his replacement Paul Weinandy, who owned a canoe-kayak called by the Germans a *faltboot* (foldboat) and thereby changed our life. He was a *vandervogl* in post-World War I Germany before he migrated to America and a counterpoint marriage to Janet, who was as realistic and restrained as he was romantic and ebullient. Paul had wandered across Central Europe and the Balkans with his lute; at our parties he blended his folk musicianship with fabulous half-whispered travel tales, such as one about his visit to a monastery in Greece where no female human or even female animal had ever set foot.

Life was good to us in those early Columbus years. We hiked, picnicked, played tennis, and went to university events in a young person's town. On fall afternoons Bee and I walked hand in hand across grassy fields to the stadium to urge on the Ohio State Buckeyes as they battled with hated Michigan and the rest of the Big Ten. Post-game we celebrated victory or deplored defeat with eagerness and sazeracs and magnificent small steaks at a local hotel, the Fort Hayes. Or we joined somebody's party. We often hosted others on the faculty and were hosted in return. Low though instructorship was on the academic ladder, we even visited in their homes full professorial demi-gods H. Gordon Hullfish, philosopher of education, and Edwin Pahlow, historian. Sometimes we would all sit at the feet of the genial hosts Rudy and Dora Lindquist. On one such occasion Rudy said, "Wouldn't it be awful if we were together, doing the same things at the school, ten years from now?" We soberly agreed, for we recognized that change ruled the world.

Mike and Mary Giles started a commune decades before the experiments in living of the 1960s and 1970s: themselves, two Weinandys, and one art instructor, Don Torbert, sharing kitchen facilities and social rooms in a big, ramshackle Columbus house. The year after our marriage they invited us to join their version of Brook Farm. Privatists as to domestic life, we unhesitatingly said "no thank you." Janet Weinandy, the only member of the household not employed at University School, did not appreciate her elevation to cook and maid—the experiment in group living was soon terminated.

Bee went shopping for the education she hadn't gotten in her trade school, Jamaica Training School for Teachers, or even in factory-like Hunter College. Ignoring degree programs, she selected professors and topics and studied with, among others, Harlan Hatcher on the American novel, H. Gordon Hayes on socialism, and Boyd H. Bode on philosophy of education.

I devoted my working life to learning to be a good teacher, not through formal courses but through day-by-day experimentation. I taught the core program on the junior high school level and settled into social studies rather than language arts teaching in the senior high school program. I tried out a variety of progressive methods and approaches.

Yet I kept telling myself that I was a writer, not an educator, even though my love affair with teaching became more intense daily. But what to write? During my first year at the University School, I had written one article on education. "The Social Scientist Wonders," a criticism of indoctrination through schools, not only was accepted by the *Phi Delta Kappan* for the April 1935 issue; it was also reprinted in *Educational Method* (the predecessor of *Educational Leadership*) in November 1935 under the title "But Should We Indoctrinate?" I defended exploration of controversial issues, not imposition of answers.

In those days I was ignorant and fearless—what have you got to lose when no one ever heard of you? So I sent a reprint of the article to America's leading exponent of reform of society through education, George S. Counts, whose support for liberal-radical indoctrination by educators I had assailed in the article. Counts had recently delivered his famous address to the Progressive Education Association, "Dare the School Build a New Social Order?" and was shaping policies and writing editorials for the exciting new, radical *Social Frontier*, a journal supportive of social reconstruction through schooling. Though Counts's reply has been long lost to a wastebasket, I shall never forget it. He thanked me politely and then, in a final sentence, said, "When you mature, I believe that you will think differently." Years later I came to know George Counts as a national colleague and a co-worker in organizations. Over a drink following one of his lectures, he recalled the letter with a twinkle and asked, "Did you ever mature, Bill?" I said, "You're as wrong now, George, as you were then."

But from my world view, shaped as it was by liberal arts training, writing about education wasn't really **writing**. Writing was literature: fiction and non-fiction, travel books, essays for journals of opinion, reviews of books and plays for the elite magazines. So during 1935 I practiced to become an author some future day by writing a caustic appraisal of the *New York Herald Tribune* and by trying my hand at reviews of New York plays that Bee and I had seen during summers: Shakespeare's *Taming of the Shrew*, Jane Austen's *Pride and Prejudice*, Clifford Odets's *Paradise Lost*, Sidney Kingsley's *Dead End*, Billy Rose's production of *Jumbo*, George Gershwin's *Porgy and Bess*.

I also taught myself to write through mimicking writers I admired. Thomas Wolfe was my newest discovery. Full of both admiration and malice, I wrote a parody of Wolfe's writing; here is part of "Subway":

> He suddenly knew that he had none. He clawed his pocket as though mad, and as he turned it inside out a dull ripping noise that shot through his viscera like a hell-bound monster assailed his ears. He had ripped the pocket. There was no nickel. He plunged both hands into a hip pocket and cursed God and the laughing angels in heaven when his bitter search-

ing glance revealed floods of dimes and quarters and pennies and halves and one dollar bills and fives and a ten but not a single nickel. Back beside his sinewy long leg he jammed the products of the United States Treasury Department. Then he pushed back his hair and plunged into the milling cursing shouting mob, the symbol of all the whirl and glamour and madness and frenzy and love and beauty that made New York. He crashed into them and he felt their flesh shrink from contact with him as he tore and bit his way to the metal booth, grey, menacing, like an ancient fortress torn from the battlements and transmuted to the boil and rush of this world.

Oh changeless change booth! You became the Mecca of all the young men—and yes the young women and the old men and the old women and the little children and the pregnant women and the bitches dressed in harlot clothes—you, the change booth became the Grail, and the love of pure women. You they struggled with before they dived into Manhattan's bowels to mole through bed rock upon which the ichthyosaurus excreted in the dim hissing days before man came. And their hearts bounded in their mouths as they individually thought of the home station. Canarsie, Prospect Park, Harlem Square, Willets Point, Kosciusko, Fort Washington, Vesey Street, Corona, Mott Avenue, all the names of joy and light and sun and sorrow that have gone into the axes of the pioneers, into the bleached bones that marked the desert trail for only hawks wheeling above in the still awful void to look down upon, into the rust of guns, and the squalling mouths of little children that have made this that we call America, this singing, yelling, wheeling, whistling entity that makes up this continent, broad and crossed by pioneers and the singing hungry voices of a nation.

He fought. He changed a dime. He strode through the turnstile. The maw of the subway sucked him down greedily and picked its teeth.

Paul Weinandy, bless his heart, unwittingly shaped the next several years of our lives when, in the spring of 1936, he said to Bee and me, "Why don't you come to Europe this summer with Janet and me?" We explained that we had no money; $2400, while a healthy depression era salary, would not finance European travel. "You don't need money," said the romantic Paul. "We'll travel by foldboat." "To Europe?" we asked incredulously. For a foldboat is a canoe-kayak about eighteen feet long, a rubberized sheath held rigid by a framework of assorted sticks and pieces. It's a folding boat which can be packed into two canvas bags and carried between rivers. Paul admitted that we would have to beg, borrow, or steal money for travel back and forth across the Atlantic on an ocean liner. But once there, costs would be minimal.

Bee's mother and father advanced us my summer salary checks. In June, 1936, ten months after our marriage, we sailed for Europe. I would write a book. It would be about our travels. The literary world would hear from me yet.

Chapter Seventeen

PORTRAIT
OF THE YOUNG MAN
AS AN ARTIST

I n Europe, during the summer of 1936, I wrote *Paris in the Spring*. We didn't set foot in Paris that year, and our travel season was summer rather than spring. Yet *Paris in the Spring* was a good title, calling up visions of eager youth and abundant expectations, of hunger for life of the young man as an artist—yet with an overtone of tongue in cheek.

I can only write of the author of *Paris in the Spring* in the third person and past tense. Not only did he live and write a long time ago; he was also so committed to becoming a litterateur, so self-consciously the player of the role of young man as artist, that he shunned dealing with his personal loves and hates, joys and sorrows, angers and fears. If we are to believe his wife and friends, he loved and hated, laughed and wept, raged and cringed like any mortal man. But *Paris in the Spring* seldom recorded his intimate emotional states, for the young man aspired instead to creative writing and literary artistry.

Paris in the Spring conveyed its ambiguity in the first lines:

> The first problem is that of orientation. What shall this manuscript be? A journal, diary, a novel, impressions, a sketch book, caricature and character sketches?...What is this to which the artist is giving birth?
>
> Perhaps the knot may be cut most expeditiously by resolving that this will be a journal which will be written in whatever form or style the author finds congenial at the moment.

"The artist...the author." The die was cast.

So the young man began a literary smorgasbord. He so shunned diary form ("They serve heavy breakfasts on British ships; today we had kippered herring") that it is hard to tell when he and his young wife sailed for Europe; diligent sleuthing suggests June 20. He wrote satirically of their shipboard acquaintances, indignantly of social distinctions between first, tourist, and third classes on Cunard's S. S. *Scythia* and of the slave wages of stewards and waiters, and soberly of impressions of Emil Ludwig's *Lincoln*, which he read on board. He saved his disillusion with the thin walls of their third class cabin, the profanity and obscenity of drunken Irish passengers, and the foul, sour smells of garbage at the entry to the dining room for a hot letter he soon wrote to Cunard, demanding transfer of return passage to a German liner.

He was lyric when, after more than a week, Ireland came into sight:

> Ireland rose softly. Ungainly humps of hills differentiated themselves from clouds low and protective. Mysteriously from the sea depth new land clawed upward. The ancient headlands appeared first, proud, a grandfather introducing his brood. Then the nearer brasher bolder lands, blacker, less fog-crowned, the strong young men of the family. Then pertly elfishly unexpectedly appeared the saucy children, the smaller nearer jagged highlands.

As Ireland rose out of the sea, he even thought kindly of the noisy Irish returnees for whom it had been "a long way to Tipperary." Then came dingy Liverpool, the flawless English countryside, intimidating London, and a stunning performance of Shakespeare's *Henry IV* in Covent Garden. In Antwerp, the first impressions of the American abroad were complicated by despair at "the major problems of the literary artist: selectivity and unity."

> What should I attempt to convey?—the old world peasant charm of Anvers, the stretching Gothic spires and antique musty splendor of the cathedral, in the manner of the travel books? Or should I draw the contrast of the old and new— twisting alley streets and Shirley Temples, bicycles and sleek channel steamers, sad-faced veterans and the young soldiers strolling the boulevards with their young mistresses? Or I might assay the humorous—my misadventures in making

myself understood, the Gargantuan meals thrust willy-nilly upon the protesting traveler, the incredible quantity of *pommes de terre*, the quaint though modern fixtures in our johnny, the solo glass of beer with its overpowering dazing effect....

Here in this cafe with lovely tired Bee at my side, I wish to sit and steep my senses in my beer, drowsy, rocked, completely uncreative. Sing ye Muse; I join not your harmony. Let the bells of the old cathedral float me through space in a land where hurry is the province only of bicycles and beer trucks.

After Amsterdam and Cologne came Saarburg, base for the forthcoming Mosel cruise with the Weinandys. The young man admitted that he was uncertain whether he was "an artist or a vacationer." The profusion of possible themes haunted him:

Among the possibilities are these—the history of the old Saarburg Castle from the builders of the Middle Ages, through the regimes of the toll-taking robber barons, into the days when the castle passed into the hands of a proud bishop, stepped perhaps out of Chaucer....

And another—the glories of the German countryside with quilted hills, vineyards pushed precariously or impossibly against the cliffs set into the hillside with a call that the rain be gentle, slow twisting rivers that have eaten into the heart of solid rock and tired, their work done, flowed slowly....

And another—a book might be made of the enjoyable way to see Europe. Again it might employ contrast. The early chapters might deal with the unpleasantness of the cities.... Then with swift transition hurl the reader into the rapids, the town appearing from beyond the bends, the high green vineyards, the Roman walls, the tomb of old Johan the Blind, the dreamy philosophy of the riverman, the duffel bag shoved into the prow, the slow pace of the days.

Once in a while it all came together and a piece of writing worked. Such was his experience on the Saar in the hills above Saarburg where he first met the Romans through miraculously preserved tile mosaics depicting conflict among gladiators, lions, tigers, and men with whips. He wrote an essay, "Roman Veteran," which recreated the life of the Romans on the frontier of empire and the reaction of the American visitor horrified by the immortalized butchery.

Saarburg, a castle-crowned jewel of a town above the Saar,

was an unforgettable romantic delight. With Bee and the Weinandys, he trained for the coming cruise through "the trip by
kayak above Saarburg, the fifteen-mile hike, the twenty-five-
mile journey to Luxembourg by bicycle. The passing of physical
pain from the rear to the feet and back again to the home of
original sin, between the legs."

After almost a week, the four launched in their two boats for
the days of their Saar-Mosel cruise from Saarburg via the Saar
and into the Mosel to Guls, just above where the Mosel meets the
Rhine at Koblenz. In his journal he wrote of the Roman ruins in
Trier—amphitheater, gate, baths, and marketplace—of foldboaters met midstream and ashore, of the best Mosel wines at
twenty-five cents a bottle, of the surpassing friendliness of the
Germans whom they met in the little towns. He wrote too of Beilstein, forgotten by trains, a slice of the Middle Ages that had
"crammed itself into the crevice of the valley, sent its streets
circuitously up the mountainside, and achieved a height equivalent to its breadth." He had harsh words for the pretentious
castle Burg Eltz, "quite sensibly, the owners of Burg Eltz do not
live there." He wrote on the ugly arrogance of the Nazis. He gave
little space to the unromantic tragi-comedy of losing his trousers
stuffed with passports and all their money at Bullay on the banks
of the Mosel following a stop for luncheon and swimming, the
frantic discovery of the loss at Beilstein, the hectic ride upriver
with a friendly driver, the happy retrieval, and the joyous waving of the pants from the car window, a symbol of success
communicated to anxiously waiting Bee and Janet.

Along with reporting the Mosel's charms were the artist's
worries. Back home in America he had read *German Summer*, a
relaxed and readable account of foldboat trips by a mother and
daughter named Parker:

> I continually realized that writing of the Cornelia Stratton
> Parker type is not for me. In it there is too much of the stench
> of the dead past, too little of the breath of the present. It is pure
> Cabellian escapism; it is not real. I will let Cornelia have her
> vineyards like giant carpets wearing thin upon the mountain-
> side, seams showing despite continual repair. I will look at the
> vineyard through other lenses. My description will be social
> and will talk of the lives of men and women.

141

He made stern resolutions:

> As the nature of my book grows more clear with the passing days, I experience a feeling of deep satisfaction at the months which lie before me in Columbus. I must guard warily against my old foe, the desire to have my cake and eat it too. If I am to create this book (or at least manuscript) I must rigidly hold to a resolution to devote only part of my waking life to the school, only a fraction to social achievement, and to devote a considerable part to writing, rewriting, despairing, cursing, melancholy, and the most intense joy I shall ever know. And I must taste now, swallow, some of the implications of this decision. Here are some. I must cut my already meager reading in half. I must read but approximately one book in two weeks. A corollary here is that my reading must necessarily become more selective. The ephemeral materials I must pass by and I must drink more deeply of the knowledge of the past, the classics of literature (not particularly fiction) and economics. Magazines I must allow but one evening weekly. I must work far more efficiently both at the office and at home. This implies that I must set conference hours, keep them, refer students to these hours, that I must set hours for office work, perform it expeditiously and get out. I must cut down on recreation in all forms. Less time for tennis, fewer parties, fewer weekend trips. And absolutely no plays in any shape, manner, or form. No acting, no directing. Because young man, you near the turning point. You are twenty-five. Literature does not know you.

After the Mosel, the four travelers hiked in the Black Forest, where the artist wrote of the distorted visions and mirages of hikers in the foggy rain. Munich made their honor roll of cities with its absence of hurry and its presence of the Hofbrauhaus. In Munich, the artist and his wife bought a brand new foldboat to replace a leaky craft; they called it Long Island Duck I. The four then separated—Paul and Janet for the mountains, the flatlanders for foldboating on the Danube and the Elbe Rivers.

The artist still rejected travel writing, yet was tempted. He wrote:

> I suppose there are times in every writer's life when he wishes that he were doing something other than that which he is doing. For if I did not scorn the travel book replete with

socially meaningless chatter—its epitaph is "so conversa-
tional"—I might write the same happy drivel on our days on
the Danube. In fact, I might try it. I shall title it "An Essay Into
Halliburtonism" or "Dear Diary":
> "The rain had poured with peasant persistence for days.
> Munich sopped and slogged through the streets, head down.
> We left it with thanks for the cavernous monument to the
> belly, the Hofbrauhaus, with thanks for its friendliness, pla-
> zas, gaiety, with curses for the rain. The slow local crept from
> the station and in far more than the twinkle of an eye we were
> at Ingolstadt. We wheeled the boat through the streets and
> through a fine park and, as we did, we received the thrill of the
> day. The sun came out." (Note: Who, except you, cares?)

So the artist wrote his essays on the monument to the belly,
the Hofbrauhaus; on Nazi persecution of a lonesome aristocrat at
Kelheim; on an evening with a rigid young Fascist met at the
canoe club and folkfest in Vilshofen on the brown Danube. Yet
sometimes, as on one soft Vienna night, he thought about the
coming return to America and the University School and addressed a message to neophytes on the faculty:

> For the Professor Doctor [Giles] and myself are the victims
> of a loathsome disease, known to the medical world as yet only
> as University School disease.... The dread disease in an ad-
> vanced stage has us. Formerly we slept with women, now
> nightly we clasp to our bosom University School, enjoy sweet
> dreams in which we stroke the delectable rump known as the
> industrial art shop, or in tempestuous mood endeavor to
> subdue her to our whim. Formerly we ate, drank, conversed,
> like normal humans; now inhumanity has such a grip upon us
> that we eat and drink of the body and blood of the school and
> it alone makes our conversation.

The last few weeks in Europe really belong in Bee's autobiography, not the young artist's. For Bee returned to her roots by
visiting relatives in Czechoslovakia. The train from Vienna ran
through golden wheat fields in free Czechoslovakia and eventually brought us to towns unpronounceably named Lnare, Kocelovice, Blatna. In Kocelovice, the travelers met Bee's uncle, her
father's brother, heir through primogeniture to the family farm
and at 75 still tearing his peasant living from the soil. Of Jan
Blaha, the artist wrote:

He knew what existed, what daily sunk its stench deep into his nose, bit lines into his leather cheeks, curled his shoulders and made his step heavy, slow, and solid. Work. The incessant demand of his boss, the seasons, his job, the land. The fordized monotony of binding grain, the awkward swing and swish of the scythe, the shovelling of manure. So he said, "You Americans do not know what it is to work." There was no self-pity in his voice, no trace of the martyr complex. He was a strong man, proud of his age and strength; his cross was idealized from burden to banner. A simple mental twist and work became the value in life. In his own eyes—and whatever other eyes matter?—he was the greater man. The younger brother, retired and now at ease—no good anymore, a weakling. The young wanderers—drifters, wasters. Cain had sinned; man's destiny was clear. Work since childhood and still he could stagger to the cows under a giant basket of clover. That which man cannot defeat he calls God.

These relatives proved to be enduring people. In Blatna, the uncle of Bee's mother was an 86-year-old man resembling a small, belligerent, shrunken ferret. While galloping up a hill in pursuit of deer, he commented of a 76-year-old neighbor, "Work is play when you are young like that."

The kindness of Bee's relatives led the artist to invent a new definition of hospitality: "Hospitality is lying awake in a too-short and too-narrow bed in a room with five other people until six o'clock in the morning in order to save you eighty cents for lodging which you would have delightedly spent." Aunts and uncles and a younger generation of cousins plied us with food and drink. On one round of visits, the travelers had a first breakfast of rolls, butter, and coffee, a second breakfast of eggs, a lunch of beer soup (no comma, that is the name of the soup) and rabbit, with a syrupy drink and cakes. Then mid-afternoon, when the rabbit had lain but half an hour, tea with rum, then Pilsener beer, followed at four o'clock by cakes, fresh baked bread and beer. All this was prior to the major meal of the day set at the hour of eight in honor of the travelers.

It was in Bee's mother's town, Blatna, in the shadow of a castle, that the young man began to recognize the handwriting on the wall:

Lately my mental attitude toward the noble art of translating mental to another type of tissue has turned dilettante. This very sentence is ample betrayal of a new frivolity. The book has grown misty; much of what I do is simply muscle exercise, frequently intricate as barwork in a *sokol*, but training for an event which won't come off. I look good in the gym.

It isn't that my writing has fallen off spectacularly in quality or quantity. I probably cover as many pages fully and illegibly after that dead spot about Munich. Too, I write more easily; the tenses hang together well, seldom launch into too tenuous air. The vocabulary has been refurbished after the prattle of the high school class. The big lack is in unity. My theme song is dead. The threat over Europe can play but a minor part in the whole unless I lapse to artificiality. Social consciousness is of course present, as in the Czechoslovakian sketches, yet I wonder if that is not too thin a thread, too undefined, to spin a good book upon. That realization has discouraged me.

Let's look seriously at what I've lined up for the epic. (Again the lightness. I sometimes wonder whether it is a mask but then I have never known where real began and let's pretend left off.)

But hope sprang eternal in the artistic breast:

Is a loophole magazine publication and eventual collection in "Essays for our Times"? Is the solution Edmund Wilson's *Travel in Two Democracies?*

In Prague, the travelers celebrated the first of their wedding anniversaries in the luxurious hotel Grand Steiner, where the drapes matched the expensive wallpaper, then cruised the Elbe River north into Germany past the town where Martin Luther's revolutionary theses had been nailed to the church door. They visited a trade fair in a city celebrated for its china and smoking factories, unaware of the coming saturation bombing that was to level the city of Dresden. Then home on the comfortable German ship, the *Europa*, and rewriting of "Roman Veteran" and "Myopia in the Black Forest." In Ronkonkoma, the young artist whistled in the graveyard:

As I suspected, the book has diminished—possibly degenerated—into articles which, if sufficiently numerous and worthy, may become a book. The articles are now a literary venture "Myopia in the Black Forest" *(Harper's, The Atlantic)*;

a social pacifist document "Roman Gentlemen" (*Harper's*.?); "See Europe and Live" for—of all things!—*The Saturday Evening Post;* "The Back Door to Fascism" (*Nation, New Republic*); "Hello!" (a humorous radical paper), "Three Man Parade" (the same), "Nationalism" (the same—what the hell will it be?); "Gospel of Work" (a serious journal); "Two Jews" (*New Masses*); "Hobi" (some humorous magazine).

Back in Columbus the young man wrote essays and short stories based on his European experiences and acquired a variety of rejection slips. *Paris in the Spring* in its totality and in separate pieces was never published. So, in the late fall, the artist died.

Before his death he put up a gallant fight for his beloved literature, his romantic impressions, his scorn and his snobbery. He was reincarnated as a young journalist who believed he could write a travel book that would hybridize social observation and carefree adventure and would derive its unity from the eternal Danube flowing through that ugly excrescence on its banks, fascism. Wait until next year, promised the young journalist. The artist was no longer around to respond.

Chapter Eighteen

THE DANUBE FLOWED
THROUGH FASCISM

Youth is resilient. The artist was dead; long live the journalist! The year between our two European river summers began with my despair as to my writing and ended with rainbows of hope. As a book, *Paris in the Spring* was a dead duck, and ducklings in the form of essays and stories never managed to swim. Essays on "My Bay," written in the manner of Edmund Wilson; a critique of the poet Mark Van Doren; and a short story in the manner of James T. Farrell were learning exercises that were never completed. But my writing for the education profession fared better. *The Social Frontier*, pleased with my April 1936 book review of James Rorty's *Where Life Is Better*, satiric impressions of California by a radical, published my reviews of novels by James T. Farrell and Martha Gellhorn. *American Teacher*, the magazine of the American Federation of Teachers, published my review of Paul Hanna's *Youth Serves the Community*.

Life continued to be good to the young couple. The parties, football games, and picnics went on and included new staff members such as Latin teacher Sam Bradshaw, one of the geniuses Terman studied and reported on in his books on the gifted child. Sam, an amiable Westerner, was carrying on a love affair with Coors beer and introduced us effete Easterners and Middle Westerners to this brew during some social occasions. My teaching of both core and social studies grew more assured, and Bee continued to tap Ohio State's supply of courses.

Yet we were impatient for the coming summer of 1937 and

our Danube trip. Now a veteran, Bee prepared for a sustained cruise. We had decided to hike to the Danube's source, put our foldboat into the stream as soon as it became navigable, and follow the allegedly blue Danube as far as we could before summer's end. I read about the river and about the Middle European and Balkan nations through which we would travel. Meanwhile, Hitler grew more aggressive and the democracies temporized. We knew that war was coming but hoped there was time for one more European river trip.

School ended in June, and we sailed on the *Hamburg* of the German Lloyd line. This time we actually saw Paris in the spring, though only briefly, for big cities, we had learned, were not for us. We had sold Long Island Duck I in America, so in Freiburg, Germany, we bought a brand new Klepper foldboat for eighty dollars plus eight dollars for accessories. We then hiked in the Black Forest area, in which the Breg and Brigach rose, and to the point where the two rivers joined to become the Danube.

On July 8, the Long Island Duck II was launched from Ulm, Germany. Thirty-seven days and 882 miles later we arrived in Belgrade. We had voyaged through Germany, Austria, Czechoslovakia, Hungary, and Yugoslavia. The Danube ran on through Romania and Bulgaria, 1,776 miles in all from the Black Forest to the Black Sea.

Bee kept a careful diary loaded with facts as to distances and places and people. I wrote daily of events, impressions, and ideas. Together we amassed the raw material for what became *The Danube Flows Through Fascism: Nine Hundred Miles in a Foldboat*, Charles Scribner's Sons, 1938, 301 pp., $3.00.

We had learned much from our river cruises of 1936; consequently, the creation of *The Danube Flows Through Fascism* worked. In the previous summer the artist had been scornful of travel books; now the journalist unashamedly wrote one that combined adventure and social observation. The artist scorned research and cherished impressions; the journalist read whatever he could about the Danube, the past of the nations and the Fascist present, and selected what he could use. The artist had been content with his own psyche; the journalist recorded details of scenery, towns, encounters with people, locales. The artist had seldom included Bee in his literary abstractions; the journalist recorded his conversations with her and, if truth be told, frequently improved on their dialogues. The artist tried to write complete essays while they traveled; the journalist took notes for later shaping into a unified book and relied on Bee's journal crammed with data on who-what-when-where. The artist waited for his return to Columbus to begin his book; the journalist left the river in mid-August with several vacation weeks still to go and began to write his book in Dubrovnik on the Adriatic Sea.

The journalist also conquered two major problems, how to handle anti-Nazis so they would not be identified and how to absorb summer of 1936 experiences into the account of the 1937 trip.

Protection of informants was achieved through a prefatory note, "Excuse It, Please," and a chapter of condemnation of Third Reich policies ironically addressed to the Fuehrer and called "Listen, Mr. Hitler." The prefatory note read:

> Men may differ philosophically but all share two extremely human desires—they want to keep on living and they want to stay out of jails. Even anti-Nazis in Germany. Therefore it is impossible for me to identify or localize some of the people whom Bee and I met as we paddled down the Danube. I don't want to write any cryptograms for heresy hunters.
>
> The shadows of the German anti-Nazis may be seen as through a mirror, extremely darkly, in Chapter Eleven. I regret that their tremendous stories must be muted—in no other dictatorial nation along the Danube did the antis or I think such a degree of caution necessary.

The "Listen, Mr. Hitler" chapter skipped all telltale identification related to Nazi German places or persons in this manner:

> "Can we come with you?" was only a cheery if tedious joke to us until we met the noisy man in the tavern. He had been drinking beer with his friends and he was several up on them.
>
> "Take me," he said. "I'll hide in your knapsack."
>
> They kidded him. There was too much of him for one small sack, they said. He would sink the boat. He'd get seasick. We would have to pay duty on him. The ambitious stowaway grew serious.
>
> "You must take me," he said. "I can't get out any other way and I won't stay any longer in this God-damned country."
>
> The kidding fled.
>
> "Shut up," they said quietly. "Close your mouth. You're drunk. You don't know what you're saying."

They began to sing. They looked about, not too obviously, to see who might have heard him and then one of them took him home and the party went on with an unacknowledged damper on the evening. Surreptitiously they looked over each person who left; it would be morning before they would know for certain if he had been heard and reported.

And when you've mastered keeping your voice down, drunk or sober, you dissatisfied Germans, learn unceasing vigilance too. Make sure that no high-school boy has bent nearby to tie his shoe while you are talking quietly of Germany. An ex-service man was careless once in this respect; he told us about it in whispers in the center of the broad Danube one sunny day. He had said to a friend, "It is too bad we do not have a free press in this country." The high-school boy no longer fumbled with shoe laces; he straightened up and went away. "Five days," the Nazis told the veteran. Five days aren't much in a lifetime, but it gave the man some time to think. He sat in a cool, quiet, damp, dark cell and he remembered that this nation which had jailed him for a passing remark to a friend was the same nation that he fought for through four years of hell on a front, and the same nation in which in 1919 he had joined an anti-Semitic organization that antedated the Nazis.

Relevant earlier experiences were incorporated in the new book. Chapter One told of how we became European foldboaters and thus incorporated a reprise of the Saar-Mosel trip. A 1936 encounter with broken and scorned Jews in the Black Forest became a flashback in the account of locating the Danube's source. The near loss of Long Island Duck I at the dangerous bridge at Regensburg helped build up suspense for shooting the rapids in Long Island Duck II. The ambiguity of the Nazi youths, socially amiable and ideologically abhorrent, met at a 1936 folksfest in Vilshofen, rescued the later account of that dung-laden little village from the curse of uneventfulness.

After we folded up the Long Island Duck II on August 13, we visited our third Danubian capital city, Belgrade. It couldn't compare with our nostalgic memories of delightful Vienna and incomparable Budapest. By great good luck we found in Belgrade a steamer that took us almost 400 miles farther down the Danube. As tourists we traveled the Cataract Stretch, through Kazan Gorge and the perilous Iron Gates. Glad that we hadn't tried to foldboat this turbulent stretch, we reached Radujevac, with Romania on one side of us and Bulgaria on the other shore. We had come 1,266 miles since the Black Forest, 882 of them in the Duck. The steamer turned back, still many miles from the Black Sea.

"You're just a tourist now; Bee's not in the kayak bow," Time hummed. "It didn't cost much either," said Bee regretfully. "How much altogether?" I asked. "I'll get out my black book and recite. Wait a minute. From Ulm to Zemun 37 days. Cost $170.29. Daily average $4.60." "Luxurious living in the cities included?" "Even Nurnberg. Even films." "Not bad."

In mid-August we took a small plane from Belgrade over the Dinaric Alps. The aircraft swooped up a narrow valley hemmed in by menacing mountains on both sides. Our taxi swerved recklessly along a coastal road in the subtropics to a delightful small hotel that overlooked, across the bay, the massive fortified walls that enclosed the red roofs of Dubrovnik. High on a cliff in a garden crammed with fragrant cedars and pines, and above the translucent waters of our swimming cove, I began _The Danube Flows Through Fascism_. At Dubrovnik, once called Ragusa, we spent our second wedding anniversary and Bee's twenty-sixth birthday. Then a tramp coastal steamer took us along the Adriatic to Venice and we entrained for Paris. Departure was from LeHavre in the massive _Bremen_, which plowed through a stormy North Atlantic.

Back in Columbus I completed the book. The opening of school that year seemed only incidental. _The Danube Flows Through Fascism_ came along fast and by January was complete. Now, amateur author, where to submit the manuscript, typed and retyped by Bee? During the fall, a traveler selling Scribner's textbooks had come by. "Writing anything these days, professor?" Since I had been promoted from instructor to assistant professor in 1936, I was still flattered by the honorable appellation of professor. I readily told him about the Danube manuscript. Though the salesman had no relationship to Scribner's trade books for the general public, he loyally suggested, "Submit it to Scribner's." I needed no urging, publication by Scribner's was the aspiration of all neophyte authors of my generation. So, manuscript completed, I mailed it to the legendary editor, Maxwell Perkins, at Scribner's. What happened then is described in one of my 1969 columns, *To Walk With Others*:

> The odds against acceptance of an unsolicited manuscript of a book by a twenty-seven year old unknown in the depression decade were astronomical. I did not know that. But had I known, it would have made no difference. I had to become a writer; the necessity devoured me. Charles Scribner's Sons was the Valhalla of young writers of the time, so I sent my manuscript, unsolicited and without an agent's blessing, over the transom to this publisher. In Valhalla, editor Maxwell Perkins was the chief Norse god. Perkins, a literary legend, had edited Ernest Hemingway and F. Scott Fitzgerald and had nursed along the titanic Thomas Wolfe.
>
> Scribner's kept my manuscript for what seemed an incredibly long time while I agonized. Life is terribly real when you are twenty-seven. In retrospect it wasn't long, only three weeks. Then I was invited to come in for "a conference."
>
> Which brings us back to the moment that made a difference. They ushered me into the office of the quiet man with his hat pulled low over his eyes—the great Maxwell Perkins. He sat barricaded against the world behind his big desk. He was surpassingly kind. But—the economic problem of publishing, the gathering war clouds in Europe, the probable reluctance of readers to accept a travel book combining the joy of river cruising with the grimness of social observation of fascism. Yet there would be a final editorial meeting tomorrow and Scribner's would let me know the outcome. But I shouldn't expect....
>
> After I left the office, I don't know how long I walked through the afternoon and into the night swallowing the bitter fruit called rejection. Years later, though it was only the next day, the telephone rang and I answered. It was no underling notifying me; it was Maxwell Perkins.
>
> Never have I heard such happiness for another human being as there was in the quiet man's voice. He said, "We've decided to publish your book." Somehow he knew what it meant; in his own way he had been walking with me through the afternoon and into the night. The essence of being a great editor like the famous Maxwell Perkins is to walk with your authors.

To be the author of a book! Wallace Meyer, the editor to whom the manuscript was delegated, was amazingly tolerant.

He deleted nothing from the manuscript except for a sophomoric sacrilegious smartassism—and I was brash enough even to dispute this deletion. He was willing to respect my phrasings and my meanings and to publish my manuscript essentially as I wrote it, a policy lesser editors were to repeatedly violate in later years. Scribner's subtitled the book, *900 Miles in a Foldboat.*

At least one traumatic happening always characterizes the making of any book; ours came early while we were in Europe. Somehow we lost the photos and negatives for pictures taken during the early weeks of the trip. Bee, the custodian, was heart-broken. We substituted some Weinandy photographs of the Saar-Mosel and the Black Forest at appropriate points and resumed our own photo coverage when the book reached Kelheim on the Danube.

During the spring of 1938 we painstakingly read proofs and caught typos. Our chores complete, we waited for publication, scheduled for August, 1938. Kudos to Scribner's! The manuscript was submitted in January and published in August, remarkably fast processing and production of a book. *The Danube Flows Through Fascism* was jacketed; two figures in a foldboat dig into the water with their paddles; no one except the author and his wife seemed to notice that the paddlers didn't synchronize their strokes, a cardinal sin on any river. Then as now, authors were seldom consulted about the appropriateness or accuracy of jackets.

The book itself was handsome, twenty-nine chapters running 301 pages in large eye-easy type with abundant white space. Scribner's spent freely for illustrations, no less than fifty-eight, including Bee's six well-drawn maps of nations through which the Danube flowed and three excellently reproduced river maps. Such an expenditure of money is prodigal in any era and especially remarkable in a depression era.

I wish I could say that the investment returned dividends to Scribner's, but I can't. *The Danube Flows Through Fascism* sold about 1,600 copies at $3.00, almost all in the single year that lay between publication and the outbreak of World War II. For a world at war, a book about carefree European travel was irrelevant. Through royalty, the book paid its author almost $500, enough to finance the trip. Scribner's, I am sure, did not get its investment back.

But who cares about money when fame is achieved! *The Danube* was given a half-page review in both the *Sunday New York Times* and the *Sunday Herald Tribune*, as well as a full column review in the weekday *Herald Tribune*. Review copies went to newspapers across the nation. Eager and hungry neophyte that I was, I subscribed to a clipping service and received scores of clippings on the book, often simply parroting the Scribner's release. In the immemorial tradition of irresponsible criticism, one Southern reviewer devoted his limited space to his outrage at my comment that the two Jews we met in the Black Forest were as cowed as Alabama Negroes. However, the large majority of the reviewers were friendly and favorable.

The travel author and his wife tried their clumsy hands at promotion. A long cozy account of the travels of the Corona couple appeared in the *Long Island Daily Star*, to the great joy of my mother and her cronies, who regarded the *Star* as a journalistic bible. Bee surreptitiously rearranged displays of new books on Brentano's, Macy's, and Scribner's counters to make my new book still more visible to buyers. Veteran salespersons no doubt nudged each other and murmured "author's wife."

So now, at 27, I was a published author. Famous too. Hadn't I been given a featured review in both major New York City papers? Naturally, there would be wonderful, delightful, and delectable changes in my life. I didn't really know what they would be, but I was confident they would be extraordinary.

However, nothing much happened. Life ran on. In the fall of 1938 I went back to University School to teach. One of my colleagues told me that, knowing me, he couldn't believe I was capable of writing so interesting a book—a dubious compliment. Local churches added both Bee and me to their lists of possible speakers. I was once introduced by a church lady as "the man who had gone up and down the Danube in a flatboat." Bee was once told by a clubwoman that there would be no honorarium for her talk, since the club was saving its money for "a really good speaker." So much for the rewards that accompany fame.

Chapter Nineteen

FOLDBOATING
AND HOSTELING
IN AMERICA

T he year 1938 goes down in our archives not only as the year in which *The Danube Flows Through Fascism* was published. Nineteen hundred and thirty-eight was also the year we tried foldboating in America and, in the process, discovered youth hosteling.

As summer approached, we considered briefly a Volga cruise and a possible *The Volga Flows Through Communism*. But the Russian reality immediately dispelled that notion; in the late 1930s Americans saw the Soviet Union only via Intourist while closely chaperoned by loyal and hard-eyed Communist guides. Maybe the Nile—but who wants dysentery or other exotic tropical diseases? The Mississippi awed us—too wide, too industrialized. So we settled for exploratory foldboat forays from our Long Island bases, Bee's parents' home at Lake Ronkonkoma and my mother's bungalow at Beacon Hill. Knowing that foldboating was almost unknown in America and fearing that overnight lodging by streams might be infrequent, we bought a tent and camping equipment to add to our "zubehor" (foldboat gear). Maybe a book would take shape—*The Poor Man's Yacht?*

If I may be permitted a classic understatement, our first American foldboat experience was not propitious. Chevy transported us from Ohio across the Mohawk Valley to the lordly Hudson. We launched the Long Island Duck above the industrial clutter of Albany and Troy; our first impression of Hudson River foldboating was of massive bridges that, like desert mirages, hung in the air miles ahead. No matter how hard and long and deep we paddled, the bridges stayed miles off. After an eternity, we reached and passed them and moved into fairer country, a series of estates. Unlike Europe, no towns cozily hugged the river.

As darkness fell, we picked a stopping place for an overnight camp and were immediately attacked by voracious mosquitos. We hastily began setting up our tent. Then the man came along. He was a security guard for an estate. "Private property. You can't camp here." But it was almost dark. He made clear that nightfall was God's business and not his. "You have to move on." So we dismantled the tent and shoved off into the blackness. Ahead no lights beckoned. We paddled a mile or two and then, in desperation, went ashore somewhere in the black unknown, frantically slapped mosquitos, hastily put up our tent and dove into it, supperless. No guard materialized.

Very early the next morning we paddled into the emptiness of the Hudson Valley. We met no one, saw no one on the river. In the late afternoon we came to a town with a lovely name, Castleton-on-Hudson. Surely here we could relive the hospitality of European river towns! But Castleton-on-Hudson completely turned its back on the river. To add injury to insult, the residents of Castleton-on-Hudson dumped their garbage on the banks of the river. No guest houses, no floats, no boat club—just stench and, most probably, rats. We landed in the revolting mess, abandoned the Duck, and walked to a small hotel near the railroad tracks. Again we met no one, talked to no one except the apathetic desk clerk.

In bed in a grim room, we dialed the radio to the Joe Louis-Max Schmeling fight, their second bout. As the fight began, a New York Central freight train went by, whistling for the crossings. For a couple of minutes, we couldn't hear the radio. When the train had passed, the fight was over—Louis had won by a knock-out in the first round. We slept fitfully.

The next morning we rose and looked at each other in silent agreement. Tails between our legs, we slunk back to the banks of the Hudson, dismantled the foldboat, and hired a driver to take us and our gear back to Chevy above Albany. We left the lordly Hudson, never to return. Flow on, lordly Hudson, past your mirage-like bridges and through your aristocratic estates and your town dumps—flow on without us.

Possibly lake cruising might be worth reporting, I thought. We teamed up with old buddies Harry and Ben and Jane, Ben's wife, for an early July trip through New England to Moosehead Lake in Maine, where the Duck again took to water. Then, since hope springs eternal in any riverman's breast, Bee and I peeled off for a Connecticut River voyage. The Connecticut was to restore our flagging faith in the potentiality of American foldboat cruising.

At Sugar Hill in the White Mountains, en route to the river, housemother Dorothy Aldrich of Cooley Farm showed us through our first American Youth Hostel. We had heard of hostels in Europe but didn't use them, since we preferred to be together rather than in separate sleeping quarters. Hostels are overnight stops for those who travel under their own steam, whether bikers, hikers, horseback riders, or foldboaters. In simple surroundings, such as converted barns and sheds, hostelers are overnight guests of families. Youth hostelers cook their own meals, wash their own dishes, and sleep in Spartan bunkrooms. At the Sugar Hill hostel, an inscription on the common room wall advised, "Cut your own wood and it will warm you twice" and "Our brooms need exercise." Come morning, hostelers of the late 1930s paid a trifling sum to the houseparents, then traveled on toward the next hostel in the loop. We recognized that hostels were a key to a friendlier way of life than that of formal tourist homes, so we immediately took out AYH passes.

The week on the Connecticut was Europe all over again: delightful sleepy towns, friendly country folks, long vistas of hills and mountains, sunshine and rain, rips, plus new experiences with covered bridges and paper mill dams and youth hostels. We cruised from Guildhall in northern Vermont to Dartmouth College at Hanover, New Hampshire, and there abandoned ship as an apparently endless rain set in. I wrote a lyric account that was published by Greystone Press in 1940 in the first anthology of American foldboating, J. Kissner's *Foldboat Holidays*. Morale high, we traveled home to Long Island, stopping off at Northfield, Massachusetts, the national headquarters for American Youth Hostels. Conversations with Monroe and Isabel Smith, the charismatic couple who founded AYH, increased still further our enthusiasm for hosteling.

From Beacon Hill, we cruised east one day beyond Hempstead

Harbor, where we knew and had names for every beach, rock, and house: Duck Beach, the Cardboard House, the Stairs for Giants, Penguin Island, etc. J. P. Morgan's magnificent yacht *Corsair* lay moored off his estate in Glen Cove; once, when asked how much it cost to maintain the yacht, Morgan is reported to have said, "If you have to ask, don't own one." We hailed the indolent crew; passed Morgan's estate guards, who were incongruously dressed in city clothes; rounded the point into Long Island Sound; passed other estates owned by magnates; rounded Matincock; portaged across Lloyd's Neck; passed Oyster Bay; and came to Northport. A good cruise, yet few people were encountered, and people were essential to my kind of travel writing.

On still another day we cruised west to Manhasset Bay, bobbing with colorful sailboats and full of life. Near Steamboat Road we met death. They were working on the body of a young boy on the beach. They persisted, to no avail. Finally they flung a couple of blankets over the body. The ambulance pulled away. But when you are 27 death is for other people, and, like Thomas Wolfe, you know that you can never die. So live, love, and foldboat.

We had heard of the Rideau, a chain of rivers, lakes, and canals that ran from Kingston on the St. Lawrence to Canada's capital city, Ottawa. As I reported in "The Rideau Canal" in the Kissner anthology, *Foldboat Holidays*:

> ...the original purpose of the Rideau Canal [was] to provide a military highway down which British gunboats might descend to attack the United States. More than a hundred years ago the Canal was begun in those good old days of 1826 when war had a comic opera touch. Tremendous vessels the gunboats must have been, for today no boat with a draft greater than five feet can use the Canal without nestling its keel snugly in the oozy bottom of lake or river. Need it be said that the Canal, as a military venture, happily is obsolete? The route is popular now with fishermen and cruisers and the region is inhabited largely by the fine breed of men known as lockkeepers, indolent fortunate fellows with all the blessings of rural life and few of the burdens.

First we cruised, landed, swam, and camped in the Thousand Islands of the crystal clear St. Lawrence, headquartering at Sugar Island, the camp of the American Canoe Association. We made short cruises to Gananoque, a quiet little town where my mother was born, to Canoe Point and the Bloodthirsty Islands, to Camelot, and around Stave Island. We reveled in the story-swapping among the canoeists as to the competing merits of the Delaware or the Suwannee or the lakes of the Adirondacks. Arguments were animated between cruisers who wanted to absorb scenery and people's views, and white-water addicts who sought thrills. The cruisers themselves were of two persuasions, the paddlers who said, "When I get so old and feeble that I can't handle a paddle, I'll buy your sailboat," and the sailors who said, "Sailing takes intelligence. Any goddamn coalheaver can handle a paddle."

One August day we paddled into the first river of the Rideau chain. Seasoned foldboaters that we were, locks were a new experience for us; only a single dam had checked the Danube on its restless movements to the sea, and we had portaged, not been locked through. The Saar and Mosel were totally unfettered. (Sadly enough, it you travel these rivers now, foldboater, expect to paddle and portage rather than run and relax and ride rips.) So we approached locks with reservations, only to learn that friendly lock-keepers and their crews would carefully carry our boat to the upper levels or lock us through. The first lock-through was memorable.

> The heavy gates before us slid open a mere crack and we stroked into a concrete vault, the first lock we had ever entered in all our 2,000 miles of cruising throughout three foldboat summers. The doors swung shut. In the great tomb we were pitiful specks, walled in and doored in, not knowing exactly what to expect. High above us the lockman walked along the stone walls toward the gray doors ahead. He wrenched at a valve. The water gurgled in and swirled insanely, without pattern, through the lock. Invisible lurching hands seemed to be pushing us upward. The gurgling and swirling stopped and the great gray gate ahead opened a crack and we humbly slid out into a new and sunny world. We had risen thirteen feet.

By journey's end we were lock-wise, for we had been carried over or locked through no less than forty-seven locks. We had met friendly lockmasters, fishermen amazed that we carried no tackle, and even an authentic descendant of Tories, Miss Nina

Burritt of the Burritt Rapids Burritts, whose family, she told us, had left the States in 1781 after "the tax revolt." We had traveled narrow, fast-running streams and wide, placid lakes, followed the buoys yet sometimes had gotten lost, slept in inns and hotels and private homes and made camp.

One night in a tent on the Rideau, Jon, our oldest son, was conceived. We celebrated our third wedding anniversary in Ottawa. No wonder that the last sentence of "The Rideau Canal" reads, "We lived happily ever after and late in the twentieth century as they were carting us away to the Old Folks Home we were still advising paddlers to try the Rideau."

Home in Columbus in the fall of 1938, with World War II less than a year away, I began to consider undertaking an ambitious community program, the establishment of a loop of youth hostels in Central Ohio. By then I wasn't a stranger to social action, though I couldn't claim my efforts had been howling successes.

Fresh from college and bent on the salvation of society, I had joined other Young Turks like Mike Giles of University School and Old Turks like Louis Raths and Edgar Dale of the Ohio State education faculty in establishing a campus local of the teachers' union, the American Federation of Teachers. The local remained small and was soon beset with the factionalism that plagued uneasy bedmates of the left during that era—liberals versus socialists versus suspected fellow travelers, isolationists versus interventionists; "let's clean up local campus problems" versus "let's issue manifestoes about international problems." In the 1935-36 academic year I edited a newsletter that Bee loyally typed and distributed to the faithful across the campus. A faction too sympathetic with the policies of the Soviet Union took over leadership of the local from those of us who had established it; I wrote a curt resignation, which was not accepted, so I gradually drifted away from union activities.

Stimulated by the 1936 European travel experiences, I had put my activist energy into Peace Action, a Columbus group united in opposition to war and, as war neared, disunited in strategies to avoid the coming international catastrophe. I took the isolationist position rather than what was then termed interventionism. As I write these words about a half century after the mid-1930s, I am well aware of the verdict of contemporary historians, endowed as they are with twenty-twenty hind-sight, that the interventionists were right and the isolationists were wrong, indeed that the interventionists were "good" and the isolationists "bad." But today's historical hindsight was un-available in the mid-1930s, and to me the case for isolation was strong. I had absorbed the views of the best analyses of the 1920s and 1930s, including Walter Millis's *Road to War*, Charles A. Beard's *The Rise of American Civilization*, Erich Remarque's *All Quiet on the Western Front*, Ernest Hemingway's separate peace of *Farewell to Arms*, and the disillusionment of other lost genera-tion writers such as Dos Passos, Fitzgerald, and E. E. Cummings.

So I went with Norman Thomas and Senator Gerald Nye in opposing the steady steps into intervention by FDR. Yet I was torn. During the European travels of 1936 and 1937 I had learned firsthand of Nazism. I loathed it. Though I was rightly skeptical of World War I atrocity stories, I had seen the nasty surface, if not the evil depths, of fascism. I hated the anti-Semitism that was apparent in Central Europe. I knew that Hitler was a menace to the world. My writing repeatedly docu-mented the ruthlessness of the brown-shirted terror.

Nor did I share the ideas of some fellow isolationists. For instance, I could not accept that Nazism was "the wave of the future," as the Lindberghs put it. I recognized that the America First Movement was attractive to reactionary forces. Yet, as a pacifist, I rejected war. Indeed, I hated war with all my heart. If it came, I wanted America to stay out. I regarded Europe's gang wars as incurable.

As an eager volunteer, I assembled, edited, and often wrote for our local *Peace Action Bulletin* from 1936 through 1938, though I never served officially on the board. Peace Action's governing group, originally strong for keeping America out of war, became increasingly dominated by intellectual interven-tionists of the political science department. Sometime in 1938 I was informed that the *Bulletin* would have a new editor and that my services were no longer needed. Since I had no political leverage, I had no recourse.

Maybe, I thought, the road to peace was through the atti-tudes of individual persons. Maybe peace must begin in the hearts of men, as the UN was later to phrase it. And maybe I was just licking my wounds from the Peace Action experiences and trying to escape my own personal confusion about the imminent war. Anyway, author that I was, I deferred action on organizing youth hostels in Ohio and decided instead that Americans might welcome a book about youth hosteling, dedicated to the youth hostel purpose, "to promote a greater knowledge, understanding, and love of the world."

But what vehicle? I had relearned in 1938 that accounts of foldboating on the Hudson, Moosehead Lake, the Connecticut, and the Rideau lacked unity. An episodic book about youth hosteling would be equally vulnerable. To carry my message I needed a unifying factor like the Danube and fascism. How could I best interrelate youth hosteling and peace? I found my unifying theme in the Rolling Youth Hostel, an American Youth Hostel-sponsored trip from Northfield, Massachusetts, to Montreal; then across Canada in Canadian Pacific colonist cars that once carried immigrants west; then by a variety of railroads down the Pacific Coast and back across America. The Rolling Youth Hostel combined stretches of train travel with intensive hosteling by bike in selected regions. In Canada, while the biking hostelers explored Montreal, Winnipeg, the Canadian Rockies, Victoria, and Vancouver, the colonist car sat on a siding awaiting pickup by another train days later. More conventional trains in the United States took the rolling hostelers to disembarkation and biking in the Pacific Northwest, the San Francisco area, the Southwestern desert region, the Ozarks, and then back East.

I sounded out Scribner's in the spring of 1939 and found Maxwell Perkins and his staff amenable but understandably noncommittal. There was always Hitler and the threat of a European war to take into account in publishing decisions.

But no Bee this time. Jon was born May 15, 1939, and, however impractical and romantic his parents might be, was clearly ineligible for a Rolling Youth Hostel trip. Bee and I agreed that I'd go and she would spend the summer with the baby at her parents' home at Ronky on Long Island.

So I went. I wrote as we rolled.

The trip was exciting and memorable and rewarding—and sometimes lonesome for me. In late August Bee and I were reunited for a gala fourth wedding anniversary and twenty-eighth

Bee birthday celebration at the McAlpin Hotel in New York City. What an anniversary-birthday celebration sequence—Prague, Dubrovnik, Ottawa, now New York City! With three-month-old Jon, we traveled back home to Columbus. I intended to write a book on hosteling and peace, and to continue my work as an educator for a better world, a world at peace. But, as Robert Burns reminds us, "The best laid plans o' mice and men gang aft a-gley."

On September 5, 1939, as we traveled toward Columbus, our car radio shrieked, "Hitler Invades Poland." World War II had begun. All bets as to everybody's life were off. We looked at our baby. We had brought Jon into a world hell bent on self-destruction.

Chapter Twenty

THE WAR YEARS

I wrote *Rolling Youth Hostel* all right. But it was never published. Forty-two years later I again reread the manuscript. It told of the experiences of the youth hostelers, sometimes adventurous, sometimes perilous, sometimes fun; of the diversity of their personalities and reactions; of colorful people met along the rails and trails; of what Canadians and Americans were doing and thinking in the summer of 1939 just before the lights went out all over Europe. The photographs were handsome and dramatic, much better than my Danube pictures, almost as good as Paul Weinandy's.

Early in 1940 the manuscript went in to my editor, Wallace Meyer, at Scribner's. He wrote back, "No." I asked, "Why?" He leveled with me: in a world at war, the financial problems of publishing and marketing a book with emphasis on peace. And the absence of Bee. On the Danube I had bounced my observations off Bee and she had responded. In *Rolling Youth Hostel*, I had no opportunity for this type of close personal interaction.

To me, the word of Scribner's was final. I accepted the verdict and I submitted the manuscript nowhere else. I didn't even try Greystone Press, which published in 1940 J. Kissner's *Foldboat Holidays*, which included my "Connecticut River Cruise" and "The Rideau Canal." Knowing what I now know about publishing, I recognize that I should have persisted, moving from the major league companies to the minors. Instead, I simply had the manuscript bound and it now sits, unread, in our family room on a shelf along with my published books.

Rejection of *The Danube Flows Through Fascism* would have devastated me; the rejection of *Rolling Youth Hostel* didn't. Put this down in part to greater maturity, in part to having previously experienced publication of a book, and in part to my recognition that the times were out of joint.

Put it down also to another sea change that was going on within me. Just as the artist had been replaced by the journalist, the journalist was now yielding to a different kind of writer. The artist had fiercely fought his demise, particularly in the fall of 1936 after Mosel-Danube-Elbe travel, when he came close to refusing to return to teaching. Instead he wanted—to do what? Travel? Free lance? Find a garret and starve? Now in a world at war, the journalist who wrote travel books had shouted his last hurrah in the form of the hosteling manuscript. An education writer was lying in wait and biding his time.

The education writer had written an article on indoctrination in 1935 and had tried book reviews in 1936 and 1937. He had been rewarded by publication and had been consequently reinforced, as B. F. Skinner puts it. Subordinate to the journalist, he went underground for a while. After *The Danube* was published, he emerged again in the 1938-39 academic year with reviews for the *Curriculum Journal* as well as the *Social Frontier* and *American Teacher*, and with a trio of articles on teaching experiences. *Educational Method* printed his account of a University School junior class trip to study industrial Detroit, *Clearing House* his article on working with the school council, and *Social Education* his account of a senior class study of propaganda. The education writer coexisted awhile with the journalist; then, with rejection of *Rolling Youth Hostel*, took over, never to be dislodged.

I had become hooked on teaching, and now I had become committed to writing about education. But this didn't mean that the idea of establishing youth hostels in Ohio, which I had come up with after the Connecticut and Rideau cruises, must be abandoned. I recognized that hosteling activism could be linked with teaching and with writing.

In the fall of 1939 I found kindred spirits sympathetic to hosteling, especially Art Robinson and Bill Guthrie. Art was a newspaperman who regularly wrote a free-wheeling column for the Scripps-Howard *Columbus Citizen*. One column was about my toughly disciplined writing habits as I wrote *Rolling Youth Hostel*; he called it, "The Professor Is Writing Another Book."

Art was out of *The Front Page*. He knew everybody in Columbus, it seemed; he went anywhere, and wrote as he pleased. I occasionally accompanied him on his quests for material. For instance, though gambling was not among my vices, I went with him one night, out of curiosity, to Columbus's largest illegal gambling house. Art wrote several readable columns about the gamblers and their ways. If I were twins, I would have liked one of me to be journalist Art Robinson. Though not himself a hosteler, Art threw himself into the establishment of our Buckeye Trails loop and supplied essential publicity. Through his column and through newspaper stories, he called our first meeting.

Bill Guthrie was the dean of men at Ohio State University, a quiet fellow of an old Columbus family, respected, knowledgeable, and of the establishment. He had mapped a hiking trail through Ohio's scenic hill country, and he helped build necessary contacts in the Columbus community.

To our first meeting there also came the YMCA man who saw hosteling as a supplement to his biking program, the young couple who had hosteled in the Great Smokies, the engineering student from the East who had taught hostelers to ski, the publisher who could not forget that the young were a substantial fraction of the unemployed in a world that they never made. We formed a district committee of American Youth Hostels.

Our techniques in establishing youth hostels followed national AYH practices. On maps, we roughed out a loop from Columbus into the hill country to the southeast. Much of our leisure time we devoted to recruiting local committees charged with selection of hostels and houseparents. We addressed meetings, showed films, sent out releases and letters, and raised seed money. At Northfield, Monroe Smith had once told me of hosteling, "It's so beautiful and simple that some people can't understand it." Fortunately, most people could. Yet there were sneering doubters like the newspaper publisher in one Ohio community who was convinced that hosteling was a subversive plot to recruit youth to nazism or communism.

I substituted for wide-ranging travel during the summer of 1940 an assignment to teach at nearby Ohio University in a workshop. Through a highly informal teaching situation, the teachers who enrolled in the workshop decided what they needed to learn. Bee, Jon, and I lived in a delightful log cabin of Civil War vintage in the hills outside Athens, Ohio.

But there was no escape from World War II. After a winter lull in the fighting, Hitler moved through the Netherlands and into France in the spring of 1940. The air raids on Britain began. The United States took step after step toward involvement. A pacifist in a time of war, I fell apart psychologically in the summer of 1940.

Yes, I taught in the workshop, and on the surface I may have appeared normal to people. But inside I was a jelly of anxiety and anguish. I was ridden by my ambiguities as to war and peace, and I was saddled with fears for the world, for the people I had met in Europe, for my family and myself. I was unable to listen to the radio or look at newspapers, aside from a glance at the grim headlines.

That summer nothing helped, not my little family, not the good new experiences of a workshop, not the work holidays when we converted an old summer kitchen into a hostel, not the successful completion of the Buckeye Trails loop that was to register 300 overnights in its first year, not the planning for a coming initial hostel trip around the loop, not the preparations for extending the youth hostel idea into my University School teaching. Locked up in myself, I suffered.

In Columbus, in the fall of 1940, I often woke distraught as newsboys on the street hawked the night's headlines about Hitler's bombing of Britain. I sought no professional help. My only anodyne was Bee, who loved me and listened to me. I hid from myself in my hybrid of hosteling activities, teaching, and writing.

But, as many before me have observed, life has a habit of going on. The realities of life eventually nudge aside phantasms of the mind for all save the genuinely mad. I emerged slowly from neurosis.

Within a year after inception, Buckeye Trails became a reality. Five hostels stretched across the Ohio countryside. In September I led the first youth hostel trip on the new Ohio loop; the hostelers were a group of University School students. I reported on the trip in *Progressive Education* in February 1941, one of four articles on hosteling I was to write, and contributed a chapter on youth hosteling to a yearbook of a department of the National Education Association. Bee hosteled along Buckeye Trails with us. Jon, at sixteen months, stayed with friends Mildred and Lou Gregory and broke his mother's heart on her return by clinging to Mildred and failing to recognize his own mother.

Soon Bee was busier than ever as the mother of an infant and a two-year-old. Barbara was born July 3, 1941. She almost lived up to Umpy's hyperbole about me as a baby, "good as gold."

Abroad, Hitler made the fatal mistake of invading Russia.

I welcomed heavy demands on my time; they took my mind off the war. Writing brought increasing professional recognition: I chaired a session of the National Council for the Social Studies at wintry Atlantic City and was appointed to a NCSS committee. During the summer of 1941 I taught a college course in social studies education and a demonstration high school class at Northwestern University, traveling home to Columbus by train each Friday and back to Evanston each Sunday night. One weekend I arrived home just in time to rush to the hospital and pace the corridor while awaiting Barbara's birth.

Bee and I were listening to a symphony via radio on December 7, 1941, when a breathless announcement came. Then I walked the streets for hours, angrily saying over and over to myself, "They must think that we're some little Balkan nation." The next day Director Rudy Lindquist assembled the high school grades to hear Franklin D. Roosevelt describe the "day that will live in infamy" and ask for a declaration of war.

I still hated war—but here it was. I was torn between my pacifism and my newly felt nationalism. On the one hand, I repudiated war's savage slaughter and I knew that I personally couldn't kill a human being. On the other hand, on the day after the declaration of war we put our meager savings into war bonds, a symbolic act supportive of the war. Was I confused? Admittedly.

The draft classification in which I really belonged was "conscientious objector." But I could not be so classified, since, in World War II, conscientious objector status was granted only on grounds of religious objection and I was a member of no church. In the vocabulary of the draft officials, I was "deferred" (they would get to me later, if they had to). They recorded me on their books as almost 31, married, the father of two children, employed in a nonessential occupation. Since I suspected that they might reach me, I applied for officer training in hope of noncombatant assignment to one of the many education programs then burgeoning. Those in charge of selecting potential officers promptly rejected me because of a weak left eye, the heritage of scarlet fever in childhood, and an undependable knee that sometimes went out and sent me sprawling, the heritage of a cartilage injury acquired on a Columbia College soccer field.

(Scraping toward the bottom of their barrel, a draft board eventually did reach me early in 1944 when I was 33. On a dismal gray day in March I was herded through the customary examination of flesh and rejected as 4F, "unfit for military service." By then I had added to the bad eye and trick knee a psychosomatic ulcer caused by worry over being drafted. Clearly, this is not the autobiography of a war hero.)

Sometime during those war years of turmoil and reappraisal, I gave up the dream of America evolving into a democratic socialist nation through the growth of the Socialist Party. I can't fix any precise date, because the realization that my countrymen would not take this road came gradually. Franklin Delano Roosevelt's New Deal had implemented many of the proposals of the early twentieth century democratic socialists: social security, unemployment insurance, support for collective bargaining, *et al.* Though Norman Thomas ran for election in every presidential campaign from 1928 through 1948, he polled his highest vote in 1932, about 880,000, and support for his party and for evolution toward socialism then dwindled. For better or for worse, the United States in my lifetime was going to be a mixed economy, a capitalist system modified by liberalism, regulation, reduction of the abuses of rugged individualism, provisions for welfare, and a limited degree of government ownership and operation. If I was to make any difference, I must work within the present system.

I had voted for Thomas eagerly in 1932, willingly in 1936, and in despair in 1940 when Roosevelt's foreign policies seemed to me to be taking us along the road to war. During the war years I came to recognize that in practice I had evolved into a supporter of substantial social change in the economic system rather than a proponent of abolition of capitalism. In working for Peace Action and in establishing youth hostels, I had behaved as a liberal activist in what I actually did, rather than as a worker for radical change. So I stopped enrolling at the polls as a Socialist and began supporting liberal Democratic candidates and liberal-left groups such as Americans for Democratic Action. Whenever I passed under the phrase from James Russell Lowell graven over an entrance to University School, I reminded myself, "New occasions teach new duties." I tried to believe it. Among the casualties of wars are ideologies.

Chapter Twenty-One

FAREWELL
TO HIGH SCHOOL
TEACHING

During nearly a decade of teaching in the University School, between 1934 and 1943, I learned almost all of what I was ever to learn about the art of teaching. Though I am not a deprecator of books, I must report that I didn't learn to teach through the printed word. Nor did anyone show me, though admittedly it was helpful to appraise my colleagues' techniques as we taught the core curriculum.

I think the key element in my learning to teach well was the freedom to experiment. University School took seriously its label, "the experimental school." To us, experiment meant trying approaches, observing and appraising their outcomes, revising and modifying procedures, then trying again. Our experimentation was not the closely controlled testing of the laboratory, and we did not develop definitive empirical proof replete with impressive statistics. Yet, in a decade when the old ways of teaching were recognized as inadequate and better ways were being sought, we pioneered along new educational trails and worked out different approaches. Thinking for oneself was a goal.

The extent of our freedom was remarkable. To cite just one illustration, once while I was teaching about competing economic and social systems I recognized that few materials about communism written from the viewpoint of the Communists themselves were available to my classes. During a spring vacation in New York, I went to Communist Party USA headquarters on Union Square to obtain free materials and to the adjoining party-line bookstore to buy Communist pamphlets. The party hacks to whom I talked found it incredible that the *Communist Manifesto* was to be read by high school students in a Middle Western school. However, without blinking an eye, Director Rudy Lindquist and the Ohio State University bureaucracy honored my duly submitted bill payable to the Communists. My students became informed opponents of Communism.

The atmosphere of trust and freedom stemmed largely from our father figure, Rudy Lindquist. In meeting after meeting he presided—with his inevitable pipe—over a faculty that differed, argued, and then reached workable compromises. Once he came out of a student body meeting that was arguing tensely over awards for merit for academic and creative student achievement through grants of letters, formerly the sacred privilege of athletes only. Perspiring freely, yet with a twinkle of the eye, he said to me, "Democracy is hell, Bill." Hell or not, the debate went on; suitable recognition other than letters was eventually agreed upon, and the athletes and academics/aesthetes of the student body were reconciled.

The faculty, too, deserves credit for our freedom. Though we argued with the passion of people of good will who were persuaded that their particular ways were the better roads to good education, we tolerated, respected, and gave way to our colleagues so that they too might try out their distinctive approaches, such as Lou LaBrant's creative writing program; Harold Fawcett's nature of proof; and the music, fine arts, and industrial arts programs that encouraged love for and competency in artistic expression.

In the social studies area we tried out and compared and contrasted chronological and topical approaches to the teaching of history. We also taught units on a variety of contemporary social problems, such as propaganda analysis, consumer problems, and competing economic systems. The school encouraged action learning through community experiences; in addition to youth hosteling work holidays, during which we improved hostels, my students became interns and apprentices to various Columbus professionals as vocational orientation, and helped harvest needed crops during war years.

We also experimented with teaching through blocks of time in which social studies and language arts were combined, both on the senior high school and junior high school levels. In one such core program of nine hours weekly, the last I would teach at University School, the seniors of the class of 1943 prior to graduating into a world at war chose to study the background of the conflict; military service, war industry, and civil defense; the home front; and economic and international organization for the postwar period. During the ten weeks of the latter unit, the students read pamphlets and heard recordings and talks before listing ninety-one probable problems of the postwar era. They wrote on "What am I fighting for and against?" On possible roads for the American economy and potential postwar international organization, they read widely on alternatives, took part in heated panel discussions, and wrote up their individual conclusions. Along the way, the brightest student in the class read six solid books and seven pamphlets, while the slowest student read one pamphlet and excerpts from five others. The class as a whole hammered out recommendations through committees, voted them up or down, and sent the agreed upon proposals to Congressmen and other influentials. As to the latter experience, I wrote later, "Eleanor Roosevelt, one of the many political leaders to whom the recommendations were sent, said well in a generous letter of acknowledgment, '...the important thing is that these young people are learning to think constructively and, though many of them may think differently in a few years, they have the ability to grow.'" What did I learn from such teaching experiences? The value of education focused on real and vital human problems.

In my nine years at University School, I found that remarkable programs grew out of interdisciplinary work, untrammeled by arbitrary subject boundaries. During its senior year, the class of 1938 wrote a book that was accepted by a major New York publishing house, Henry Holt. *Were We Guinea Pigs?* described the experiences of this class from the seventh grade, when they furnished and equipped the home economics suite as part of a teaching project called "Making My House a Home," through the twelfth grade, when they cooperatively wrote the book while carrying a full program of high school courses.

Each year the weeks just prior to Christmas were given over to preparation for an all-school program. The gym was converted into a historical setting, typified by a medieval European town or an Athenian agora or an English marketplace of Shakespeare's era. On our festival day the entire faculty and student body, grades one through twelve, each appropriately costumed, ebbed and flowed through the village, sometimes as actors and sometimes as participants. Food was vended, soldiers marched, knights conflicted, peasants marketed, and artisans practiced their crafts. Vocal choruses and instrumental groups performed and dramatic productions were staged. Each festival had its surprises; revolutions and invasions even took place. On one occasion members of my core class became a traveling troupe of actors who presented an early English miracle play about the Biblical flood. In a long white sheet, I played God, an example of highly inappropriate casting to type. Through a memorable opening line, I addressed the populace from the steps of the Noah's ark set we had built, "Forty days and forty nights rain shall fall for your unrights."

At University School the faculty designed the curricular framework. However, within each class the students participated with individual teachers to varied degrees in planning content to be learned and methods to be used. After his talk on teacher-pupil planning, my colleague Mike Giles was once asked a hostile question by a conference-goer who found it difficult to believe that students could participate in determining their own learning experiences. "Mr. Giles, in this 'teacher-pupil planning,' which is more important—teacher or pupil?" Mike memorably responded, "The hyphen." During the years that followed my first fumbling 1934 ventures into planning ("What do you want to study?"), I learned to develop criteria with students so that the content jointly selected would be based on their needs, would throw light on social realities, and would help them clarify their values.

In addition to one junior high school block of time for a core class each semester, I usually taught two sections of senior high school social studies and served as counselor to one senior high school grade. Thus I was usually responsible for working annually with students on either the junior or senior class trip. The words "class trip" usually call up visions of Washington, D. C., in cherry blossom time, with desultory visits to the Congressional

Gallery, a photo with the home district representative, and hijinks. Not at University School. Our programs were social travel, each trip an intensive week of interdisciplinary study of a selected social problem in a carefully chosen community. The possibilities usually included Detroit, Chicago, Pittsburgh, Philadelphia, New York, and the TVA area. After the central social problem and the community were selected through class business meetings, committees appointed by the class president assumed full responsibility for trip planning: transportation, trips within the city, entertainment, hotel and food, finance, group agreements, plus a coordinating committee made up of chairmen. Committee members recognized that sloppiness would penalize the group as a whole. So members worked hard and effectively. Progress reports were made weekly in a class business session. In an article, "Youth Visits Industrial Detroit," I quoted from a class letter to parents and cited some foci of discussion:

> In February the parent-student committee dispatched the following letter home:
> "The Junior Class this year has planned to go to Detroit. The general purpose of our trip is to study life in an industrial city. We plan to stop at Toledo to see a glass factory, which is a subsidiary of the Ford Motor Company. In Detroit, we intend to visit the Ford plant, the Chrysler plant, the General Motors Research Laboratory, Greenfield Village, art galleries, museums, and housing projects.
> "We will hear representatives of the Ford and Chrysler motor companies, a speaker for the United Automobile Workers Union, a representative of the government on the relations between industry and labor...."

Each afternoon of the four-day trip, students returned to the hotel early enough for a rest; then in the hour before dinner they wrote answers to questions on scientific and social aspects of the day's experiences.

Learning the Ways of Democracy, a publication of the Educational Policies Commission of the National Education Association, included an account of this Detroit trip and cited it as a promising practice in community participation.

A combination of factors accounted for some people deciding

175

to regard me as "a promising young educational leader." In my favor was teaching in a fishbowl. (University School classes were always conducted before rows of observers from the college, the state, and sometimes the nation.) The Ohio State University School had become one of the thirty schools of the Eight Year Study by the Progressive Education Association; our faculty was used to interacting with Ralph Tyler and Hilda Taba of the PEA's evaluation staff, and we were accustomed to dropping in after school to have tea in the home economics suite with a variety of distinguished national visitors. Convention attendance helped my reputation too; I attended the Progressive Education Association conferences when they were held in the Midwest, and I regularly gave over Thanksgiving vacation to the meetings of the National Council for the Social Studies, at which I began to appear on convention programs in subordinate roles. I wrote about "war adaptations in the guinea pigs' school" for *Progressive Education* and even an empirical research article with Professor Louis Raths, sonorously titled "The Influence of Social Travel on Relations Among High School Students" for the *Educational Research Bulletin*. I expanded my reviewing beyond the education journals to the *New York Herald Tribune* books section, for which I reviewed river books: *Exploring the Rivers of New Jersey, Sailing to the Sun, Twin Rivers*.

My work began to be known beyond the walls of University School. Northwestern University, having tested me as a teacher on campus during a summer session of 1941, invited me to the staff of Northwestern's summer workshops held in Springfield, Missouri. Under gallus-snapping, "I'm a country boy" Harry Study, superintendent of schools in the Ozark capital, Springfield had developed a progressive education program that even made the pages of *Life* magazine. Ernest Melby, one of the great education deans of the first half of the twentieth century, sent some Northwestern faculty members, plus an invited few from other campuses, to Springfield in 1942 to work with the system's program on the scene. No Springfield teacher could claim, "My administrator won't let me do it," and no Springfield administrator could say, "My teachers won't do it"; both groups were in daily attendance at the sessions. The workshop was replete with study, discussion, trips, art opportunities, and fun; it was a magnificent learning experience for all involved. Despite the conflict raging in Europe, Bee, Jon, Barbara, and I spent a rewarding summer in the pleasant little city and the surrounding Ozarks.

Even the hateful war helped my career as an educator. After America entered the war in December, 1941, many other "promising young educational leaders" were swallowed up by the armed services through officer training programs or the draft or by the governmental bureaucracy needed to conduct such wartime programs as price controls and psychological testing. Put both brutally and accurately, my career benefited from reduction in the competition.

Despite my increasing visibility, I couldn't help recognizing that my salary remained monotonously the same. I had begun as an instructor in 1934 at $2,400 a year and had become an assistant professor in 1936 at $2,772. Then I was frozen at that level and salary.

When Rudy Lindquist left the school in 1938 to become director of an elite private boys' boarding school, Cranbrook School near Detroit, Michigan, he wanted me to come with him. Never one to worry much about the ethics of switching jobs late, he offered me the leadership of his new social studies program in September 1938, just before the opening of University School. When salary and living expenses were taken into account, my promised income would represent a substantial financial increment over my University School income. While scouting the position, I asked him whether some expensive materials, a superlative set of maps, could be purchased for my social studies instruction at Cranbrook. He responded, "If it can be bought with money, we can get it. Here at Cranbrook it is the things that can't be bought with money that are hard to get." I considered the switch to becoming a well-paid teacher-servant of the sons of millionaire automobile executives—and decided to stay with my $2,772 at University School.

But when salary determination time came around again in the spring of 1939, 1 asked Harold Alberty about a raise. At the invitation of the University School faculty, Alberty had crossed the playing field that separated the College of Education, where he was a nationally recognized professor of curriculum, from the

University School, where he was to serve temporarily as director. Intellectual, honest, experienced in university affairs, Alberty wasted few words; he said that he'd check with the powers that were, the dean and his cohorts. When he returned, he told me that, without a doctorate, I wouldn't get a salary increase until hell froze over, despite his personal support. It was apparent that he regarded hell freezing over as an unlikely event.

I held off for a year, since youth, growing self-confidence, and proximity to professors had persuaded me that I had little to learn from the professoriate and that, indeed, they had more to learn from us at University School. Being assured in the spring of 1940 that hell had still not frozen over, I began to combine full-time teaching with all the courses the Ohio State University Graduate School would allow me to take while fully employed.

Alberty, who was personally cool and reserved, yet a passionate pleader for the core curriculum, became my advisor. I respected his mind and his philosophy, and from 1940 through 1943 I loaded up on courses with him along with social scientist Frederic Landsittle and historian Edwin Pahlow, philosophers of education H. Gordon Hullfish and Boyd H. Bode, and other professors of education, along with the few liberal arts professors whom discriminating Alberty respected.

I found that the doubting young laboratory school teacher could learn a lot from the professors. Alberty usually turned me loose to read widely and to implement the core curriculum through study of theory and through building of teaching units that included many possible activities and procedures. Hullfish contributed humanity and deep personal interest in doctoral candidates. The liberal arts and the social science people beefed up my knowledge of the social sciences.

But the most provocative professor was Bode. Boyd H. Bode, tall, angular, hawk-faced, was a philosophical gadfly who combined wit and wisdom as he conducted his classes through folksy Socratic dialogues. Here is a sample.

"Ma'am" (Bode called all females Ma'am), "what are you trying to do in your teaching?"

The lady would flush and then venture bravely, "I guess, Dr. Bode, I am trying to meet the needs of my students."

"All their needs?"

"Yes sir." Then, recalling her child development courses with Zirbes, "I try to meet all their personal, emotional, and physical needs."

"That sounds good. But the other day I was visiting an elementary school class" (a fabrication; Bode didn't visit elementary or high school classes), "and a boy named Johnny had a real need, which Dr. William Heard Kilpatrick would call a felt need. He needed to hit his neighbor right on the nose. Ma'am, would you gratify that need?"

Indignantly, "Not in my class, Dr. Bode."

Bode would look crestfallen. "I'm discouraged. I thought you gratified all needs of your students? Why not little Johnny's felt need?"

"Because it isn't *right*."

Turning to the class, Bode would say sadly, "You see, no matter how you curtain the windows or stuff up the cracks under the door, questions of right or wrong seep into the classroom. A philosophy is inescapable." He might add, "Mr. Van Til, you are a progressive educator. Do progressive educators have a philosophy?"

So it went, needling child-centered progressivism, science, authoritarian religion, any and all of the sacred cows. Bee had included Bode in her smorgasbord of courses, and she and I often continued far into the night the intellectual struggles initiated by Bode's dialogues.

The graduate education program of Ohio State University did well by my education. I have only two demurrers. My professors were so dedicated to the method of intelligence and so committed to the intellectual component of education that they minimized affective aspects; this encouraged the born onlooker aspect of my personality and led me to prize objectivity and deprecate feeling tone. Paradoxically, these adherents of the rational allowed me to escape taking substantial courses in statistics; mathematics-fearer that I was, I eagerly embraced mastery of the Spanish language as an alternative.

By 1943 I had completed most of my course work leading to the doctoral degree, though I had taken no time off from my regular year and summer session teaching. I needed only a few courses at another institution, required by the Graduate School to reduce the curse of academic inbreeding. Then the dissertation would loom ahead. Hell had still not frozen over, though University School had a new director, Robert Gilchrist, a friendly man and an experienced public school administrator who served from 1941 to 1946.

A Washington, D.C., job as a writer materialized in 1943. So I left the University School and Ohio State University. They granted me a leave of absence and I fully intended to return. However, despite my love for both alma maters, I was never to come back to Columbus to teach.

Chapter Twenty-Two

THE CONSUMER
EDUCATION STUDY

ashington at the midpoint of World War II pulsated with clerks, politicians, lobbyists, and the omnipresent military. The bars and restaurants and movie theaters were crowded; the lights in government buildings burned late. As FDR put it, Doctor Win-the-War had replaced Doctor New Deal.

On my way to the squarish brick National Education Association building at 1201 Sixteenth Street, Northwest, I was daily reminded of Washington's diversity; government workers from the Virginia suburbs disembarking from their buses at the old post office on Constitution Avenue; the serene White House set on its expansive grounds; the newly constructed Statler-Hilton Hotel; the well-guarded Russian Embassy, which ironically resembled a robber baron's Fifth Avenue mansion; the long, sleek building housing the work and exhibits of the National Geographic Society; the genteel little Jefferson Hotel opposite the NEA building.

We had rented a $75-a-month two-story unit in the sprawl of Fairlington, a middle-class housing project across the Potomac in the Virginia countryside. Unlike Columbus's single-residence housing, each unit was cheek by jowl with its identical brick neighbor. Fraternization was inevitable, and particularly exciting for Jon, 4, and Barbara, 2, whose playmates included the wolf children, so-called because of their behavior rather than their family name. Our closest friends were Doug and Caroline Ward and their non-wolf children, ages 5 and 7. Like me, Doug was a

181

former laboratory school teacher, Colorado his turf; he was now my fellow writer for the Consumer Education Study. Doug was a long, lean, humorous Middle Westerner of my own age. Our families exchanged baby-sitting chores weekly; we got the best of the bargain, since Bee's sister-in-law, then with MGM, supplied us with a weekly pass to Washington's Capitol Theater. If Bee and I are ever scheduled on a quiz show, we'll choose as our category World War II movies. We saw them all.

Each day Doug and I propped our *Washington Posts* before us on the bus from Fairlington to downtown Washington, then walked to the National Education Association building. In those days the NEA was not the vigorous wage and teacher welfare oriented union that it became later. In 1943-44 the NEA was self-consciously a professional organization that held conferences and issued publications in the interest of improvement of education.

The very word "professional" was pronounced with awe by the school administrators of the NEA's influential American Association of School Administrators and the executive secretaries of the various suborganizations of the NEA who enjoyed virtual lifetime appointments. It was rumored that the executive secretary of executive secretaries, Willard Givens, was chauffeured to work by a liveried driver; I can't vouch for the accuracy of the rumor, for Givens checked in later than migrant workers like Doug and me. In the impressive lobby, an old codger, apparently left over from the nineteenth century, maintained a formidable book in which all employees recorded their names and times of arrival and departure. A time clock would have looked too unprofessional in the National Education Association entrance hall.

In the lobby beside the elevator stood a massive statue of Horace Mann. Horace had his hand thrust forward, palm upward in a graceful gesture. The statue was emblazoned with his words, "Be ashamed to die until you have won some victory for humanity." Doug and I were fond of Horace and secretly admired his slogan, grandiloquent though it was. One day after an NEA-sponsored federal aid to education bill had suffered still another resounding defeat in Congress, the incorrigible Ward signed the book, then plunked a dime into Horace's palm. "Here's a start on your federal aid money, Horace," proclaimed Doug loudly. When we went home that night the dime was gone. The old codger frowned on such irreverent humor and for the rest of the year ignored both of us as we checked in and out. Whenever Doug was asked what the National Education Association conception of education was, he would soberly respond, "According to the NEA, education is something that you try to get federal aid for." To us, the NEA brass seemed heavy on formality but light on philosophy.

Doug and I were employed as writers for the Consumer Education Study of the National Association of Secondary School Principals of the National Education Association, a study funded by the Better Business Bureau. To its credit, the Better Business Bureau, funded in turn by ethical business establishments, never interfered in what the staff wrote and published, despite our anticipation that the business-oriented organization might do so. Had the bureau attempted to influence our production of consumer education materials for high school students, they would have been cowed by crusty Thomas H. Briggs, creator and director of the Consumer Education Study.

Briggs was a hard-bitten professor emeritus of Teachers College, Columbia University, an educational conservative, a learned man, an impeccably honest person, and a prickly personality. Of middle height and beginning to get heavy, he looked like a prosperous businessman. Though his early writing took the form of specialized textbooks, *Reading in Public Schools, Formal Grammar as a Discipline, A First Book of Composition*, he had become in the twenties and thirties of the century Mr. Secondary Education and one of the leaders of the junior high school movement. He was a scholar who could casually inject knowledge of the classics into his education books. Briggs would write (without further elaboration) "As Sanderson of Oundle said," leaving lesser mortals like me baffled not only as to who Sanderson was but also where or what in hell Oundle was.

Tom Briggs—but we always called him Dr. Briggs—sat in his office, answered high-level mail about project financing, strolled regularly to his beloved art museums, had long lunches at the Cosmos Club, and left daily operation to his able associate director and editor, Fred T. Wilhelms.

183

Briggs was at his best when he would call a staff member into his office for conversation. Once he required my presence with, "Has it ever come to your attention, Mr. Van Til, that angels in fourteenth century paintings created in Siena have square halos?"

"No, Dr. Briggs, that never came to my attention."

"I'm going to find out why," he said. The next day he triumphantly explained the aberration to me; unfortunately, by now I have forgotten why the Sienese angels were crowned with square halos.

On another occasion Briggs asked hopefully, "Mr. Van Til, you are a student of the social sciences. Why does the state of West Virginia have that strange shaped hook of land to the north?"

"I'm afraid that has never come to my attention, Dr. Briggs."

Comfortingly, "I'll find out and tell you tomorrow." It turned out to have something to do with the Ohio River and the western boundaries of William Penn's Pennsylvania Charter.

I never adopted Briggs's conservative views of secondary education, but I learned to respect and act on one of his cardinal educational principles that was congenial to my progressivism: Follow up on what interests you, try to search out the answer to anything about which you become curious, and do it now. In my family, many fruitless disputes have been avoided by my version of Briggs's doctrine. "Let's look it up," I would often say, and out would come the encyclopedia, atlas, dictionary, or other reference book.

On the other hand, Briggs was at his worst when he reverted to the impatient sarcasm that had terrified his graduate students. One day Doug was ten minutes late for a "seminar," as Briggs liked to call his occasional staff meetings. As Doug sat down, Briggs began to make calculations on a pad. There was a silence with things going on in it. After several minutes, Briggs looked up and said severely, "I have been calculating the cost of ten minutes of our salaries. Mr. Ward, your lateness has just cost the Consumer Education Study . . ." And he specified a sum. But Ward was no graduate student. He said politely, "Dr. Briggs, did you include the time you devoted to making that calculation?" The meeting began, and thenceforward was never again referred to as a seminar.

Briggs was relatively innocent of the mysteries of economics.

Midway in our year of production of consumer education material, he came to the conclusion that we needed to base our material more firmly upon the scientific principles of economics upon which all economists agree. Vainly we protested that economists did not agree, that they held to schools of thought such as laissez-faire, Keynesianism, Marxism, etc. Briggs couldn't believe that economics wasn't an exact science and that economists were inclined to differ, even as were educators. "I'll lock up the best economists in the nation for a long weekend of discussion," said Briggs, "and I'll bring you back the agreed-upon principles." Some weeks later he locked them up. He came back on a Monday morning strangely silent. We waited. Then he told us indignantly, "Would you believe it? Those damned economists couldn't agree on a thing!"

More worldly in the ways of economists and writers was his associate and our editor, Fred Wilhelms, a tall, relaxed, soft-spoken Nebraska educator with a remarkable gift for the pithy phrase. Once while I was writing *Economic Roads for American Democracy*, a book for high school students on competing economic systems, I came up with a precise but harsh page of judgment on some particular economic approach. I was confident that I was accurate, yet was troubled by the toughness of my appraisal. Fred studied my page and then memorably advised, "Vague it up."

On another occasion I proudly showed Fred a section of my manuscript that had gone through several drafts by me and through editing by him. I liked the end product. I boasted, "That's really good writing in that section." He glanced at it and said, "It is. I wrote it." I went back to my original draft and the subsequent rewritings and found that he had. Fred Wilhelms is the only editor I ever worked with who could edit my work so skillfully and so much in my spirit and even phrasing that I couldn't tell where my writing left off and his began.

There were eight of us on the staff of the Consumer Education Study: Briggs and Wilhelms, Doug and I, and Leone Heuer, Effie Bathurst, Miss Weeks, and a secretary. Leone was a poised and urbane career woman on loan from writing pamphlets for the Household Finance Corporation. Effie Bathurst looked like her name; she was a farm woman who might have stepped out of a Grant Wood painting. Miss Weeks, our librarian who gathered pamphlets and did research for us, may have had a first name, but all I can remember her for now is her stories of the strange doings of her cat. The secretary, Elinor Dixon, was bright, charming, and adept in transcribing our crabbed writing. We wrote and rewrote, the secretary typed and retyped, and Fred edited and reedited and saw through to publication our dozen pamphlets and one book.

In my consumer education year I wrote *Time on Your Hands*, a pamphlet on "consuming" leisure for high school students. I also wrote a hardbound book, *Economic Roads for American Democracy*, which McGraw-Hill published with a title page that gave full credit to me as author, a characteristically generous gesture by Briggs and Wilhelms. Doug and I collaborated on a consumer education article for *Civic Leader*, an education newsletter. In preparing manuscripts we worked both at our NEA desks and in the magnificent Library of Congress, where we had the selfless help of the gifted staff. I always felt a tingle of intellectual excitement in the presence of the drones and geniuses who used the incredible resources of that august building.

A wonderful and productive year! We were doing what we loved: writing. And we were being paid salaries for doing so.

Yet it wasn't all milk and honey—writing never is. One day, going home on the bus, Doug looked gloomy, unusual for him. He had been making some calculations on the margin of his newspaper.

"What's the matter?"

"I just figured out that today I was the world's highest paid writer."

"How come?"

"Though I worked all day, I came up with only two sentences that are remotely publishable."

I checked his statistics. He was right. My own output that day had also been low. We included my output in his calculations and realized that even Margaret Mitchell of *Gone With the Wind* had not been paid more per word than Doug and I were paid that day. To cheer up, we got together over drinks with our wives in Fairlington. We all toasted the world's two highest-paid writers. Fortunately, there were many other days in which we more than earned our keep.

Chapter Twenty-Three

HOME AGAIN

H ad I wanted to, I might have stayed with the Consumer Education Study at least another year, but I received and welcomed an offer in the spring of 1944 to return to New York City, this time as Director of Publications and Learning Materials for the Bureau for Intercultural Education. As in most of my job switches, our motivations for the shift were mixed. Yet prominent in our thinking was that the new post opened the door to our hopes of a house for Bee and me and Jon and Barbara.

After marriage, Bee and I had been gypsies, moving every year or two to a new apartment in Columbus, primarily to avoid paying summer rent while we were abroad or I was handling workshops. We began our life together at 464-1/2 Vermont Place, a second floor with a round bedroom topped by a cupola in which Mr. Henderson's ghost lived. Mr. Henderson was the late husband of our landlady and the father of Faerie, both of whom lived downstairs. At our parties, a favorite midnight recreation of our guests was climbing with candles into the dark, dirty, and drafty cupola in search of Mr. Henderson's ghost. Fortunately, we didn't burn down the house.

The fall of 1937 found us in northern Columbus on the second floor of a house on East Duncan Street. Two wonderful old ladies in their sixties lived downstairs: the owner, a kindly farm lady, and her gruff-voiced friend Babe, who usually wore mannish clothing, hung out at the horse stables, and drove sulkies in trotting races. Neighbors with little knowledge of Krafft-Ebing described Babe as a "morphodite." We dearly loved both of the old ladies and never inquired. Nor did our visitors, Bee's mother and father and my mother, who silently marveled at the odd couple yet discreetly kept their own counsel. We lived in this house for two years and in May 1939 brought home another tenant, Jon.

California Avenue was our first two-story rental; then came rental of a house in the country on East Cleft Road near the dam on the Scioto River. At that stage in our lives country living didn't agree with us. Bee's isolation during recovery from a miscarriage, followed soon by pregnancy with Barbara, plus my war-related jitters, plus a balky coal stove—even wandering hunters who might mistake yardbird Jon for a rabbit—brought Bee and me as close to domestic unhappiness as we were ever to come in our marriage. But our relationship was too solidly based to develop major cracks; the long period of "going together" had anticipated and eliminated many potential rough spots.

Luckily, our arbitrary landlady unexpectedly demanded her property, despite our long-term agreement. Life was better for us on Midgard Road in a Columbus neighborhood, despite trains rushing by our house only a few feet away and despite wintry drafts seeping through the floor. Bee's mother and dad stayed with us for months while Bee wrote her master's degree dissertation, "The Relation Between the Content of Children's Literature and the Times of Writing." Mother Blaha baby-sat Barbara, a model baby; and father Blaha, rechristened Popsie, counted freight cars with Jon, who terminated each count with a definitive "caboose."

One spring day in 1942, when the newspapers headlined General MacArthur saying of the Philippines, "I shall return," the front page of the *Columbus Citizen* pictured a 1942 rarity, Bee Van Til, mother of two, proudly wearing her academic robes at commencement. Suppose I **did** get drafted and killed; now we had family insurance, Bee's master's degree.

We said farewell to renting; we bought a little house on Beechwold Boulevard, and became householders. Jon tutored Barbara on the proper boundaries of our property; I cut grass with other owners of little plots of land. Our cost was $4,300, and we sold it during that pre-inflation time at $4,700.

After the family traveled with me to a Northwestern University workshop for the Kansas City, Missouri, schools, I headed east to begin the consumer education year and buy springless furniture for our living room in Fairlington, Virginia, since metal had gone to war. Bee trekked east by car with a good friend, Ray Heiks; our two wide-eyed children squeezed between baggage and roof on the back seat. Once again we were renters.

So when in the spring of 1944 an offer of a New York City job with no termination date came along, we leaped at the opportunity. The opportunity to renew old friendships. The proximity of our parents, daily becoming no younger. A chance for me to make a difference through a crucial area, relationships among Americans of varied races, religions, nationality backgrounds. And once again a house. A place for Jon and Barbara and—since Bee was pregnant again—little Jill to grow up in. I fully intended to call the new baby Jill Van Til, a lovely tinkly name, though Bee predicted she might be called half-pint. Our research was faulty—a gill happens to be a quarter of a pint. When the baby did arrive on a bright February day in 1945, we called him Roy. That settled that.

Flush with a new salary of $5,000 for a full year, we bought a home in Baldwin, a pleasant suburb on the South Shore of Long Island. Jones Beach was only a few minutes away and the town railroad station only a mile or two distant from our home. We fronted on an athletic field and a wooded area was at our side. The large yard was well-fenced and was overlooked by a sun deck. Home at last.

Stewart Cole had employed me to develop the publications program of the Bureau for Intercultural Education. Stewart was a Protestant clergyman who had become persuaded of the necessity of intercultural education. He had entered the field in the 1920s during what I was later to describe as the missionary stage of intercultural education when men of good will like himself stumped the country calling for education for better human relations and an end to prejudices and discrimination among Americans. He had taken over a private agency, the Bureau for Intercultural Education, and had written, with my predecessor William E. Vickery, a competent book called *Intercultural Education in American Schools*. The book argued persuasively for cultural democracy, a middle way between the melting pot philosophy and unbridled cultural pluralism lacking shared goals.

The essence of cultural democracy was ethnic, religious, and racial freedom to differ within a framework of commonly held democratic purposes. It made sense then; it makes sense now, though sadly, few today are familiar with the concept. Harper and Brothers, under an outstanding innovative editorial statesman, Ordway Tead, published Cole and Vickery's book and contracted for a series of publications on problems of intercultural education. I was to develop the series as part of my work as Director of Publications and Learning Materials of the Bureau for Intercultural Education.

Shortly after we had bought the house and I had reported for work, I casually asked Cole how the bureau and its offices on Fifty-Seventh Street in Manhattan were financed. Cole said, "I raise the money."

"Oh. How?"

"Through people of good will. The board helps too. We now have money on hand that will see us through the next couple of months."

My face fell several feet. The next couple of months! And my wife pregnant with our third child, our new home bought and heavily mortgaged. This was permanency? Flabbergasted, I silently cursed my blindness and naiveté in assuming a stable financial base at the bureau. I had grown too accustomed to the stability of university finance. Privately, I thanked the gods that I was still on leave from generous Ohio State University.

"No problem," said optimistic clergyman Cole. "I've been getting along in this way for years. I'll raise the money for your salary."

He did. The bureau was financed primarily through two Jewish organizations that had been helpful in Cole's earlier endeavors, the American Jewish Committee and the Anti-Defamation League of B'nai B'rith, plus wealthy women such as socially conscious Marian Ascoli of the Rosenwald family and fortune, who was a member of the board. During my three years with the bureau, first with Cole as director, later with H. H. (Mike) Giles, my University School colleague and friend, sufficient financial support was always available.

So our mortgage payments could be met on our $7,500 house. Our Baldwin home became the staging area for shared experiences. In summer my family often met my commuter train and we hied off to swimming and picnicking at Jones Beach or the Baldwin Harbor Club. In the fall we went to football games on the adjoining athletic field and once rode out a hurricane that hit the South Shore and toppled some of our trees, to Jon's amazement. In the winter we used the good Baldwin Public Library, which made available both books and records. In the spring I taught Jon to field and bat. During any and all seasons, we enjoyed Barbara's growing from age 2 to 5. Throughout the years we exchanged visits with old friends and relatives who welcomed with us the arrival of Roy, a strong and healthy infant always ready for a trip anywhere.

We had our rough spots too. At 6, Jon came down with a rare medical problem called megacolon. As he fretted over not being up and about, the marvelous local doctor, Charlotte Schneider, made house calls and worried about the harassed mother of three as well as about Jon. In New York City's Polyclinic Hospital, either Bee or I stayed with him throughout one long day and night, whiling away the hours by reading with him the telephone book and counting Smiths, Browns, Van Tils, *et cetera*—for Jon, brighter than I, read and was adept with numbers before he attended school. Needles were slipped into him and suddenly he was well, and back home to the yard, school, and baseball. A year later we lost a beloved oldster when Bee's father died. Bee traveled from Springfield, Missouri, by train for his funeral, bearing with her infant Roy, who was never to know Popsie's strength, good humor, versatility with tools, and gentle, quiet love for his family.

Yet, all in all, we remember fondly our Baldwin years.

Chapter Twenty-Four

INTERCULTURAL EDUCATION

I threw myself joyously into the work of the Bureau for Intercultural Education. Joyously is the right word. The bureau provided an outlet for my social conscience, acquired during college, and my activism, developed during the Ohio State University years. Now I could center on doing whatever I could about a crucial American problem, the development of better human relations among American people of different races, religions, and nationality backgrounds. By the summer of 1944 the time was ripe; the race riots of June 1943 had shocked the nation and the world.

The philosophy of the Bureau for Intercultural Education embraced both democracy as a guiding concept and progressive education as a vehicle, and the Board of Directors of the Bureau was a democratic progressive educator's dream. The chairman was the man from whom I had taken a challenging course while I taught delinquents, William Heard Kilpatrick, the master teacher of philosophy of education; professor emeritus of Teachers College of Columbia University; long-time president of the John Dewey Society; a leader of the socialist-oriented League for Industrial Democracy and the vital black progress organization, the National Urban League. The vice-chairman was Ernest Melby, soon to become dean of the School of Education at New York University, a democratic, community-conscious administrator whom I had known from my relationship with Northwestern University. The board's secretary was Frank Trager, a dynamo who knew and influenced the program of many Jewish organizations. The board members included top educators and influentials with access to philanthropoids who controlled financial purse strings.

I was a writer, and the assignment called for as much individual writing and as many edited publications as I could produce. However, I had no experience as an editor. Yet I had participated in the publication of my travel book, experienced the handling of my articles by editors, and learned much from Fred Wilhelms at the Consumer Education Study. After all, editing is largely a matter of good judgment, skill in human relationships, knowledge of techniques, and common sense. My major editorial weakness was in the technical realm; I didn't know my em from my pica, and still don't. Fortunately, bureau fund-raising was so successful that an addition was soon made to the publications staff, an adept in the language of printing who was experienced in all aspects of editing. My secretary, the first of a series of secretarial blessings from then into retirement, was a black woman from the West Indies who was demonically productive.

At the bureau we believed that three great world ideas were on the side of those of us who worked for better human relations: democracy as a way of life, the Judaic-Christian religious heritage, and the findings of science. As we saw it, our job was to develop, try out, and disseminate promising practices for use in schools. They included creating a democratic atmosphere in schools, permeating the curriculum with intercultural content, using the insights of group dynamics, and learning through both study of and direct experience in communities.

Our publication bow had many arrows: the books for the Harper series, our journal, a clearinghouse, staff-written articles, yearbooks. If one didn't hit its mark, others might. We developed our publications program through simultaneously attacking on all fronts.

Future Harper publications at various stages awaited my arrival. In press was the first book on intercultural education ever written especially for high school students, *Probing Our Prejudices* by Hortense Powdermaker, anthropologist of Queens College. *They See for Themselves* by Spencer Brown, an Ethical Culture School teacher, was in manuscript form; it described research by high school students that culminated in the writing and production of documentary plays. Anthropologist Ina Corinne Brown's *Race Relations in a Democracy* was being written. To keep manuscripts coming, I promptly invited Irene Jaworski, a teacher at Forest Hills High School in the New York City school system, to develop a book on immigrant backgrounds, *Becoming American*. I tried to save a book by a Penn State sociologist, yet eventually had to recognize that it was unsalvageable; I hated the chore of rejecting manuscripts, for I knew what it felt like to be in an author's shoes.

The Intercultural Education News always breathed down my neck during the three bureau years. We issued it quarterly, and deadlines remorselessly rolled around. We converted it from house organ puffery to serious discussion of intercultural issues. For instance, the June 1946 issue carried contributions by such eminent scholars as Lawrence K. Frank, Fritz Redl, Gordon W. Allport, Kurt Lewin, Louis E. Raths, Robert J. Havighurst, Carl R. Rogers, and Beardsley Ruml. The *News* also carried lesser-known contributors whose ideas merited dissemination. I labored at putting out the *News* and enjoyed the solicitation of articles and the editing, proofreading, and cutting and pasting that goes into the production of a small journal.

The bureau bequeathed me a clearinghouse of materials in the form of a large room with many shelves holding books, pamphlets, articles, and reprints from a wide variety of intercultural sources: civic organizations, religious groups, school systems, universities, etc. A full-time clerk answered requests for free and low-priced materials from our shelves. We sought to break even on our service. Periodically I added materials, reduced overly sentimental or ineffective approaches, and reprinted the catalog of available materials.

But the work of director of publications and learning materials went beyond editing and dissemination. During the 1944 to 1947 period, publication outlets were hungry for writing about intercultural education. In the writer's market that prevailed, the only question for the writer was, "Which editorial invitation should I accept?"[1]

---

[1] I joined the staff of the bureau in June 1944; by August an article of mine was published in the *Newsletter of the New Jersey Good Will*

During World War II the major educational organizations had become acutely aware of the importance of intercultural education. The National Council for the Social Studies decided to devote its 1945 yearbook to the field of democratic human relations. Recognizing that there were two major educational organizations in the field, along with a variety of smaller fry, the NCSS leaders decided to invite Hilda Taba of Intergroup Education in Cooperating Schools and Van Til of the Bureau for Intercultural Education to jointly develop a yearbook on promising practices.

Hilda Taba was a veteran of the evaluation staff of the Eight Year Study of the Progressive Education Association. The staff had been headquartered at Ohio State University, and I knew her from her visits to University School and from occasional faculty parties in Columbus. During the war she became the director of our tough competitor, Intergroup Education in Cooperating Schools, financed by the National Council of Christians and Jews, an organization that annually sponsored Brotherhood Week and that seemed to us at the bureau to have more money than brains. With Taba, NCCJ acquired an intellect; she developed field work in public school systems and an ably written series of books reporting the field studies of her staff members.

Taba and I were uncomfortable in our collaboration. We readily agreed on a structure of chapters and could easily mine school systems for outstanding promising practices. I didn't have much trouble with her independently written chapters, nor she

---

Commission. Selecting outlets more wisely as to their potential national influence, I soon published articles in *Childhood Education, Harvard Educational Review, High School Journal, Educational Administration and Supervision,* and, with H. H. Giles, in the *Annals of the American Academy of Political and Social Science*—a reputable roster. My editorials led off issues of *Social Education* and *Clearing House* as well as appeared in *Intercultural Education News*; my pamphlets, *The Workshop* and *America's Stake in Human Rights,* were published by the American Education Fellowship (formerly the Progressive Education Association) and the National Council for the Social Studies, respectively. To obtain publicity for the bureau, I wrote pamphlets on its work and publications and developed a selective bibliography in the field of intercultural education.

with mine on school activities and community utilization, for on our own individual writing we could arrive at a separate peace. However, jointly writing the introductory chapter was an onerous experience for both of us. I was an educational journalist, a popularizer and simplifier. Taba was an evaluation scholar, an obscurantist and a complicator. Born in Estonia, she was still having difficulty with English communication in 1944. I must have redrafted that first chapter nine times before we got a version acceptable to both of us. We both suffered. Yet *Democratic Human Relations: Promising Practices in Intergroup and Intercultural Education* (the subtitle was another of our compromises) was well received. To write my own chapter on developing democratic human relations for the next NCSS yearbook (1946), *The Study and Teaching of American History*, was easy in comparison.

More pleasant than the collaboration with Taba was the preparation of the 1947 yearbook of the John Dewey Society, published by Harper through Ordway Tead. William Heard Kilpatrick, president of the John Dewey Society, was appointed to the editorship of the society's yearbook on intercultural attitudes. Since Kilpatrick was also the chairman of the bureau board, I became, at 35, the leg man, conductor of correspondence, and subeditor for the 75-year-old Kilpatrick.

In educational circles, after people talked of the preeminent John Dewey, they ranked next his disciple Kilpatrick, known in the press as "the million dollar professor." Not that the underpaid Kilpatrick ever earned a million dollars in his long lifetime; the press was referring to the million dollars Kilpatrick brought to the coffers of Teachers College, Columbia University, through the hundreds of students he taught year after year in each of his mammoth classes. Years later, in 1959 during the centennial celebration of Dewey's birth, I recorded on tape Kilpatrick's oral description of how he personalized those gargantuan classes, which were limited (!) to 450 students. Here is a verbatim unedited excerpt:

> I'll tell you what I tried to do with my class. It demonstrates what I think Dewey would stand for. I had a large class, so large that we had to do the thinking largely in advance. So I did the thinking as best I could. As to what topics I would

take, were they the important topics? Then I asked a number
of questions. I tried to ask those questions so they couldn't tell
how I would answer them. I gave a number of statements, which
might or might not be true, for them to criticize. I tried to
arrange them so they couldn't tell which way I would criticize
the statement. In other words, they would have to think.

The class was divided into discussion groups and they had
to meet an hour outside for every hour they met inside. The
discussion group must be not more than eight nor less than
five, so they could talk things over together. Each group was to
have a person of the group to report what the group thought on
each question in each statement. Mr. A would report on
question one, Mr. B on question two, and so on. Then when I
met the class I would plan to say, "Question one, groups 7, 28,
35 will answer it, question two..." Then I would go right on
through. Then when we came into the class, I would say, "We
will take question one. Now number 7, what do you say? What
did your people think?" He gets up and tells it. "Twenty-eight,
what did your people think? Thirty-five, what did your people
think?" If they disagreed, then I had them argue it out and it
was thrown open for the whole class to take part in the
argument. If they all agreed and I agreed, then we went on to
the next questions.

Kilpatrick was a Southerner, a soft-spoken Georgian, cour-
teous and even courtly, formal and intent, as gentle as Taba was
abrasive. He had a mane of long white hair, an unlined pink face,
a frail body, and a presence that commanded attention. He was
gifted in presiding at meetings in which he heard out ideas and
created syntheses that led into further action, reconciliations
that, incredibly, seemed reasonable and acceptable to all of the
contending forces.

Only once did I see him unable to work his magic rapproche-
ment; on this occasion he knew that no synthesis was possible
with the authoritarians who confronted him. Immediately after
the publication of Spencer Brown's *They See for Themselves*, a
group of self-appointed censors, both clericals and laypersons,
called on Kilpatrick to protest a student documentary play in
Brown's book that was critical of Father Coughlin, a widely
followed radio priest who broadcast reactionary, indeed some
said fascist, doctrines. The visitors' comments were abusive. Kil-

patrick heard them out and then said courteously, "You have given me an insight into the sensibilities of some people that I did not have before. I thank you for this." The meeting was over. The dedication of the bureau to the free play of intelligence was unchanged; distribution of *They See for Themselves* continued.

To develop the John Dewey Society yearbook, *Intercultural Attitudes in the Making*, Kilpatrick used an effective technique. First he called together the best scholars of intercultural education that he could muster. They met to determine that book's central thrusts and structure. Only then did he select and call together invited writers, who were not necessarily synonymous with the scholars.

During the year of preparation of *Intercultural Attitudes in the Making*, I traveled weekly from the bureau's office to Kilpatrick's apartment overlooking Morningside Heights. On my first visit he greeted me courteously and waited. I thought that it was necessary for me to make some small talk. So I told him that a decade earlier, while I commuted to Teachers College from the reform school at Warwick, I had been a student in one of his big classes. He excused himself, went to a file in another room of the apartment. Returning, he said, "And you got a B +."

I soon learned that small talk with Kilpatrick was never solicited by him and was quite unnecessary. Week after week we went directly to work on my reports on progress and problems. He had done his homework on the manuscript in the interim. His mind worked incisively, and problems that had seemed large in my office were resolved. An hour fled by and I had a whole week's work to carry through before the next meeting and Kilpatrick was turning back to another project for the League for Industrial Democracy or the National Urban League, or to his current book in progress, or to reading yearbook chapters, including my own chapter, "The High School Teacher."

For our last meeting on the yearbook I brought him the entire manuscript, ready for composition by Harper and complete with title page, "*Intercultural Attitudes in the Making*, edited by William Heard Kilpatrick." He said, "I want you to make a change on the title page. It is to read, 'edited by William Heard Kilpatrick and William Van Til.' If I make any other changes, I'll call you." The 35-year-old legman had become the full partner of the 75-year-old world leader in education. The generous and totally unexpected decision was characteristic of the man.

Mustering as much objectivity as possible, I can only report that in retrospect my production during the three bureau years now seems to me to be remarkable. I must have eaten much red meat in the years when I was 33 to 36; never again did I write so much. I even wrote my doctoral dissertation at home and on weekends and holidays throughout 1944 to 1946. And during summers I conducted intercultural workshops for NYU or Columbia or participated in a Northwestern University workshop in Springfield. Ah youth!

Through the dissertation, philosophic and speculative in tone, I developed a curriculum theory that has been my guide throughout my career. From my liberal arts courses, doctoral program, and independent reading, I had accumulated social information and theory. From the decade of teaching at the University School and from study of psychologists came psychological insights. From study and work with Bode at Ohio State University and with Kilpatrick at the bureau and through reading of Dewey, whom I once heard but never met, came my philosophy. I drew from the major curriculum thinkers of my time: Ralph W. Tyler and Hilda Taba, program evaluators for the Progressive Education Association; Henry Harap and Hollis Caswell, proponents of curricula based on social functions; Harold Alberty and V. T. Thayer, supporters of emphasis on the needs of learners.

Throughout my coming of age educationally, three theories had struggled for primacy in the progressive education movement. The social reconstructionists contended that the content of the curriculum should be based on social realities. I listened to Harold Hand, read and heard George Counts, and edited a book by Theodore Brameld. I thought they had part of the truth when they contended that social problems were of high importance, though I rejected any overtones of indoctrination of students in liberalism or radicalism. Meanwhile, the needs-oriented theorists emphasized the wants and interests of learners as a basis for selection of content. I studied and worked with Kilpatrick and encountered the child-centered theorists who dominated the progressive education movement well into the 1930s. I thought that they too had part of the truth, especially if needs were conceived as personal-social, as Alberty and Thayer advocated. A third group of theorists conceived of progressive education at the crossroads, torn between child-centered approaches and education for the democratic way of life; they opted for value-laden content. Those who saw value clarification as to competing alternatives as central were typified by Bode and his follower, H. Gordon Hullfish. But I thought that even philosophers like Bode would bake poor bread without taking into account the needs of learners and the social realities of their times.

I came away from my studies and my first decade of teaching with a belief in interaction among social, psychological, and philosophical foundations, and argued that curriculum content should be based on social realities, needs, and values. My dissertation described sixteen clusters of content or centers of experience for high school education. You may be sure that consumer education and intercultural education were among the sixteen and that the centers ranged from immediate personal needs such as boy-girl relationships through social imperatives such as war and peace, all permeated by value comparisons and contrasts. The dissertation carried a long title, as dissertations often do: *A Social Living Curriculum for Postwar Secondary Education: An Approach to Curriculum Development Through Centers of Experience Derived from the Interaction of Values, Social Realities and Needs.*

Ohio State University, through a committee made up of Alberty (major advisor), Landsittle, and Hullfish, approved the thesis. In absentia I became an Ohio State doctor of philosophy in 1946. My excuse for missing the doctor of philosophy ceremony was that I was too busy. I was.

Red meat was not the only explanation of my productiveness. As ever, Bee took over with respect to the household and enabled me to enjoy the children in the time I spent with them, which was considerable despite the dissertation. The bureau proved an ideal milieu for high production, and my colleagues were a stimulating crew.[2]

---

[2] The role of energetic, incisive, tough-minded (in the Jamesian sense) Helen Trager, director of special services, was to "salt in" intercultural

We drafted people for temporary studies, such as social reconstructionist philosopher Ted Brameld, who wrote a Middletown of intercultural education, *Minority Problems in the Public Schools*, an account of administrative practices in half a dozen school systems disguised with pseudonyms to avoid personal embarrassments; and psychologist Marion Radke, who collaborated with Helen Trager on a Philadelphia experiment, *They Learn What They Live*, which documented that children are more aware of cultural differences and more sensitive to the prejudices spread by adults than we had thought. These books too were shepherded through the Harper series of publications.

I had suggested that my former colleague Giles succeed Stewart Cole as director of the bureau; after a search, the board chose him and he took over as the coordinator, planner, and fund raiser. Though still called Mike, he had increasingly become H. H. Giles, human relations executive, rather than the bohemian Mike of the ratty fur coat and skeptical eye whom I had known at University School. He trusted me and I trusted him, but our relationships became increasingly professional. We were never alienated from each other, yet were never as close as when we sought together for Mr. Henderson's ghost in the cupola at 464-1/2 Vermont Place. Was it Henry Adams who said, "A friend in power is a friend lost"? I had faith in my area of work and wanted to expand it because of my belief in the importance of publications in fighting prejudice and discrimination. Mike believed that consultation in the field was the better bet, however intangible the results of person-to-person work might be. So despite friendship and good will, we didn't always see eye-to-eye.

In retrospect, I realize that each of our emphases was important. The pioneering bureau made an initial impact on the

education so that human relations insights would permeate selected children's books, radio programs, even movies and plays. Professors-to-be Jim Tipton, Marion Edman, and Whit Brogan and my friend from European travels, Paul Weinandy, had the difficult job of helping school systems like Detroit and Gary in crisis situations. Victor Pitkin tried to develop evaluation techniques so that we might tell, while in the process of medicating, what was the more effective treatment. Ethel J. Alpenfels was our specialist in anthropology, Lester Dix administrative associate, and Mildred Biddick special consultant.

American school curriculum both through publications and field work. Yet full acceptance of education for democratic human relations was still a long distance away.

Among the things we learned from our intercultural movement prior to Supreme Court decisions on school desegregation and to the civil rights movement of the 1950s and 1960s was that human relations education through American schools was not enough. School and community organization and participation leading to desegregation were also needed. Not either/or but both/and. Education and social action were one and inseparable if America was to have a fighting chance of achieving democratic human relations among people of varied backgrounds. I came to recognize too that Americans must go the second mile beyond physical desegregation in school and community if we were ever to achieve true integration, the full acceptance of all human beings as persons. Kilpatrick was right: You learn what you live.

Social developments punctuated those exciting and dramatic years at the bureau. One night in 1945, from our new office on Fifty-Second Street that had a magnificent view down Broadway to Times Square, I watched the joyful celebration of the end of the war. I didn't go down into the ecstatic crowds to rejoice, for I was busy putting finishing touches on still another publication, the *Intercultural Education News* or a Harper book or a yearbook chapter—I can't remember which. Below, on the streets, the postwar era was being born.

By 1947 financial support for intercultural education from private sources had crested. As funding grew more difficult in a postwar world with fewer racial clashes in American cities, director Mike grew more weary of fund-raising and its attendant requirement of fawning upon foundations, organizations, and rich donors. He began to look for a university to absorb the bureau program. Universities had begun to accept intercultural education as one of their responsibilities. Soon after I left the bureau, the board accepted the predictable adoption of the bureau as an integral part of Dean Ernest Melby's School of Education of New York University. But I had decided to enter the university job market as an independent, not as a component of a package.

Chapter Twenty-Five

THE YOUNG
PROFESSOR

S urrounded by an impenetrable clutter of books, papers, and documents, Harold Hand sat in his office in Gregory Hall, University of Illinois, and lit one of his foul-smelling cigars. He looked and sounded like a handsome, macho truck driver rather than a professor of education who had been designated to act for the new dean in filling several positions. In 1947 Harold was 46, fourteen years older than when he had supervised my student teaching at Teachers College, Columbia University. He said to me, "I want you to join the staff of the University of Illinois as a full professor."

Should I tell him? Of course, for this was Harold Hand. "But, Harold, I've never even been an associate professor. I was an assistant professor when I left Ohio State University four years ago for the Consumer Education Study and the Bureau for Intercultural Education."

Hand said, "That doesn't make a damn bit of difference. You've written a lot of stuff and you deserve to be a full professor. With tenure, of course, so that the bastards can't fire you because of your wild ideas."

I asked, "What would I have to do to lose my tenure and be fired?"

Hand puffed on his cigar, thought for a while, then said, "The charge would have to be fornication with the dean of women on a public highway in broad daylight. All four factors would have to be substantiated."

I promised to avoid the daylight hours, and Hand sent me

over to see President George D. Stoddard and his aides. "They want to be sure that you don't have two heads. Then spend the rest of your visit casing the joint. Talk to anybody you want; we'll make appointments with anyone you want to meet."

No one had ever told Harold Hand that a temporary designate is not supposed to make crucial decisions on rank and tenure. Despite his revulsion for desk work, he had been dragooned by recently appointed Dean Willard Spalding (who was absent on a six-week talent-scouting trip) to employ education professors needed immediately. He was proceeding expeditiously to fill these posts and was impatient to get back to his plane, in which to date he had flown the equivalent of a couple of times around the world for speaking engagements and consultation in school systems across America.

President Stoddard and his aides apparently noted that I did not have two heads, so I went back to New York City with an offer of a full professorship of social studies education from the University of Illinois. In those days strong administrators selected new staff members. No affirmative action quests were undertaken, and even faculty consultation was minimal. The salary offered me was almost twice what I had earned at Ohio State University. When summer teaching at Illinois or elsewhere and anticipated speeches and consultation were included, the Illinois income could amount to more than three times OSU's invariable $2,772. I was to let Hand know my decision "soon."

By 1947 I had accumulated some limited experience as a college teacher. In addition to my summer workshop at Ohio University (1940), and the three Northwestern University workshops at Springfield, Missouri (1942), Kansas City (1943), and again Springfield (1946), I had taught a demonstration class and an accompanying graduate course at Northwestern (1941). During the bureau years I had taught intercultural education programs for both New York University and Teachers College during summer sessions. During the final bureau year, 1946-47, I had also been invited, to my surprise, to teach a curriculum course at night at Teachers College. Apparently Gordon MacKenzie, pivotal in curriculum work at Teachers College and a leader in a new national curriculum and supervision organization, the Association for Supervision and Curriculum Development, had decided to scout me in preparation for a possible TC offer.

Sure enough. Shortly after my return from visiting the Illinois campus, Hollis L. Caswell, director of the Division of Instruction at Teachers College and later to become TC's dean, then president, invited me to a conference in his office, which was as well organized as Hand's was chaotic. "Cas" was a preeminent curriculum leader, author of the widely read *Curriculum Development* with Doak S. Campbell. He was also a likable human being and an administrator par excellence.

Cas offered me an associate professorship in curriculum and instruction at TC. Deferentially, I mentioned that Illinois had just offered me a full professorship. Cas's eyebrows went up, and he told me that a full professorship at Teachers College for a 36-year-old who had last been an assistant professor was unheard-of. I told him that I understood that. Yet I did have an offer of a full professorship from Illinois. We looked at each other for a while. Cas explained to me that coming in as a full professor would surely be hard on my personal relationships with staff members. I said that I would have to chance that. No doubt it also occurred to administrator Caswell that my coming in as a full professor would also raise hell with his own relationships with the Teachers College staff. We both could visualize enraged hordes of associate professors storming his office to protest that the director had lost his mind and, if repelled, to devise booby traps to blast the reputation of the undeserving young full professor.

Then Caswell made a difficult decision that still seems incredible to me. He offered me a full professorship in curriculum and instruction at Teachers College at a salary comparable to the Illinois offer. A mannerly man, he didn't describe the conditions under which my tenure might be terminated. And he wanted my acceptance right away, so that he could start the necessary process of confirmation with the dean and the president.

By phone, I talked with Ruth Kotinsky, my editorial associate. Ruth was an intellectual's intellectual; she yearned to reconcile John Dewey's and Sigmund Freud's theories in a synthesis of the cognitive and affective realms. In the last bureau year, she had become a confidante whose opinions I respected. Naturally, she recommended jumping at the TC offer.

I called an SOS to Bee, and she came into the city from our

Baldwin home. During the afternoon we talked for hours on a park bench along Morningside Heights. The pros, the cons. Comparative salaries, courses, students, colleagues, academic specializations, expectancies, consultation, writing opportunities, comparative intellectual stimulation of the two environments, life-styles, residences, community participation opportunities for both of us, neighborhoods, schools, and where it was best for children to grow up.

Exhaustion on our faces, we walked to the Kotinsky apartment near the Columbia campus; she had urged us to stop in when we had made our decision.

At the door, Ruth marveled at our appearance. "You two kids have the whole world in your hands. Bill has just had two unbelievable offers. Yet you both look as woebegone as though you had been sentenced to prison."

Worn-out, I went to the phone and made two calls. One went to Illinois, saying "yes." The other went to Teachers College, saying "no." The crucial factor was that we preferred to raise our children in a small city in the Midwest rather than in the metropolitan area of the city of our birth. "Educational history was made today," said native New Yorker Kotinsky. "A 36-year-old assistant professor has just refused a full professorship at Teachers College, the Mecca of education and the center of the educational universe in the greatest city of them all. I wish I could have seen Cas's face when you rejected his offer."

"Maybe he was glad," I said.

So the summer of 1947 became a time of transition from the East to the Midwest. I traveled back to an old stamping ground, Springfield, Missouri, this time to staff and direct an independent school system workshop unaffiliated with Northwestern. All of the workshop staff members batched it in an old house.

I had brought to the workshop a science educator, a young New York City private school teacher named Herbert S. Zim. Herb was beginning the writing career that eventuated in book after book popularizing science, including little Golden Books sold in supermarkets, and that crested with the Herculean task of writing *Our Wonderful World*, an encyclopedia in multiple volumes. One night we sat on the porch in Springfield and Herb showed me a chart of past and possible future publications with projections of royalties. "By the time I'm about 40," said Herb, who was then about 30, "I'm going to be financially independent. Then I'll stop teaching and I'll write full time." And damned if he didn't, for some time in the 1950s he resigned a professorship at Illinois and moved to an island in the Florida Keys where he established a home, a writing workshop, a staff, and a library building equipped with Xeroxing facilities and jammed with books.

That summer Bee stayed in Baldwin to sell the house at $16,000, a whopping profit reflecting the demand for housing during the postwar inflation. Then she flew to Illinois to buy another while I was concluding my bureau work. On a summer dog day she bused from Chicago to Champaign-Urbana and was hosted by Hand and his wife, Katherine, with ice cream and a bed in their guest cottage, a Quonset hut beside the wildly whistling Chicago express. The postwar housing shortage in Champaign-Urbana was so severe that real estate agents had only three possible houses in our financial bracket in the twin cities. She bought a house within twenty-four hours, then came home in tears. "I paid far too much ($15,500). It's too little, and I can't remember whether the bathroom even has a window." In the interest of our mental comfort, she flew back with a tape measure and made drawings of all of the rooms. However, 909 W. William Street turned out to be a fine home for us, especially after the euphoniously named local firm of Matska, Kachapa, and Bough—try saying it—converted a porch into a study for me.

We made no mistake in choosing the University of Illinois. The education staff was among the best in the nation.[1]

---

[1] It included B. Othanel (naturally called Bunnie) Smith, a brilliant student of curriculum and social foundations and one of the faculty's influentials, William O. (Bill) Stanley, a social reconstructionist and dogged scholar who once told me, "I had a wonderful day today; I validated two footnotes"; and Harlan Shores, an elementary education and reading specialist who later became president of the Association for Supervision and Curriculum Development. They were in the process of collaborating on *Fundamentals of Curriculum Development* (1950), possibly the best curriculum book based on social reconstruction theory that has ever been published. Lee J. Cronbach and Nathaniel Gage were initiating their research in educational psychology that later made them widely known. Kenneth Benne in philosophy of education

The vigorous Hand helped with the addition of three others to the secondary education staff: John DeBoer, editor of a language arts journal, past president of the National Council of Teachers of English, present president of the American Education Fellowship (a reincarnation of the Progressive Education Association), a lovable man and a stubborn radical who cooperated with all shades of political opinion for causes in which he believed; R. Will Burnett, a lively and skillful science educator who promptly built a modernistic house never before contemplated in Champaign; and Walter Kaulfers, a masterly foreign language educator and writer and a delightful eccentric (when undergraduate girls knitted in Walter's class, he posted a sign, "Expectant mothers are permitted to knit in this class" and thus terminated all knitting). A year after we arrived, Kenneth Henderson became a professor of mathematics education; he shared the same office with Hand and pulled out a deodorant bottle complete with air wick whenever Hand lit up a stogey.

At 46, Hand was the old man of the faculty. Hand and Bill Sanford created an Illinois secondary school curriculum improvement program that brought old and new staff members into Illinois communities to develop programs in cooperation with secondary school teachers and administrators in the public schools. Individual professors among us adopted communities; Decatur was one of my several responsibilities. Hand and Sanford were an odd couple—Harold colorful, brimming with ideas, acting on democratic and progressive ideologies and principles, indifferent to details, and Bill Sanford, sober, less interested in abstract ideas, highly skilled in operations, patient, well orga-

---

was writing *The Improvement of Practical Intelligence* (1950) with Bunnie and co-authors. Archibald Anderson was the Henry Luce of the campus; he edited *Progressive Education* and was associate editor of the *History of Education Journal* and *Educational Administration and Supervision*; he was about to take on *Educational Theory* as editor. J. Lloyd Trump, later to develop team teaching for the National Association of Secondary School Principals, taught classes on student activities; Francis G. (Griff) Cornell carried on the Strayer-Engelhardt survey tradition as director of the Bureau of Educational Research; Celia Stendler in child development was publishing a social class study, *Children of Brasstown*.

nized. During my Illinois years, 1947-1951, they held a series of weekend conferences of University of Illinois faculty members and school people in state parks. Individually and in groups we worked in the field on bettering the Illinois secondary school curriculum. Through meetings, over meals, and through after hours in taverns with names like "The Blue Goose," the Illinois education staff came to know each other and school people as they never had before.

Illinois had a fleet of planes and a number of student pilots who flew those professors who didn't fly themselves. Flying madness infected our faculty. Cornell already flew, Burnett was learning to fly, and even mechanically inept Arch Anderson and John DeBoer tried their wings before being discouraged by unanticipated forced landings in corn fields. I was content to be transported throughout the state by student pilots, though alarmed once by a young pilot coming in for a landing, then heading up again with an explanation, "Wrong airport." I never again believed the flight director's invariable greeting on our returns, "You've been safe with our boy, professor. But be careful of those cars on your way home from the field!"

Even the community of Springfield, though located in Missouri rather than Illinois, became familiar with the University of Illinois staff. In the late 1940s the Springfield school system ran into criticism from parents who supported traditionalism and were hostile to progressive education; under the direction of Griff Cornell, the University of Illinois conducted a Bureau of Educational Research survey of the system by professors and graduate students. The protesting parents objected to my membership on the survey team, since, as they saw it, I was a progressive educator who had contributed to ruining the system through my participation in the summer workshops of 1942, 1946, and 1947. As a condition of making the survey, Hand and Cornell insisted that I remain on board. I did.

The young Illinois faculty not only worked together on campus and in the field. They enjoyed each other socially. Saturday night parties brought together the newcomers and their wives, the DeBoers, the Burnetts, the Hendersons, and the Van Tils, along with longer-time staff members, Kenneth Benne, Celia Stendler, and Arch Anderson. The Smith-Stanley-Shores team and their wives sometimes joined us, and Bee and I also frequently paired with the Cornells, Trumps, Hands, and many more.

Vignettes persist in memory. Historian and editor Arch Anderson listening to Richard Wagner's music in the small hours of the morning long after the hosts, Bee and I, had retired. The abortive lion-hunting expedition by Henrietta DeBoer, Bernice Burnett, and Bee, who brought a national celebrity to one of our parties after his campus folk song concert, only to be disillusioned by his vulgarity and crudeness. The New Year's Eve our scientist Will Burnett tried out a new rifle and was politely informed by the police of the illegality of discharging firearms within the city limits. The flight back from the Springfield survey, with Griff Cornell at the stick, when Cornell complained bitterly to me that because of survey responsibilities he was not prepared for his next class; when I next saw him I asked him what he had done about the class meeting and he responded, "I wasn't prepared. So there was only one thing I could do. I talked." The senility party celebrating my fortieth birthday when the guests were required to appear in costumes different from their present ages. Bee and I dressed up as aged antebellum Southern plantation owners, complete with powdered hair; attractive Henrietta DeBoer came as a dowager in a dress with a lace fichu; Fred Barnes squeezed into his World War II sailor uniform and Florence appeared as his waterfront floozy. Kenneth Henderson discreetly wore a raincoat to the door before unveiling his complete costume, a diaper.

But life at the University of Illinois wasn't all fun and games or field work and flying. To the best of our abilities, we taught and counseled our undergraduate and graduate students and inducted our graduate assistants; social studies education was my specialty. By now I could phrase abstractly as an educational credo what I had learned concretely from University School and the Bureau for Intercultural Education experiences. I believed:

—that the overall purpose of American education is to develop the understanding and practice of democracy as a way of life;
—that the salient characteristic of democracy as a way of life is faith in the method of intelligence;
—that the best learning experiences are those that begin with the needs of the learner, illuminate the social realities of

the times, and contrast competing ways of living;

—that teacher-pupil planning is desirable and feasible;

—that controversial issues are the life-blood of general education learning experiences;

—that indoctrination of set answers to controversial issues is
an abuse of the method of intelligence and thus undemocratic;

—that by thinking through problems, using facts, and applying values, students can reach conclusions for themselves;
they need not and must not be innocuous neutrals on
human issues;

—that, if mature men and women are to act, young men and
women must learn to act.

I continued publishing in the field of intercultural education
through a resource unit for high school student use, *Democracy
Demands It*, a collaboration with DeBoer, Burnett, and graduate
assistant Kathy Ogden; wrote a chapter for the 1951 National
Council for the Social Studies Yearbook, *Education for Democratic Citizenship*, with graduate assistant George Denemark;
and chaired a National Council for the Social Studies committee
that sponsored a pamphlet, *America's Stake in Civil Rights*.
Other intercultural education articles appeared in the *North
Central Association Quarterly* and the *NEA Journal* and, again
with graduate assistant George Denemark, in the *Review of
Educational Research* in the form of a sustained review of
research in intercultural and intergroup education. Since I was
concerned about public understanding of contemporary education, I chaired a commission on communication of democratic
education of the John Dewey Society and wrote a Bureau of
Educational Research and Service pamphlet with graduate
assistant Evelyn Luecking, *What Popular Magazines Say About
Education: 1946-1948*.

The opportunity to collaborate with these graduate assistants had introduced a new element into my writing program. I
never forgot the lesson learned from Tom Briggs and Fred
Wilhelms of the Consumer Education Study when *Economic
Roads for American Democracy* was published by McGraw-Hill
under my name and from Kilpatrick when he took me into
editorial partnership on *Intercultural Attitudes in the Making*—
always give full credit and bylines to one's young associates. At

Illinois they were a varied and interesting lot.

Through field work in Harvey, Illinois, I encountered George Denemark, a young high school teacher who was handling himself and his work remarkably well despite his unpleasant and unsympathetic department chairman. As a graduate assistant he was solid, reliable, and scholarly, and in time he became executive secretary of the Association for Supervision and Curriculum Development, education dean at the University of Milwaukee at Wisconsin and the University of Kentucky, and president of the American Association of Colleges for Teacher Education. Evelyn Luecking joined me at Illinois through core program contacts and Kathy Ogden (Brondyke) through mail correspondence, in effect over the transom; they too collaborated on my writing projects before they returned to teaching. Vernon Replogle came from teaching on Chicago's North Shore, wrote the first dissertation for which I served as advisor, and began a long career as principal of the laboratory school at Illinois State University at Normal, Illinois. Edward Weir, teacher in a community near Champaign, became a professor at the University of Pittsburgh.

My first graduate assistant was the memorable Charley White. Charley, a social studies teacher, first came to my attention at the opening of Northwestern University's second Springfield, Missouri, workshop when he moved to the piano to provide music and patter. He was soon in unofficial charge of the workshop recreation and entertainment program. After the independent 1947 workshop, he came to Illinois for a two-year hitch as graduate assistant. Charley had been an aide-de-camp to a general in World War II, had carried out such assignments as clearing out a Paris hotel so that General DeGaulle's staff might be housed, and was completely capable of performing academic miracles. For instance, one day I commented wistfully that life would be better in our office if we had an additional filing cabinet. I contemplated a requisition and months of processing. However, the next day a filing cabinet materialized. Charley never told me how he did things like that.

He became a close family friend. Whenever I returned from a trip, even if after midnight, he would be waiting at the airport to pick me up. When Bee and I needed some time to ourselves, he made reservations at the Blackstone Hotel in Chicago, where undoubtedly he knew the manager, and baby-sat our children, who adored him. His tastes were expensive, and he encouraged our frugal selves to spend a wedding anniversary at the Waldorf-Astoria Hotel in New York City and buy a Pontiac for $3,200, a fearsome price at a time when American full professors often were paid $5,000 for the academic year.

Charley's Achilles' heel as a scholar was, in his own words, that he "never knew who wrote it." Eventually a faculty committee judged his doctoral candidacy not feasible. Unhappy ending? Not at all. I recommended him as an assistant to the harried dean of the School of Education of the University of Houston. In his new post Charley earned more as assistant dean than the degree-laden full professors.

The graduate assistants learned the ropes as they shared my writing, research, field work, and attempts to cope with the mysteries of the academic universe. They participated in all of my work except teaching; as a matter of honor and conviction, I met all of my classes myself and arranged out-of-town schedules so that I seldom had to rebook a class. The contributions of my assistants were highly valuable to me; since loyalty is one of my virtues/vices, I helped them in job placement and fostered their careers in every way I could.

In 1947 more than one million war veterans enrolled in colleges under the G. I. Bill of Rights, and Illinois got its share. As our staff expanded, I brought to the University of Illinois as instructors or assistant professors in social studies Arno Bellack, who later became executive secretary of ASCD, a Teachers College professor, and an editor for McGraw-Hill books; Doug Ward, my Consumer Education associate, who had worked abroad for AID, and who later was to be a dean at Miami University and the University of Virginia; and Lawrence E. (Larry) Metcalf, who in time became an Illinois full professor and co-authored a brilliant yet unfortunately largely ignored book, *Teaching High School Social Studies*.

As I worked with both graduate assistants and additions to staff, I remembered Kilpatrick's answer to my question, "How does a person make a difference through education?" Kilpatrick said, "Through writing. And through working with a few graduate students and colleagues who learn from you while you learn from them." Mutual learning, not discipleship. I frequently warned doctoral advisees and associates, "You become an educator in your own right when you kick your advisor in the teeth." Indeed, an occasional one did.

Much of my writing time I spent on two projects on which I soloed. By now my relationship with the Association for Supervision and Curriculum Development publication program was so well established that Robert Leeper, editor for ASCD publications, entrusted me with writing a column for *Educational Leadership* called "The Importance of People." Thirty-two years later I wrote in *Writing for Professional Publication*:

> ...[W]riting columns for a magazine that speaks to members of one's own profession is the nearest thing to pure pleasure that authors like us can experience. Imagine being able to write whatever you please. Imagine being allowed to choose your own genre, whether satiric, pleading, angry, humorous, commendatory, condemnatory, descriptive, analytical, emotional, or whatever. Yet you are guaranteed that what you write will appear in print with regularity. Columnists are free to say what they want to say in the style or manner they prefer to use. They are limited only by their own abilities and space restrictions. A happy situation! Columnists are the freest of all writers for professional publications.

For *Educational Leadership* I wrote satiric columns on which I received substantial mail, "The Remarkable Culture of the American Educators" and "The Ladder to Success in Universities." An autobiographical column, "He Went Back," reported my return to my high school, and a column titled "John Dewey's Disciples" twitted some of my overly orthodox colleagues. Several columns urged public participation in shaping the educational process, "People and Policies," "The Community Won't Stand For It," and "Let's Communicate Democratic Education." Aware of rising reactionary criticism of contemporary education, I wrote "The Climate of Fear" and "Cheaters of Children."

Educational Leadership also carried a vigorous criticism of traditional textbooks titled "Fable of Textbook Strategy." Whether this article had anything to do with McGraw-Hill inviting me to edit a series of social studies books for high school students and write some myself, I don't really know. Publishers are unpredictable. At any rate I signed up to co-edit a series of social studies books with Dorothy McClure, a national colleague active in the National Council for the Social Studies.

It was a good life at Illinois in the late forties of the century and the late thirties of my life. We took our responsibilities as educators and citizens seriously. The times were beginning to get rough for people who supported progressive education and people who were willing to stand up and be counted on behalf of social and civic causes in which they believed.

From one flank the educational beliefs of the Illinois group were being vitriolically criticized by liberal arts professors. Historian Arthur E. Bestor of the University of Illinois nationally assailed programs of progressive education through his *Educational Wastelands* and locally criticized the secondary school curriculum proposals of the Illinois education professors. He termed social studies "social stew" and attacked problem-oriented teaching. Conflicts flared in campus meetings and committee sessions. Campus debates were held. Hand and Bestor exchanged memorandums frequently across campus. Bestor's criticisms were the opening guns in a war on modern education by academic critics.

From another flank came blanket condemnation of professors who supported liberal and radical social causes. Censorship of books and materials used in school was proposed. Joseph McCarthy came on the national scene in 1950 through his Wheeling speech; there were legislators with similar views in the halls of Illinois government. State Senator Broyles proposed a series of bills mandating loyalty oaths and authorizing red hunts. Our colleague John DeBoer was a prime target for Senator Broyles, since John stubbornly exercised his right as a citizen to work with whomever he wished for causes he regarded as just. Though his campus friends did not share his faith that one could work with Communists (with a capital C) in coalitions that included independents, progressives, liberals, and socialists, they defended his right to do so if he saw fit. We knew John as a man who did not indoctrinate in the classroom and as an independent activist who disliked all forms of totalitarianism.

One night the Broyles viewpoint and method came to town

for a red-baiting speech. We knew that John would be under attack. The speaker did a version of the "I have here in my hand the name of such a man" tactic that McCarthy made famous on the national scene. As he inched toward naming John as a Communist conspirator, we found ourselves angrily and lustily booing the attack on John's citizenship right to support causes in which he believed. John took a beating in the press but held to his post and his convictions.

Governor Adlai E. Stevenson vetoed the Broyles bill. His veto read:

> The stated purpose of this bill is to combat the menace of world Communism. That the Communist Party—and all it stands for—is a danger to our Republic, as real as it is sinister, is clear to all who have the slightest understanding of our democracy....
>
> Agreed upon ends, our concern is with means. It is in the choice of methods to deal with recognized problems that we Americans, in and out of public life, so often develop differences of opinion. Our freedom to do so is a great source of strength and, if not impaired by mistakes of our own, will contribute greatly to the ultimate confusion of the enemies of freedom....
>
> [The message then observed that another provision of the bill required a complex loyalty oath of all state employees, of all applicants for state jobs, and of all teachers.]
>
> By such provisions as these, irreparable injury to the reputation of innocent persons is more than a possibility; it is a likelihood. If this bill became law, it would be only human for employees to play safe and shirk duties which might bring upon them resentment or criticism.
>
> Public service requires independent and courageous action on matters which affect countless private interests. We cannot afford to make public employees vulnerable to malicious charges of disloyalty. So far as the employers are concerned—heads of departments and of schools and so on—the only safe policy would be timid employment practices which could only result in lowering the level of ability, independence and courage in our public agencies, schools and colleges....
>
> The whole notion of loyalty inquisitions is a natural characteristic of the police state, not of democracy....
>
> Basically, the effect of this legislation, then, will be less

the detection of subversives and more the intimidation of honest citizens. But we cannot suppress thought and expression and preserve the freedoms guaranteed by the Bill of Rights.

In this torrid atmosphere, a bill was introduced to censor, through a legislative appointed committee of unspecified size and composition, all textbooks and other materials used in Illinois schools. The bill was supported by right-wing forces, including the *Chicago Tribune*, self-styled "the world's greatest newspaper," and the Illinois American Legion. No opposition materialized. My colleagues assured each other that the bill was so bad—it would even have required censoring the *Chicago Tribune* itself—that it would "die of its own weight." So nobody did anything about it and the bill moved toward committee hearings.

I waited for somebody to do something about it. Nobody did. It took a while for me to realize that bills, however bad, don't die of their own weight but are killed. Eventually I realized that my role as professor of social studies education at the major state university meant that I had a social responsibility to build a coalition to kill the bill. Unwillingly, since I was a peaceable man and a political amateur, I did. I brought together others who were opposed and yet were hesitating to become "involved" in an era of nasty retribution in which irresponsible politicians struck with smears at any head that showed itself. The Illinois Civil Liberties Union, the Illinois League of Women Voters, the Illinois Parent-Teachers Association, and the Illinois Education Association agreed to testify against the bill. We traveled to Springfield, Illinois, and talked up in the hearings. The bill died in committee. My good friends said, "We told you so. That bill was so bad that it died of its own weight." But it really didn't. We killed it. I learned an unforgettable political lesson.

Chapter Twenty-Six

THE SIT-IN
BY ALTON'S
BLACK CHILDREN

I n Champaign one winter day during January 1950, I had a phone call from the right-hand man to the governor of Illinois. He told me that an explosive racial situation was developing in Alton, Illinois. Negro children were sitting in at all-white schools and groups of white adults were clustering outside the schools. (The word "Negro" was then standard and will often be used in this account; "black" didn't become widely used until the late 1960s.) Governor Adlai E. Stevenson wanted me, as a representative of the Illinois Interracial Commission, to go immediately to Alton to mediate.

Stevenson, who later ran twice for the Presidency against the unbeatable Eisenhower, had been elected governor of Illinois in 1948 and had been inducted into office early in 1949. The state of Illinois had created an Illinois Interracial Commission in 1947 during the Republican Dwight Green administration. A new unsalaried twenty-member commission was appointed in the summer of 1949 by Stevenson, who included me as a member, no doubt at the suggestion of intercultural agencies in the state. The duties of the commission were to

> investigate the most effective means of affording opportunity and profitable employment to all persons, with particular reference to training and placement; cooperate with civic, religious, and educational organizations in promoting tolerance and good will; report to the governor and the legislature biennially, on or about the third Monday in January of each odd-numbered year, the results of its investigations.

I knew there was a law on the Illinois books that segregation in Illinois public schools was unlawful, and I knew that state funds could be withheld from school systems that practiced racial discrimination. The Jenkins amendment authorizing the withholding of state aid was passed in June 1949 during the Stevenson administration. These state laws, of course, substantially antedated the crucial U. S. Supreme Court decision of 1954, *Brown vs. Board of Education*, outlawing public school segregation nationally.

I knew too that in many Southern Illinois communities black elementary school students went to public all-black schools and white elementary school students went to all-white schools. Paradoxically, in some communities, black students often attended desegregated public senior high schools; separate high schools for blacks would have cost taxpayers too much, as small communities saw it. (Later I was to learn that this was the situation in Alton; only the senior high school was desegregated.)

Alton and East St. Louis are industrial communities across the river from St. Louis. The press reported that East St. Louis had initiated grade-by-grade desegregation beginning with grade one in January 1950. The East St. Louis desegregation had gone smoothly; a three-day sit-in in 1949 had been followed by a year of careful preparation by school and community groups. But in Alton the situation was different. I later described the Alton situation at a 1953 meeting on desegregation at Highlander Folk School in Tennessee. A tape of my talk survives and is drawn upon liberally here:

> In Alton, under all of the legislative pressures, the school and community people did practically nothing to attempt integration. Then came a time shortly after East St. Louis integration when some of the leaders of the Negro group in Alton, and possibly nationally, lost patience at this repeated—I won't call it temporizing; Alton just didn't do a blessed thing—inactivity on the part of Alton. The strategy was conceived in the office of the [Alton] National Association for the Advancement of Colored People, with some advice from beyond [primarily from NAACP in East St. Louis] to have the Negro children go to the school nearest to their homes and request admission at the schools. So there came a particular day [during the beginning of the second semester, January 23, 1950] when the

219

Negro children of the community went to the schools nearest their homes, requested admission, and were refused admission by the principals after very worried calls to the superintendent's office, which responded, "No, of course we're not going to do that." The children were then instructed by their parents to stay in the nearest schools—in effect, to use the labor terminology, to conduct a sit-down.

In some schools they were received by the administration coolly, coldly, and they sat along the walls and in the corridors outside the office. In other schools they were received by the administration warmly, and they played with white youngsters out on the playground during recess, or they waited more or less comfortably in the libraries or elsewhere. In other words, the sit-down was made comfortable in some cases and uncomfortable in others.... In one school they weren't allowed to go to the bathroom and had to run home or go outside and then come back to their sit-down....

As soon as this happened, Alton, which is an explosive community, learned about it through its newspaper, which was markedly unsympathetic to the sit-down.... Outside of each of the schools where the Negro youngsters were sitting, knots of white people gathered and stayed all during the school day.

No one has made a sociological study of these white people—it wasn't the kind of situation for that kind of cool sociological study—but to my naked eye, the white people were...obviously of the working-class and lower-middle-class population—not very often the collar-and-tie type. They did nothing at first except stand outside the schools, fifty or sixty or seventy of them,...and just talked to each other, usually across the street from the school. The Alton police came to the scene of each of these schools. A few policemen, very few, just stood around at each school, sometimes talking with the men, sometimes not.

It was at that point that obviously some in the community...got in touch with the governor's office and said, "This looks like hell might break loose here any moment. Here are the little kids inside the schools, brought there by their mothers as of that morning, and here are threatening groups of whites outside the school. If some Negro kid hits some white kid, or some white kid hits some Negro kid, all hell might break loose in Alton, and we may have the beginning of a full-fledged race riot on our hands."

Governor Stevenson got in touch with the Illinois Interracial

Commission, which sent down one of its salaried employees, a black man. The school people, in effect, refused to talk with him. They required proof of his identification, and even afterwards he continued to meet hostility. So someone at the Illinois Interracial Commission suggested that I go to Alton as a mediator, not to achieve the end of segregation but to restore some degree of quiet and to try to keep the lid on the situation. (Nearby East St. Louis had been the scene of a major American race riot in 1917.)

I packed, took care not to include a red tie, and drove to Alton. First I scouted the knots of whites gathered outside the schools. Then I went to the office of the superintendent of schools.

The superintendent accepted me as a fellow educator but said, "They've got to get out of there. We can't have this potentially explosive situation." I asked him what he proposed to do and he said, "Not a thing. Just get them out of there."

I saw the chairman of the school board. His attitude was even worse. He said, "We'll get along without state aid if aid means we're going to have Negroes in the same school as whites." I pointed out that this meant an inferior quality of education, that he knew how much the state was putting into education on the local level, that the educational system would be crippled. He said, "We don't care what happens " With menace in his voice, he reminded me that Alton was the community that had lynched Elijah Lovejoy, an abolitionist, after local residents had destroyed Lovejoy's presses. What should I do? "Get them out of there; get them back where they belong." He wasn't going to give an inch.

I went to a meeting of the nearest thing there was to a liberal group in Alton, a human relations group made up mostly of whites. The participants that evening were Christian clergymen, people from social service agencies, a representative from one of the Jewish agencies who had come down from Springfield, Illinois, after he had learned of the sit-in, and a few Jewish and black citizens. What could they do? They didn't know what they could do. If they made a public statement, they would personally be exposed to pressures in the community. The most courageous of the group was a Protestant minister who wanted to go public. The few Negroes in the group were not themselves among the community leaders who initiated the sit-in. The group was predominantly made up of white, liberal, Christian/Jewish, interculturally concerned and religiously oriented people. I decided that I would find sympathy here but little tangible assistance in the mediation process. I mentally categorized the group as "living-room liberals."

Strange as it may sound, my greatest single problem was to identify and find the Negro leadership. I was white, so I didn't have access. So I got acquainted with some of the Negroes of the living-room liberal group, won their confidence, and went along with them after the meeting to meet still other blacks late into the night and through the next day. My goal was to meet the Negro leaders and persuade them to offer to sit down at a conference table to get out of a situation that was hourly becoming more untenable for both groups. Continuing with the Highlander Folk School tape:

> I felt a little bit—the nearest I suppose I would ever feel— akin to a conspirator.... I began to have a vague understanding of what people might live like if they were American Communists. Because I would go to one group of the Negro population in Alton and we would meet somewhere in somebody's room and they would talk with me and tell me that what they wanted was to get integration, and my job was to explain to the superintendent about this integration. I would say, "Would you sit down with him?".... But they didn't quite have the authority.
>
> Finally—and this was in a matter of hours—...I found the true leadership.... The whole sequence took place over about two and a half days. I'm not sure whether I ever slept [I probably got a couple of hours sleep.] And remember, you have an unskilled mediator here.... I didn't have sense enough even to see the mayor. Later on I wondered how I forgot....
>
> At one time I did see the chief of police, because the member [chairman] of the school board...thought maybe it might be impressive to me in some way to bring in the chief of police. I said something that irritated him and he said, "Well, by George, we'll get the chief of police here." So he got the chief of police there, and the chief of police—after the school board chairman blustered a little bit—made it quite clear that his job as he conceived it...was to keep order, and what he was going to try to do was to keep order. He didn't have anything to do with this mediation business. He was just a cop; his job was to

keep order. I tried to get the police chief at one point to see that maybe it would be a good thing to dissipate the threatening knots as good police practice. But, you see, the threatening knots denied being threatening knots; they were people who were just there as mothers and fathers to see that nothing happened to their children while the colored kids were in school. When I referred to them one time, a bit untactfully, as a group of threatening knots or a group of poorly dressed people, the school superintendent said to me very indignantly, "They certainly are not! Now, my wife went to one..." [laughter].

After the search for leadership, I found it centered in the office of a dentist, a very bright young man, a recent college graduate, a relatively prosperous member of the Negro community. He agreed that the time had come now to reconsider the strategy they had initiated and that they had better talk it over as a group.

I met him at four o'clock in the afternoon. He said, "We will have a meeting of the Negro community at seven o'clock." I said, "How will you have a meeting of the Negro community tonight at seven o'clock?" And he said, "Well, now"—he smiled a little—"you watch." The way they did it was by careful organization. They had one person whose job it was to call fifteen people, and these fifteen people in turn each had a list.

So at seven o'clock that night, completely unbeknownst to the white citizens of Alton, a meeting was held in one of the Negro Protestant churches. It was a well-attended meeting; it didn't have all of the Negro citizens of Alton, but it had a great many of them. Meanwhile, the paper was stewing and fulminating and people were talking and rustling. The situation was deteriorating in one of the schools where the white people outside had decided to go inside to make sure that Negro children didn't use the restrooms; it was an attempt to break the sit-down through control of the toilets....

It looked like a good prayer meeting; people just came from all around to the church and the leadership took over. They raised the question as to what they should do. It was as fine a democratic discussion as I've ever heard. There were a lot of emotional overtones. You'd get a mother who would stand up and say, "I just don't want to go on with this. This is too much for Rick. These people are not going to yield; you know that they're not, and I'm just not going to risk my little boy in that situation. I don't care too much what you decide; I think I'm going to keep him home tomorrow." Others would say, "The only way to do this is to dramatize it to those white people. We've got to keep on for several more days so they see what the situation is."

The majority sentiment by the group went toward calling off the sit-down—having done, the leadership said, what they hoped to do. They had...local publicity; they had...national publicity; they had brought the question to the attention of the state and of the governor.... The superintendent wasn't going to give; the board wasn't going to give. There wasn't anything to be gained except trouble, as they saw it.... "We are going to very carefully initiate legal proceedings against the board." The NAACP lawyer was there. He pointed out that they could probably sue the members of the school board. This was received with great enthusiasm.

I was the only white person in the group and I took a bow and that kind of thing.

When I went back to the white educational leadership, I told them there was a possibility that the Negro group would be willing to call off this sit-in and that they were going to institute legal action. "Well, they shouldn't. Tell them not to." I said that I had nothing to do with that decision, that it was up to the Negro group to sue if that was what they wanted to....

By this time the pressure on the liberal minister had developed to such an extent that...his board was demanding his resignation from the church. I offered a type of trade—I didn't have any enforcement power—if they'd call off the war on the minister as part of the total mediation as the thing moved into the law courts.... They blustered, but there wasn't much they could do. Certainly they didn't like the notion of being sued. They were conscious, too, of the poor publicity. They were conscious of the riot threat, etc.... So it ended at that point, with the determination of the Negro community to sue in the courts.

The next morning, three days after the sit-in began, no black children went to the white schools. I mustered what remained of my energy, reported by phone to Springfield, and drove back to Champaign to get some sleep. One of the nation's first sit-ins by black children had ended. The quest for admission to the schools moved from the streets to the courts.

The lawsuit was filed on February 3, 1950. The night after the suit was filed, two fiery crosses were burned in the city. One was located in the Negro area of the city, the other across the

Mississippi River in Missouri, clearly visible in Alton. Governor Stevenson denounced the action as the work of the Ku Klux Klan. On the night of May 17, 1950, more crosses were burned. During the summer the Alton Ministerial Association attempted to institute some community planning. Little resulted from this. Shortly afterward, in September 1950, the liberal minister who had been active in the living-room liberal group with which I met was dismissed by the Unitarian church. *Time* magazine ran a sympathetic story on his dismissal. In July 1950 the Alton Forum, a human relations group, was initiated by fifty citizens and held meetings throughout 1950-1954.

Faced with the possibility of losing about $300,000 in aid from the state of Illinois, the Alton Board of Education, during the fall of 1951, reconsidered the problem of desegregation. A "school of choice" policy evolved. Since the white schools were opened up for attendance by black children in January 1952, the Negro suit was no longer pertinent and was dropped by Alton's blacks. The black children of Alton had won in the struggle against the white establishment.

At the first meeting of the Illinois Interracial Commission that I attended following the January 1950 sit-in, I reported on the Alton experience. Thereafter I met monthly with the other members of the commission until late in 1951, when I left Illinois. We dealt with many instances of discrimination, the most sadly absurd being the refusal of a concessionaire to serve food to black children in a state park honoring the memory of the Great Emancipator, Abraham Lincoln. The commission made short shrift of that and other cases of discrimination brought before us. Governor Adlai E. Stevenson, always generous with praise, wrote me, in accepting my resignation, "I do want you to know how much I appreciate your cooperative and helpful spirit, and how grateful I am for the intelligent and loyal service which you gave to the Commission during my administration." No part of that attempted service had given me more personal satisfaction than had that first assignment to mediate in Alton, avoid racial violence, and move the conflict into an arena where the Alton black children could triumph.

Chapter Twenty-Seven

AT PEABODY COLLEGE
IN THE SOUTH

N ever doubt the wisdom of Dame Rumor. Though people often bad-mouth her she frequently knows whereof she speaks. At the annual conventions I attended in the winter of 1951, friends would sidle up to me and say in hushed confidential tones, "I hear you're going to Peabody." I would respond blankly, "Where's Peabody?" (I really knew), or say with simulated anxiety, "Is Illinois trying to get rid of me?" Back in my classes I used my friends' comments as an illustration of the worthlessness of rumors.

What was happening, of course, was that Peabody was considering making me an offer. The administration had instructed the Peabody staff to get reactions to me and my work. In the spring of 1951 I was offered the chairmanship of the Division of Curriculum and Teaching at George Peabody College for Teachers.

In Nashville, Tennessee, modestly self-titled "The Athens of the South," George Peabody College for Teachers had earned a reputation as the Teachers College of the South. The private college had an excellent faculty and a lovely campus. But to philanthropic foundations across America and to much of the educational world Peabody was President Henry H. Hill.

In 1951 President Hill had just achieved another coup. He had persuaded the General Education Board (Rockefeller money) to finance the appointment of heads for each of four newly created divisions at Peabody. In 1949 a committee made up of Hollis L. Caswell, George D. Stoddard, and William F. Russell (chairman), president of Teachers College, had developed *Pro-*

posals for the Future Development of George Peabody College for Teachers. The proposals envisaged "...a whole new plan—the Peabody Plan. It calls for the abandonment of present departments and many of the course offerings and for the creation of four *Educational Task Forces* to sail through partially uncharted seas and to bring the full firepower of education upon our enemies—poverty, disease, immorality, ignorance, selfishness, hatred and intolerance, inequality of opportunity, and tyranny. We suggest for these task forces the titles of *Teaching and Curriculum Development, School Administration and Community Leadership, Human Development and Guidance,* and *Education and Social Progress.*" As the 1950s opened, the General Education Board supplied funding to pay the salaries of four people brought in from across the nation to head the new divisions.

President Hill sought and secured the services of the legendary Harold Raymond Wayne Benjamin as head of the Division of Social Foundations (a retitling of Education and Social Progress). Ben's career is almost impossible to capsule. Once when I introduced him to a summer audience, I asked myself and my listeners which Harold Benjamin I should describe. The educator who was a teacher-principal and superintendent in Oregon and then a university teacher and administrator at Stanford, Minnesota, Colorado, and most recently dean at Maryland? The scholar who wrote on Latin American history and leaders? The advocate of democracy in education and American life who wrote *Under Their Own Command* and *The Cultivation of Idiosyncrasy?* The J. Abner Peddiwell (his pseudonym) who wrote the marvelous fable, *The Saber-Tooth Curriculum?* The liberal who battled unflinchingly for academic freedom? The military man who fought in a Mexican campaign as a muleskinner, in the trenches during World War I, as an officer in World War II? The man of peace who was technical advisor at the inception of UNESCO and on postwar missions to Japan and Afghanistan? The man who rolled his own cigarettes with one hand? The speaker whom everyone in education wanted to hear? Ben was versatile, colorful, and outspoken.

Willard E. Goslin, engaged by President Hill to head the Division of Administration and Community Development, had just resigned as superintendent at Pasadena, California. Reactionary forces had engineered his dismissal because his Pasadena school system taught about peace, race relations, environmental abuses, and similar "subversive" matters. Goslin, who had been the president of the prestigious American Association of School Administrators, had come into national prominence because of the Pasadena case. A trade book, *This Happened in Pasadena*, was being written about the Pasadena affair. Willard liked to tell his audiences that he was just a simple country boy; in reality, he was a highly knowledgeable and sophisticated man who had served successfully as superintendent in suburban Webster Groves, Missouri, and urban Minneapolis. He was a spellbinding speaker with the ability to bring audiences to their feet. Willard was a crusader, a liberal, and a charismatic leader.

The third of the division heads was Nicholas Hobbs, already well-known as a psychologist. Nick had been an associate professor at Teachers College and chairman of the Department of Psychology at Louisiana State University. The youngest of the group, his work as director of Kennedy Center for Research on Education and Human Development, his national honors on Presidents' panels and national advisory boards on mental health, his presidency of the American Psychological Association, and his role as provost at Vanderbilt University were still to come. Nick was quiet, soft-spoken, and reflective; less widely known than either Ben or Willard, he was obviously destined to become a national figure.

For his fourth division head, Henry Hill decided on me. I suspect he may have had his reservations. Henry Hill, born and bred in the South, was an administrator, a gentleman and a churchgoer, a moderate who prized the golden mean and the middle road. In his office I saw on his wall the quotation from Alexander Pope that guided him, "Be not the first by whom the new are tried, nor yet the last to lay the old aside." President Hill had already moved substantially toward "the new" in employing such mavericks as Ben and Willard. Now me?

It wasn't simply that I was a Yankee; after all, so was the sainted George Peabody, whose philanthropy had funded the college after the War between the States, as the South still called it. But I was also a New Yorker born and bred, unchurched, a left liberal, a member of the Illinois Interracial Commission, a prolific writer on race relations, and a person who had worked on desegregation of schools and communities. My wife's activities included leadership of an American Association of University Women's survey on race relations in the Champaign schools and active support of Catholic interracial programs. Little wonder that as our initial interview progressed Henry Hill expressed his hope that we wouldn't live in a Negro neighborhood. In turn, it was little wonder if he was startled when I asked about a written contract. A contract? There were no contracts at Peabody. At Peabody, Henry Hill's word was the only contract.

Many things militated against acceptance of the Peabody offer. I was happy as the proverbial lark as a professor at the University of Illinois; I liked my teaching, my university, my social life, my state roles, and my academic freedom. A generous letter from my Illinois friends, received after I accepted Peabody's offer, summed up the attractions Illinois had for me.

The letter reached me in California, where I was teaching during the summer of 1951. My family and I liked the opportunity Illinois afforded me to teach across the country during every second summer session; we had lived in the mountains when I taught in 1949 at the University of Denver and were now living in Altadena while I taught at the University of Southern California's summer session. In Champaign the older children were well settled in good schools, and Roy was about to enter school. Bee was scheduled for the presidency of the local Parent-Teachers Association.

True, Peabody offered more money, $9,500 for the academic year plus $2,500 for the summer, a whopping salary for the times. At Illinois I had risen from a $5,000 academic year salary in 1947 to $6,714 in 1950. With summer teaching and frequent consultation, I was earning between $10,000 and $11,000 annually.

But Peabody was a tremendous challenge. The post invited me to put my social and curricular beliefs into effect in a higher education institution and in a new (to me) region of the country. The headship offered me the opportunity to work with Ben and Willard and Nick to implement the rhetoric—"to bring the full firepower of education upon our enemies—poverty, disease, immorality, ignorance, selfishness, hatred and intolerance, inequality of opportunity, and tyranny."

A college president tipped the balance. Not Peabody's president but Charles S. Johnson, president of Nashville's famous black college, Fisk University. I talked to him by phone and asked whether a white Yankee could help to make a difference in the South at this stage. Johnson said yes. I became a teacher and division head at Peabody in the fall of 1951 and took responsibility for curriculum leadership of the largest division, Curriculum and Teaching.

At Peabody I had an ideal teaching program that included large and small classes. I usually taught a high-enrollment course in curriculum that reached most of the graduate students regardless of their fields of specialization. The course opened with challenges through films on school and society. For instance, *And So They Live*, a film created by a commission of the Progressive Education Association, portrayed the starved and barren existence of a mountain family in the nearby Appalachians and the total irrelevance of the schooling of the children to family and community living. At the film's close, I would simply ask my shocked students, "What's a school for, anyway?" Discussion would rage. Only after concern for a meaningful curriculum had been created did we move into lectures, discussions, and readings on conflicting ideas on curriculum and into proposals for a balanced and significant school curriculum as developed by subcommittees representing all teaching fields. Summers limited me to the Peabody campus, yet gave me the opportunity to work closely with doctoral students year round and to foster the future careers of a favorite few who were to rise high in the profession.[1]

---

[1] They included DeGroff Platte, who became a California curriculum director; Richard Gibboney, commissioner of education in the East and professor at the University of Pennsylvania; Gordon Vars, core curriculum leader at Kent State; John Lounsbury, the dean at Georgia College in Milledgeville; Harold Turner, professor and chairman at the University of Missouri; Bill Hedges, professor and chairman at the University of Florida; Bob Thurman, professor at the University of Tennessee; Jack Blackburn, dean at Auburn University; and John Groebli, Peace Corps, dean at Santa Barbara, and a successful entrepreneur. David Turney came in as my assistant as I was leaving Peabody; Blackburn's Peabody M.A. preceded his NYU doctorate with me.

From earlier experiences at Ohio State, Illinois, and visiting summer professorships, I was at home with teaching. The novel challenge to the Peabody division heads was, however, to improve the graduate and undergraduate college curriculum and to do it without carrots and sticks. The president, the two deans, and to a lesser degree the chairmen of the departments within the division held all the carrots and sticks; the division heads had no relationship to hiring/firing, salaries, promotion, or tenure.

How best to work with the Peabody faculty? Walking the campus one day early in the fall with Peabody's veteran sociologist, H. C. Brearley, I asked about the power structure in Peabody's faculty. What were the factions? Brearley replied memorably, "At Peabody every man is his own faction." He was right. Unlike Illinois professors, Peabody faculty members usually worked as individuals, not in teams. As soloists, they taught and counseled their students, wrote their textbooks, worked through their organizations, drove to individual appointments to consult within the state. Those in high demand often flew afield to speaking engagements, consultation, and conferences; a professorial joke was that Peabody divisional meetings should be held in the Nashville airlines terminal. Opportunities to work together as a faculty were few.

The Russell-Caswell-Stoddard proposal had been double-barrelled:

> The Peabody tradition, the continuing need for top-level leadership in education, and the importance of giving attention to the regional problems of education in the South lead us to recommend that Peabody firmly accept as its central function the maintenance of an advanced professional school for educational personnel and that it undertake nothing that diverts its facilities, resources, or faculty from this purpose.

> Specifically, we recommend that the general undergraduate program, as now organized, be dropped in its entirety and that the advanced professional program be made the focus of attention. We believe that the advanced program may be supported by a two-year senior college program open only to students who have chosen teaching as a profession and to experienced teachers who do not have the A.B. degree.

The response of the Peabody administration had been (a) to

secure financial support for four division heads yet (b) to continue rather than drop the four-year general undergraduate college. Tongue in cheek, some faculty members dubbed the new division heads the Four Horsemen.

The resultant divisions were lopsided as to membership. As Ben put it, whenever he needed a meeting of the Division of Social Foundations, he would go to the office of Professor Clifton Hall and sit on his desk, for Ben and Hall were the entire social foundations faculty. Willard and Nick divided twenty-five other faculty members. However, when a meeting of the Division of Curriculum and Teaching was needed, I would convene 91 faculty members of Peabody's 118, for the division included all teachers in the undergraduate departments of the four-year college, all teachers of the demonstration school, and a large majority of the graduate professors. Thus a Division of Curriculum and Teaching meeting was almost as large as the regular total faculty meetings that President Hill called occasionally to share information of general interest with the faculty.

The new division heads moved into program improvement through both divisional activities and facultywide programs. Two years later I could write in my annual report, "The most significant achievement of our young Division of Curriculum and Teaching to date is the general education program. The past two years have seen a general education program grow from a hope to an actuality on the Peabody campus. The Division of Curriculum and Teaching, in October 1951, named general education as one of six major problems for emphasis. At that time there was little optimism among the Peabody faculty about the possibility of instituting a general education program." Action was swift, for the faculty had been stung by the repeated use of the word "ordinary" in the Russell-Caswell-Stoddard report:

> The undergraduate college is an ordinary college of liberal arts, less conservative than many Southern colleges and with more than the usual emphasis on education, librarianship, and nursing education. Nevertheless, it is apparently not organized to demonstrate modern trends in general education....
>
> It is certainly not in the forefront of modern experimentation on problems of collegiate education. The college was developed to meet financial needs, especially in the wake of the

depression of 1929-35....

Inspection of the catalog reveals that the organization of courses and departments, and the types of courses offered, resemble more those of an ordinary college (with an exceptional offering in education) than of a truly advanced professional school.

During the first two years, the division also achieved an interdisciplinary degree in the social sciences, agreement on the functions of the Demonstration School, establishment of blocks of time in its elementary school program, and a core curriculum in its junior high school years. The college catalog, which had been published by the dean of administration as a record of the past, was now to be published before the opening of each academic year. The Division of Curriculum and Teaching worked on improving the student teaching program, revising the undergraduate program in professional education, and exploring possibilities of service research. Still to come was a development of a program for the education of college teachers, examination of service courses, and writing of descriptions of positions for which Peabody trained.

In the second year, monthly divisional meetings were succeeded by meetings of the departments to carry out new all-college programs. The four division heads had helped to develop a five-point program for faculty study; a working paper titled *Peabody in 1965* was issued in May 1952. The selected five points were tightening up administratively, a creative teaching program, a selected student body (especially urged by Nick Hobbs), a service-research program, and a program for international education (ambitiously limned by Harold Benjamin).

In the fall of 1952, the faculty gathered for an unprecedented two-day conference at Montgomery Bell State Park to move the five-point program forward. Faculty members chose one of five work groups and came up with recommendations.

At the opening of the first of a series of faculty meetings called to consider the conference recommendations, President Hill commented that the meeting had turned out well, better than he expected, and that he had noticed "euphoria" after the conference. He pointed out that the committee had proposed ideas and suggested policies; now the results should be channelled to existing committees. In a preface to my report on the conference, he wrote, "Perhaps an educational venture will find the longer way of presentation, discussion, and modification a better procedure towards a better goal than any quick or non-matured move." In this atmosphere, faculty consideration of the recommendations began.

Since I had chaired the Montgomery Bell conference, I took responsibility for a progress report on the five-point program at the end of the academic year in 1953. Necessarily, I reminded some administrators and faculty members of faculty actions that had been implemented and other faculty actions that had been ignored. Such a report was undoubtedly a way of influencing people, but it can't be recommended as a way of making friends. The role of serving as the conscience of a college guarantees opposition from those dedicated to letting sleeping dogs lie. As one sage had said, changing a curriculum is like moving a grave-yard; until you try it you don't realize how many friends the dead still have.

In October 1953, back to Montgomery Bell State Park came the faculty for another two-day conference, this time on creative teaching. During the third and fourth year of my chairmanship, the Division of Curriculum and Teaching worked on the general education program, initiated an Ed.S. degree, achieved a fall quarter for student teaching, and worked on improving our use of community resources.

During 1955 I urged the division to work on the liberalizing content of the curriculum, the delicate problem of relating liberal arts courses to the professional needs of teachers. This was essential to achieving curricular balance among general, profes-sional, and liberalizing content. We had reconsidered and recon-structed general education and our professional programs. Now we needed to examine the liberal arts component. But to some faculty members the reexamination of liberalizing content threat-ened favorite courses and established ways of handling classes and content. So the division discussed but was unwilling to appoint *ad hoc* committees or to make recommendations to established all-college committees.

By now the vigorous pace of the 1951-55 meetings and programs of curriculum reconstruction had begun to tell on the faculty. Many changes had been instituted in the program within the control of the professors. Changes calling for substantial funding, such as released time to develop service-research, or an ambitious program of international education, or eliminating some students by raising standards of admission, were stymied at the administrative level through Peabody's perennial lack of funds. As the faculty saw it, without substantial funds for venturesome programs they had gone about as far as they could go.

In such a situation, faculties are inclined to attempt to pass responsibilities for major curricular changes to administrators and heads. So I tried a proposal to the Ford Foundation to help on the liberalizing content problem; it was rejected by the philanthropoids. I developed a proposal for service-research that involved released time for staff members so that they might work in the field. The college administration couldn't underwrite the necessary released time from teaching.

Substantial curriculum changes had been made in four years, despite the difficulties inherent in the change process of any college. By about 1955, Peabody ran out of curricular steam and the energy investment of leadership was diverted into other fields. Henry Hill focused on fund raising, particularly from the new philanthropic power, the Ford Foundation. Ford did finance a fifth-year program for liberal arts graduates; I taught some classes in this special degree program. The division chairmen collaborated with the president on still other proposals to foundations. Most were not funded. Harold Benjamin went off on a mission to South Korea, 1954-55, and Willard Goslin soon followed. Nick Hobbs concentrated on obtaining support in Washington for mental health and human development centers at Peabody. I continued to plug along at whatever curriculum changes could be made within Peabody College's financial limitations.

Peabody offered a much better program in the academic year 1955-56 than it had in 1951 when the Four Horsemen rode in. But the halcyon days of curriculum development at Peabody were over.

Chapter Twenty-Eight

AGAINST
REACTIONARY FORCES

oday's fashion in ideas is to describe the 1950s as a passive decade, a time of apathy, an era in which nothing happened. I didn't find it so, for I got involved in two sharp social conflicts: first the 1950-1954 struggle against the reactionary forces that were attacking education and later the 1954-1957 struggle against racism and public school segregation.

In 1950 Senator Joseph McCarthy rose to national prominence with his charge that the State Department was "thoroughly infested with Communists." His accusations via radio and television became increasingly reckless, mounted further when he chaired the Senate permanent investigations subcommittee, and culminated in 1954 with his contention that the Secretary of the Army had concealed evidence of espionage. In December 1954, the Senate, acting on a motion of censure against him, condemned McCarthy and ended his influence. During this period of sensationalist tactics and unsubstantiated accusations by McCarthy, education came under fire by reactionary individuals and groups that used the tactics of McCarthyism.

Understandably, the media paid more attention to Joseph McCarthy and his political invective than to the educational McCarthyites who attacked modern elementary and secondary school programs. McCarthy worked primarily on the national scene to create suspicion and fear through irresponsible charges against individuals and groups; the McCarthyites assailing public education did their dirty work primarily in communities through attacks on local systems and personnel.

The educational McCarthyites passionately hated anything that related even faintly to progressive education, which they denounced as an un-American, subversive, godless, atheistic, Communist conspiracy. Their special *bêtes noires* were John Dewey, William Heard Kilpatrick, George S. Counts, Harold Rugg, the Progressive Education Association, and the National Education Association. Armed with lurid pamphlets that catalogued the sins of the progressives, promoters of national right-wing crusades descended upon local communities, organized meetings, and attempted to attract grassroots support. Their meetings initially included solid citizens critical of weaknesses of public schools, conservatives who rejected excesses in modern education, and traditionalists in religion who preferred nonpublic schools. But the more moderate members of such groups frequently became disillusioned, so the hard core adherents who remained true believers were usually a mixed bag of economic royalists, tax cutters, superpatriots, and religious zealots, plus assorted racists, bigots, and other monomaniacal kooks. Following preliminary agitation, publicized by the media, their representatives attacked school programs and personnel at school board meetings packed with vocal supporters of the critics. They hurled charges of radicalism and subversion, atheism and irreligion, treason and un-Americanism. Having created their stir, organizers often moved on to new territory, leaving local dissidents to follow through with vitriolic campaigns.

Educators were frequently unready to respond to character assassinations through guilt-by-association techniques. Supporters of the public schools were often taken by surprise. It usually took considerable time to rally moderate individuals and groups and to respond to wild charges that utilized the Hitler technique of the big lie.

The assault on educators and public education by reactionary forces came early in my Nashville stay. The Illinois struggles against the Broyles bills threatening academic freedom and the bill to censor textbooks and other learning materials had warned me of what might be ahead. As early as October 1949 I wrote an Importance of People column in *Educational Leadership*, "The Climate of Fear," which was a tongue-in-cheek satire through which I suggested that the Communists had taken over highly conservative right-wing organizations. How else, I asked, can we explain right-wing advocacy and use of Communist techniques: censorship of textbooks, espionage on colleagues, avoiding open discussion of controversial issues?

Irony is a tricky weapon; some readers took seriously my fanciful contention that the far right had been infiltrated by the far left and even told me in dead earnest of far rightists whom they suspected to be representatives of the Communist Party. Rather than helping to dispel the climate of fear, my column may possibly have contributed to its spread, for the country was on its way to paranoia. My later columns were more explicit: "Let's Communicate Democratic Education" and "Cheaters of Children."

In the early 1950s, with McCarthyism a reality and little McCarthys yapping at the heels of educators through publications and legislation, I joined with kin spirits in urging national organizations in education to recognize the threat. The John Dewey Society responded with a 1953 yearbook, edited by my former Ohio State University professor, H. Gordon Hullfish, and sponsored by a yearbook committee made up of Hank Hullfish, me, and V. T. Thayer, long affiliated with Ethical Culture Schools, a veteran of the progressive education movement, and a gallant defender of freedom. I contributed an introduction to *Educational Freedom in an Age of Anxiety*.

> ...*Educational Freedom in an Age of Anxiety* is about old and enduring issues. Its contributors are not neutral. They believe in freedom of inquiry. They believe in the right of individuals to decide from among alternatives. They believe in educational freedom. They believe in the democratic method of intelligence. They dislike totalitarianism in any shape. That includes communism. They believe that it would be tragic if in combating communism in this age of anxiety our nation should embrace totalitarian means and ends. They believe that we cannot save democracy by jettisoning freedom of inquiry. For freedom of inquiry is central in the meaning of democracy. Freedom of inquiry is what differentiates us from the totalitarians....

The Association for Supervision and Curriculum Development, larger and more influential than the John Dewey Society, also developed a 1953 yearbook on reactionary forces and the schools.

The foreword traces its evolution:

> The yearbook had its origin in the late nineteen-forties when
> William H. Burton of Harvard University tirelessly attempted
> to rouse the concern of the educational profession over new
> developments in forces affecting education. Few heeded him
> until the nineteen-fifties when marked criticisms of outstand-
> ing school systems attracted nation-wide attention through
> newspaper, radio, magazine and book coverage. Burton, weary
> and in poor health, for a time literally a casualty of the struggle
> for freedom of the mind, was unable to continue as editor of the
> yearbook which he had proposed after several years as chair-
> man of an ASCD committee on forces affecting education.

In 1951, the ASCD appointed me chairman of the yearbook committee. The committee members recommended that the manuscript be prepared by educators located in the same general geographical area, thus affording opportunities for the writers to meet together and develop a common point of view. The twelve-person yearbook committee included Harold Benjamin, Willard E. Goslin, and me; the committee recommended that the writing committee be made up of the three of us from Peabody plus Charles S. Johnson, president of Fisk University in Nashville, and Robert A. Skaife, field secretary of the National Commission for the Defense of Democracy Through Education, sponsored by the National Education Association. Bob's offices were in not-too-distant Washington and contained extensive files on supporters and destructive critics of public education. The non-writing segment of the yearbook committee included Bob's chief at the commission, two superintendents of schools, a curriculum director, a former president of the National Congress of Parents and Teachers, a laboratory school director, two professors, and Bill Burton.

In the yearbook we used a variety of approaches to try to counter the forces that were affecting education at the time. My first chapter, "The Task of the Educator," set forth the democratic philosophy on which the book was based. Charles S. Johnson then described "The Culture Affecting Education." The longest chapter of the book, "Groups Affecting Education," was written by Skaife. In it he described organizations and individuals attacking public education, the national organizations that were supportive of schools, and how support for the schools developed in conflict situations at the local level. In his chapter he named organizations and individuals who were active in the current controversies. Harold Benjamin, in "Communication Affecting Education," wrote on the American tradition in communication and on communication agencies today. I then reported on "Research Affecting Education." Willard E. Goslin closed the book with "The People and Their Schools," in which he stressed that the schools belong to the people. He set forth a program of community participation, described responsible citizen groups, and closed with a challenge to educational leadership.

The yearbook committee participated in each step in the development of the book. The committee originated ideas, criticized over-all outlines, revised the basic draft, and corrected galley proofs.

The authors met together occasionally, shared outlines, and criticized each other's work. The writers worked together on the whole book, from developing a preliminary draft to revising galley proofs.

Forces Affecting American Education was published early in 1953, and all involved braced themselves for the inevitable vitriolic attack from right-wingers. The custom at ASCD was to present the annual yearbook to the membership through a session of the national conference that was held yearly. The writers of the yearbook took turns in talking to a session attended by the entire ASCD conference in 1953 in Cleveland, Ohio.

I opened with a summary of my first chapter: the struggle between democracy and authoritarianism, the major social realities of our times, the impact of scientific findings in psychology. I gave most of my time to the great debates on education: on modern versus traditional education, on the child-centered school, on philosophic direction, on the school and society. I closed with advocacy of full citizenship rights for teachers and a free play of intelligence, rather than indoctrination, in classrooms.

When Willard Goslin, as final speaker, took to the podium he completely surprised the audience, shocked the yearbook committee and the writers, and stunned me. In effect, he repudiated the yearbook that he had helped to develop at all stages and to which he had contributed a chapter. He said (the excerpts are direct quotations from a tape made at the conference):

> If you say what I said, use the same words...
> ...This yearbook, it's dangerous. It's dangerous for what isn't in it. The chips are down in America....
> I don't believe that this organization through its committee and those who did the writing, and remember I'm one of them, lived up for a minute to the dreams and ideas of Bill Burton when he began to develop this concept three or four years ago. The committee itself, or the writing segment of it, was tempted to go over to the promised land and do something about this job. But each time we passed away. Then if, in addition, we ever did get an idea written down that had some punch in it, it was only a matter of time till we talked ourselves out of it....
> ...One of the insidious forces is inside the teaching profession. I refer to superintendents who'll administer.... They're not going to have anything to do with the program.... I'm talking about nearly every one of us who are just playing it safe waiting for it to blow over....
> There are no bald, clear-cut statements in this yearbook telling about the struggle that's on in America about changed relationships between citizens of different racial backgrounds and its impact on the school system ...in fact, that several states are cocked and primed to do away with their public schools.... Charlie Johnson [the black president of Fisk University] covers it in the broad, fine language of a magnificent sociologist (laughter)....
> There are not ten lines in this yearbook on the great struggle and tension that blows up in America on the relationship of religion to other organized phases of American life.
> ...But I'm afraid of this yearbook because it will lull too many people to sleep or keep them from waking up. Because it doesn't deal with sufficient realism on the rough, rugged internal pressures that are on this school system here and now.
> It's done in good language.... There are only two or three grammatical errors in it (laughter).
> Bill has a wonderful time with his great debates.... The chapter Bob Skaife wrote six or eight months ago and that he delivered here tonight is good. The one in between sags a little.... Ben didn't write about communication like he talked to me going up on the plane (laughter). I didn't do any better than the rest of them. So make sure that you read this yearbook understanding that it is a good step in the direction

of understanding forces operating on education. But it is an elementary course (laughter).

At the close of the session, admirers swarmed around Goslin. One disbelieving ASCDer asked me whether Goslin's talk was a ploy developed by Ben, Willard, and me to insure wide readership. I confessed my complete surprise. Goslin had never indicated any dissatisfaction whatsoever to the committee or the writers at any time concerning the content or the process of development of the yearbook. He had participated in all its stages since the inception of the yearbook committee. In his own chapter he had not dealt with racial or religious issues, nor did he name destructive forces.

Why did Goslin repudiate the book he had played a major role in creating? To this day I don't know for sure, and I am unwilling to speculate here.

I talked with Willard about the matter only once. Willard and I were scheduled to present the yearbook to the American Association of School Administrators at their convention in Atlantic City a few days after the ASCD meeting. I told him that I had scheduled him to speak first. If he chose to denigrate the book, I would tell the audience that he had voiced none of his criticisms during the making of the yearbook, despite abundant opportunities to do so. I would detail his participation in the development of the book and his acceptance of the manuscript, the editing, and the galleys. I would point out the opportunities he had to speak out in his chapter for whatever he believed.

At the AASA convention Willard spoke first. He delivered a completely different speech from the one he made at ASCD. His talk contained no criticism of the book. I then delivered the same talk I had given at the ASCD; I had no need to use the special version I had prepared that dealt with Goslin's criticisms at the ASCD conference.

Though the comments by Goslin were unanticipated, the onslaught on the book that came from the right-wing forces was no surprise. *Forces Affecting American Education* hadn't minced words. The book had named names and cited conflict situations.

Right-wing journals such as *Human Events* reviewed the book negatively. The most venomous of the reviews were included in the *Congressional Record* by right-wing congressmen. One individual whose attacks on a local school system Skaife had described wrote an eleven-page, single-spaced letter to me and ASCD officialdom. The letter was notarized and sent by registered mail; a libel suit seemed imminent.

Though Goslin had said that "There are not ten lines...on the relationship of religion to other organized phases of American life," the most persistent onslaught on *Forces* was conducted by James Francis Cardinal McIntyre, archbishop of Los Angeles. In 1953 *Current Biography* wrote of Cardinal McIntyre that in 1951 he "attracted national attention when he stated the Government was 'devoid of principle,' a situation for which he blamed 'whimsical evaluations of justice and equity...based on a purely social concept' by Supreme Court Justices Oliver Wendell Holmes and Felix Frankfurter (New York *Times*, January 29, 1951). The following December the prelate again roused controversy by questioning the fitness of Mrs. Franklin D. Roosevelt to be chairman of the United Nations Human Rights Commission because she had expressed uncertainty as to the exact form which personal immortality might take."

In 1953 Cardinal McIntyre was highly critical of the National Education Association. The *Houston Chronicle* reported that in an interview after a Houston speech, the cardinal "recalled that in recent lectures in Dallas and Fort Worth he had decried apparent tinges of Communist philosophy in the 1953 yearbook of the National Education Association."

The United Press covered Cardinal McIntyre's Dallas speech, aided by a release of his talk from the *Catholic Tidings* in Los Angeles. As reported in the *Washinglon Daily News*, October 28, 1953, under the headline "Cardinal Finds Red System in NEA Book," the UP story said:

> DALLAS, Tex., Oct. 28—A Catholic cardinal says a new book from the National Education Association preaches a kind of "progressive" education similar to "the philosophy of communism."
>
> James Francis Cardinal McIntyre, Archbishop of Los Angeles, Calif., attacked the book in a speech before the annual Christian Culture Lecture series last night.
>
> Altho he did not name the book in his speech, his secretary

said he was referring to the 1953 yearbook of the Association for Supervision and Curriculum Development, a department of the National Education Association.

Brain Washing

The book is titled "Forces Affecting American Education."

Cardinal McIntyre referred only to "our largest educational association."

He called "progressive" education "an education without God, without soul without immortality."

He said the same principles that guide "progressive" education were the basis of the brain-washing of American Korean war prisoners by communists.

The book, published recently by proponents of "progressive" education, claims "there is nothing immutable, fixed, stable, enduring, permanent in their system, there is nothing to learn from history, the riches of the past, the experience of the race," he said.

As a result of this philosophy of education, "we may soon hear that stealing is not wrong," the Cardinal said.

Similarity

He said because the system advocated in the book has "such a strong affinity in its outlook to the philosophy of communism, it is reasonable to see in the movement a danger of great magnitude to the stability of what we treasure as sound American education."

Cardinal McIntyre noted the similarity between beliefs held in the book and "the experience of our hero-sons brainwashed in Korean communist prison camps."

"According to the book we are considering, the so-called 'democratic' form of education considers it essential to progress that men should argue, even endlessly, hypothesize, even senselessly, advance proposals, even recklessly, experiment, even goallessly, destroy old values and reconstruct new ideals without necessarily final formulation," he said.

The executive secretary of the ASCD immediately issued a reply. As George Denemark commented later to the membership, "As is so often the case in such matters, the initial sweeping charges against the yearbook received wide national coverage on the radio and in the press, while the reply documenting what the book actually says appeared only spottily." The statement by Denemark read:

James Francis Cardinal McIntyre is quoted by the press in criticism of *Forces Affecting American Education*, a publication of the Association for Supervision and Curriculum Development, a Department of the NEA. The Cardinal ascribes to the book a point of view which it specifically rejects. He is reported to have said that the "book claims there is nothing immutable, fixed, stable, enduring, permanent in their system, there is nothing to learn from history, the riches of the past, the experience of the race." No such statement appears anywhere in the book.

Reference to the first chapter of *Forces Affecting American Education* would have disclosed the philosophic statement upon which the book is based, as follows: "...Democracy as a way of life is deeply rooted in world and American tradition. Its principles are based on man's experience. Thus democratic principles derive not only from contemporary life but also from man's long history, from the insights of religion, from the great ethical convictions of man. The democratic principles of worth of the individual, of widening the area of shared interests, of working together for common purposes commonly arrived at, and of using the method of intelligence have a distinguished lineage. These world ancestors of democratic principles include....Jesus...."

A further misinterpretation by the Cardinal may be found in his reported comment that "there is a similarity between beliefs held in the book and the experience of our hero-sons brain-washed in Korean communist prison camps. They were obliged to discuss proposals, to destroy ideas, to question ideals, and then after indoctrination to reconstruct the mind again."

Such a philosophy of indoctrination is diametrically opposed in the book criticised by the Cardinal. The right of the student to think, to reach his own conclusions without the imposition of ready-made ideals is clearly indicated in the following statement from the book: "Commitment to the method of free intelligence does not mean that today's teacher never expresses an opinion. But it does mean that when he expresses his viewpoint he labels it as his own. He indicates that other men may disagree. He requires no one to conclude his way. He rejects all mental straitjackets, especially those he might unconsciously create. *He has no party line of left or right to be forced on learners.*"

Although the Cardinal's address purports to review the entire book, *Forces Affecting American Education*, he quotes only four words from its text.

245

Shortly after the cardinal's Dallas condemnation of *Forces Affecting American Education*, I was nominated as one of three candidates for the presidency-elect of the Association for Supervision and Curriculum Development. I was defeated.

Did the yearbooks and the gallant defenses of public education by such individuals as Ernest Melby and V. T. Thayer and such groups as the NEA's Commission for the Defense of Democracy turn back the reactionary attack of the early 1950s on public schools? Or was it belated yet effective responses at the community level by long-time supporters of public education such as the League of Women Voters, the National Congress of Parents and Teachers, the labor unions, the Anti-Defamation League, the American Jewish Committee, the American Association of University Women, and such newcomers as the National Citizens Commission for the Public Schools? Or was it the extremism of the attackers and the discrediting of the father figure, irresponsible Joseph McCarthy himself, that accounts for the retreat of the reactionary forces? No one knows for sure. We do know that by the mid-1950s McCarthy was stripped of power and the educational McCarthyites disappeared locally into obscurity, at least for the time being. Public education weathered the reactionary attack.

During the period of writing and publishing *Forces Affecting American Education*, I noticed that I was developing numbness in one leg. One of my feet dragged. I sometimes stumbled over carpets that rose even fractionally above the floor level. I checked with a doctor. Psychosomatic, he said. I didn't want to join Bill Burton as a casualty of McCarthyism. Nor Archibald MacLeish, who, as my guest following his Peabody lecture, chose milk rather than spirits because of an ulcer attributable to McCarthyism. So I sought out a psychologist to help me learn to live with conflict. "Teach me to expect and handle criticism," I said. He couldn't. After some visits over a period of months, I decided that I would have to go it alone. After a time my foot no longer dragged.

"If you can't stand the heat, get out of the kitchen," said Harry S Truman. Obviously, heat was hard on my emotional economy. Yet to stay out of the kitchen was unthinkable; it ran contrary to my beliefs and my self-image. So in the mid-Fifties I reentered the kitchen to work toward desegregation of Nashville's public schools. But first I took a holiday.

246

Chapter Twenty-Nine

TO EUROPE
AS A FAMILY

S ince our Danube and youth hosteling days, most of our vacations had grown out of side trips during my summer teaching in such locales as the Ozarks, the Rockies, and Southern California or had taken the form of visits to our parents on Long Island and to my sister in Virginia Beach. Now we decided upon a long holiday abroad during a semester of sabbatical leave from Peabody. So "We Went to Europe as a Family," as the following light-hearted account of our travels, published years later in *The Making of a Modern Educator*, Bobbs-Merrill, 1961, phrased it:

...Suddenly one cold day in 1954 I was 43. I don't know whether the Greeks have a word for it. But the Americans sure do. The word is not young. The word is middle-aged.

I was a college professor, well established in my chosen field. I was a suburban householder with a mortgage and a wife—same wife—whose age I have no intention of revealing to snoopers. I was par for the course as to children: Jon, fifteen; Barbara, thirteen; and Roy, nine [as of mid 1954]. My insurance was high and my cash was low. All in all, I was a respectable middle-class citizen. And the merciless travel bug chose this time to bite me fiercely again.

A humane policy of my college allied itself with the bug. Once every three full years a professor is granted a few months off with pay. His only assignment is to refresh his weary soul by drinking at whatever springs of knowledge and experience he chooses. I was due for fall 1954 and I knew what springs I needed. The Moselle. The Danube. A Long Island Duck III.

Maybe a microscopic car for jogging about The Continent.

But Europe in the Fall? Europe with my family? Particularly, Europe with my three children?

Respectable middle-class families have many ties which bind. In our home the phone rings madly. Often it brings tidings of the League of Women Voters. Bee is on "the board." Otherwise, it is for Barbara, blonde and budding at thirteen, whirling in her orbit of early teen-agers all engaged in learning who they are and whence this strange new power over boys.

Jon at fifteen also had his ties. As a high school sophomore he was scheduled to begin geometry, biology, and French, and to continue English. But it was a love affair my older son shares with Tallulah Bankhead which caused him the greatest pangs of parting. For as spring and summer wore on, the New York Giants hung grimly to first place in the National League. Jon was sometimes heard moaning, "Of all years to go to Europe—with the Giants ahead by seven games! With a World Series coming!"

Only Roy was a free man. At nine, he was as uncommitted as the weather. When he was emancipated from the fourth grade at school's end, with summer vacation and European fall lying ahead, he waved airily to his friends, "So long, boys; see you on January 3, 1955." They drooled and uttered strange cries into the soft May air.

Our best friends were as skeptical as they were tolerant. The literary among them dropped titles into their conversation: "You Can't Go Home Again," "The Revolt of the Middle-Aged Man." One bounder even suggested "Fire in the Ashes." Good souls warned us that we couldn't re-create the romantic atmosphere of Europe in the Spring, seventeen years previous. They assured us kindly that they meant that Europe had changed. But they didn't fool us even for a minute.

As to traveling with the youngest generation, Robert Benchley once contributed the definitive statement, "Traveling with children is like traveling third-class in Bulgaria." This is best understood by people who have traveled third-class in Bulgaria.

So—the five of us decided to go to Europe in the Fall as a family.

There remained the matter of money. How much was all of this going to cost, Professor, and where was the money coming from?

The same thought apparently occurred to many of our acquaintances. We would say, while trying hard to look like the

248

sophisticated people in the travel folders that flooded us, "We're going to Europe as a family. No, it's not a mission or a job abroad. We're just going to live in Europe awhile. Just...live." Glazed looks would slide over the faces of our listeners. Sometimes speculation took over. They hadn't heard news of my mother in a long time. Was she well? In fine health, never better, thank you. Had I published a textbook lately? No, I hadn't. I didn't own a Geiger counter, did I? Strike an oil well? Some people are too genteel to come right out with things.

I buried myself in guides for poor men and treatises on traveling on a shoestring. I consulted the standard travel books also, but found them too rich for my thin-blooded wallet. They advised: "...for unobtrusively wealthy travelers...where Farouk sometimes spends his nights...center for the international set...top of the heap in Venice is ..." You feel flattered but flabbergasted.

The rock bottom figure for a family-style ocean crossing is not hard to find. One hundred and sixty-five dollars was then the cost for each person each way between New York and The Continent, tourist class, off-season, on the best of ocean liners. Children under twelve are as blessedly half-fare as on your local railroad line.

Some beg, borrow, or steal $165 times X. More thoughtful people save. Others—and here I am carefully mentioning no names—use retirement annuities [from Ohio State University] in the firm but foolish conviction that they are immortal.

But there is an all-important figure that is harder to come by. Once off the boat, how much do we spend? What is the Daily Average Per Person In Europe or, as we came to call it familiarly, DAPPIE? This is strictly an Irish Sweepstakes question. Some travel books calculate your DAPPIE anywhere from $20 to $50, transportation extra.

I consulted my crystal ball, gulped rapidly, and decided our Daily Average Per Person In Europe would be $5.50, gasoline included.

Our planning was strange and wonderful. I worked out elaborate itineraries to which we paid no attention once in Europe. Bee prepared as though for a rocket trip to the moon. Would you think of bringing to Europe—take a deep breath— a pencil sharpener, Scotch tape, flashlight, extra shoelaces, a hard ball and a rubber ball, baseball hats and fielder's gloves, sneakers, moc sox, jeans, sunglasses and extra eye glasses, bathing suits, raincoats, color film, travel literature, *Huckle-*

berry Finn, Palgrave's *Golden Treasury*, geometry textbook, French textbook, playing cards, ball-point pen and fillers, document bags, plastic shoe bags, cigarettes, flatpack tissues, Noxzema, Old Overholt, instant coffee, Suave for cowlicks, bobby pins and curlers, money belt, Energine for spot removal, a knee supporter, sewing kit, hair clipper and scissors, iron and press cloth, five diaries, ten packs of gum and ten rolls of Life-Savers for European children as well as—time for another deep breath—aspirin, a thermometer, vitamin pills, nose drops and ear drops, S. T. 37, dramamine, and antibiotics? I wouldn't either. She did.

All of our worldly goods for August through December we packed into seven remarkable bags: a Japanese paratrooper bag, a Boy Scout duffel bag, a veteran canvas Valpak, a seventeen-year-old Yugoslavian straw bag, a worn-out brief case, a gaudy plaid shoe bag, and a sturdy item from an Army Surplus store. Porters turned pale at the sight of us. We didn't mind. We were mobile. Among the five of us we could carry all we brought to the European world. No, I don't know either how Bee got everything in.

For a hundred and fourteen days we were to sail the seas, paddle our foldboats, jaunt by car, and live in celebrated and forgotten towns and cities across France, Austria, Germany, Switzerland, and Italy. Before we got back, each of us, save our official postcard collector, Roy, was to write thirty to forty thousand words in our personal journals concerning how the world looked to us.

The *Ryndam* of the Holland America Line was so reassuringly like a resort that Roy gave up saying forebodingly, "Don't forget the *Titanic*." Paris was conventional tourism and the children's introduction to the mysteries of European hotels:

> ...They were enchanted with the pigmy elevator, a mirrored coffin which could hold three people if they were well acquainted. The elevator, passenger-operated, had a button labeled "stop." The children used it liberally for halts at such mythical levels as three and a half, three and three quarters, et cetera, on their trips between our rooms on floors two and five until a hotel employee made an impassioned address containing words not found in Jon's French textbook. Our promising scholar of French reported to me proudly, "I was able to answer, '*Je ne comprends pas*.'" I instructed my young in my best fatherly way, "But you shouldn't play with the

ascenseur." Barbara asked, " Isn't the *ascenseur* the man behind the desk in the lobby?" "That's the *concierge*," I responded wearily, wishing the French were sensible enough to use English. "He's cute, whatever his name is," Barbara said. But it was the plumbing of our Paris hotel which the younger generation found most strange and exotic. Of an antique toilet with pull chain, Roy wrote indignantly, "Even Grandma's fifty-year-old plumbing works better than that." I assume he was referring to what the French describe as the plumbing of the house of his grandmother.

Incidentally, none of the guidebooks are helpful on how to interpret French plumbing facilities to the growing mind of American youth....

...We would have needed a solid-gold shoestring if we had stayed long in Paris. So one gray morning at 5 o'clock, less than a week after we landed, a little Simca station wagon loaded with Van Tils and baggage stole from Paris. We were bound for Germany and the rivers. Yes, we bought a French car, confident that three months later we could sell it if we wished for $300 less and—let's see now—that would cost the family $3.33 1/3 cents per day or 66 2/3 cents Daily Average Per Person In Europe. Our Simca came to be called Marilyn, for reasons obvious at a glance....

...So after one long day—and seventeen years—we came again into Germany, the land of Dr. Jekyll and Mr. Hyde, of the honest friendly people who run amuck with militarism every second generation and take on the world. Saarburg was our destination, a lovely country town with castle ruins that look down on the Saar River, cobblestoned crooked streets, and precise patterns of grapevines that blanket the hills. In the best hotel, over one dollar dinners of rump steak, blue trout, *Wiener Schnitzel*, beer, and cokes, with three big bedrooms boasting four-foot-square fluffy featherbeds, our faith in the power of our shoestring was renewed. The owner of the *Hotel zur Post* was a dignified little old lady who perpetually bowed to us as she backed out of any room. She always addressed me as Professor New York and my family swears I don't know the difference between my name and my place of birth on the long registration form one fills out at every German hotel. When the little lady presented us with a bottle of Moselle wine on our departure, we hoped that Mr. Hyde was dead and that decent Dr. Jekyll had come back home to Germany to stay.

We bought two foldboats at a sports store in Trier, one a

vivid red and silver and the other a blue and silver descendant of earlier Long Island Ducks. ("Stop worrying, dear; we can sell both of them at a profit in America.") We left our car at the local canoe club. For nine blissful days we drifted and paddled 112 miles down the Moselle River to the Rhine.

To describe foldboating to one who has never cruised on a European river is hopeless. It's lolling deliciously in the sun in the fond belief that a paddle is something to lean on. It's waving to peasants on the steep shale slopes of the vineyards. It's riding the rips that flash around stone jetties that narrow the river and speed its current; it's whirling into backwaters and spinning out again into the main stream.

At noon we landed in little towns and stretched our legs in market squares that looked like the backdrops for Shake-spearean plays. Each evening we found rooms for the night in a local river-front hotel. Our boats we left overnight in places as various as a river bank, a dark cellar, a grand ballroom of a hotel, and a giant jail of a boat house under a bridge. After dinner we often climbed to the inevitable ruined castle brood-ing over the town. (Barbara once found it diary-worthy that "Today we passed a town with a **whole** castle.")

And sometimes, truth being truth, we noticed the little spots on the river, as Jon put it, and we grimly sat it out, covered by raincoats or whatever, until rain, the arch enemy of the river man, moved on to new conquests. Then there was the matter of our landing places. Jon holds that the old Captain was not at his best here. "One thing must be understood. Dad has a good eye for picking the dirtiest, slimiest, most mucky, icky, gooey spots in which to dock." Removing river ooze from under her toenails one night, Bee said briefly, "Sometimes I wonder." I always claim it's the unexpected which lies around the corner that gives life its tang....

...Where the Moselle met the Rhine, we packed the fold-boats. Marilyn was driven to us by an employee of the sports store where we bought our boats. The cost was his rail fare home plus a tip. We tied the foldboat sacks on top of the car and headed south. For the nine-day cruise on the Moselle, our Daily Average Per Person In Europe was $3.35.

In the Black Forest, cuckoo clock madness overcame us. Roy recorded, "We saw a cuckoo clock shop and then it started." How can madness be avoided when Black Forest clocks sell for ninety-six cents up? When the delirium had passed, we had added to our baggage eight clocks, elaborately carved, sur-

mounted by proud birds, and telling the hour at the slightest
provocation.

We might have stayed forever hiking in the Black Forest
or foldboating on Lake Constance to a reconstructed Stone Age
village and to an island with tropical vegetation in the shadow
of the frozen Alps. But the Danube still ran. So we came back
to our brown river and a brush with the Angel of Death. But not
on the old growler, which we found in flood. The brush came
nearby in a little walled town with clock towers dating from
1200 over each of its three entrances. Kelheim, beside the
German Danube, was our low point. There Roy, our youngest
and strongest, came down with pain.

It is a desolate feeling to be alone in a foreign land with a
sick child whose illness the local doctor cannot diagnose.
Nothing helps—medicine, time, reading *Huckleberry Finn*
aloud, planning ahead. For stabbing hours you try to turn back
the irreversible past and look into the unknowable future.
When your child jolts in a Red Cross ambulance to the hospital
in the nearest city and three deadly serious, quiet doctors tell
you they are not sure but they will have to cut in at once to
look—their words are "exploratory operation"—you are trapped
in the dead end of your emotions. Now everything depends on
the foreign-tongued people, your late enemies. As they get
ready to take your youngest to the operating room, he says to
you only "Go with me as far as you can" and all the lights of your
life seem to go out inside you.

An orderly comes in and carefully carries the wasted body
to the operating room. You say to your wife, "Now you can cry."
After the crying is done, you can only wait and try to persuade
yourself that your world couldn't possibly end this way. Other
people maybe. Not you. Ages later the stretcher goes by with
its silent cargo. Appendicitis with peritonitis. Peritonitis means
only one thing to you.

Now time becomes eternity. Then the doctors come out
and you see in their eyes a look you know well. It's the look of
the professional who has done a difficult job, a look that says
no one else knows what we've done or how well we did it, but
we know and that's enough. Then you know it's only a matter
of waiting for him to be well.

While waiting eighteen days for Roy's recovery, family teams
ventured out on side trips while either Bee or I stayed with Roy
in the *Kinder Klinic* in Regensburg near Kelheim. Bee, Jon, and

Barbara saw Munich and Nuremberg rebuilding, as well as Dinkelsbuhl and Rothenburg, towns out of the fairy tales. Jon and I paddled a stretch of the flooding Danube and Jon and Barbara cruised the quiet Altmuhl Canal. Then we all went on to Austria to stay for a while with a niece and her lieutenant husband on an army installation.

...The cold came on and we fled further south. On the day we crossed Switzerland's Saint Gotthard Pass to the new vegetation, architecture, and people of the Mediterranean world, Jon, a tolerant fifteen, wrote, " I have come to know the German language and have come to know the three types of German people, all very different. The Germans doubtful of their former enemies, the simple Austrians, and the modern Swiss. I seem to catch the liking of these people."

I sometimes wonder if Roy, at nine, ever quite caught "the liking of these people." Germanic or Mediterranean, they deviated from America's way, especially as to sanitation, and he disapproved. Thinking about the hospital, he said, "They kept scrubbing the floors all the time. But they didn't change my sheets and they didn't swat the flies. Don't they understand about germs?" Of Italy, he asked, "How long have these people been in business?" I tried to tell him. "Why don't they build more bathrooms instead of so many churches?" These are hard questions for nine to answer—or even forty-three. Whenever we talked about the noticeable Americanization of Europe, Roy had one comment, "Good."

The days grew shorter in mid-November, but we put a foldboat together again for a week on Lake Como. Home base was a little pension intimately inhabited by a father, mother, old grandmother, and little Marialena, exactly Barbara's age. Marialena was learning English in school through stilted little sentences, and we traded vocabularies. The two thirteen-year-old girls later corresponded and traded photographs.

Eventually we packed Long Island Duck III and hit the tourist trail, the eternal triangle across the top of Italy to Milan and Venice, down to Rome, and up to the Italian Riviera. We might be tourists from now on, rather than foldboat vagrants, but we were going to pick and choose foldboat-style. So, in Milan we had a single purpose—to see *The Last Supper*. Barbara wrote, "A single long, white room—at one end a complicated picture of the crucifixion and at the other end *The Last Supper* by Leonardo da Vinci.... In 1945 the whole building but the two walls where the paintings are were ruined by bombs. What detail. Almost three dimensional. I tried to grasp the fact that I was standing in front of the 500-year-old painting right where it was painted by a man who knew everything. Engineer, architect, astronomer, politician, sculpturer and artist. Jesus accepting the fact that he must die, but the Apostles trying to figure out how they can save their King. The hands and the faces in such detail. This is religion alive. I could have spent hours looking at this piece of art, never equaled. The beauty beyond words. 500 years old. Judas sitting forward, while Peter and John whisper. Each face different and beautiful. A real experience never to be forgotten...."

We spent our last nine days on the shore of the Mediterranean Sea:

...Should I tell you the name of the place and ruin my chances for staying there when I come to Europe in the Winter seventeen years from now? I might as well. Seventeen years is a long time. The hotel at Paraggi. I guess it means Paradise. P.S.: In accordance with Emerson's Law of Compensation, it rained abundantly on the Sunny Riviera. But we read *The Sea Around Us* and *The Golden Treasury* at the fireplace, paddled a foldboat, hiked along the sea, and swam luxuriously in the Mediterranean on December third.

We chose a ten-day trip which contained a Mediterranean cruise in the bargain. We embarked at Genoa, sailed west to Cannes, then southeast to Naples, thence to Gibraltar and through the Azores. I wanted to take a ship that stopped at Halifax too, but then I never have known what enough means.

On the high seas, the father of the family spent some hours with pencil and paper. Later, he proclaimed some figures. The Daily Average Per Person In Europe was $4.77.

Our DAPPIE included all food, clothing, shelter, hospital and medical costs. (Blessings on you, Red Cross, for the ambulance. Thank you, Blue Cross, for the hospital insurance. From now on, you will be two crosses we will be happy to bear.) Our Daily Average Per Person In Europe included gas and maintenance for Marilyn, shipping the foldboats by rail across the Alps, phony lemonade and gourmet's wine, a stream of tips, riotous living, and heaven knows what all. The works. Also included was our loot: eight Black Forest clocks, three Swiss watches, two Austrian leather briefcases, four paintings, a rosary from Rome for one Grandma and hand-embroidered

Italian linen cloth for the other, a score of little gifts such as Hummel figurines for friends and relatives, and an abundance of souvenirs, including Jon's pennants and wood-pictures, Roy's miniature cars and planes, and Barbara's glass menagerie.

Naturally, DAPPIE did not include what we brought with us to Europe in the seven remarkable bags, nor ocean transport, nor foldboats salable at a profit. Nor did it include an immigrant, Marilyn. To buy, equip, document, insure, and ship her home cost two thousand one hundred dollars. In place of our venerable 100,000-mile Pontiac, now Marilyn daily ran the roads at 27 miles to a gallon and parked in places where nothing else fit.

But no one cared any longer about the DAPPIE, and no one listened to the poor man tell the average for each nation: France $7.52, Germany $3.89, Austria $4.07, Switzerland $8.86, and Italy $5.53. We had been to Europe, hadn't we? Who cared what it cost?

You know what people say when they come home, "Being away was wonderful. Now it's great to be home." So you know how we felt when we sailed into New York harbor. Jon put it with starry-eyed sincerity on the inside back cover of the only space remaining in volume 2 of his 40,000-word journal. "We are in New York, America. We have found out that there is no country in the world like America. I believe that we must continue to help the European nations. It has been a great wonderful experience and I'm certain I shall return to Europe. I shall never forget Fall, 1954." Roy said, "When we passed the Statue of Liberty on our way to Europe you said I would look at it different the next time I saw it again. I didn't know what you were talking about then. But now I do."

Then we slipped back into the life of Suburbia. The phone rang madly again. It was the League of Women Voters for Bee and the First Teeners' Club for Barbara. Jon worried about the Giants. Roy built menacing model airplanes, probably as protection against foreign people who spit in the streets and don't wash their hands after going to the bathroom.

The three children went back to school again, and made the same grades they used to make. Barbara mined her journal for the fifty words she misspelled abroad and made these her spelling list for the first two weeks of school. The industrious ant of the family, Jon, having carried his textbooks abroad, moved back smoothly into his high school classes. I like his understatement, "It isn't easy to learn geometry by yourself traveling in Europe." The fiddling grasshopper of the family, Roy, looked at me solemnly while going to bed on the night of January 2, 1955. He said: "Dad, an awful thing has happened. I've forgotten how to divide and multiply. And that's what school is all about." It took the whole evening of January 3 to bring him up to the level of his classmates.

Though our middle-class responsibilities swallowed us up again, we had our memories.

Anybody else in this family besides me want to go see the rest of the world sometime?

Chapter Thirty

TOWARD
DESEGREGATION
OF SCHOOLS

T he second major social conflict of the 1950s in which I
became involved was the struggle toward school desegregation. School segregation was challenged in 1954 by
the U. S. Supreme Court in its historic *Brown vs. Board
of Education of Topeka* decision that "separate educational facilities are inherently unequal" and that the nation's public school
systems must be desegregated. In general, school systems in the
border states complied, but school systems in the South resisted
the Court's decision. For instance, in 1956 one hundred and one
Southern senators and representatives published a manifesto
calling on states to disobey and resist "by all lawful means" the
Supreme Court's ruling on desegregation in public schools. In
Tennessee the state legislature strongly opposed desegregation;
bills ranging from extremist to moderate segregationist approaches
were introduced in each session of the legislature. Southern school
systems, including Nashville, faced momentous decisions in an
atmosphere charged with fear, anger, and violence.

As a private institution, George Peabody College for Teachers was not legally required to desegregate. But the moral obli-
gation of Peabody was apparent. The mission of the college was
leadership in teacher education in the South. Peabody, like other
Southern colleges, had an all-white administration, faculty, and
student body. And the South was at a crossroads.

Summer sessions at Peabody provided the best and the
easiest opportunities for initial desegregation. The summer
student body was made up primarily of experienced administra-

tors and teachers from across the South, unlike the largely undergraduate student body that attended during the academic year from the area around Nashville. A lecture series that I had developed provided an entering wedge.

During my first summer session on campus in 1952, I had noted that the strong Peabody music department offered pleasant musical events under the stars in the open campus area in front of the Social Religious building. A characteristic offering was a musical comedy such as *Carousel* or an orchestra or a quartet or individual musicians and singers. The summer student body and many community residents flocked to these occasions; weather permitting, the camp chairs and even the greensward were occupied on many balmy summer nights. The audiences, of course, were white.

Why not add to these programs one night weekly for the life of the mind? So I dreamed up a series for the summer of 1953 titled "Great Human Issues of Our Times." Peabody professors, including division heads Willard Goslin and Harold Benjamin and such campus stars as James L. Hymes in child development, Kenneth Cooper in history, Clifton L. Hall in social foundations, and Claude Chadwick in biology were invited to speak. President Henry H. Hill also agreed to talk. My role was to organize and arrange each program and to introduce the speakers. So I got out notices of the lectures and hoped that somebody would come. Fortunately, they did; the Peabody summer student body and the local community members embraced the new program as enthusiastically as they had the musical events. The Great Human Issues of Our Times became an accepted part of Peabody's summer program; seven or eight professors spoke during each of the 1953-56 summer sessions. Following every summer session, the lectures were published in book form by Peabody.

A Peabody precedent was unobtrusively broken early in the evolution of the lecture series. I sent notices inviting attendance at the lectures not only to the faculty of Vanderbilt University and Scarritt College for Christian Workers but also the staff members of the black universities, Fisk and Tennessee A&I. A few phone calls to friends and acquaintances among black academics insured that the recipients would not interpret the communication as a clerical error. Peabody officialdom and faculty were alerted to the coming breakthrough. I was confident that I had touched all bases. But I had overlooked a venerable night watchman whose usual function seemed to be routing romantic couples from cars parked on campus. On the crucial first night of desegregation, while a sprinkling of blacks under the protection of darkness (no pun intended) were seating themselves throughout the audience, the night watchman headed toward me, with fire in his usually lackluster eyes. "There are people here who don't belong here!" A good old country boy, despite his mantle of years, he was primed to oust them. I told him that some "colored people" had been invited and that Dr. Hill knew about it. Shocked and incredulous, he said, "Dr. Hill **knows**?" Torn by divided loyalties, he hesitated, then retreated into the darkness of the night and his spirit. I breathed a sigh of deep relief. All else went splendidly throughout the evening.

Thereafter some black intellectuals regularly attended our summer night programs. After a while, people no longer noticed them. Desegregation had come to Peabody; a small opening had been made in the campus racial barriers. Yet the sky did not fall.

Then Willard Goslin, in collaboration with the president and the division heads, brought a small group of black administrators to campus for an all-black seminar during a summer intersession. Rumor has it that there was consternation in the registration offices when the blacks officially enrolled in Peabody. But the institution survived. The doors slowly opened. After a time, a few blacks enrolled in the regular summer and academic year programs. The Peabody student body had been desegregated.

By necessity, desegregation of Nashville public elementary and secondary schools became a more public matter than the quiet desegregation of private Peabody. Before the Supreme Court decision of 1954, there was no movement whatsoever toward desegregation of Nashville public schools. During the year after the decision there was much gossip and viewing with alarm in the community but no planning or forward movement by either the school system or the citizenry. Everyone seemed to be waiting. People of good will waited too. As I had learned earlier from the Illinois textbook censorship controversy, it takes time for people of good will to realize that what they are waiting for is themselves.

One year after *Brown vs. Board of Education*, the presidents of the United Church Women and the Council of Jewish Women agreed that something should be done to educate the community about the Supreme Court decision. These organizations decided to offer a program. Thirteen additional organizations were invited to co-sponsor a workshop. Only seven accepted; the honor roll read: American Association of University Women, B'nai B'rith, Citizens Committee for the Public Schools, Council of Colored Parents and Teachers, League of Women Voters of Nashville, Nashville Association of Churches, and Young Women's Christian Association.

Since presidents are loaded with other organizational responsibilities, a trio of women developed arrangements. They were Catholic, Protestant, and Jewish; two white, one black. Bee Van Til was one of the three. To find a meeting place was not easy. Only the Jewish Community Center was willing to host a meeting; Christian churches were "unavailable." (Three years later, the Jewish Community Center was dynamited by racists.) The topic of the workshop was "The Supreme Court Decision and Its Meaning to the Community." Though the sponsors had anticipated 150, some 500 uneasy people, two-thirds white, were in attendance. As they gathered, the tension in the air was apparent. One could tell that people were wondering who else was there.

As moderator and chairman of the meeting, I reached into my bag of group process techniques and said, "Good evening, neighbors. Good of you to come out tonight. Let's see who's here. Put up your hand if your relationship is to"—and I tolled off the nine sponsoring organizations. "How about some relationship to Vanderbilt; it's all right to put up your hand twice...Fisk... Peabody..." I ticked off the universities, public school personnel, labor unions, businesses, social services. You could feel the tension ebbing as the 500 realized that "our people" were there. Only then did I introduce the speakers: Whitworth Stokes III, a local attorney (the Third is highly important in Nashville); Charles S. Johnson, the black president of Fisk; and George Mitchell, director of the Southern Regional Conference, a long-established race relations group. The next day, 180 people communicated across racial lines through small workshop groups. Following this May 1955 workshop, luncheons for discussion and fellowship were held and were attended by Nashville organization leaders of both races. Out of the sharing grew two goals, another community workshop and a permanent community organization on human relations. Then the second workshop was held on a night in February 1956, this time in a Protestant church. The sponsoring organizations had grown to twenty-six and the topic was "Integration—How and When." At the time, the Baltimore and St. Louis school systems were developing successful desegregation school programs. So I suggested two of their administrators, Harry Bard and Frank Sskwor, as speakers. Leadership people in the Nashville public schools, both school administrators and board of education members, wanted their advice, but, because of probable Nashville community reaction, the school people wanted any such meeting to be off the record. An unpublicized daytime meeting was scheduled; as in Alton, I became again the conspiratorial arranger.

That night Bee and I drove to the church in the second-hand Cadillac we had bought from President Henry Hill (despite my initial reservation that driving a Cadillac was inappropriate for a curriculum worker). Since I was again to serve as moderator, we arrived early and parked in front of the church. Six hundred people turned out to hear Bard and Sskwor; the meeting was orderly and thoughtful. People were more at ease than they had been during their first workshop.

After the meeting ended and the usual details were wrapped up, Bee and I emerged into the February night. By then, most of the people who had attended the meeting had driven away. The street was now dark and deserted except for a few remaining cars. Racists had ice-picked the tires of several cars. One of them belonged to our Peabody colleague, Jimmy Hymes. We hastened to our Cadillac to inspect it for damage. The cars parked directly in front and directly behind it had been disabled through tire-slashing. But the Cadillac was untouched. The racists had apparently decided that our Cadillac belonged to a Nashville influential, possibly the mayor or a powerful business executive. They had decided not to touch it.

About twenty of us, drivers and passengers in the cars with the slashed tires and the immune Cadillac, huddled under a street lamp. We called a garage and then waited for the Ku Klux

Klan or White Citizens Council members to come out of the bushes swinging their clubs and brandishing their ice picks. They didn't materialize. Ages later, after repairs and changing of tires by the group and the garage men, we drove home. Before we went to bed we closed the Venetian blinds so that if the windows were shattered, the glass wouldn't fly. We took our nameplate off our mailbox. We had to remind ourselves that we were living in the United States of America. We didn't report the tire slashing to the police because we preferred responsible and unsensational coverage of the talks to headlines about the ice-picking of the tires. In Nashville, desegregation supporters were already fearful enough.

The next evening we went back to the Protestant church for discussions held by 360 people. Nobody got ice-picked that night.

During the winter we worked on identifying Nashville leaders who were white, Protestant, of "old" families (that wasn't so hard), and courageous (that was hard). We hoped to develop a permanent group on human relations. Approximately a dozen of us had taken the lead so far, but we were largely "outsiders" who were not born and bred in Nashville, or we were blacks or Jews. Few of the Catholics and Protestants or unchurched among us could claim to belong to the Nashville establishment. For a successful group on human relations, we needed indigenous establishment leadership. Well-recognized community leaders agreed to sponsor an organizational meeting; 120 individuals came together to organize the Nashville Community Relations Conference. Long-established black and white community leaders accepted offices: the president of a local foundry and machine company, an attorney who was the son and grandson of Tennessee lawyers, a head of a university department of medicine, a state PTA officer, the wife of a black college president, and an active community worker of the Jewish faith. The rest of us who had initiated the desegregation workshops participated through a thirteen-person executive committee, fifty-member board, and eleven subcommittees.

In August 1956 the executive committee of the new Nashville Community Relations Conference urged the school board members to formulate a plan for desegregation. The school board delayed, but in October 1956 began work toward 1957 desegregation. The committee on parent education of the Nashville Community Relations Conference tried to persuade the local PTAs in white schools to hold meetings in preparation for the coming desegregation. The efforts of the committee were unsuccessful because of the unwillingness of the white PTA Council to foster meetings of any type concerning desegregation.

Early in 1957 the state legislature came to town for its sessions. Fiery members promised vigorous segregationist legislation. After several lengthy sessions, the executive committee of the Nashville Community Relations Conference developed a release that said in part: "We firmly believe that no legislation on this subject should be passed at this session of the Tennessee General Assembly." Each legislator received a copy of this statement, which was also brought to the governor and sent to the various media of communication.

Nevertheless, Governor Frank G. Clement proposed two bills, one allowing boards of education to provide separate schools for white and Negro children whose parents voluntarily elected to send them to such schools, and a second giving boards of education the power to assign pupils to schools for a variety of reasons. Representatives of the Community Relations Conference held two meetings with the governor but couldn't change his position. The conference decided not to testify as an organization against this segregationist legislation, since basically the conference conceived itself as an educational organization rather than as a pressure group. Some executive committee members agreed that the governor's bills were the best that could be expected under the circumstances and predicted that they would be found unconstitutional anyway.

The only two white males to testify against the bills were a clergyman of the Southern Baptist Church and me. We testified as individuals rather than as representatives of the Nashville Community Relations Conference. At the January 15, 1957, public hearing of the Senate and House Education and Judiciary Committees, I read a statement and was asked only one question by a member. "Professor, where were you born?" I replied truthfully, "New York City." That settled that; obviously, my testimony could be ignored.

The bills passed overwhelmingly and were soon declared

unconstitutional by the Federal District Court in Tennessee. The same court in January 1957 accepted the Nashville Board of Education proposal that integration be instituted in the first grade beginning in the fall of 1957. The conference sponsored a public lecture by Omer Carmichael, superintendent of the Louisville school system, which had successfully integrated and had received national publicity. The Nashville superintendent of schools cooperated and Carmichael talked to 400 teachers and then to 400 community people.

In 1957 a Tennessee community east of Nashville exploded into violence. The newspaper headlines read, "Clinton Prepares for Negro Students...Twelve to Enter High School: No Trouble Reported...Pupils Integrate Without Trouble...Outside Agitator Stirs Clinton Melee...Clinton Race Agitator Held in Jail...Clinton Pleads for State Aid...Tear Gas Routs Clinton Mob...New Racist Leader Stirs Disorder...Trouble City, USA Blames All Disorder on Outsiders...Mob Member, Guardsmen Wounded As Strike Spreads...Oliver Springs Mob Calls for March on Clinton...Clinton Passes Tough Measures...Students Return to Clinton High...Last Guard Leaves Clinton." Consequently, during the summer of 1957 the Nashville Community Relations Conference sponsored a statement supporting law and order. The statement did not endorse integration; it simply called for law enforcement. Though the statement was signed by 600 Nashville leaders, some prominent people, including some eminent educators, found reasons for not signing. A last effort by the Nashville Community Relations Conference to sponsor community meetings for discussion of the coming desegregation foundered when the white PTA Council found such meetings "inadvisable."

Opposition to the coming desegregation accelerated. Opponents included the Tennessee Federation for Constitutional Government, whose leaders included a nationally known professor of English at Vanderbilt University; the Ku Klux Klan, whose meeting of fifty white-robed Klansmen I observed at a respectful distance from the cross-burning; and John Kasper, on trial for bombing at Clinton, who harangued, rope in hand, before the state capitol in Nashville.

In September 1957 the racists demonstrated and threatened as nineteen wide-eyed Negro six-year-olds went to formerly all-white schools in Nashville. On the morning of September 10, 1957, a bomb blew up Nashville's new Hattie Cotton School. The blast blew many solid citizens of Nashville out of their comfortable beds. The police cracked down and the demonstrations dissolved. The six-year-olds went back to school. Nashville citizens explained to each other that the trouble was the fault of "outsiders" such as John Kasper who made the trouble at Clinton. The bombers were never identified or apprehended.

Nashville won acceptance of a grade-by-grade desegregation plan that began with integration of the first grade in 1957. Some commentators reported that the existence of the Nashville Community Relations Conference explained in part why the Nashville story, 1957, did not become the Little Rock story, 1957. (After crowd violence at Little Rock, President Eisenhower had sent in the National Guard to protect black enrollees at Central High School.)

Nashville desegregation of schools proceeded peaceably over the years that followed. I played no part, for I left Peabody in the summer of 1957. As a kind of farewell to my participation in school desegregation in the South, I wrote a letter to the *New York Times* suggesting the establishment of an American Conscience Fund to support future college attendance by the courageous black high school students who had laid their lives on the line in Little Rock. An organization headed by Harry Carman, formerly dean at my alma mater, Columbia College, took up the suggestion and invited contributions.

My son Jon got in his parting shot, too. In an editorial in the Peabody Demonstration School newspaper, which he edited as a high school senior, he called for desegregation of the school that it not become "a haven for bigots." Later, the Demonstration School, too, desegregated. By then Jon was a Swarthmore College student, Bee was a school board member in Mountain Lakes, New Jersey, and I was a teacher-administrator at New York University.

Chapter Thirty-One

BACK EAST
WHERE WE CAME FROM

N ashville in the 1950s—and maybe in any decade—was a delightful place for economically comfortable white families. Our suburban/exurban home was a half-hour south of the city and just short of the soft, rolling hills. The ranch-style house with its long living room and adjoining book-loaded family room was conducive to entertaining; a big garage became a recreation center for Van Til and neighboring kids. Our yard had trees made for flying swings and solid platforms; little-traveled lanes and roads provided safe bike riding; an unfenced baseball field was a few steps away; a basketball court on the nearby school playground featured such events as the Slavery Bowl (so-called because school followed that New Year's Day) where my agile children battled an aging giant, their father.

The roads near 900 Tower Place had such wonderful names as Grey Oaks and Granny White Pike and Leland Lane. Early in our Nashville stay I tried to tell a guest, Dr. Crabb, how to reach our home. Alfred L. Crabb was a long-time Peabody professor and a Kentucky-born novelist who wrote of the Civil War—pardon me, the War Between the States. "Ah yes," he said, "the general area of a gallant struggle by _____," and he named a Confederate officer. The well-informed author of *Breakfast at the Hermitage, Dinner at Belmont, Supper at the Maxwell House,* and novels with less gustatory titles could have found his way to that battlefield blindfolded.

The Peabody faculty, though still overly inbred (so numerous were Peabody graduates on the faculty that in earlier years the college catalog reported only faculty degrees, not the awarding institutions), now included many cosmopolitans. We became acquainted with all faculty members and close friends with some.

Our most intimate friends were the Allen, Drummond, Hymes, and Hobbs families. Intense and alert Jack Allen was a man of the New South, a writer of history textbooks and a president of the National Council for the Social Studies, a Kentuckian who joined Peabody five years after receiving his doctorate at the college and who taught there till retirement. Humorous, quizzical, and unflappable Harold Drummond was educated in the West, wrote geographies for elementary school students, and became president of the Association for Supervision and Curriculum Development while teaching elementary education and assistant deaning at the University of New Mexico following his Peabody years. A vigorous critic of school and society, Jimmy Hymes was a New Yorker, an editor and executive secretary during the progressive education movement, then president of the National Association for the Education of Young Children; he became a retiree at 57 to work as a full-time independent author, lecturer, and consultant. Nick Hobbs was a South Carolinian whose work in psychology, human development, mental health, and administration I have already described when commenting on the Four Horsemen.

The geographically disparate but ideologically compatible men, however different in personalities, formed a cordial and cohesive group. Our wives varied too: Cherry Allen, who loved her immaculate home and her ceramics hobby; Kay Drummond, who focused on her family and assistance with Harold's publications; Lucia Hymes, an artist and craftsman who was converting a barn into a comfortable, informal home; Mary Hobbs, a career psychologist; Bee, family-oriented and active in community organizations. We partied together on weekends and mourned together in our living room on election nights when Adlai Stevenson twice lost to Dwight Eisenhower. My regret was particularly deep on the second occasion, for I had campaigned actively for Stevenson through writing editorials that were boilerplated and published in weekly newspapers throughout the country.

We had many "less intimate" friends too, such as the Kenneth Coopers (history), the Roosevelt Baslers (secondary educa-

268

tion), the Fremont Wirths (author of a high school history book which sold so well that his Peabody salary was used primarily to pay his annual taxes), the Henry Haraps (Henry was the father of consumer education and a pioneering curriculum man), the Benjamins and Goslins when the peripatetic husbands happened to be in town from lecturing far afield. A night with Ben sometimes included his performance on the organ and his son's skirling on bagpipes.

The South and Nashville and Peabody were hospitable. So were the Van Tils. Our entertaining was extensive, though largely confined to the faculty. After many of the Great Human Issues lectures, we entertained cross-sections of the faculty at receptions. When celebrities such as Archibald MacLeish came to town for lectures, we also held receptions in our home. Our children learned to be co-hosts and able tray handlers. The only time in my life when my income tax was questioned came when I claimed 1953 entertainment expenses for these receptions; the auditor asked whether the occasions were a "required" part of my work and, when I said no, disallowed them. Required or not, the receptions went on every year, along with a monster breakfast at our home as the final meeting of each of my larger classes, another self-imposed requirement.

Despite the heat of the kitchen from reactionary forces and racists, and despite the occasional heartburn of curriculum leadership, life in Nashville was good. We attended campus cultural events and followed the George Peabody Demonstration School basketball team, on which Jon played guard and for which Barbara led cheers. We visited the state parks and Kentucky Lake and Nashville's Parthenon and Andrew Jackson's Hermitage. We had our family sabbatical in Europe. Bee worked particularly with the League of Women Voters on consolidation of city and county school systems and on desegregation of schools. With like-minded associates she brought some black women into the local American Association of University Women (a byproduct was a rise in the proportion of members holding doctorates) and persuaded a downtown hotel to permit integrated luncheon meetings. After some of us on the Peabody faculty organized a chapter of the American Association of University Professors, I helped to develop occasional joint and integrated meetings with our colleagues at other Nashville institutions of higher learning including Fisk University.

At the Demonstration School, Jon moved steadily toward scholarships that allowed him to choose among Yale, Oberlin, Carleton, and Swarthmore upon graduation; once when a basketball teammate taunted him on being a brain, Jon replied, "That will never bother me, Roger, as long as I can outscore you." Barbara was a cheerleader and a social leader, popular and never lacking dates. Even as an adolescent she was the family psychologist, with an uncanny and penetrating understanding of adult and youthful personalities. During summer vacations she became my able salary-earning secretary. In elementary school, Roy followed his interests into conquest of mathematical abstractions and the elaborate mapping of Siberian and Southeast Asian rivers; Jon tutored him in athletic prowess and eventually created a Frankenstein's monster able to defeat his older brother in tennis.

The attendance of our children at the Demonstration School precipitated another struggle in my family's apparently inescapable Wars over Religion, a conflict that was particularly hard on Bee. In 1956 an edict was issued by the Nashville area monsignor that all Roman Catholic children under his jurisdiction must attend Catholic schools. Part of Bee's and my hard-won compact prior to our marriage was that our children would be brought up in the Roman Catholic faith but would not attend parochial schools. Bee explained our agreement to the local priests; our children continued to attend church with their mother, receive religious instruction, and attend the Demonstration School, which was included in my Peabody division. Then a sterner ruling came down from the monsignor's office in that era two years prior to the accession to the papacy of the gentle reformer, Pope John XXIII. Parents of Roman Catholic students who did not attend Catholic schools were to be denied the sacraments. For Bee, this meant that she could no longer receive communion or enter the confessional. She talked to the parish priests, who could not yield; she was barred. She suffered, yet held to our compact. Sensitive to her deprivation by Catholic officialdom and aware of her feelings, our adolescent children became increasingly alienated from the church in which Jon and Barbara had received communion.

I still found some time to write, though not as much as I had during my years with the Bureau for Intercultural Education. The difficult *Forces* experience may have slowed down my momentum somewhat. Yet I edited a special issue on human relations for the *Review of Educational Research*, wrote two editorials for *Educational Leadership*, did two house organ pieces for the *Peabody Reflector*, and wrote articles relating to reactionary forces and to the academic critics of education for such journals as those of the National Education Association and the History of Education Society. I also wrote on delinquency and discipline for the *NEA Journal* and *Educational Leadership* following my testimony before Senator Estes Kefauver's subcommittee on juvenile delinquency in 1956, on the gifted child for one of the last issues of *Progressive Education*, and on my last year of University School teaching for the *Peabody Journal of Education*. Mostly, however, I taught, worked on the improvement of Peabody's curriculum, and consulted throughout the South during my six years at Peabody.

If life in Nashville was so good—despite reactionaries, racists, and authoritarian religionists—why did I leave? As usual, the reasons were multiple. One was Alexandrian—hunger for new worlds as curriculum development at Peabody slowed. Another stemmed from my role as the bastard cat at the family reunion, as Charlie White used to put it; since I was the administration/faculty needler on campus and one of the sponsors of the unpopular crusade for school desegregation in the community, the role would have done me in sooner or later—and I knew it. Too, Bee hoped to find more humane church administrators elsewhere (and did).

The term of the General Education Board support for the salaries of the division heads ran out, I believe, after five years. Since President Hill told me not to expect salary increments, the $12,000 for the academic year and summer term Peabody paid me in 1951 still remained my salary in 1956 and might have remained at $12,000 from here to eternity.

I could have followed the lead of other Peabody professors less well salaried than I and increased my income through more consultation, a full lecture schedule, or commercially rewarding textbook writing. However, I chose to make known that I was available for another post. By now I knew how to do this, and in the fall of 1956 I told my friends (the currently fashionable word now is network) that I was ready to leave. Nibbles, sometimes eventuating in offers to become director of teacher education or dean of education, came from Hunter College and Queens College of the City of New York, Tufts Civic Education Center, the University of Toledo, and Boston University. (UNESCO had offered me a post abroad a year earlier.)

When I left Peabody in 1957, I received many friendly letters from friends and professional acquaintances. But the one I cherish most came from Myles Horton, the courageous founder of Highlander Folk School in Tennessee, which had defied the segregation practices of the South and held desegregated meetings and classes for years before the Supreme Court decision. Myles wrote, "Just having you so near has added to our own strength and assurance that we are not alone. You will perhaps never fully realize what your presence in Nashville has meant for the South. We also will always be indebted to you for helping us with our first integration workshop. Your analysis did much to put us on the right track."

I signed with New York University as chairman of the Department of Secondary Education at $12,000 for the academic year and with additional salary for summer school teaching. George D. Stoddard was dean of the School of Education, following his University of Illinois presidency; Walter Anderson, whom I had known from my summer work for Northwestern University, was now associate dean; I had many friends at NYU from Bureau for Intercultural Education days. The cynics who claim that it's whom you know rather than what you know may be right, though I don't want to believe them.

Stoddard had been president of the University of Illinois when I first became a professor there, and our relationship had been excellent. The most important of our connections was a conference of a national commission supportive of UNESCO, an organization that President Stoddard then headed, despite virulent criticism from Illinois provincials who repudiated any international cooperation. He had entrusted me with bringing together top leadership in social studies for a conference at Allerton, the University of Illinois estate, to make recommendations on preparation of world-minded textbooks. I had written to college

272

presidents asking them to send specified educators with outstanding credentials to this summit conference (for instance, Jack Allen, history, and Russell Whitaker, geography, came from Peabody)—and to pick up the check for their travel. The gambit worked nicely, the presidents came through with travel expenses, and the conference was a resounding success. Stoddard had a good memory.

At NYU I soon found that the major policy decisions were made by the dean and his associates or by the governing bodies of the faculty, especially the august, highly politicized faculty government, lightly referred to as the College of Cardinals. Though some who buried themselves in department administration may deny it, department chairmen at NYU were largely implementers of decisions made by others. Much of the work of department chairmen was administrivia. With the half-dozen established professors and the two or three instructors who made up the department, I worked out teaching schedules and released time for projects and research, rated faculty members and recommended salary increments (final decisions were made elsewhere), and worked on revision of course offerings. I employed part-time teachers and secretaries and replacements for senior professors working temporarily abroad, encouraged grant proposals, and tried to keep peace among those department members who clamored for more secretarial help and for teaching assignments that fitted into their selected life-styles.

Let no one tell you that higher education institutions are alike. Institutions have personalities of their own. NYU was quite different from Peabody, even as Peabody differed from Illinois. To cite a small item, at Peabody alcoholic beverages were strictly prohibited on campus, whereas cocktails were part of the luncheon menu at the NYU Faculty Club. More important, when an education professor at Peabody suggested an educational innovation, some students were sure to try it out in their classes. So did some suburban teachers at NYU. However, many NYU students who taught in the New York City school system would explain at the drop of a hat why the new idea couldn't possibly be adopted: the NYC Board of Education and the bureaucracy wouldn't let them, they said. Most Peabody students lived on campus or at least stayed around the college to use library resources. Most NYU students were subway riders or suburban commuters; they necessarily rushed in and hurried home. To make a difference through teaching was harder for professors at NYU. New York University professors, like many of the students, were often commuters. Because of faculty dispersion, social occasions for faculty members in our home were less frequent than when we resided in Nashville. We lived out in New Jersey, and our invitees lived way to hell-and-gone out Long Island, up in Westchester, centrally in Manhattan, or in scattered New Jersey communities. It takes potent drinks and epicurean meals and oodles of charm to compensate for bucking traffic from Long Island through Manhattan to the Jersey boondocks.

NYU had to accommodate to its dispersed faculty. Department chairmen scheduled an individual's academic year teaching over a four-day period weekly. With an eye to student convenience, chairmen programmed the majority of graduate classes on Saturday or on weekday afternoons and nights, four to six, six to eight, or eight to ten. Naturally, the office hours of professors seldom overlapped with the hours of their colleagues. So Mondays were the periods of assembly for monthly faculty meetings, committees, department meetings, and such miscellany as faculty government and department chairmen's meetings. Aside from Mondays, the best opportunities for faculty socialization took place during June in Puerto Rico, where a segment of the NYU faculty lived in the Condado Beach Hotel in San Juan and taught Puerto Rican master's degree aspirants. Surveys also helped socialization; during my NYU decade, I took part in Puerto Rican, Virgin Islands, and Iranian surveys. Fine people, many of these New York University professors, if you ever found a chance to get acquainted.

Faculty dispersion and eccentric hours encouraged professorial individualism, including mine. One's own classes, national organizations, research, and publications were of high importance in the professional lives of NYU faculty members. They took their teaching and counseling seriously, but collegiality through the school and the departments encountered harder sledding. The typical School of Education professor was bright, competent, nationally recognized, wary of administrators, and as independent as the proverbial hog on ice.

My own New York University work schedule, handcrafted

and self-determined, was a far cry from that of those Peabody old-timers who still reported daily at nine A.M. and went home at four P.M., a heritage from clock-conscious former Peabody President Bruce Payne. After *New York Times* reading on the Lackawanna Railroad and the Hudson Tubes from Mountain Lakes, New Jersey, I arrived after an hour and twenty minute trip at the conventional nine A.M. for Monday meetings. I administered the department and saw students, then taught from six to eight P. M. Many Monday nights I traveled by subway to Corona, which was closer to NYU than my New Jersey home. There I visited with my mother and slept overnight. Sometimes I stayed at sleazy fleabag hotels or the respectable Grosvenor in Greenwich Village. I got to the office early on Tuesday morning for the day's administrative chores, then taught a class from four to six and another from six to eight. After classes I occasionally met Bee for a Broadway or off-Broadway play; then I returned to Mountain Lakes. By Tuesday night I had usually worked about twenty hours. So I stayed home Wednesday and wrote. Thursday I put in a normal nine-to-five office day on administration, relationships to national organizations, class preparation, miscellaneous correspondence, or whatever else came to hand. Friday I either came into the office or wrote at home. Weekends usually included the equivalent of a day of writing or paper marking or preparing speeches.

As an administrator I must have kept my nose and desk clean and my staff relationships tolerable despite occasional conveyance to faculty members of administrative nay-sayings. In a school reorganization in 1966 I was promoted to the chairmanship of a newly created division, the Division of Secondary and Higher Education. However, I didn't enjoy being an administrator.

Yet I have many good memories of my decade, 1957-1967, with New York University. Of them all, I remember most happily:

—my cramped office in the firetrap Press Building from which I could overlook Washington Square and the roofs of Greenwich Village while I heard the powerful horns of the ocean liners on the Hudson River. (One night Bee and I were reading galleys in the office before the president's reception at his apartment across the park. Suddenly all the lights of New York City went out. By the light of matches we daisy-chained with others down the stairs from the sixth floor and joined the gala that President James Hester had moved to the candle-lit lobby of his apartment building. That night of the Great Blackout, New York City was on its best behavior. Mugging was abandoned as adolescents directed traffic by flashlight on street corners. After we crept through the Lincoln Tunnel, the lights of New Jersey were dazzling.)

—the doctoral candidates and instructors with whom I worked closely; among them the mature and sober John Amend, a curriculum leader from the state of Washington; young and promising Jack Blackburn, who joined me from Peabody graduate work and, in time, became dean at Auburn; Paul Warren, a handsome and able New Yorker who went on to an eventual deanship at Boston University.

—the professors I recruited after department campus influentials retired: Virgil Clift, a top black educator from Morgan State who became my close friend and collaborator on John Dewey Society programs; Jack Brooks, former director of Lincoln School and active international educator; reliable Ron Doll, who wrote on supervision and curriculum improvement; relaxed Sam Keyes, who left New York's Manhattan for the deanship at Kansas State at Manhattan, Kansas; Earl Peckham, who shunned full-time appointments yet was always available to fill in as an adjunct professor; Hulda Grobman, capable evaluator and research scholar. And who could forget a long time department member, colorful Jack Robertson, an incredibly patient counselor and grant-getter par excellence who adopted a Brooklyn slum school and built his own APEX staff (some said empire) for curriculum experimentation.

—the successful curriculum improvements when the Educational Theory and Application undergraduate program began emphasizing social realities, needs, values; the chairmanship of the School of Education's curriculum committee; the personalization of doctoral advisement that accompanied decentralization of the program and reassignment of advisement to all secondary education professors.

—the months of June in Puerto Rico: the eager Puerto Rican teachers gathering an hour before classes began, the late afternoons with Bee and the staff at the Condado's beach, the drinks and dinner with cordial colleague Ellis White and his wife Helen; a trip across the mountains in a reck-

lessly driven publico with colleague Herb Schwartz, who
was teaching for NYU on the south shore of the island; the
summers when our kids discovered Puerto Rico through
stays in San Juan and in Ponce.

—the leadership of Walter Anderson, the well-loved dean who
succeeded Stoddard after the latter ascended to the executive vice presidency and chancellorship at NYU. His office
door was always open to Puerto Rican and other students,
as well as to the professoriate.

Andy led by his own example. For instance, during NYU's
Puerto Rican survey, he saw to it that staff members were roused
out of bed early to jaunt with him into the mountains or across
the island on our survey visits to schools, and to return exhausted to the Condado Beach Hotel for a late dinner.

Our family life-style also became somewhat different from
earlier Peabody patterns. Bee, now a veteran house-buyer, had
found us a house in Mountain Lakes, New Jersey, a pleasant
upper-income community for commuting executives. She had
phoned me from the East during Peabody's summer session in
1957. I asked, "What kind of architecture?" There was a long
silence. "Mountain Lakes architecture," she said.

The house was a big old rambling tree-shaded monster with
a delightful sun room, a second-floor deck overlooking azaleas
and a garden-surrounded gazebo, a covered area for ping-pong
duels, and abundant space for entertaining. Our home was two
blocks from a lake for boating and swimming, though a substantially longer distance from the door of my office. A family legend
has it that I placed the point of a compass on Washington Square,
swung the pencil to take in all of New York City, Nassau County,
part of Westchester and Suffolk Counties, and New Jersey almost halfway to the Delaware River, and said, "Anywhere in this
circle." The legend has it that Bee bought a house on the outer edge
of the pencil mark—indeed may have even widened the circle a tad.

Since my colleagues were scattered throughout the metropolitan area, we made our new friends in Mountain Lakes, population 4,300. Roy, entering the junior high school years in the
local public school system, had little difficulty in adjusting to the
new environment. At 16, Barbara had more of a problem at
Mountain Lakes High School, for cheerleading and social lead-

277

ership roles are not automatically transferable, particularly when school cliques are already well established and when local belles fear potential competition from an attractive new girl. Yet Barbara kept adding to her already substantial list of boys dated. High school graduate Jon chose Swarthmore College in Pennsylvania and, during vacations, brought home new friends.

Best of all was Bee's adaptation. She found local priests who were indignant at the policies of their Nashville colleagues and who welcomed her back to the Catholic sacraments. She switched from the Nashville League of Women Voters to the Mountain Lakes branch, worked with the American Association of University Women, took part in a community survey, was appointed to the Board of Education of the Mountain Lakes Public Schools to fill out a term, and then ran for the board as a strong supporter of public education. Her platform was simple and direct: do whatever would most help children and youth. Despite such disqualifications as being female, Catholic, liberal, and Democratic in male-dominated, heavily Protestant, conservative, and Republican Mountain Lakes, she led the ticket by a wide margin and regularly spent Monday evenings with the "boys on the board."

Bee's local friendships sufficed for me, and we led a good social and community life. Each Christmas season we held a reunion at our home for forty or fifty members of Bee's immediate and extended family; as matriarch of the clan, her mother welcomed the chance in her eighties to see again nieces and nephews as well as children, grandchildren, and great-grandchildren. For February birthday parties for my mother, we gathered her Corona buddies and some of my cousins. In warmer months our foldboat came out of mothballs and we boated, swam, and fished in the lakes that were readily accessible.

We were back where we came from, at least as to the general area. Yet socially, economically, and culturally we were a long distance from Corona where Bee and I had grown up. During the Mountain Lakes years our children, each in his or her own way, ceased to attend church, Jon through intellectual confrontation of supernaturalism, Barbara through a gradual drifting apart once away from home, and Roy through active rebellion. The church authorities in Nashville had won a skirmish and lost a battle. Maybe a war.

278

Chapter Thirty-Two

WORKING
WITH NATIONAL
ORGANIZATIONS

T
he mail to Mountain Lakes brought good news early in
January of 1960. By membership ballot, I had been
elected from among the three candidates for the presidency of the Association for Supervision and Curriculum Development.

I readily admit to being delighted. I liked working with national education organizations almost as much as I disliked
doing the chores that went with a departmental chairmanship.
The election meant that I would become president-elect at the
March 1960 meeting in Washington, D.C., would become president in Chicago in 1961, and would preside over the convention
at Las Vegas in 1962. Then, as past-president, I would become
vice-president until the close of the 1963 conference. Three years
to try to make a difference through the most influential curriculum organization in the nation; three years on the executive
committee to work for a forward-looking ASCD program; three
years of opportunities to speak up nationally for the version of
modern progressive education to which I held.

The central role that national education organizations play
in American education is often underestimated. Along with textbooks by university professors and journals published by universities, their yearbooks, periodicals, and pamphlets dominate
educational publishing. Textbook authors and journal editors
are themselves usually active in their chosen national organizations, influencing and themselves being influenced. Their commitments to their professional organizations in education are some-

times stronger than their identification with their universities.

The meetings of national educational organizations are rallying points for the profession. Conferences are major vehicles for publicizing new practices and disseminating established procedures. Resolutions reflect the social, political, and educational beliefs of members that staff personnel attempt to implement. In a nation like the United States, with no centralized ministry of education, the influence of educational organizations is impressive. True, the culture is the most potent shaper of the nation's schools; yet organizations can to some degree accelerate or slow down societal trends.

My apprenticeship in working with national education organizations had begun during the 1930s. During the 1940s and 1950s I had become an active participant in several educational groups through publications, talks, and committee and board assignments. In the decade of the 1960s my work in educational organizations was to include presidencies of the Association for Supervision and Curriculum Development, the John Dewey Society, the National Society of College Teachers of Education, and leadership of the Spring Conference.

The apprenticeship began shortly after I joined the faculty of the Ohio State University School in the 1930s. For us, the great educational organization of the era was the Progressive Education Association, a loose coalition of theorists and practitioners with varied interpretations of progressive education ranging from child-centered through social reconstructionist views. When PEA conventions were held in such cities as Chicago and St. Louis, which were within our geographical and financial reach, a carful or two of University School teachers would drive to the conferences. There we would listen to the demigods of the progressive education movement, leaders such as Harold Rugg, a social reconstructionist with a wide intellectual range; Carleton Washburne, the moving spirit in the progressive Winnetka, Illinois, school system; and our own OSU Laura Zirbes, Harold Alberty, and Boyd Bode. We would also attend subgroups on teacher-pupil planning, creative writing, problem-oriented social studies, or whatever else was relevant to our teaching. Once we attended a protest meeting against the mandatory retirement of William Heard Kilpatrick by ungrateful Teachers College and hotly debated among ourselves the legitimacy of mandatory retirement. Sometimes we skipped sessions to worship at pagan shrines, such as those presided over by clarinetist Benny Goodman or drummer Gene Krupa.

Each Thanksgiving vacation the National Council for the Social Studies separated social studies teachers from their loving families. I regularly left Columbus late in bleak November to sit in audiences in East Coast cities such as Boston and Atlantic City as well as nearer Midwest centers. Most of the social studies leaders described and advocated skillful teaching of separate history, geography, economics, and other social science courses, and still others called for more integrated, topically oriented, or problem-centered social studies programs. My teaching experience inclined me toward the latter group. But I had little opportunity to express my views, since my NCSS participation was limited to occasionally introducing a panel of speakers or recording the proceedings of a subgroup.

In the middle 1940s a combination of factors opened the door to my wider participation in the National Council for the Social Studies. My writing on University School teaching was being read, since, as an eager beaver, I sent out reprints to leaders. My assignments in Washington and New York City resulted in acquaintanceship with Wilbur Murra and his successor as secretary of the NCSS, Merrill Hartshorn. To achieve inclusion of consumer and human relations programs in school curricula, the Consumer Education Study and the Bureau for Intercultural Education welcomed relationships with such groups as the NCSS. A committee of the NCSS put me to work on a pamphlet, *The Social Studies Look Beyond the War*, which the Consumer Education Study published in 1945, and the publications committee of NCSS authorized the Taba-Van Til 1945 yearbook, *Democratic Human Relations.*

Yet I was never elected as a director or to an office, and never became an influential in the inner circles of National Council for the Social Studies governance, despite my full professorship in social studies education at the University of Illinois. At the time, I thought I had been passed over simply because of my relative youth and the superior qualifications of those who were chosen. Later, with more experience in the politics of organizations, I recognized that the mainstream of the governing influentials of NCSS differed from my views on social studies education. They supported teaching the social studies as separate subjects. Many of them wrote widely sold textbooks on American history, world history, geography, civics, and economics, which were adopted by states as required reading in elementary and secondary schools.

On the other hand, I was an advocate of highly integrated, problem-centered social studies programs, and I encouraged the development of interdisciplinary core programs that tore down the barriers separating the social studies from English, the sciences, and the several arts areas. I reflected doctoral advisor Harold Alberty's contempt for textbooks. Progressives like me threatened vested interests in the teaching of social studies. Such mavericks might write occasional dissenting chapters in NCSS yearbooks with such titles as those to which I contributed, *The Study and Teaching of American History* (1946) and *Education for Democratic Citizenship* (1951), or might chair an occasional committee on such inescapable social problems as race relations or human rights. Yet few were permitted to become members of the inner governing circle.

Even while I worked at the Bureau for Intercultural Education, I began to shift toward organizations more ideologically compatible with my views. William Heard Kilpatrick and Ernest Melby, chairman and vice-chairman respectively at the bureau, were also influentials in the John Dewey Society for the Study of Education and Culture. The JDS was made up of educators who admired Dewey and who wanted to build on his ideas. The major activity of the organization was publication of yearbooks such as the one I had edited with Kilpatrick.

The John Dewey Society practiced direct democratic electoral processes. The membership list was distributed to all members, who then voted for whomever they wished. To take the place of board members whose terms had expired, those members with the highest number of votes were elected.

Yet pure democracy has its drawbacks too. Those elected were almost always the nationally known veterans of the progressive education movement. They already were committed to many heavy responsibilities. Consequently, in the interest of injecting new blood, Melby sponsored a constitutional amendment allowing the board to "co-opt" organizations that wished to merge with the society. A co-opted group was entitled to representation on the board. I belonged to a group of Young Turks who called themselves "By Way of Comment" after a column we contributed to a journal of administration and supervision. We accepted an invitation to merge. Ike Thut of the University of Connecticut and I found ourselves appointed members of the John Dewey Society Board of Directors, along with the elected greybeards. Ike was soon appointed secretary of the society, and I became a committee chairman; these roles carried with them indefinite continuing tenure on the board. Ironically, the pure democracy of the John Dewey Society had to be compromised if the society was to be youthful, alert, and active.

The John Dewey Society, then as now, was small, never more than a few hundred members. To reach a wider audience, the society used an approach irreverently termed by us the cuckoo technique. The cuckoo, you may recall, lays its eggs in other birds' nests. The small John Dewey Society sponsored intellectually alive talks on the eve of large conventions of major organizations. The most notable, indeed notorious, of their meetings was held (well before my time with the society) at an American Association of School Administrators convention at Atlantic City. Before a large audience made up of a few John Dewey Society members and many school superintendents who had arrived early for the meeting of the school administrators, the noted historian Charles A. Beard declared of William Randolph Hearst, whose newspapers had been attacking progressive education, that "no decent person would touch him with a ten-foot pole." The Hearst press raged, the organization of school superintendents panicked; the John Dewey Society was no longer welcome on the eve of AASA conventions. However, the cuckoo is a resourceful bird; officially ignored by the AASA, independent JDS meetings at Atlantic City continued for several years while the small organization looked for hospitable new nests.

In search of other places for progressive education eggs, the John Dewey Society in 1949 appointed me chairman of a commission on meetings, and I promptly initiated an annual John Dewey Society meeting on the eve of conferences of the Association for Supervision and Curriculum Development, a less nervous organization than AASA. Each year several educators talked on the year's most controversial issue to ASCD influentials, many of them board and committee members who had arrived early for preconvention meetings. The titles of the current issues read like a history of contemporary education.[1]

No speaker was ever paid; the invitation soon became a sufficient honor. In 1963 I was moving into the responsibilities of a president of the John Dewey Society, so Glen Hass of the University of Florida took over the planning and the chairing of the meetings; after 1968 I resumed my former role as meeting developer since Glen, in turn, found himself busy as president of the JDS. Under Harold Turner, my successor in 1974, the meetings of the John Dewey Society in cooperation with ASCD continued, now as an integral part of the annual ASCD conference.

Serious though the issues were, the meetings sometimes had a droll side. Once ASCD's *News Exchange*, through a gorgeous blooper, announced the coming meeting of "The John Society." Vice-president Ernest Melby wrote to ASCD Executive Secretary Arno Bellack that he wanted to join this fascinating society

---

[1] 1950, "Why General Education in the Public Schools?"; 1951, "Education for a World Society"; 1952, "Educational Freedom in an Age of Anxiety"; 1953, "What's Ahead for Progressive Education?"; 1954, "Education for American Freedom"; 1955, "Report on Integration and Segregation"; 1956, "Religion and Education"; 1957, "The Intellectual Component of Modern Education"; 1958, "Rockets, Satellites, and Missiles: Their Meaning for American Education"; 1959, "John Dewey: Exponent of Intellectual Discipline"; 1960, "What Can We Really Learn from Russian Education?"; 1961, "Who Is Being Heard on Education Today?"; 1962, "The New Educational Technology and Organization—For What?"; 1963, "How Can Our Profession Achieve Better Salaries and Conditions?"; 1964, "The Education of American Teachers: Agreements and Issues"; 1965, "Poverty in the United States: What Can Education Do?"; 1966, "Assessment of Federal Aid Programs: Are We Developing a Third School System?"; 1967, "Education Technology and Professional Practice"; 1968, "Troubles and Triumphs—And What to Do Now?"; 1969, "Teacher Negotiations in the Curriculum: The Curricular Rights and Responsibilities of Teachers"; 1970, "Consequences of Confrontation"; 1971, "The Counterculture: What Can We Learn?"; 1972, "Compulsory Education Under Fire"; 1973, "Relative Influence of School and Society on Inequality."

because "The John Society will meet in a place where people
know what they are doing." Another time a poster carefully
lettered by faithful Bee unfortunately included EVERBODY
WELCOME. A *Chicago Tribune* reporter spied it and sent off for
a photographer to lampoon the illiterate progressives. Getting
wind of this, our friends tore down the poster before the photographer's arrival. On still another occasion a celebrator a bit
worse for the wear occupied the otherwise empty front row, then
slowly withered across several chairs. Unperturbed, the panel
addressed their remarks over his prone body.

The American Association of Colleges for Teacher Education
annually held a meeting in Chicago for the college and university
administrators who primarily constituted the membership. To
attract more college professors to their meeting, AACTE leadership encouraged smaller organizations to meet during the convention. Consequently, another John Dewey Society commission
sponsored and published an open John Dewey Society Lecture
Series for the benefit of AACTE members.[2]

In the late 1940s, while at the University of Illinois, I took
part in the activities of my earlier group, the Progressive Education Association (American Education Fellowship). The Progressive Education Association, founded in 1919, was fading through
a combination of factors summarized by Lawrence A. Cremin in
The Transformation of the Schools. I frequently sat in with PEA
leaders at the University of Illinois when they were trying to
resuscitate the organization through a strong injection of societal emphasis into a child-centered organization: John DeBoer,
president; Arch Anderson, editor of *Progressive Education;* Bill
Stanley and Bunnie Smith and Kenneth Benne as volunteer
planners. We sponsored a convention and too few people came.
Child-centered progressives didn't like a heavy emphasis on
society's problems. The organization plunged deeper into debt. I
learned from the PEA experience, and thereafter became a

---

[2] The speakers/authors included: Ordway Tead, Oscar Handlin, Seymour
E. Harris, Gardner Murphy, Loren Eiseley, R. Freeman Butts, Huston
Smith, Abraham H. Maslow, Robert J. Schaefer, Donald U. Michael,
Bentley Glass, Robert Nisbet, Theodosius Dobzhansky, Lawrence A.
Cremin, David Hawkins (1958-1977).

spokesman for fiscal conservatism in the affairs of the other educational organizations, as strong an advocate of a balanced budget as any right-wing Republican.

The Spring Conference was ebullient and healthy. I was elected to membership in 1949, and it's still my favorite organization. The way of working of the Spring Conference was unique; a few years ago one of my *Kappan* columns summed it up:

> The Spring Conference is an informal discussion group of seventy people—mostly educators, with a sprinkling of editors, community workers, and government officials—who meet for a weekend in Chicago each spring for "free trade in ideas," as Justice Oliver Wendell Holmes memorably put it. No program is developed in advance, for the members organize their own program at the meeting. No papers to be read to the membership are toted to the conference, for no one, including the factotum, knows till the meeting is well under way which members will provide springboards to discussion. No minutes or proceedings are printed; no publications are issued; no resolutions are considered or adopted. The Spring Conference members simply come together to discuss whatever is on their minds concerning education and the culture.
>
> The factotum? He's the nearest thing the Spring Conference has to an officer—and that's not very near. For a factotum, according to the dictionary, is "a person employed to do all kinds of work, as the chief servant of a household."...At the annual meeting, the factotum presides over an irreverent membership which enjoys overruling him. No one takes the factotum too seriously, including the factotum.
>
> But discussion is taken seriously....
>
> In response to the factotum's "What's on your mind these days as to education and the culture?" each of the forty or so members who happen to attend that year speaks up on his deepest concerns and hopes. Just to hear these varied views is often worth the price of admission. Before noon a committee is appointed to identify four central issues which have emerged from the personal statements that Saturday morning. During the lunch hour the committee selects and then invites members to introduce one or another of the four issues. The selected springboarders, who are not aware in advance that they will be asked to talk on that issue, must then reach into their hearts and minds, rather than into their briefcases, for their forthcoming commentary. They are warned that their comments

are to be brief and to the point, so that there will be abundant time for discussion.

When the conference reconvenes after lunch, the first panel sets the stage with three or four viewpoints from people of varied persuasions. In mid-afternoon the conference turns to the second issue, next morning to the third and fourth. Each discussion is open to all and, at its best, is earnest, argumentative, good-humored, and marked by mutual toleration and respect.

Memorable meetings were assured when the discussants included such vigorous spokesmen for controversial ideas as Myles Horton of Highlander Folk School; Morris Mitchell, an eloquent advocate of community schools; Goodwin Watson, a Teachers College societal reformer; and Earl Rugg, Harold's irreverent and earthy brother. Myles was once asked by an ambitious educator what the Spring Conference was and how one became a member; he drawled dryly in response, "It's a self-appointed elite."

Why allow the Spring Conference to be unique in its procedures? The John Dewey Society members too needed the mutual support that comes from informal talk about issues and ideas. So my JDS commission on meetings sponsored for the JDS membership an annual day for discussion, modeled on the Spring Conference. I tried to introduce the same approach into the Professors of Curriculum conference that annually preceded the ASCD conference, but the Professors of Curriculum repeatedly regressed to formal stuffed-shirt presentations.

Consequently, I entered my three-year span of leadership of the ASCD with some experience in educational organizations: the NCSS, the PEA, the Spring Conference, the Professors of Curriculum, and the JDS, in which I had served as vice-president, 1957-1960, and acting president, 1958-59. I had also worked in community organizations: the teachers' union at Ohio State University, Peace Action, the Illinois Interracial Commission, and the Nashville Community Relations Conference.

Chapter Thirty-Three

THE LIFE
OF AN ORGANIZATION
PRESIDENT

Yet the Association for Supervision and Curriculum Development was different. For one thing, it was big. The quarter of a million dollar annual budget supported a paid staff headed by an executive secretary and associate secretaries in charge of publications and state relations; the expenses of a dozen or two committees and commissions; an annual publications program made up of a yearbook, a half dozen pamphlets, and a monthly magazine; and an annual conference with extensive exhibits. The ASCD had a large board of directors, made up of sixty-two state representatives and eighteen educators elected at large from the nation. It had a small executive committee of seven that included the three officers.

Unlike many of my predecessors in the presidency, I had not served earlier on an ASCD Executive Committee and had instead come to the presidency-elect via the board and the committee/commission route. In 1951 and 1957, I had been elected at large to the board, each time for three-year terms. Theoretically the board was the governing body of the organization; the mandate of the executive committee was to serve in the year-long interim between annual board meetings. Yet, since the board was large and their meeting time before and after the conference limited, the board more often served as a forum for opinion while the executive committee made most major policy decisions. As chairman of the Publications Committee, 1953-55, then chairman of the Intergroup Education Committee, 1957-60, I knew how it felt to appear before the ASCD Executive Committee, hat in hand, with requests for authorization of activities with attendant funding.

As president-elect I soon learned where the power in the organization was lodged. George Denemark was in a good position to tell me, for he had both been my close associate as my graduate assistant at Illinois and later had been executive secretary of ASCD during the travail over *Forces Affecting American Education.* He advised, "The effectiveness of an ASCD president depends on the quality of relationships with the executive secretary." During my term Margaret Gill, bright, capable, and sometimes tense, was executive secretary. Her initial appraisal of me was that I would become a strong president, not easy to work with, who might, in effect, "move from New York to Washington and try to run the organization." We both worked to achieve mutual trust.

The other power center was the executive committee, which met before, during, and after the convention and, in addition, for two to five-day periods twice annually. Feeling my oats as the people's choice, early in my term on the executive committee I urged financial support for acquisition and dissemination of kits of materials on ethnic and racial relationships that had been assembled by the Intergroup Education Committee. The executive committee demurred. I pressed. They still demurred. I forced the issue. I lost. My motion was tabled; mine was the only vote in favor of the intercultural kit project, even though I requested only a measly $350 appropriation. The executive committee had made clear to me who was in charge. I mended my aggressive ways and thereafter, with greater tact, managed to get most of what I wanted.

During my term the times were difficult for defenders of modern education, for Admiral Hyman Rickover had just denigrated American education through his *Education and Freedom* (1959). The nearest public education came to a nationally known defender was James B. Conant, whose twenty-one recommendations in the *American High School Today* (1959) were traditionally oriented. In the era that immediately followed the launching of the Soviet Union's Sputnik (1957), science and math were supported by the National Defense Education Act while other areas, notably the social studies, English, and varied arts areas,

My Way of Looking at It

were minimized. Projects were developed by liberal arts scholars ignorant of hard-won curriculum knowledge and unable to recognize the difficulties of dissemination that their new programs would inevitably encounter. When I began my three-year span for ASCD, Jerome Bruner in *The Process of Education* (1960) was urging an oversimplified approach to curriculum building that focused on teaching the structure of the separate disciplines and teaching students the ways that the scholars within each discipline think and work. Unfortunately, the theory ignored the reality of interdisciplinary problems.

And what was it that I supported? Speaking out by the ASCD to the profession and the public on the modern schools we need. Being heard in the halls of government for a balanced curriculum rather than one that went all out for science and mathematics. Defending equal educational opportunities for minorities and the disadvantaged. Developing disciplinary and interdisciplinary programs based on the interaction of needs, social realities, and values, a curriculum that insisted on relevant knowledge.

Even before I became president in 1961 I began to shape the coming 1962 Las Vegas conference as to program and participants. To support education based on social realities, needs, and values at the conference at which I was to preside, I urged major addresses at Las Vegas by Max Lerner, scholar of society; Arthur Combs and Earl Kelley, humanistic psychologists; and Harold Shane, a philosophically oriented generalist.

Ironically, a few years earlier I had voted as an ASCD board member against holding our 1962 conference at Las Vegas; after living in the South, I recognized that, in Bible Belt areas, some boards of education would not sanction expenses for travel by public school employees to a wicked, sinful gambling hell. But the ASCD went ahead anyway, and I inherited the responsibility to preside over the first conference to be held in Las Vegas by a major group of educators. (Happily, the convention was to turn out to be one of our largest—3,015 curriculum leaders participated. Despite Las Vegas lures and however bleary-eyed, our members scrupulously attended even the early morning convention sessions.)

At the close of the Chicago ASCD conference in 1961, I became president of the organization. Wells Foshay of Teachers

290

College was president during the conference and made a well-received speech, "A Modest Proposal," in which he attempted to reconcile the structure of the disciplines theory with the long-time commitment of ASCD to meeting the needs of learners and dealing with social realities. Many in the audience, curriculum workers under pressure from supporters of varied projects in the separate subject fields, were grateful. Structure of the disciplines proponents, including some who made regular pilgrimages to Cambridge to sit at the feet of an unlikely guru, Jerome Bruner, heard only Wells's advocacy of structure of the disciplines and ignored his coequal endorsement of a curriculum related to the concerns of learners and the problems of the surrounding society.

At Chicago I was busy. There were decisions by the executive committee on budget and on the length of time any executive secretary should be engaged to serve the ASCD, a meeting of board members eager to spend ASCD funds for creative ideas, a talk to the John Dewey Society, a reception sponsored by the Curtis Publishing Company, a proposal for cooperation with the newly created Peace Corps, state unit and college breakfasts, parties, visits to meetings of committee and commissions, an NYU reception, the business meeting for adoption of resolutions, more executive committee meetings to hear committee and commission reports. One afternoon I went to the Chicago studios of CBS to appear as a TV panelist on Kup's *At Random* program, in which I disputed with a Mr. Gavrikov, a representative of Soviet Russia's embassy. The broadcast was taped and aired at midnight just after the ASCD conference closed. I watched from an easy chair in the deserted Conrad Hilton.

The spring and fall executive committee meetings in Washington in 1961 were effective. In the first, still more socially oriented publications were planned. The Las Vegas meeting was outlined and planned, letters to the *New York Times* setting forth ASCD positions were developed, and I even got authorization for my intercultural kits on racial and ethnic relationships. At the second meeting, in addition to regular business that included consideration of the reappointment of Margaret Gill as executive secretary for a three-year term, we developed ways in which ASCD could speak out on educational issues through the presi-

dent, executive secretary, and executive committee. We breakfasted with Roy Wilson, media specialist for NEA relations; the
program of "speaking out" we developed included my appearance on a national TV show on March 11 on NBC. We lunched
with Commissioner of Education McMurrin and urged a joint
curriculum committee appointed by his office and the ASCD to
reduce organizational overlap.

Early in 1962 I prepared my presidential address to the
coming convention at Las Vegas. I decided to stress that undra-
matic yet essential element in curriculum construction: balance.
Panicked by the Soviet Union's 1957 Sputnik, the U. S. Congress
had passed a National Defense Education Act funding science,
mathematics, and world language programs but had neglected
the social studies, English, and the several arts. My talk was
intended to strengthen the hand of educators and legislators who
were attempting to correct this imbalance. I also called on schools
to be sensitive to the needs of students and to deal with crucial
interdisciplinary social problems such as war and peace, intercultural education, and conservation of the environment, rather
than limit their instruction to teaching the separate disciplines
as advocated by the sponsors of science and mathematics projects.
The address was scheduled early in the conference to provide a
keynote.

We were the first major educational organization to have
held a meeting in Las Vegas. As the convention closed I tore up
a press release I had carried with me day and night throughout
the convention in readiness for possible mass media criticism of
our selection of Las Vegas as a meeting place. The release sancti-
moniously pointed out that such eminently respectable groups
as organizations of surgeons and of Catholic women had preceded us in their Las Vegas meetings. The anticipated press onslaught never materialized; I had no occasion to use my constant
companion. For the first time during my Las Vegas stay, I visited
the casinos, where I dribbled away some nickels in the slot
machines. Gambling was never among my vices. Then I slept the
sleep of the totally exhausted.

I went on to Los Angeles for some talks, then flew to Hawaii.
For a celestial week, which began with my first visit to a VIP airlines club, Pam Am's Clipper Club at the L.A. Airport, I enjoyed

Hawaii's charms and the warm hospitality of Hawaiian ASCD members. The soft odors of exotic flowers filled my room at the Princess Kaiulani Hotel; I breakfasted daily on papaya and pineapple; I swam at Waikiki and rode the outriggers. Then to the State Department of Public Instruction, visits to schools, a New York University alumni meeting in a gorgeous valley home, and several talks to the ASCD state unit. I hosted a party in my room for ASCD leadership, enjoyed magnificent South Seas dances at a Polynesian panorama sponsored by a Mormon college, took a round-the-island tour with my hosts and hostesses, regretfully packed for my return home, and waved a lei-garlanded aloha to a delegation that accompanied me to the airport. My term as ASCD president closed with this regal fringe benefit, a working vacation in Hawaii.

Chapter Thirty-Four

IRAN
ALL THE WAY

G oing to Iran wasn't my idea. The Iranian Teacher Education Survey was the brainchild of the New York University administration, and I got talked into it. The timing was terrible, May and June of 1962, just after the Las Vegas ASCD conference and Hawaiian trip, just after the publication of "Is Progressive Education Obsolete?" by *Saturday Review* in a February issue, just when resultant TV guest appearances to talk about education might materialize, and just when Barbara was to graduate proudly from Douglass College and Roy was about to walk away with many prizes at his high school graduation in Mountain Lakes. Too, I couldn't shake a strange, uneasy premonition of personal disaster. And, I had read enough about Iranian history and contemporary life to conclude that the box score of any survey of teacher education in Iran would read no hits, no runs, several errors. But I went. Pan Am brought me to Germany, then to Istanbul on May 6, where I wrote Bee communication four of the twenty-eight I was to write home:

> At a very golden six o'clock of the evening of a blue-sky day in Istanbul, I sit on my balcony looking across the Bosporus from Europe to Asia and I write the one who should be with me here as always. It's a strange feeling for one who knows a little history to sit in the last of Europe and look over to Asia. Darius the Persian came through the region in the sixth century B.C. heading west to conquer Europe. Alexander the Great captured the area, going east to take Persia (and destroy Persepolis).

Constantine I made this city the capital of the Roman Empire in the fourth century A.D.... The Ottoman Turks got it back in 1453 and it has been Turkish since.

To see it, think of Budapest gone Byzantine. The same massive buildings, nearness to water, picturesque (poverty-stricken) side streets.

I toured the bazaars and the Sultan's Palace, took a ferryboat ride from Europe to Asia, and pampered myself at the Istanbul Hilton. Pan Am took me to Beirut then gorged me in first class with Iranian caviar, beef stroganoff, champagne, and brandy en route to Teheran.

At the Teheran airport I was met by John Payne, NYU's associate dean and the leader of the survey team; Herb Schwartz of science education, NYU; and Paul Regan, an educator with the Agency for International Development, A.I.D. for short. John Payne was a good human being, a hard-working fullback type who worked by day and wrote our report by night. Herb Schwartz was a humorous and amiable man, an incessant shopper who constantly mailed merchandise home, a swarthy native New Yorker who could have readily passed for a Near Easterner in Iran, even as he readily passed as a native in Puerto Rico. Paul Regan was a gentle, patient, and aware professional in international education.

Of our quarters, the Abe Karaj compound with its view of the snow-topped Elburz Mountains, I wrote home:

...The internal architecture could be called barracks-dormitory. Bare walls, passable cot beds, a couch, tile floors, a shower that occasionally achieves "luke," an occasional cockroach, an occasional naked bulb and occasional shade, a refrigerator with a pitcher of drinking water. As Mercutio pointed out when wounded, "Not as deep as a well nor as wide as a door—but 'twill serve."

We regularly rose at six A.M. and learned the ropes from the thirty educators on the A.I.D. staff of several hundred. I wrote Bee that the A.I.D. staff:

...are pleasant people who have learned patience, who work long hours and are pleased with small results. They are international pros, a modern version of the Wandering Jew, who go from a two-year assignment in Iran briefly home, then to another two-year assignment in Tripoli (a secretary left for there today) or to Nepal (where Paul Regan will head shortly). What their motivations are, I know not. They are said to live well, in villas, etc. They are the new "British," the nineteenth century moved into the twentieth.

With A.I.D. top man Hendershot, we paid a ceremonial call on the Minister of Education of Iran, who had been head of the teachers' organization that won a strike and doubled teacher pay to $700 a year for elementary school and $900 for high school teachers. He had been rewarded by appointment as Minister. During our visit, which was marked with much "taroof" [ceremonial behavior], he urged that some A.I.D. money for research be transferred to audiovisual equipment for schools. Toussy, a young Iranian intellectual who was to be a constant companion on our journeys, translated impassively. Only later did we learn that Toussy, holder of a Ph.D. degree from Michigan State, was the most vigorous protagonist in A.I.D. for spending more money on research.

Within two days we were off for Shiraz, Isfahan, Kerman, and Zahadan. I wrote Bee:

...Once Teheran was left behind, we crossed some of the most fearful, awesome country I have ever seen. The plateau land is barren, desolate, achingly dry, just short of a desert. It is occasionally edged with red mountains that rise out of what seems miles of dust. As you look down, you see occasionally a patch of spotty green and beside it what looks like an acrostic made of mud. This is a mud brick village with a mud brick wall. The sheer fact of survival in the surrounding immensity and waste makes you marvel at man's tenacity. Your next reaction is horror at what life must be like in those mud walls. It looks like excrement on a starved, parched landscape. So you fly for an hour and see maybe twenty such patches in the nothingness.

Suddenly your plane comes to a much larger patch, partly mud houses, partly concrete, with occasional gleams from pools, recurrent grass. This larger entity in the vast dryness is a city....

Shiraz was first:

We call on the Ostan chief—county superintendent is the nearest description in our language. Underlings open doors, precede us to the great man's presence. He sits behind a king-size desk with no papers. Above him, the pictures of the handsome Shah look down on us. We proceed through our translator. He grants us permission to visit. We drink tea in glasses served by an illiterate and deferential underling. All is ceremonial.

We visit the schools. A class of 21-year-old girls in the thirteenth year program is learning to teach reading. I ask them where they want to teach. Unanimously, Shiraz. But first they must go to their Siberia, the villages, for several required years. (Like New York teachers in the Negro and Puerto Rican slum schools.) If they survive, they may return to Shiraz. Out in the pest holes of the villages there are no health facilities, toilets, or supervision of teaching. Survive three years and back to Shiraz. Meanwhile 16- and 17-year-old boys are also being trained in normal schools.... They are village boys. Most intend to teach their required years and get out to Teheran, Shiraz. One tells me, "In this country, we lack dedication." And seventy percent of Iran lives in hovels in villages, they say.

To a school for training young men to teach in tent schools that move with the tribes. And a surprise! I am back in Oklahoma! These tribesmen are the equivalent of American Indians. They are strong, leathery, grave, tough, quiet, respectful. They live in a neat boarding school out of town. They are quietly contemptuous of city Iranians, who are, to them, corrupt, soft, cowardly, pale. I ask whether they would rather teach in Teheran, Shiraz, or with the tribes. They chorus, "With the tribes."....

As the work day closes, we return to the Ostan chief. He has gathered his subordinates. He has an audience. He talks and is translated for one and a half solid hours. He is a superintendent. He has problems...the Ministry, the teachers who do not read the manuals. 4:00 to 5:30 PM. One gets tired of drinking so much tea. John Payne attempts to conclude and the chief says dolefully that Americans have not learned patience. We will come back, we say. Bring more patience, he says.

Shiraz itself was fantastically lovely in the spring of 1962:

Shiraz is the land of the two poets of seven centuries ago, one a poet who traveled widely and wrote with humor as well as with sad celebration of the infinite, the other a poet alone who never left Shiraz and who wrote symbolically of the eternal through songs of roses, taverns, veils, gardens, journeys begun and ended. Omar Khayyam lived here too, but Shiraz does not celebrate his poetry; they think of him as a mathematician.

But for Hafiz and Saadi, they have tombs in gardens joyous with flowers. Saadi's tomb has an astonishing green tile top against contrasting blue sky. The dome is supported by long, graceful wooden columns. Hafiz's tomb is in a garden run riot with tremendous roses bordering grass plots, bordering pools, bordering myriads of flowerpots with geraniums massed together. The people come and stroll the paths and read the poems on tiles set in walls. They do not even see the beggar who holds a boy child with legs spindle-thin from rickets. Seeing a tourist, he snaps open the boy's mouth with a finger to point with piteous fawning to a supposedly aching tooth in the child's mouth. I am told the beggars often rent such children. It is easy to believe, and it helps you not to see him. So you believe it. If you don't see him, he doesn't exist for you. But the child exists.

Shiraz is most amazing because it is set squarely in the heart of aridity. They won't call it desert, because a trace of vegetation can be seen here and there. But when you enter Shiraz you encounter greenness and flowers gone mad beyond any description I can achieve.

Nearby was the incredible Persepolis:

...thirteen high columns elaborately carved, surmounted by legendary beasts. Thirteen left of literally hundreds of columns that held up the palace roof. Also there are remains of great court rooms. All were destroyed by Alexander the Great, some say to please his courtesan, who wanted to set fires after a drinking party. Bas-reliefs remain on walls and two keep recurring to remind the viewer of the brutal nature of the age. One is a winged and scaled lion sinking his teeth into the haunch of an agonized unicorn. The other is a king sticking his sword into the belly of a mythical beast that has reared up on its hind legs. This was the realm of Darius, King of Kings, and Xerxes.

One prowls for two hours without completely crossing or circumscribing the vast acreage of ruins. And you look at the surrounding barrenness and think of armies going from Persia to conquer Greece, from Greece to conquer Persia.

So back to the hotel by jeep and a walk through a precise and perfect Persian garden. A pool with a spraying fountain, fabulous and mammoth roses everywhere, a cage of love birds and doves (about 150 birds), oranges growing, a mulberry tree, tea out of doors. Now time has caught up and I must stop.

We moved on to Isfahan:

298

Monday, we labored. The ceremonial call on the Ostan chief (superintendent), the labored translation, the slow progress, the curious students.

The high or low spot was a visit to an emergency program for training teachers for Isfahan Ostan (county) villages. The battered chairs were occupied by thirty women huddled under their chaddors (long body-length shawls covering the head, clutched nervously to cover the mouth, covering the entire body to the dust) and ten men. Ages: 16-21, about 17; 21-26, about 10; over 26, about 13. Average education: seven to nine years in school. Mostly villagers, mostly mothers. Due to teach at 100 rials ($1.33) a day. (If Ed Welling [superintendent in Mountain Lakes] is short of teachers, you might tell him they're available.) I asked them what kept people from teaching in villages and guess what they said? Yes, money....

At a **good** teacher education program for girls in their thirteenth year of education, the activity program had been introduced—and had gone mad. Units, projects, charts, charts, charts! The girls proudly reported two projects via charts on walls. One was *Foods of Iran*. The charts showed magnificent foods, clipped from American magazines. The second was *Life in Iran*. The charts contained pictures of an Iranian engineer's family at a $20,000 a year income. I gently suggested that the poverty-stricken children of the villages couldn't **conceive** of such foods and living. I suggested charts that would help **improvements** of living conditions. It was a new idea to the girls. They listened seriously, then told the translator of a great block to following this idea in a project. He translated, "They would be unable to get pretty pictures to put on their charts if they followed my suggestion."

Of the giant square of Isfahan called the Maidan, once used as a polo field by early shahs, I wrote to Bee:

Imagine fifteen Washington Squares joined. Imagine most of the body of water called Mountain Lakes made long and oblong. You have some idea of the square. At one end is the Shah Mosque, poetry of tiles in green and blue mosaic. The minarets outside face north. But proper minarets point to Mecca. So beyond the squareness at the end of the park, beyond the minarets that bound the Maidan, comes the mosque itself turned "catty-corner" so that the minarets and the entire inside open area may point to Mecca. There is a blue dome with a wonderful seven-fold echo when you yell up into it. The pool is central in the interior yard; the mosque rises on four sides of you as usual. In the mosques surrounding the courtyard, there are no chairs; Muslims bow to the floor on prayer rugs.

I wrote home at length of the road to Zahadan:

This is a letter about The Road to Zahadan. The phrase calls up memories of the zany antics of Bing and Bob, joined by the beauteous Dorothy at crucial moments and rocking by camel along a Hollywoodized road to mirth. But this is not my Road to Zahadan, though my Road has its lighter moments too, as you may see.

My Road to Zahadan is a story of some experiences on a trip east to the corner of the world where Iran, Afghanistan, and Pakistan join. **The** road runs from Kerman to Zahadan. **The** road is used advisedly; for 400 miles there is no other road. No road parallels it; no road crosses it. The gravel road of small broken stone and dust goes remorselessly east, across deserts, in the shadows of mountains, through winding mountain passes, through dead-level, straight-ahead hours too.

There is another level of the Road to Zahadan that I hesitate to tell you about. But I must, for it is part of the truth and necessary to an honest narrative. I think you know, for you are highly sensitive to what I think, that I have been struggling against—let's call it forebodings of personal disaster in connection with this trip. With that part of my mind that has rejected spookery and supernatural manifestation since the time of my father's death when I was fifteen, I know that forebodings are part of mankind's over-active imagination, reflections of the temporary state of the psyche. A minority contender for my mind encourages me to wear my comedy-tragedy pin (and way of looking at the universe) on days when I need the breaks.

The camel of our light-hearted jests (the traffic in Iran is heavier than in New York; watch out for trampling by the camel traffic) became in my mind the symbol of Nemesis, the embodiment of the foreboding. He became it playfully, lightly— and yet seriously. So when John Payne mapped as part of our travels a long jeep ride from Kerman to Zahadan, the most eastern part of our trip, a desert journey, the foreboding on occasion zeroed in on me. My single resolve was, "Be careful. Forebodings don't bring disaster—falls do, bacteria do, crashed steel does, violence does." I thumb my nose at the irrational—I say.

Two jeeps and two drivers, Ali and Hossein, an Iranian

300

Laurel and Hardy, an Abbott and Costello, in that order. For Ali was thin and wispy-wistful; Hossein solid and of Falstaff's build. Four passengers—me whom you know too well; Herb Schwartz, science education NYU, a pleasant boulevardier sentenced to Great Neck; Dave Laird of A.I.D., a California schoolman of 56, reflective, knowledgeable of the region; Toussy, Iranian middle-class son of a small landlord, Ph.D. Michigan State, translator, general factotum, upwardly mobile for socially significant purposes in the Ministry.

The Road led east. We left Kerman, undistinguished mud-brick houses and streets of tiny shops, and it turned gravel. First it ran through New Mexico, a sandy floor between substantial mountain ranges, a long valley plain. Then a patch of green ahead, which grew into Mahan, a town twenty-five or so miles out. Then the green was punctured by the inevitable mud color of all residences and institutions, and finally by the delicate blues and greens of the priceless and memorable minarets....

The Road ran east. New Mexico gave way to Utah, purple bluffs with highly visible stratification, some salt flats, some sizable and made, naturally, of mud-colored mud. The drivers pushed the jeeps hard. We jolted and swayed and talked. The Road ran through the authentic desert. We were again reminded of the excess of geography which is Iran.

We reached Bam. Not Pow or Zowi—but Bam. The desert becomes punctuated by squares with mud walls. Barely topping them are palm trees—date palms. The squares thicken and coalesce—that's Bam. It's near Guk.

In the lead jeep, Schwartz and I were driven by Hossein (yes, Hardy not Laurel) into twisting streets to our predestined rendezvous, which was totally unanticipated. Take one of the several castles you have wandered through—Richard and Blondell's on the Danube or perhaps Aggstein will do. Flatten out the land a bit but still make it a sizable hill. Then, most miraculous of all, transmute every battlement, tower, hole for pouring arrows at enemies, symbolic decoration, into plain unrelieved mud shaped with cunning by a supernaturally precocious child, add at the foot of the castle but within the great mud walls a village that he built, got tired of, and slashed into near destruction with a few strokes of his hand—and you have the ancient city of Bam. It is undisturbed by archeologists, tourists, locals, time, life, history. The brick that underlies the plastering of mud over the square mile of the castle and town has baked placidly in the desert sun for centuries. The best estimate we could get was that it was 2000 years old (at least begun 2000 years ago) and that it was inhabited up to fifty years ago. What Muslim century was its crest—the thirteenth, the seventeenth? No one knows, or indeed cares. In Iran they say sagely, "Old, very old," and go back to eking a living out of the desert or to manipulating people....

Outside the ancient city of Bam lay the new village only centuries old. Beyond the desert, the shapes and forms of buttes and escarpments, the landscape Herb calls Krazy Kat, calling back visions of Hermann's strange buttes before weird mountains, background for the sage remarks of Krazy Kat....

Back through the twisting alleys. But a jeep was overheating, and as the drivers tinkered, another jeep came by. A school man of Bam, a specialist on fundamental education (literacy). They were waiting for us. Dinner was "ready" at his house. The judge was there, the agricultural specialist. He had word from the Ostan chief (county superintendent) that we were en route. We must stop.

We protested. We had planned to eat in the desert far along at a lonely stop for trucks. The outcome was foregone. We went to his house. It was a middle-class (upper section) Iranian home. Like all homes, it was down a narrow, twisted, dusty street, one jeep wide. The door in the mud stucco wall opens and you are in the sanctuary, the house, and shortly in the garden. The garden has two stages, a gravel area with a pond surrounded by concrete slabs and small trees. Just beyond a wall another garden through which the jube flowed. At its meanest, the jube is a gutter through which grey water slowly sloshes. At its best, the jube is a near creek, also grey, but forceful in speed. Everything happens beside a jube. Clothes are washed; parts of people are washed; litter is disposed of; dusty feet are dangled. Children pee. Water is drawn for household purposes. Sophisticated people boil it for beverage. In the jube I washed with soap carefully laid by and dried with a towel on the tree.

The living room is spacious, perhaps fifteen feet by thirty-five feet. As everywhere in Iran, from pictures high on the wall, well beyond touch, two men look down. One is Ali, the dark-eyed, bushy faced son-in-law of Mohammed. The other is the Shah—in military dress, or smiling at his son, or stately with his wife, or fierce. The Shah is everywhere. Over administrators' desks, he signs papers; in homes he gazes kindly at his son....

Two P.M. and the Road to Zahadan leads east. Now we

cannot arrive before nine P.M. even at forty miles per hour by jeep. The desert takes over, flat, endless. We watch the lovely lakes and ocean shores formed by mirages. We particularly enjoyed the Jones Beach causeway mirage!

We stop now and then to "rest the engine"—actually to rest the driver and us. I get a sick feeling as the key is turned off and the comforting motor stops out in nowhere. Now we have only one jeep; the overheated one was sent back at Bam with Ali (yes, Laurel). We cram all of our baggage, large Hossein, and the four travelers into the space not pre-empted by the gasoline cans and water barrels. The Road runs east....

Gendarmes on duty in isolated outposts in this wild Baluchi country, the Baluchistan that Iran shares with Afghanistan and Pakistan, checked our passports, wired ahead that we were coming. Cars have been waylaid in Iran. A few years ago an A.I.D. couple, the Carrolls, traveling to investigate thefts of American wheat going east, were murdered by bandits, and all Iran was aroused. The murder was in Baluchi country; they are like your Red Indians, we had been told. The road ran east toward the mountain passes before Zahadan.

At one gendarme check point, a camel was tethered. I went over to look at him. Let no one tell you that the camel is a good, bland animal out of Walt Disney. Ask any camel driver. Camels are mean-tempered, arrogant animals that hate men. I took his picture and he showed his teeth in a snarl and made unfriendly noises that combined a growl, snarl, and groan. The camel—my symbol on the Road to Zahadan.

Dave Laird, A.I.D. veteran, decided to be pictured riding him. The gendarmes saddled the protesting beast, forced him to fold. And Dave mounted. Great mirth. First the front legs reared up and Dave lurched back. Then the rear and Dave lurched forward. There, even keel, high above us. The camel walked to the water hole, dipped his head, still keeping keel even, and drank. The gendarmes pulled the camel down. The lurch front and back. Dave dismounted. The camel snarled. Herb mounted, beret atop his head. The camel grew angrier and pettier and noisier.

I decided that I had taken enough from this camel with his bared teeth, his ugly sound, his nasty beady eyes, his hostility to life. So I mounted him too. The gendarmes forced him up and as one set of legs unfolded, I lurched front and rear on what passes for a pommel on the stack of old carpets that makes the saddle. A picture taken while I was up. Then the camel broke the string binding the saddle to the beast, alarming the gendarmes, who could do nothing about it. The camel grew more hostile. They forced it down and I dismounted. Toussy and Hossein decided then to have their pictures on the **kneeling** beast thereafter, for they are intelligent Iranians. As for me, some obscure necessity required me to tell death that life was to be lived fully till its end and that death for this individual or for the world was to be denied even the courtesy of credibility, denied till it prevailed as it must. Meanwhile, ride the camel.

Light-hearted, we traveled east. The road ran toward Zahadan and dropped miles behind us. We grew tired. It was eight P.M. Hossein grew sleepy and the jeep began to sway. We turned off the motor in the desert. It kicked off again. The moon was full and the high mountain passes were full of ghosts of Baluchi warriors.

At the height of the pass, lights ahead. A mirage, we suggested. But we knew it was Zahadan, in a forgotten land, forgotten by all save its residents and A.I.D., a town that no one knew existed in the wild Baluchistan desert. The Road had brought us to Zahadan.

...The superintendent lives in a lovely house that cost considerable to build. He entertains lavishly in a region where, we heard, some Baluchis have been reduced literally to eating grass in order to survive the drought. He has a clean-cut philosophy of education. Hot lunch. Give him power to administer the hot lunch money and the Baluchis and village people will attend school. Do not give him the administration of this money and they will not come to school. He can talk of no problems of curriculum, selection, other ways of recruiting. Only hot lunch. In America, he would be calculating football receipts and entertaining the community elite.

Back in Teheran and the surrounding area we saw many more officials and more schools. I went to Tabriz near the Soviet Union border where, with Paul Regan of A.I.D., I visited city schools and a small village:

There were two institutions and two institutions only in the village and they are symbols of the fight between old and new going on in Iran. They are the school and the carpet factory. Our interpreter asked some 8 to 10-year-old boys (like everybody else on holiday Friday, Muslim style) what they did during the week. Seven out of eight said they worked in the carpet factory.

The carpet factory is the only "modern" building in the village. Small, of yellow brick, one floor, with roof vents, a few glass windows. It was locked. It was owned by an absentee landlord (the curse of Iran) and managed by his foreman. A few yards away was the school. Two rooms of mud and stone separated by an entrance hall. Two small windows in each room giving insufficient light. Dirt floor, very dusty. Black long benches, whittled and scarred. Long black desks for the benches on which four could crowd. On the wall, a map of Europe. Up front, the teacher's table and chairs. Long pages for attendance records. Nothing more. No materials, no nothing. The light filtering into the darkness, the dust, the black scarred benches, the little room. The other room its twin.

In the village of Matanag we met a mullah. Years later, when the Iranian fundamentalist religionists held the Americans hostage, I often thought of the authority the mullah exercised in that village:

And along came a wizened old man, with greying beard, creased forehead, black leathery skullcap, tattered long brown coat over blue-patched trousers. He was really an old man, about 45. (Life expectancy in Iran is 52. Half of the children born die before age 5.) People fell back deferentially. Would we have tea? Of course. He was the old mullah, the Muslim religious man who read religious books and can use the abacus. We followed him up the hill to a hut no different from the rest....

What did they need in Matanag, population 800? They now had a bathhouse, but they needed more water supply. He understood that in America people had electric blankets. He would like to know more of this. He had also heard that we killed people by electricity.

We asked him how bad people were handled in Matanag. Some were brought to the gendarmes. In other cases the people handled the matter themselves through a third party. A theft for instance. What third party? Himself. He was also the judge. Where? This room.

Did the people vote? Yes, on occasion. Where? This room. They brought their ballots and left them on the floor of his room. Sometimes they reached this high (he demonstrated). On such a day he served much tea. (In Iranian villages the landlords instruct the peasants whose names to write on the ballots. The names are always those of the landlords and their cronies. In villages where the people own part of the land their votes are bought for one or two terman (10 to 20¢) by the landlords or other candidates.)

By the survey's end, our team had visited 84 percent of all of the teacher institutions in Iran.

Personally, I ran all the way.

Chapter Thirty-Five

IRANIAN CHARACTER AND THE SURVEY REPORT

I ranian character and our survey report were inextricably intermingled. I wrote to Bee:

The cultural historians debate whether national character exists. Meanwhile the Iranian character grows clearer and clearer and more and more difficult to crack. To reverse roles, Imagine if you were an Oriental sent to America to "aid" and faced with the problem of slowing Americans down to the Oriental pace and developing a philosophy of fatalism in place of one of progress and forward movement. Your leverage is the educational system. How do you do it?

In Iran, democratic values (except individualism) are not comprehensible.

Sit side by side a centuries-old ability to adjust to the conqueror, the imperialist, and in time absorb him. Alexander destroyed their Persepolis; his warriors married Persian women; Persia absorbed the Greeks and went on being Persian. The Arabs conquered Persia and brought it the Muslim religion. The Persians developed a splinter religion based on Mohammed's son-in-law, Ali, and made their deviant interpretation prevail. The Turks and the Mongols invaded; Persia absorbed them. Britain drove for India across Persia; Russia looked for warm water to the south. Iran acquiesced in their influence. America moved in. And again on the surface Iran accepted the newcomers. She did in a haphazard fashion what the newcomers wanted her to do. But she accepted because it was what **they** wanted; she did not do these things for herself, because they were things **she** wanted.

Add carefully wrought negative explanations as to why

307

things cannot be done, neatly developed in the interest of face-saving, and you can understand why a scholar of national character finds it necessary to say (Vreeland on Iran):

"Adroitness and expediency are highly valued."

"Insecurity and distrust permeate attitudes toward each other, toward the government, and toward outside powers. Persians are skilled dissemblers... A profession of altruism is usually considered rank hypocrisy (and often correctly so)."

"In contests they try to choose the winning side, and often promptly desert a loser."

"The strongest attachments are based on mutual self-interest."

"He must not lose, if he is to preserve face... He cannot admit failure."

"The things which are beyond the powers of men to cope with are in the realm of fate."

"A Persian admires dead heroes, but he ordinarily has no desire to become one immediately."...

Yet this letter is skewed so far. It leaves out many charming national characteristics. The pleasant humor of people when not defending or striving. The deep-rooted courtesy. The enjoyment of beautiful weather. The way they prize little gardens and carry flowers. The patience with adversity. The charm of the laughing children. The endless rote recitation by students memorizing as they walk. The endless fight against the encroaching dryness, against admitting the horror of the emptiness. The enraged dedicated few who feel immobilized. The helpfulness to strangers. They often seem like strangely old, preternaturally tired, wise children. We will see you again, we say. If Allah wills it, they respond. Fate is in charge and directs mankind.

Yet a survey report was inescapable:

The time has come when the jaunts, long as the Road to Zahadan or short as yesterday's to Dardasht (literally "place in the desert"), are ending. We turn now to the hard intellectual work of any survey: determining about fifty recommendations, phrasing them tightly, defending them for a page or so in a land of contradictions where statistics are lacking, wrapping all into *The Survey Report.*

So my mind turns to administration in Iran, a near relative to Erewhon and unrelated to Edward Bellamy's scientific Utopia.

In the beginning there was the Ministry of Education. (I suspect in the end there will be the Ministry.) Physically, it is set in pleasant formal gardens. Humanly, the Ministry is an aggregation of mutually suspicious human beings, number indeterminate even to the paymaster, because some on the payroll never put in an appearance at the Ministry Building. Some say they could not, even if they wished, since they are shades. Others are tangible, the "outs" who remain on the rolls. One brave researcher, however, has estimated 700 employees, of whom more than 200 are servants...

Ministries come and go. When a minister falls, all down to the level of principals throughout the country (but not including principals) become the "outs." They go back to being professors at the University of Teheran, teachers in cities, workers for A.I.D., Peace Corps, Fulbright, Near East. Skillful politicians stay on the payroll. A new group becomes the "ins," giving up their duties temporarily as professors at the University of Teheran, teachers in cities, workers for A.I.D., Peace Corps, Fulbright, Near East. Skillful politicians stay on the payroll. Rather nice arrangement. One ministry lasted two weeks; the present one has lasted long, over a year, and dark muttered rumors are being heard: "The minister is not an educator." (I do not know what this latter calculation is based on, but am certain it is exact. I don't know what it means, either.) "The minister loses his control."

I have met the three top men. Number one was the leader of the teacher organization that successfully struck a year ago. Salaries were almost doubled and he was made Minister. He looks like a hard-bitten American politician. His right-hand man looks a bit like Harpo Marx and talks like an angel (American style). The opponents of this second man say he does not practice what he preaches but has learned to preach well for American ears. The third power is the Farley-Curley-Louis Howe-Robert Kennedy of Iran. Rich, personable, persuasive, friend of the Shah, he heads vocational education and skillfully sabotages training vocational teachers in favor of turning out "engineers" through teacher training institutions. He struggles to build expensive vocational schools that are not used and scarcely attended through lack of teachers to man them. So he builds new unused schools, Pharaoh's monuments in modern dress.

Here is a typical administration struggle. With American planning and funds, plus Persian funds, a center for vocational

309

education was planned and built at Dardasht, twenty minutes from Teheran in the baking desert. Elaborate vocational shops (not to be confused with industrial arts)—automobile, foundry, machine shop, etc., about eight in all. About forty classrooms seating about thirty each. Big auditorium. Big gym. Big circular cafeteria. Big administration building. Right for vocational education. Built for 1500 students.

In Teheran is a teacher-training institution for vocational education called Teheran Institute of Technology. At the insistence of the third man, it gives dual degrees, teaching and engineering. So almost all of the students want to be "engineers." Only five of 200 want to go with the institution in the fall when it moves to Dardasht in the desert...

So, reasons the second man, let us transfer the Teachers College, now housed in a rented Teheran hotel, to Dardasht for next year. As the vocational school expands, using the magnificent shops as intended, the Teachers College will withdraw. (I am reminded that, in Marxist legend, the state will "wither away.") But will it, once the camel has his nose in the tent? Withdraw where? Who knows? Perhaps new buildings.

The third man wants the school to be vocational (and for engineers?) only. "Put beds in the classrooms and tell Teachers College we have no room. Make it a boarding school."

The second man wants it to be the place for the Teachers College, despite vocational layout. "Not enough classrooms?" A quarter of a mile away is a new high school for the youth of Dardasht community, just being completed. The second man saw it on a visit to Dardasht a few days ago. "We will take over this high school building for the college too. This will give us enough rooms."

It is June 8. Dardasht vocational center, the "place in the desert," stands completed. Each single shop cost $200,000 (there are eight shops); each has top American and German machines installed. It opens in September. It has no director or student body yet. No one knows whether it will be a vocational center or the home of Teachers College. The nearby high school, approaching completion, will open in the fall (I presume). It has no principal, no staff, and no student body. "We will take over this high school building for the college too."

The first man, the Minister, makes an announcement. "No decision will be made on Dardasht till we have the recommendations of the NYU team." The NYU team, learning to play Iranian, say, "But we are not building site experts." "We will await your pleasure," says the Ministry. "There is plenty of time."

A few days later I wrote:

We are now also in the inescapable phase of the survey—attempting to agree on recommendations. The difficulty is less that there are disagreements among ourselves; we have a fairly broad ideological base of agreements. The difficulty is instead that recommendations are hard to develop because of lack of money in Iran, the amazing lack of data and information, and the way one approach affects another. We have, for instance an eminently sensible plan for training village teachers through a village curriculum in a rural setting for work in village schools. But the authorities say they have no money for building schools of this sort and have an excess of high school graduates for whom there isn't room in jobs and who must be used up somehow, preferably by mandatory assignment to teach in villages. But the high school graduates are city-bred, hate the idea of going to the villages, even hate the idea of teaching, have no village contacts or sympathy or insight.

We call this kind of problem, "you can't get to Poughkeepsie from here," after the old joke about the farmer who unsuccessfully attempted to give a motorist a pattern of directions to Poughkeepsie, "Stranger, you can't get to Poughkeepsie from here." Again and again those we interview and who "advise" us come to this conclusion. So far our recommendations on rural elementary, for instance, have gone through six drafts. We now have a proposal—till we meet our next analyst, who will expose the flaw in this one too. Seriously, it is much more complex than Puerto Rico, incredibly more so.

So we wrote and rewrote and presented our survey report, as described in my last communication home:

In the beginning there was the Word. So let's start with the contract. It was wrought in the U.S.A., somewhere in the bowels of the great digestive system of New York University and Washington bureaucracy. It was wrought, no doubt, by a good American citizen (or a committee of citizens) who had never seen Iran and who writes pure English. Yet the contract is written in the most delightful Iranian. It would please the heart of any good Iranian who is attempting successfully to be all things to all men.

For our contract plainly says that we as a survey team are to do three quite different and mutually contradictory things. Clear? As an advance party, we need only explore the territory lightly and always be sure that we so proceed as to clear the way for the depth approach that follows upon our scouting. But interpretation two says there are four specific areas in the wide realm of teacher education that we must conquer completely and report on sagely. But interpretation three reveals the survey team as supermen conquering the total picture of teacher education in its entirety, missing no nook nor cranny, rendering the judgment of Solomon, and the devil take the advance party concept...

Back home at the ranch, Uncle Andy and Uncle George and all our little cousins of the New York University happy family are licking their chops and waiting for us to bring home the bacon. Survey-shmurvey. To them we are a brave scouting party, inspecting the terrain, avoiding ambushes, at all costs clearing the way for the coming NYU invasion, for the true Armageddon when we battle for the Lord.

Out in the vast desert, punctuated by oases, we prefer this role. It's a big country; it's a complex, confusing system. Anything jiggled here causes something to fall there. True, we know a lot, have been in every ostan, have physically, tangibly, been in and have been served tea in fifty-six of their sixty-seven teacher training institutions. But one is reporting on a delicate web of relationships, and something gently poked here bleats over there. We have to watch for ambushes at the passes; we have to bring home the bacon...

Thus thinking, the scouting party approached the passes and the potential ambushes. The strategy was clear. Watch out for the Iranians. Play Solomon, yet be reasonable with their viewpoints. After all, it is their country. Remember? Onward group process!

Out of a pass came Taslimi [the second man]. He's the deputy minister who looks like Harpo and talks like an angel. It's a hung jury on whether he practices what he preaches.

At two long conferences we explain our views, hold to our basic principles, make concessions on smaller points in the name of realism. And Taslimi joins us. He becomes Tonto, the good Indian. We have a love feast.

But hark! Out of the pass comes another deputy, Nafici [the third man]. He's the one who combines Farley-Curley-Kennedy and could charm an Eskimo into installing air conditioning at the North Pole. He explains that we have neglected him, that he has seen many of us only socially. So we give him two days and he shows us his fortifications. He has a strange penchant for building magnificent buildings with good equipment—and he trains no teachers who know how to keep people in his buildings or know what to do with the equipment. We skirmish. He retires back into the hills to think some more. He may be neutralized; he's not sure; we're not sure.

We proceed cautiously into the mountains, bravely showing our tentative recommendations to Iranians we encounter. Sometimes we fight confused skirmishes with the Iranians. But fortunately we have Tonto with us on our side.

We enter a deep defile. The noise of powerful forces! We look up alarmed. But joy quickly spreads. Riding toward us on their powerful steeds come our Allies, the Americans, the A.I.D. education professionals of Iran. Support has come to us. Victory is ours! NYU, the Contract, and the Truth forever! Viva U.S.A. Oh say can you see—?

At the head of the column, wearing his Mounty uniform, is General Hendershot. At his right, out of a Nelson Eddy operetta, is Dave Laird. In the ranks are our buddies with whom we have been eating, drinking, traveling. Good old Don of business education! Good old Art of trades and industry!

But something strange is happening. Bullets begin whizzing by us. We whirl and look about for hidden Iranians. Then the horrid truth dawns. The American A.I.D. troops are shooting at us, their own people! They invited us originally to take part in this war. They housed us and equipped us. We are buddies. These are our boys! What the hell—?

We take to the hills and escape under the cover of night. We regroup our thin, pitifully ragged band. We try to figure it out.

Why this rigorous, slashing, intolerant attack on our most basic recommendations?....

We fight gallantly and wearily, a tired little band. The truth—I use the word timidly, for here truth is slippery—begins to appear as to why the American A.I.D. attacks, not aids, its loyal ally. They believe the gallant scouts are too conservative, not bold enough in recommendations. Naturally we disagree. We are steering, we honestly believe, a way that reconciles boldness and realism.

Also, there is our old friend semantics. We want village youth to teach village people through a village-oriented curriculum. We say it is bold. They say it is conservative. This is probably the country and the place in which to point out that one man's Mede is another man's Persian.

We were on the watch out for Iranians. We wrote for them...so we would have a fighting chance for implementation. We didn't write for American consumption. But General Hendershot says that if we are to give him a weapon he can use, it must be written for Americans too, with long explanations of backgrounds of education in Iran and the findings of the team and many "and so forths." And if not—no contract. The General has a large gun there.

So under a flag of truce and tired from the long fight and the surprise attack, we try to gather more data to shape back at the ranch, in overtime no doubt.

Meanwhile we met a whole passel of Iranians today at Dry Gulch, the Ministry. We gave them our recommendations. They reacted impassively as the Sphinx. Tonto wasn't with them. He had disappeared.

We had worked hard. We hadn't sat on our butts in Teheran. Instead we had planed and jeeped throughout the country from the capital to the borders with the Soviet Union, Afghanistan, Pakistan, and the borders of the Persian Gulf. We had personally visited the overwhelming majority of Iran's teacher education institutions; we had talked interminably with superintendents, teachers, and ministry personnel; we had read documents till our eyes bugged out.

We cared about the Iranian common people and we worried about their inadequate educational system that helped most the monied and corrupt. Our recommendations for reform were hard earned and well thought through; the recommendations for training village people to teach the village children who constituted the bulk of Iranian common folks were sensible and practical, we thought.

But so far as I can tell our recommendations were ignored. I know of no action on our proposals by the Ministry or the American representatives abroad and no follow-up through New York University assistance to teacher education in Iran. Instead, the Shah and his educational functionaries presented and publicized a half-assed program whereby some Iranian soldiers did some inadequate "teaching" in village schools. Our recommendations were filed and forgotten. One more survey.

Chapter Thirty-Six

TALKING
AND WRITING

laska never invited me to talk or advise on education, nor did Montana or Idaho. The other forty-seven states did. Speaking and consulting, which became part of my life when I first became a professor, peaked during the New York University years. Only later did I realize that I had talked too often.

Prior to college teaching, I spoke occasionally to church and social organizations in Columbus and to teachers in Bureau for Intercultural Education field centers, including Gary, Detroit, and Cincinnati. At Illinois my intercultural education and Illinois Interracial Commission background led to talks in Midwestern communities through the Anti-Defamation League and the National Conference of Christians and Jews.

Texas had become another turf while I taught at Champaign-Urbana. My Texas consultation dated from 1948, when L. D. Haskew, then dean of the college of education, invited me to Austin. Haskew, a mover and shaker in Texas education, later to be university vice president and university system vice chancellor, was initiating a state unit of ASCD. In introducing me, he apologized for my relative youth, explained that I would soon get over it, and told his confreres at the opening session that, since this was my first trip to Texas, they should show me some Texas hospitality. They obliged with alacrity. That evening we made the rounds of Austin bottle clubs. The morning after, on the speakers' platform, I asked my chief host of the night before, a curriculum director from a community on the Mexican border, how he felt. He replied, "I'm going to be all right if nobody pushes me."

Surviving the initiation and accepted as an adopted son of Texas, I was scheduled during the next four years for two ten-day workshops of the Corpus Christi schools with teachers who worked and played hard; an Austin public schools workshop; a week at the University of Texas; a meeting of Texas elementary principals; and a swing through northern Texas, Austin to Waco to Dallas, during a January blue norther. When, on my return from such safaris, Bee asked me why I looked tired, I explained that it was not the work but the hospitality. After Texas, Midwestern consultation in corn-fed Hutchison, Kansas, or Ronald Reagan's college town, Eureka, Illinois, or the baby food capital, Fremont, Michigan, seemed mighty dull to me.

Annually, from 1955 through 1957, I directed a human relations workshop for black Langston University in the black community of Langston, Oklahoma. I found that my greatest problem was to help those of my staffers who were white to adjust to the brand-new experience of being white minority members in totally black and largely low-income surroundings. Through an evening in her upper-middle-class living room, Dit, a Langston faculty member and the daughter of a black college president, once saved two white women staffers who were afflicted by white panic from fleeing home to their Northern residences. Needless to say, I didn't reemploy them. Those June days the staff learned more about human relations than did the black participants.

The Peabody assignment resulted in many consultation invitations from black and white education groups in the South. The civil rights movement was rising. In 1956, in a small Louisiana community, a teachers' meeting opened with a talk by an arrogant state education official, white of course, who praised segregation, pointed out how grateful "nigras" should be to benevolent whites, told why "the colored should stay in their place," and warned against outside agitators. He was followed by a glorious chorus of black school children. They sang with passion and conviction a civil rights marching song that began, "This is my country, land of the free." I prefaced my talk with an invitation to the audience to give still another ovation to the children. They did and the building rocked. The moment was unforgettable. The state official glowered and left early. A great experience!

Talks and consultation increased during my NYU decade, 1957-1967. Not only did I talk to ten state units of the ASCD, as well as unforgettable Hawaii; now there came invitations from superintendents, school boards, and principals. They came from school systems, local teachers associations, colleges, foundations, educational associations, human relations agencies, and community groups. I did a workshop for the Tulsa, Oklahoma, schools; taught at the University of Utah for a month (and vacationed weekends at Grand Canyon, Zion, Phoenix, San Diego and Tijuana); and taught a TV course for the University of Wisconsin at Milwaukee.

A lecture bureau, Program Associates, Utica, New York, tempted me with comfortable fees; the assignments seemed largely to be up back roads in Pennsylvania communities that no doubt were pleasant to live in, yet not easily reached from either Mountain Lakes or New York City. Stroudsburg, Butler, Reading, Erie, Wilkes-Barre, Pottsville, Penn Argyle, Millersville, Bedford, Selinsgrove, Ridgeway, Warren, Honesdale—still with me?—are a considerable distance from major airports.

Like Ado Annie in *Oklahoma*, I couldn't say no—not even when I ought to say nix. Not counting surveys or Puerto Rican teaching, I took on twenty to thirty engagements on the road each year. They ranged in duration from a day to a month.

I was pulled in two directions. One pull was centrifugal—toward presenting my ideas on education before large audiences and thus representing New York University, ASCD, and myself. The other pull was centripetal—toward staying home with my family and taking care of the store through teaching, administering, and writing.

New York University was no help in resolving my ambiguity. The administration of both the university and the school was pleased that I was in demand at conferences and for talks. NYU as a private institution was hungry for enrollment and eager for favorable publicity; the university welcomed my multiple presidencies and speaking engagements and encouraged my roadwork. Yet, simultaneously, New York University expected me to carry a full load of teaching, administration, research, and writing. At no time during the ASCD term, nor during the presidencies of the John Dewey Society and National Society of College

Teachers of Education that followed, did the university adjust my assignment or provide me with supplementary help.

So I responded to both centrifugal and centripetal pulls. I packed field work into spring and winter vacations and free summer periods. During regular sessions, I used some weekends and nonteaching days for work on the road. I avoided whenever possible any overlap of field demands with my days for administration and my classes.

Weekends are favored times for conferences; I hurried back from Washington meetings for Monday responsibilities. Occasionally I talked in the East or Midwest on a Monday or Tuesday morning, yet flew back in time for late afternoon and evening classes. Without sightseeing in the Northwest, I hastened home from long trips to Spokane, Washington, and Medford, Oregon. When classes had to be missed, I rescheduled them for the next week through doubling up class meetings or shuffling times. To me, it was a point of honor to do my own teaching and to depend minimally on graduate assistants or pinch-hitting department faculty members. I managed time for administrative chores to the satisfaction of myself and the deans and the department members, save for two inveterate gripers who demanded miracles of a largely powerless department chairman while they themselves skillfully avoided department-related responsibilities.

Yes, I found time for my family too, including short vacations and trips to special occasions with Jon and Roy at Swarthmore and Barbara at Douglass, though I missed such major occasions as Barbara and Roy's Mountain Lakes High School graduations and Barbara's college graduation from Douglass—Iran and Puerto Rico were simply too far away for any return home. But I did manage to break away in the middle of the Tulsa workshop to attend Jon's college graduation and then return to Oklahoma. By the end of the NYU decade I had logged almost a million miles by plane.

Looking back with the twenty-twenty vision of hindsight, I now recognize that I should have taken on fewer speaking engagements and less consulting during the New York University decade, 1957-67. I learned that you don't move the educational universe toward the achievement of the ideas you support through one-shot speaking engagements to teachers or through brief consultation in a miscellany of school systems—at any rate that I couldn't and didn't. Writing, when well targeted reaches the right people and endures. The spoken word quickly dissipates.

John Lounsbury and Gordon Vars had studied with me at Peabody and now, after my 1957 shift to NYU, became my collaborators on a textbook, *Modern Education for the Junior High School Years*. Both were already well launched on their careers as leaders in junior high school education. We approached the development of a textbook for junior high school teachers with extreme caution.

I had been burned by my one earlier venture into textbook writing. While at Illinois I had entered into an ill-fated agreement with McGraw-Hill to co-edit and to contribute volumes to a series of social studies textbooks for junior and senior high school students. Though I had been attracted by the reputation of the company and its ambitious plans for the series, and though McGraw-Hill had been attracted by my reputation as a progressive educator and by such prior publications as *Economic Roads for American Democracy*, the project didn't come off. My manuscript for the first book of the series, a junior high school civics book, never satisfied McGraw-Hill, despite my laborious revisions.

For instance, the editorial staff and I disagreed interminably over my insistence on including information on social class in a book for junior high school students. I wanted to acquaint young learners with the six-fold stratification ranging from upper-upper to lower-lower developed by W. L. Warner in his *Yankee City* series and August Hollingshead in *Elmtown's Youth* and used by Allison Davis and Robert J. Havighurst in their analyses. I hoped to help students to see how social class influenced their daily life, including friends, dating, schools attended, etc. The McGraw-Hill editorial group maintained that junior high school students were too young for acquaintance with social class data and might be emotionally disturbed by such insights. But I thought I smelled censorship.

Eventually, editor Russ Fraser and I looked across the table at each other, ruefully suggested that perhaps we should publish our voluminous correspondence, and terminated publication plans for the series. A few years later I tried to revise the civics book with Fred Wilhelms as my collaborator, but we never completed it. Russ and I retained friendly relationships. But the textbook series died aborning. Maybe it was just as well; Harold Rugg once told me that writing textbooks for high school students was "a life sentence," and my doctoral advisor Harold Alberty regarded writing textbooks for elementary or secondary school students as a form of prostitution.

As the 1950s closed, the experience was still a sore spot, for I had invested countless hours at Illinois in planning the series and writing the projected first book. So, as senior author, I counseled Vars and Lounsbury on a publisher-proof approach (I thought) to writing a book on junior high school education for teacher educators. We would write half of the book, inquire of some publishers as to whether this was the book they really wanted, then sign a contract with the company and editor most amenable to our views and ideas. A second unit of the publication package would be a collection of my shorter writings. The collaborators agreed.

The plan worked. We wrote half of the book on junior high school teaching and sent it to half a dozen publishers. Some indicated that, for varied reasons, our junior high school book didn't "meet their editorial needs"; some expressed interest but suggested modifications, yet two definitely wanted the book we wanted to write. We chose Rinehart as our publisher after becoming acquainted with editor Bill Hackett. He liked what he had read and he bought the two-book package. We signed the contracts and turned back to finishing the junior high school book.

But Robert Burns has oft reminded us of what happens to the best-laid plans of mice and men. The ganging a-gley came about when, out of the blue, Rinehart merged with Holt and Winston. Holt had been one of the publishers that had expressed interest but wanted substantial educationally conservative modifications, including less emphasis on the integrated core curriculum and more on separate subject fields—which was precisely what we didn't intend and couldn't accept as good junior high school education. Nevertheless, the merged new firm assured us that all existent contracts of the combining houses would be honored.

Editorial disagreements over the content of the junior high school book soon emerged. Nor could the tough-minded, sales-oriented new management, Holt-dominated, wax enthusiastic about the sales prospects of an anthology of my shorter writings. The roof fell in on August 4, 1960, when I was informed that the company had decided against publishing the selections from my writing, since "circumstances had changed" and they "couldn't merchandise it." Yet the company did want to continue to "work with us" toward "probable" publication of *Modern Education for the Junior High School Years.* I pointed out that our agreements clearly called for publication of both books. Yet they handed me back the manuscript of my collection of shorter writings. I readily acknowledge that the newly merged firm was on defensible legal and business ground throughout the process of cancellation. But nobody was happy about the whole matter.

Bill Hackett, our original Rinehart editor, had left the merged firm for Bobbs-Merrill. I called him and told him that the contracts with his former company might be cancelled through the action of the new management and that he might be able to bring *Modern Education for the Junior High School Years* to Bobbs-Merrill. He said that he could do better than that if the contracts were cancelled: "I'll take both of them." I talked to Vars and Lounsbury. They agreed to the switch. So I went to the offices of the merged firm and in a somber, silent ceremony our agreements to publish both books were cancelled. I called on Hackett and shook hands on publication of both books by Bobbs-Merrill.

Modern Education for the Junior High School Years was published in 1961 and enjoyed good sales. A revision, in the form of a second edition, the hallmark of commercial success, appeared in 1967. The book, though now obsolete, was still in print in the 1980s.

My collection, titled *The Making of a Modern Educator*, was also published in 1961 and, despite the dire predictions of Holt editors, sold well enough to make both Bobbs-Merrill and the author feel pleased. I had grouped twenty-eight articles under the headings titled Teaching in an Experimental School, Learning Through Travel, Laughing at Ourselves, Meeting Forces Affecting Education, Working for Better Human Relations Among Groups, Bringing Up Our Children, and Participating in the Great Debate. Included were the unpublished "We Went to Europe as a Family" and an article by Jon on his observations on desegregation upon returning to Nashville. Harold Hand wrote a characteristically warm and generous foreword.

Distribution of both books was helped through appearances on radio stations WBAI, WEVD, and WMTR in New York and New Jersey, and through two guest appearances on Betty Furness's program, *At Your Beck and Call*. On Betty's show, my role was to respond extemporaneously to any question on education that any viewer happened to phone in. My three specializing fellow panelists were to respond to questions on antiques, veterinary medicine, theater. For the first program, I prepared frantically, stuffing myself with facts in a vain attempt to become an educational encyclopedia ready for any question. I soon found that a typical question phoned in to our charming hostess was, "My daughter is having trouble with her courses at college and what should I do about it?" I relaxed and had a good time as an Ann Landers and a philosopher-at-large during the shows.

During the early NYU years I had a close working relationship with the Anti-Defamation League. Stirred by the conflict over segregation of schools, I wrote *Prejudiced—How Do People Get That Way?*, an ADL pamphlet for high school students; wrote and narrated a video tape on human relations education; and published the script with ADL under the title of *Challenge to America*. I wrote up the Nashville story, edited an issue on experiences in cultural integration for ASCD's *Educational Leadership*, then served as editor for a guide to intercultural education for the Pennsylvania Department of Public Instruction. As a reporter, I summed up what research had taught us about instructional methods in intercultural and intergroup education for the *Review of Educational Research*, wrote the entry on intercultural education for the 1960 issue of the *Encyclopedia of Educational Research*, and prepared a paper on research dealing with the development of education for desegregation and integration, which the Southwest Center for Human Relations Studies published as a pamphlet.

Then, in effect, I retired from writing about intercultural and intergroup education. I had said all that I could say about building better human relations among Americans of varied religions, races, and ethnic backgrounds. I saw no point in repeating myself, and suspected I was in danger of doing this if I persisted. A writer can say just so much—they either hear you or they don't.

I made my farewell to intercultural education through activism. In the mid-Sixties, the era of LBJ and the Great Society programs, money was available for programs to achieve equal educational opportunities, to help the culturally disadvantaged, and to bring about desegregation. I never was much for grantsmanship; I even repeated some of the cynical humor of the period, "While you're up, get me a Grant [a popular Scotch whiskey]." However, I applied under Title IV, Section 404 of the Civil Rights Act of 1964 for $43,776 for a special training institute on problems of school desegregation.

The institute brought to NYU in the summer of 1965 forty hand-picked principals, supervisors, and curriculum leaders from both the North and the South to develop skills necessary to the achievement of desegregation and integration of public schools systems. Our staff included blacks and whites; of the participants, nine were black, one Indian, and thirty white.

The follow-up of the institute took the form of visits to help the participants in their own communities. I visited twenty-eight participants during the 1965-66 school year. Paul Warren, assistant director, and staff members Charity Mance and Juliette Bursterman visited the rest; the remaining staff members, Prudence Bostwick, William D. Hedges, and Harold Turner, were at the time unavailable for follow-up trips.

My most memorable visit was to New Orleans to work with two Roman Catholic participants, Sister Caroleen and Sister Colleen. The day before my arrival in New Orleans, a Mr. Nesson of the United States Justice Department informed my New York University office that a U.S. congressman, acting on behalf of a constituent, had reported to the department that someone was impersonating me in Bogalusa, Louisiana. Apparently, the Ku Klux Klan had gotten wind of my Louisiana visit; prior to my arrival, a segregationist had posed as "Dr. William Van Til of President Johnson's Committee on Racial Unrest" (a nonexistent organization), presumably to gain entree into the local human relations group.

I learned of the situation from a phone conversation with my secretary after my evening arrival in New Orleans. So I called the sisters and found that they had scheduled me for an off-the-record conference at Bogalusa the next morning. I talked with my associate Paul Warren at NYU and found him doubtful as to whether the caller genuinely represented the Justice Department. The purported Justice Department caller had asked for a full and complete description of me, which Paul had readily given. Now he had misgivings that the call might be an attempt to gain a description of me on the part of persons unknown for purposes of easy identification of the Yankee outsider when I reached Bogalusa the next day.

That evening I called the FBI in New Orleans and told them about the impersonation. FBI man Otis Paige called me back with word that (1) a Mr. Nesson of the Justice Department did exist, (2) that the FBI contact in Bogalusa had no knowledge that anyone was impersonating me in Bogalusa, and (3) that I'd best get in touch with the Justice Department myself. It was then midnight and the Justice Department was closed. I left a message with the switchboard and the next morning Mr. Nesson of the Justice Department confirmed his original call to my office. He had been told that someone was passing for me in Bogalusa. I might be met by violence.

The next morning at the Convent School of the Sisters of Notre Dame, Sister Caroleen and Sister Colleen called a Catholic colleague in Bogalusa. Using Aesopian language because the Klan, they told me, had access to phone conversations to Bogalusa, they informed their contact that they were "cancelling the delivery of the package"—namely me. A return call from a Catholic sister asked cryptically, "Has the party in question left New Orleans safely? If not, advise him **not** to leave from the New Orleans airport this morning." On reporting this to the New Orleans Office of the FBI, I was told that no action could be taken by the FBI at this point. Apparently one had to be injured or killed to merit "protection" by the FBI.

With the sisters, I traveled to Baton Rouge for a conference with leaders of the Catholic archdiocese and the black community. I then flew under an assumed name, William Andrew, a resurrection of my long-lost middle name, from Baton Rouge to Greenville, Mississippi, for my next follow-up visit with participants. I used the pseudonym because I knew from my Nashville experiences that segregationists played rough and because I could apparently expect no help from the FBI.

324

Back home, I wrote a full report on the episode for the FBI. Years later, after revelation of the hostility of J. Edgar Hoover toward Martin Luther King, Jr., in particular, and civil rights workers in general, I asked through a *Kappan* column, "Can Educators Trust Representatives of Government?" I had fully trusted the FBI and told them all I knew of the situation. Only later did I ask myself whether or not I had been naive in trusting the FBI during the civil rights struggle of the Sixties.

As I terminated my intercultural publications developed for educators, my writing began shifting toward a wider reading audience. The breakthrough came when I made a speech on progressive education at a John Dewey Society-promoted and New York University-sponsored meeting celebrating William Heard Kilpatrick's ninetieth birthday, November 20, 1961. Though I was virtually certain that a defense of progressivism would be rejected in a post-Sputnik climate of opinion in which progressive educators were receiving the silent treatment, I submitted a version of the talk to editor Paul Woodring of *Saturday Review*. To my surprise, Woodring accepted it, ran it with pictures of John Dewey, George S. Counts, Boyd H. Bode, and William Heard Kilpatrick in their middle-age prime, improved the title by rechristening it "Is Progressive Education Obsolete?," and featured it on the cover of the February 17, 1962, *Saturday Review*. When I told him of my surprise, Woodring responded that Harold Taylor, former president of Sarah Lawrence College, and I were the only progressive educators he knew about who could communicate effectively with a wide audience. I doubted that.

Publication of "Is Progressive Education Obsolete?" by *Saturday Review* triggered me. It seemed that everyone I met at the Las Vegas ASCD convention or months later had read the article or the condensation in *Education Digest* that followed. A subsequent *Saturday Review* issue carried several letters to the editor that were supportive and a few that were critical. Despite my supersensitivity to criticism since the *Forces Affecting American Education* affair, this time I enjoyed the debate that the article stirred.

I became hooked on writing for the general reader concerning current curriculum controversies. A dormant dream of my post-college years was revived; I would earn my bread as a free-lance writer! Yet, busy as the proverbial one-armed paperhanger with the itch, I deferred the dream until my year-long sabbatical from NYU, the 1963-64 academic year.

When that welcome respite from Washington Square arrived, I worked out a new schedule. Each weekday morning I kissed Bee good-bye and headed, not for the Lackawanna Railroad Station, but upstairs to my study and sun deck or outside to the little summerhouse under the trees. There, save for coffee breaks and lunch, I became a free-lance writer. I started a novel and wrote articles on education for mass circulation magazines. Only on Thursdays did I head for the city, where I became a Visiting Scholar at Teachers College, Columbia University, sitting in on courses taught by Lawrence Cremin on history of education, Phil Phenix on philosophy of education, and Gordon MacKenzie on curriculum. Before going to classes I systematically visited and eagerly absorbed the holdings of the Museum of Natural History and the Metropolitan Museum of Art. Weekends were reserved for family, guests, and reading.

Like most first novels, the novel I started was autobiographical. I plugged away only to find that, for me at least, age 52 was too late to learn the novelist's trade. My editorial eye recognized that what I wrote simply wasn't good enough. All that survives of the novel is the first chapter, converted into a short story about the wolves and punks of my reform school days. The manuscript of that story grew dog-eared from repeated rejections by magazines.

Writing articles on education proved more productive. Aiming for widely read periodicals, I wrote on the frontiers of education, dropouts, and the characteristics of a good high school curriculum, and I developed outlines on how to pick a college and on working mothers for women's magazines. As a result of these efforts to free-lance, *Saturday Review* published "The Genuine Educational Frontiers" in April 1964; *Woman's Day* ran "What Makes a Good High School Curriculum?" in October 1964; and *Parents* carried "Five Bold Ways to Attack the Dropout Problem" in March 1965. Articles that the commercial world shunned were converted into contributions to educational journals. For instance, "What Knowledge Is of Most Worth?—A Reassessment," too toplofty for general readership, appeared in *The High School Journal.*

Yet when I totaled my income from my sabbatical year of free lancing, it came to $1,250. Of course, I could readily rationalize that I took substantial time out for reading, family life, and visits to my sister, ill with cancer in Virginia Beach. I could tell myself that I also talked during the sabbatical year at—here we go again—Montgomery County, Maryland; Steubenville, Ohio; Rutgers University; Warren, Pennsylvania; New Haven; Hammond, Indiana; East Texas State University; the University of Houston; San Antonio; El Paso; University of Toledo; University of Akron; and a local school system near Syracuse, New York—I told you that I couldn't say no. I could explain to myself that John F. Kennedy's assassination immobilized all of us for days, that I helped lead a human relations committee in Mountain Lakes, that the attempted denial of free speech to Carey McWilliams of *The Nation*, scheduled to talk in our community, had to be combated. I could also point out that I participated in the ASCD conference in Miami, developed a chapter for the 1965 ASCD yearbook, became president of the John Dewey Society for a two-year term in 1964, and nostalgically returned to familiar European haunts with Bee for almost two months during that sabbatical year.

Yet, however I rationalized about interruptions of my free lancing, the stubborn fact remained that I wasn't going to switch careers in midstream. Clearly, I had best stay with the university world for my daily bread—to say nothing of the college education of my children and of my Mountain Lakes mortgage. Three hundred and fifty dollars from *Saturday Review*, $500 from *Woman's Day*, and $400 from *Parents* wouldn't suffice.

Yet my sabbatical was a blessing—it enabled me to survive a middle-life crisis. Rather than blindly resigning and plunging into a new occupation, I had tried out a new career. I had learned that I could not make it as a free lance; I needed a more dependable vocation and source of income.

Chapter Thirty-Seven

TO THE BANKS
OF THE WABASH
FAR AWAY

I should have returned from the sabbatical with fire in my whiskers and full of piss and vinegar, as the salty Harold Hand would have phrased it. After all, the sabbatical year had included not only my attempted metamorphosis from administrator-professor to free-lance writer but also sufficient rest and relaxation. From mid-April to early June, Bee and I had retraced our steps to locales we had earlier enjoyed together or with our children: England, Holland, the Black Forest, Switzerland's mountains, Austria's villages, Venice, Bavaria, and even a foldboat cruise on the Mosel River. Surely nostalgia for lost youth and past travel experiences would now disappear; surely the venture into free-lancing would purge me of middle-life career crisis.

However, the dictionary definition of sabbatical year specifies "a year of release from duties," and "release" is not permanent emancipation. In July 1964, I returned to the familiar combination of administering and teaching at NYU, to talks and consultation, and to work with national organizations.

My sabbatical writing chickens were coming home to roost. In September 1964, while Bee and I vacationed briefly at Cape Cod, *Woman's Day* published my "What Makes a Good High School Curriculum?" for its eight million readers, and I was faced again by my ambiguity about writing. I wanted to—indeed I had to— stand up and be counted for the ideas in which I believed. I had to communicate my convictions; speaking out was integral to my self-image. Yet the nakedness of self-exposure to an observant world, the irreversibility and permanency of cold print, scared me. For me, the process of writing was and is a joy, but publication increasingly had become a terror. On Cape Cod, imaginary people whom I had injured by my words lurked in every cranberry bog; unreal assassins hid behind every sand dune. In the *Woman's Day* article I had written of the views on education of actual, though unidentified, neighbors; now, irrationally, I thought that I must have hurt them, wounded them somehow by so doing. It did no good to tell myself that publication is like dropping a rose leaf into the Grand Canyon and waiting for an echo, or to reassure myself with Franklin D. Roosevelt's wisdom, "The only thing we have to fear is fear itself." I was sure that back home I would be regarded as a pariah. I had to live through this attack of writers' fright and, on return to the cocktail parties of Mountain Lakes, find myself a temporary celebrity among those neighbor ladies who had read my supermarket opus. Nobody assailed me; nobody suffered except me.

My rabbit ears as to my writing didn't get in the way of sharing leadership in Citizens for Johnson, a local Mountain Lakes group that helped shift the 14 percent for Kennedy in 1960 to a 41 percent vote for Johnson in 1964. Not bad for that bulwark of conservative Republicanism, Mountain Lakes, once described by Jon as aroused only by such issues as whether dogs should be permitted to run at large.

In the fall, our New York University department meetings were characterized by complaints about such matters as lack of secretarial services, low enrollment, and dispiriting teaching assignments. A couple of negative faculty members can depress and immobilize an entire department. Too, a proposal for reorganization of the structure of the colleges by high university officials was troubling the entire education faculty; my diary reports that normally optimistic Dean Walter Anderson admonished the faculty in its meeting of October 19 to overcome the low morale that was creating poor college and community relations. Andy was at his warm, vibrant, and eloquent best that day in what proved to be his last message to the faculty. For on Sunday, October 25, 1964, he died.

In an Importance of People column in ASCD's *Educational Leadership*, I wrote:

The essence of Andy was relationships to people. Andy smiled at people. Andy accepted people. Andy liked people. Andy believed in people. By just being Andy, he made people feel good—good about being with him, good about life, even good about themselves. Andy, beyond any man I have ever met, understood the importance of people....

How often we must have let him down. How often we must have put the asking price of our cooperation too high. How often we must have failed to give the gift of appreciation. But he never said so and he might deny it if he were here now. He seemed to see only the good in us. And that made us better people.

Andy's death crystallized my thinking about the direction of my career. I decided that I would move elsewhere when I could—and **if** I could, for career changes in academia are not as easy at age 53 as at 43. I didn't like the departmental quarrels over turf that had always existed but were now exacerbated by the shuffle in administrative leadership; jurisdictional disputes occur among academics as they do among building trades workers. In the reorganization process, our department's program of preparing curriculum workers and supervisors was being shifted from secondary education to the educational administration department, which already controlled programs for developing high school principals. The secondary education doctoral clientele was thereby reduced and dissatisfaction of some secondary education department members increased. If I couldn't readily move elsewhere, I planned to settle for an NYU professorship sans administrative quibbles.

Even the 1964 accession to the acting deanship by John Payne, with whom I had cordial prior working relationships in Iran and at Washington Square, didn't change my mind. For the new administration, which took over in 1965 with Daniel E. Griffiths as dean, was more research-oriented and grant-minded, while I was closer to Andy and John's orientation toward teaching, guidance, and local and national service. In addition, I wanted time to write for a wide readership. From earlier relationships with Dan as the School of Education associate dean, I recognized that our styles were different. Nor did my 1966 promotion by the new administration to the headship of the division combining the secondary and higher education departments persuade me that my better course would be remaining as an NYU middle administrator.

I didn't apply for any other posts, but I did let the word go out that I was available. Meanwhile I continued my crowded schedule of administering, teaching, talking, consulting, working with national organizations, and writing. My diary sometimes reported "very tired" or "took a tranquilizer."

Yet there were enjoyable experiences too, such as developing effective action and communication programs through national organizations. I became president of the John Dewey Society for a 1964-66 term and discovered that in a small society a president was less fettered in access to funds for program development than in a larger society like the ASCD. In one relaxed JDS board meeting early in my term, I was authorized to use a substantial part of our limited treasury as I saw fit. So we launched a little magazine, a quarterly called *Insights*, to allow John Dewey Society members to say what was on their minds. Our editorial policy appeared in the first issue that I edited and prevails to this day:

> We intend to launch an experiment in communication among the members of the Society. Its success will depend squarely on you....
>
> Geographically separated as we are, we need widespread, prompt, informal *free trade in ideas*. We need to share terse and hard-hitting ideas on our current concerns and our opinions.

For John Dewey Society members, *Insights* supplemented the annual conference day of sharing, modeled on the Spring Conference, through which the members could discuss with each other issues in school and society.

JDS board member Harold Benjamin, prosperous through his advisory editorship of a successful series of McGraw-Hill teacher education books and personally indifferent to wealth accumulation, was readily persuaded to contribute $500 annually for a financial gift to a doctoral student whose work was outstanding. He specified only that the award be named for the man John Dewey once called the father of progressive education, Francis W. Parker, and that the donor be anonymous. The society also created two honors annually announced at the John Dewey Society lectures at AACTE, one for outstanding service to education during the past year in the spirit of John Dewey and the other for outstanding lifetime service to education, also in the spirit of John Dewey.

In an era in which Kilpatrick, Melby, and Counts were still among the elder statesmen of progressivism, the earliest of the lifetime awards were easy to bestow. Choice of the educator of the year was more difficult, and the selection of Francis Keppel for his achievement of substantial federal aid to education as Lyndon B. Johnson's commissioner of education stirred controversy among our membership. "In the spirit of John Dewey" proved to be a slippery phrase; Keppel himself, in accepting his award, indicated that he had never seen himself in quite that light. When an elder statesman took umbrage at not receiving a lifetime award and when a new generation of Young Turks in the society were angered by the selection of Sidney Hook, an able early John Dewey scholar who in the yeasty late Sixties and early Seventies was opposing the student revolt, the awards were dropped, despite my resistance. *Insights*, the John Dewey Society day of discussion at AACTE, and the Parker award continued for years.

Administration might be tedious and teaching master's degree classes pleasant yet uneventful. Yet there were always exciting encounters with doctoral students and good experiences in family and community life. Bee and I were steady playgoers, patronizing both Broadway and off-Broadway. In Mountain Lakes we were partners in swimming and foldboating and rivals in table tennis. Entertaining in our community was relaxing, pleasant, and sufficient.

During our decade in Mountain Lakes, Jon's visits home were frequent, first as a Swarthmore undergraduate, then as a master's degree student at the University of North Carolina. On our sabbatical trip to Europe, he guided his parents about London, where he was a student at the London School of Economics. Jon returned regularly even after he became a doctoral candidate in sociology at the University of California at Berkeley. When he returned to Swarthmore as an instructor, we again often saw him and his wife Sally, a Californian sociologist whom he married while in the West. Barbara spent weekends with us on her frequent returns from Douglass College, to which she had gone without much enthusiasm at first. Post-college work with

332

exceptional children in New Jersey schools turned her on emotionally and intellectually; she lived at home while enjoying
teaching special education, then readily gave a year to graduate
study at Peabody that helped her become a master teacher in her
chosen field. Her Nashville extracurricular activities included
becoming engaged to Bob Nichols, a New Jersey friend studying
for a doctorate in clinical psychology at the University of Tennessee. Roy lived with us till high school graduation. He went to
Swarthmore for undergraduate study, shifted from a mathematics major to economics, and wielded a powerful tennis racket
under Ed Faulkner's tutelage. He began graduate study at
Boston College that eventually led to a doctorate in economics.
Both colleges were near enough for his frequent visits home.

We loved and enjoyed our children, exulted with them in
their academic, social, and athletic accomplishments, suffered
with them through their inevitable struggles with school and
society and with life and love, and interminably talked things
over with them. It's a great experience to have children who are,
respectively, sociologically, psychologically, and economics oriented. For instance, with Bee, they converted me from my
original lack of opposition to the Vietnam War, which stemmed
from my anti-communism of the Thirties and Forties and which
had been enhanced by absorption of propaganda in Washington
at a persuasive State Department Conference in 1966. Shame-
fully late, I joined them in outspoken opposition to the war in
1967. To that date, though I certainly hadn't supported the
Vietnam War, I hadn't spoken out or written against it.

After I became head of the new Division of Secondary and
Higher Education at NYU, opportunities to move to a new post
materialized. However, because of my Peabody and NYU assignments and my offices in educational organizations, I found that
I had been typecast by higher education institutions as an
administrator. For instance, the University of North Carolina
was seeking a dean for the School of Education; Bee and I met
with the faculty committee and university officials. In December
1966, Brooklyn College made me a firm offer to become director
of teacher education and, in the City University hierarchy,
associate dean of teacher education, a post of power, prestige,
and substantial remuneration. Yet I withdrew my candidacy for

the North Carolina deanship before the committee ended its deliberations and I refused the Brooklyn College offer.

Despite the obvious attractiveness of Brooklyn's offer of $26,000 for ten months of service while NYU was then paying me $18,000 for nine months (summer session pay was additional), I found reasons to say no. I suspect I even invented reasons. A slow learner, as I have observed earlier, I came in time to understand that I didn't want to be a dean. Nor did I want to be a director of teacher education. Nor did I want to be any kind of administrator. Instead, I wanted to live the professor's life.

On March 31, 1967, I took the plunge and notified Dean Dan Griffiths and Associate Dean John Payne of my resignation from the chairmanship of the department and the headship of the division. As of September 1967, I would become a professor of education at NYU. My intention was to serve as a professor at NYU until retirement.

Just then along came Alan C. Rankin. Dr. Rankin was president of Indiana State University, Terre Haute, Indiana. Indiana State had been a normal school, then a teachers college, then a state college. In 1965 the college had been retitled a university. Now it offered the Ph.D. degree in elementary education and in guidance and psychological services. Doctoral programs were to be added in secondary education and educational administration in 1968. But President Rankin had a problem. Accreditation agencies couldn't help noticing that Indiana State University, including the doctoral degree granting School of Education, still resembled an undergraduate college with master's and specialist graduate offerings, not a university. Few faculty members carried on significant research. Still fewer published, and these primarily in state journals or through minor publishers. Offices in national organizations were rare. Indiana State University was strong in teaching, counseling, and field service. That was fine yet not enough.

So Alan Rankin came up with an idea. As one of his many contributions to making ISU a true university, he established two Distinguished Professorships. In universities, distinguished professors are usually retirees who have achieved distinction in their long academic or public careers. In Rankin's version, the distinguished professorships were to be held by individuals who were currently publishing, who were established as leaders in national organizations in their fields, and who had a considerable number of years to go before they reached mandatory retirement age. He looked for people in their fifties to hold Distinguished Professorships, which he named for graduates of Indiana State who had become college presidents. To work in the field of guidance and psychological services, Edward C. Roeber, past president of the American Personnel and Guidance Association, came from the University of Michigan in 1966 to become the Raleigh W. Holmstedt Distinguished Professor. In 1967, a distinguished professorship in secondary education seemed to Rankin a logical strategic step.

I had resurrected and revised my credentials in 1966, and they were available from the placement office of my alma mater, Ohio State University. In April 1967 I visited the Indiana State campus for the customary round of interviews with faculty members and university officials. I liked what I saw and heard. President Rankin was open and pleasant; my colleagues were able and amiable; the university was obviously on the move; the state legislature had decided to build further the programs of second-level institutions like Indiana State and Ball State rather than contribute to the increased giantism of the two Big Ten schools, Indiana University and Purdue University. ISU promptly sent me an offer of a professorship at $20,000 for the academic year, plus the potentiality of $6000 for summer sessions.

Yet I had some questions. Was the post to be a "distinguished" professorship? The brief message had not specified this. Tenured? I had held tenure since my University of Illinois professorship in 1947. Secretarial assistance and graduate assistants? I knew that I owed much to having a full-time secretary since the years with the Bureau for Intercultural Education and to having the help of graduate assistants since Illinois. Teaching load? As a middle administrator, I taught three graduate courses a semester for NYU. Increases for merit? I readily recalled the freezing of my salary at Peabody and at Ohio State University when I taught at University School. Summer school? I wanted guaranteed employment for both summer sessions. Outside professional activities? Consultation and work with national organizations were important to whatever contributions I might make. Convention attendance? I wanted financial support for participation in several national meetings. Who would become dean of the School of Education? Currently, the post was open.

President Rankin responded frankly and specifically. The post would be titled a Distinguished Professorship and would be tenured after a year. The teaching load would be two courses a semester. Salary increases for merit "could be anticipated." Summer employment could be divided into teaching two courses in one session and carrying on research and writing during the second session. Outside activities one day a week. Limited support for convention expenses. He waffled only on secretarial help. The university would supply secretarial assistance. But most senior people at ISU did not have private secretaries, he wrote.

I came back with Bee on May 10 to explore the housing situation and to negotiate further. The one-year probationary period before tenure didn't trouble me, though perhaps it should have. I belonged to a generation that had experienced education as a growth industry; self-confident, I never worried about tenure at ISU or elsewhere. If necessary, I would tip my hat and tug my forelock to all officials met on campus until confirmation of tenure in March 1968. But the question of secretarial help did worry me (fortunately, it was resolved by agreement on the equivalent of full-time service through student secretaries, and they proved to be jewels). Support for convention attendance also seemed bothersome (it was resolved through putting me on the administrative budget for travel). But the largest fly in the ointment was whom the university would appoint to the post of dean of the School of Education.

I asked folksy Byron Westfall, acting chairman of the Department of Education and Psychology—everybody at ISU, including Acting Dean Fred Swalls, seemed to be an acting something-or-other—about a reliable Terre Haute real estate salesman. He recommended equally folksy Olis (Oley or Jamey) Jamison, former head of the department, now retired and growing rich in the real estate business. Oley was a man about whom legends clustered. Once, during an exam that he was proctoring, he came upon an apprehensive nun nervously telling her beads. "No outside help, Sister," enjoined Oley. We told Oley and other agents that we had to have a house on water; the proximity to

336

boating in Mountain Lakes had corrupted us. Perhaps along the Wabash? Only chemical plants and fertilizer factories, they warned us. We went and looked: They were right. Maybe you should have gone to Indiana University in the lake region, professor, the agents said.

House or no house, dean or no dean, I accepted ISU's offer, asked Oley to find me a house on water, and returned to Terre Haute weeks later with Bee and the children on our way to a last wonderful summer of teaching in the American West. During our brief Terre Haute stay, we appealed to the greed of the real estate lads and lasses by informing them that we intended to buy a house—on water—within 24 hours. Only Oley came through; he found an owner who hungered for $39,000 cash paid in full to finance some apartments he was building.

As we turned off a dirt road south of Seelyville, twenty minutes from my campus office-to-be, we drove up a lane beside a lake and through pines, sycamores, and cottonwoods. The lane stretched two-tenths of a mile from the mailbox to the house. Mentally, I bought the house before it came into view and hoped it wouldn't be a hovel. It wasn't. Our new home was a brick ranch-style house on one and a half acres on the shore of half-mile-long Lake Lure, ideal for swimming, boating, and catching bluegills, crappies, and largemouth bass. The lake and the adjoining property through which we had driven were privately owned by five families, one of which could be us. The region was once a strip-mining area. Now the giant floor-to-ceiling panes of glass in the living room overlooked a lovely lake, and the common property was riotous with countless trees and shrubs. After brief and rapid negotiations, we bought the house.

While we were cruising back to Terre Haute with Oley, who favored pointing out new houses while driving at fifteen miles an hour in the fast lane, he mentioned to Bee and me that the School of Education had just appointed the new dean. We came to complete attention; I thought of some of the possible sons of bitches they might have appointed.

"Where is he from?"

"Ohio." Not bad, our former stamping ground.

"What's his name?"

"Turley or Turner, something like that."

"David Turney, assistant dean at Kent State!?"

"That's it."

Bee and I fell on each other's necks in joy. David Turney had come from the state of Washington to be my graduate assistant at Peabody, only to have me leave for the NYU post immediately after Dave's first summer on the Peabody campus. Dave Turney, low key, affable and able, with whom we had cordial relationships at many conventions over the past ten years!

So I became the sonorously titled Coffman Distinguished Professor in Education at Indiana State University. They named the post after Lotus Delta Coffman, an outstanding university president who developed one of America's first programs of general education at the University of Minnesota and whom Harold Benjamin (whom I revered) worshiped. Praise the Lord that Admiral Hyman Rickover or Senator Homer Capehart or President Warren G. Harding didn't attend Indiana State University and didn't become college presidents. The more I learned of Coffman the more pleased I was to try to walk in his big footsteps.

Now I was no longer an administrator. I was free to live the professor's life. All I had to worry about now was how to keep my colleagues from hating me. Wouldn't you hate a colleague who was labeled "distinguished" while you were not, who drew more salary than you, who had the equivalent of a full-time secretary, who carried a light teaching load, who was helped by graduate assistants, who had funds to attend conventions, who had time to write while you did not, who carried no administrative responsibilities, who could in general call his own shots? I don't know about you—I certainly would.

Celebrating our acquisition of a new house, a new dean, and a new post, the Van Til family headed west for the last summer during which I was free to be a visiting professor. I had arranged for summer 1967 teaching on three college campuses in the Rocky Mountain area. But first a gala family reunion was to take place, scheduled prior to Barbara's coming marriage to Bob Nichols. In our new blue Chrysler Newport, Bee and I, with Barbara, now 25, Roy, now 22, arrived at Yellowstone and the Grand Tetons where Jon, now 28, and his wife Sally joined us. We climbed trails, ran rivers, and had a glorious vacation. Then our descendants returned east, while Bee and I went on to my teaching assignments, two weeks at the University of Wyoming in Laramie, two weeks at the University of New Mexico at Albuquerque, and a week at Colorado State College (later rechristened Northern Colorado State University) at Greeley. The life of a visiting professor is good: concentration on teaching and on students, no committees, hospitable hosts, opportunities to explore the scenic and cultural offerings of the area.

We hastened home for Barbara's wedding in August and for the attendant preparations and parties. Barbara's white satin wedding dress with long train was lovingly created by Bee. Both grandmothers attended the wedding in the local Roman Catholic church, St. Catherine of Siena. That evening, when the father of the bride temporarily vanished to pick up the tab for the wedding reception held at a lodge, Victoria Inn, in Boonton, he was inadvertently left behind while revelers returned to his house. The abandoned father called home plaintively, identified himself despite the hubbub, and was eventually retrieved and restored to his hearth. Fathers of the bride are expendable.

The Mountain Lakes house, purchased at $27,500, was put up for sale and eventually brought us $32,000. Bee and I left the region of our birth and headed for the banks of the Wabash far away.

Chapter Thirty-Eight

WRITERS AND EDITORS OF TEXTBOOKS

B yron Westfall, acting chairman of the Department of Education and Psychology, was a competent and benevolent old-time school administrator. During the first semester I discussed my next semester assignment with him in his orderly office lined with books, all of which he gave to faculty members on a first-come first-served basis the day he retired. During the first semester I had taught two doctoral-level social foundations courses, one of which was a rewarding team-teaching venture with W. Richard Stephens, an outstanding student of society soon, unfortunately, to be lost to the field of social foundations as he moved on to the vice presidency, then presidency of Greenville College in Illinois. Byron asked me what I liked to teach. I named several foundational and curriculum courses, then had an afterthought.

"Would ISU be interested in my teaching a course for doctoral students on writing for educational publication?" I had taught such a course (so far as I know the first ever offered in the nation) at Peabody for a couple of years during the 1950s.

"Very much," said Byron. Then he too had an afterthought. "Might some faculty members sit in, if they want to?"

I hesitated, for "sitting in" implies observation, not participation, and people don't learn to swim in the living room. "Only if they'll write and subject their writing to criticism by the entire group."

"Good," said Byron. "I'll send out an announcement to that effect to the faculty."

When the writing class met during the spring semester, there were two doctoral students and twelve faculty members in attendance, and that's the way it went for a decade. Faculty members always outnumbered graduate students. Doctoral students are immersed in required courses and dissertation preparation; publication seems remote. On the other hand, university faculty members hunger for help on writing for educational publication.

I kept my office door open and word soon went out via the grapevine that the new man, despite his formidable title, was willing to help aspiring writers. My connection with Houghton Mifflin also attracted some campus professors ambitious to publish books.

Just before we left for Europe during the NYU sabbatical, William MacDonald of Houghton Mifflin had recruited me as the secondary education specialist on an editorial committee in education, national in composition, made up of Samuel A. Kirk (special education), C. Gilbert Wrenn (guidance), Van Cleve Morris (foundations), Charles S. Benson (administration), and Robert H. Anderson (elementary education). The editorial committee's role was to suggest possible authors to editor Bill MacDonald, read manuscripts on which he asked advice, criticize and improve company-edited material on the way toward publication. In return, we were to receive a 1.5 percent royalty on paperbacks and 2 percent royalty on each hardback book published in our area of specialization.

Bill was an able and effective editor. I fed him early a list of potentially promising authors of secondary education textbooks. During the six years of the editorial committee's existence, prior to its termination by Houghton Mifflin as an economy measure in 1970, I sponsored ten varied books in secondary education. All were deserving of publication; I tried to choose manuscripts with an eye to the importance of the content. The most popular proved to be *A Writer Teaches Writing*, by Donald M. Murray; *Secondary Schools Today: Readings for Educators*, by Frederick R. Smith and R. Bruce McQuigg; *Education for Relevance*, by Carlton E. Beck and a team; and *Supervision for Change and Innovation*, by Adolph Unruh and Harold E. Turner.

I was particularly happy with Harold Turner's participation in the publication program, since he had been my graduate assistant at Peabody where he had written a fine dissertation comparing Alton's and East St. Louis's approaches to desegregation. Bill had originally expressed doubts about the supervision manuscript, and I had put much time and effort into editing the volume. When Harold's book sold well, I remembered the classic legend of Papa Scribner and young Maxwell Perkins. The story goes that Scribner gave Perkins some manuscripts to read. At the ensuing editorial conference, Perkins's analyses were flawless. Papa Scribner then asked, "How many copies shall we publish of each?" And Perkins replied "My God, sir, I haven't the faintest idea." The legend has it that Papa Scribner shook his head sadly and said, "I never know either—but I thought one of you young fellows might know." I remembered, too, Bill Hackett's comment on my collection of short writings, *The Making of a Modern Educator,* "The guys at Holt told me we'd never sell more than 500 copies." Instead, the collection sold almost 5,000.

The course called Writing for Educational Publication was offered once each year. During my decade with Indiana State University, about half of the School of Education faculty enrolled and a few from other schools of the university trickled in, along with some ambitious and farseeing doctoral candidates. Our batting average was highly creditable. About 85 percent of the writing undertaken by members of the writing groups was eventually published, including Houghton Mifflin books by professors of administration and secondary education and the associate dean of the Graduate School. I had developed the course to be helpful to students and colleagues, yet a fringe benefit that accrued was my personal acceptance by the faculty, despite being an outsider brought in under a pretentious title.

Settling in at ISU included teaching social foundations courses open to all doctoral candidates, curriculum courses for the emerging secondary education doctoral program, and a self-assigned responsibility to develop working papers of advice on aspects of the new doctoral program for the use of Dean David Turney and implementing committees. That, along with the presidency of the National Society of College Teachers of Education, the editorship of *Insights,* participation in conventions, work on subcommittees on curriculum of the graduate committee, and the newcomer's inevitable willingness to be drafted to speak on campus or in the state, kept me busy during the first two years on campus.

Yet I had come to Indiana State University in large part because the new position would afford me greater opportunities to write. So in the fall of 1968 I instituted a column for the Indiana State University journal, *Contemporary Education,* and in the summer of 1969 I began two books for possible publication by Houghton Mifflin. Through the column I would primarily reach Indiana educators; through an introduction to education textbook and a curriculum anthology, I would attempt to communicate to the profession as a whole.

I had an additional motivation for writing the Houghton Mifflin textbooks: For the first time in my life I needed more money than was yielded by my professorship and my consultation and Bee's remarkable ingenuity in money management and household maintenance. The combination had sufficed for our peripatetic years as a young married couple, for the decades of child-rearing, for financing the college education of our children (scholarships helped too), and even for summer trips to Europe or through the American West as college graduation gifts to Jon, Barbara, and Roy. Until I decided to write textbooks for Houghton Mifflin, the only education royalties I had ever received from my 200 or so publications had been royalties shared equally with my collaborators Gordon F. Vars and John Lounsbury on two editions of *Modern Education for the Junior High School Years,* which had sold about 21,000 copies, and the slim returns from *The Making of a Modern Educator* and the sabbatical-related articles. But in 1969, my mother, at age 89, had to be cared for through a nursing home. She was the last of the children's grandparents, for Bee's mother had died a year previously when she too had reached age 89.

Umpy's fall in her bedroom in the Terre Haute house had done what nothing else in life had been able to do to her, taken away her independence through making it impossible for her to move about on her own. An extra bedroom built onto our Nashville house hadn't lured her away from her beloved home in Corona. Nor would Umpy come and live with us in Mountain Lakes until she couldn't cope with illness while living alone. In New Jersey, Bee gave her unbelievably faithful care and taught her to clump along with a metal frame called a walker. Even in her mid-eighties she occasionally returned to Corona and her faithful neighborhood cronies or visited my sister in Virginia Beach. In 1966 my sister died of cancer following several years of pain—the accordion and the piano were stilled forever. Flo once told me that her killer had taught her to hate three things— the mirror, the clock, and the calendar.

Umpy came along with us to Terre Haute and lived in our house until her fall two years later. Let no one tell you that Medicare fully covers the medical expenses of the old; Medicare ran out a few months after my mother was hospitalized, then transferred by ambulance to a nursing home. The minuscule remainder of the savings she and Will had miraculously managed was swiftly swallowed up. In 1969 I needed several thousand dollars a year for her care; medical costs were steadily rising higher as bills came in from Meadows Manor, where we visited her daily.

In the late 1960s, arrangements for writing education textbooks were easily made. Teacher education enrollment was high; education books sold well; Nixon was too busy with Vietnam to attack the heritage of Lyndon Johnson's Great Society program. So I simply told Bill MacDonald about the books I wanted to write and he readily agreed. During my time available for writing in the late summer of 1969, I began laboring in my study and on campus on an introduction to education and a curriculum anthology.

Education: A Beginning was to be a long book that covered the waterfront in an attempt to introduce neophytes to education. Because of the necessary variety in the content, I urged that each chapter in first draft be read by a specialist in the field dealt with in that chapter, since this would be more helpful to the author than the customary procedure of review of the entire draft by three or four generalists. Bill MacDonald was persuaded of the usefulness of this unorthodox approach, and nineteen outstanding people in their fields criticized and helped with the chapters. I revised and met my deadline, with a manuscript ready for Houghton Mifflin's editing in 1970, a year after I began work on the book. Meanwhile, I had been developing the anthology, *Curriculum: Quest for Relevance*, which drew heavily from the March 1970 issue of the *Phi Delta Kappan* on curriculum that I had guest edited. Though different, each book fed on the other; for instance, short quotations from authors whom I included in the anthology were sometimes used in the introductory book, and ideas discussed in the introduction to education influenced the structure of the book of readings on curriculum. To deliver both manuscripts in time, I sharply reduced speaking engagements and social life, and I regularly worked seven days a week.

Editors and authors prize timeliness. So when Bill MacDonald proposed that *Education: A Beginning* be published in the spring of 1971 I readily, though unfortunately, agreed to "crash publishing." In this case, crash publishing meant full speed ahead—prompt editing, early return of galleys by the author, and no opportunity for the author to see and check page proofs. As is the custom in the making of books, editor Bill MacDonald delegated copy editing to subordinates, particularly to a copy editor who will here be called Susie, since that was not her name.

I met Susie only through correspondence and really know nothing of her background. Yet I always visualize her as just out of one of the Eastern colleges called the Seven Sisters, an English major specializing in Chaucer and Beowulf. In turn, she visualized me, I am sure, as an obsolete old dodderer who was, in the bargain, ignorant and uninformed. As the galleys came in, I found that Susie had repeatedly "improved" on my work. Highly aware that the historical usage was "Negro" and the post-1960s usage is "black," I referred in my manuscript to Negro colleges when I was writing about the nineteenth century and to black leaders of the civil rights movement when I was dealing with the mid-twentieth century. Susie blithely changed all to "black." And so it went. Humor intentionally introduced to lighten the reading was invariably deleted. Worst of all, Susie quite unintentionally inserted historical errors into the edited copy. For instance, in dealing with the early American colonies I described education in the New England, the Middle, and the Southern colonies. Apparently Susie had never heard of the Middle Colonies—New York, New Jersey, Delaware, Pennsylvania—so she changed Middle to Middle Western. She shifted Puerto Rico over into a listing of foreign countries; I protested that my Puerto Rican students would be appalled that their ignorant instructor didn't know that the enchanted island was a United States commonwealth.

I complained vigorously. Bill, loyal administrator that he was, defended his copy editor, though he accepted corrections of her errors. However, some "improvements" by Susie found their way into the editing and, when the galleys arrived, I had to revise them substantially. Now it was Bill's turn to protest; he pointed out that galley changes are expensive and, if too numerous, would postpone publication by a year. I fretted, fumed, and fulminated and continued to make changes in the galleys. I could only hope that my corrections and restorations would be transferred to the final copy. To facilitate crash publishing, I had agreed to forgo checking page proofs, and I rued that day. Meanwhile, under a less omniscient copy editor, the anthology *Curriculum: Quest for Relevance* proceeded splendidly. Copy editor Ann made only minor changes in introductions to the sections and each was referred to me for consideration.

Bill brought the first copy of *Education: A Beginning* to the ASCD conference in March of 1971. It was a handsome, well-printed 591-page volume of which I at first felt proud. But shortly afterward, when I read it for "errata and corrigenda," an author's chore following publication of a book anticipated to go into further printings, I was horrified and crushed by the carryover of some errors despite my revision of the galleys. A few were mine; others derived from Susie's "improvements" and to inadequate proofreading in the transition from galleys to page proofs. To cite only one, a prejudiced paragraph by the educational historian Ellwood P. Cubberley, which ascribed inferior stock to late nineteenth-century immigrants, was not set off in the blue type reserved for quotations and thus appeared to be my own position. I agonized. Bill calmly assured me that no one except me as the author would ever notice the errors and that anyhow they would be removed when the next printing was run. Whether anyone noticed or not, I'll never know; if anyone did, they forbearingly didn't call the errors to my attention.

But I noticed, and that mattered most of all. I hate typographical and factual errors with an unbelievable passion. My writer's neurosis returned, and again I fell apart emotionally as I had after the publication of *Forces Affecting American Education*. For months I dreaded the arrival of every mail delivery, sure that it would contain scathing excoriations and denunciations. In anticipation of nasty reviews, I suffered every time I opened a journal. Incredible as it sounds, I even had suicidal thoughts. One error in particular—my own—haunted me. I had attributed authorship of a vitriolic book attacking progressive education to the wrong, though equally vitriolic, attacker. In imagination I became the laughing stock of the profession and a contributor to the downfall of the entire modern education movement. Meanwhile, the book, seldom reviewed and then always favorably, was selling very well. That only added to my misery—would that no one had seen my cursed book, that albatross about my neck!

My confessor, a local psychologist whom I consulted, didn't help. He was dedicated to a therapy that advised the client to silently shout "stop!" whenever the client flagellated himself about his inadequacies. Print-lover that I am, I found salvation not in his office but in a book, *Reason and Emotion in Psychotherapy*, by Albert Ellis. Ellis lists among irrational ideas that cause disturbance: "The idea that it is a dire necessity for an adult human being to be loved or approved by virtually every significant other person in the community; the idea that one should be thoroughly competent, adequate, and achieving in all possible respects if one is to consider oneself worthwhile." Ellis advises that, when beset by fears, the client ask himself, "What is the worst possible thing that could happen to me if the worst of my fears actually comes about?" So I contemplated the worst—derogatory reviews, mocking words at conventions, the scorn of scholars. I came to realize that I would still be alive, I would still have my family, my dog Smokey, my friends, my work, my travel, my escapes. I cursed my insane self-expectation that I must be perfect and my writing flawless. Slowly I recovered. The new printing came out; the errors were banished and I found no additional ones. Bill was right about nobody noticing. And I went on living. And writing. But never again would I be seduced by crash publishing.

I did an anthology on education for high school students with Rich Stephens, my partner in team teaching. We enjoyed our leisurely labor of love and never expected *Education in American Life*, published in 1972, to sell. It didn't, since the number of high schools that teach about education is microscopic. But, as one of Shakespeare's numerous noblemen remarked about begetting his bastard child, it was good sport at the making.

Since the introduction to education and the curriculum

anthology sold briskly, my publisher requested second editions. My revisions were sweeping but comparatively uneventful because, by the luck of the draw, the copy editing was excellent. I have sometimes accused myself of being prejudiced against the entire race of editors. To refute self-slander, I can cite happily the impeccable and highly helpful editing of the two second editions. When in 1974 both second editions were published, I reacted as normal authors, perennially dissatisfied, usually do, criticizing my publishers for their ineptness in publicizing and promoting my books (including the cardinal sin of not having copies available at the sales booth at the 1974 ASCD convention) and deploring the turnover of editors, rapid as that of football coaches or college presidents, that successively deposed several editors with whom I had worked effectively and appreciatively. My neurosis had vanished. But I still kept some xeroxed pages from Ellis in my bureau drawer against horrid night thoughts at three A.M.

In the six years between the first publication of *Education: A Beginning* and *Curriculum: Quest for Relevance* and the end of 1976, about 80,000 copies of my two teacher education textbooks had been sold. They said to the world what I wanted to say about a good modern program of education. The royalties more than covered my mother's expenses for medicine and nursing care until she died at 93, flickering out like a spent candle one spring night in 1973.

Chapter Thirty-Nine

CONFRONTATION
IN CHICAGO

I n American life, the years 1967 through 1973 were stormy. Two revolts overlapped: the demand for civil rights by blacks and the anger at the Vietnam War by the young. In 1967 there were riots by blacks in Cleveland, Newark, and Detroit. Fifty thousand people demonstrated at the Lincoln Memorial in Washington against the war. In San Francisco, the black and the youth movements coincided, as Martin Luther King, Jr., led an anti-war march. In 1968 King, the great black leader, and Robert F. Kennedy, the presidential candidate admired by the young, were assassinated. Vigorous protests by demonstrators and brutality by the police turned Senator Hubert Humphrey's nomination in Chicago into a nightmare. In 1969 Richard M. Nixon, narrowly elected, was inaugurated President. Senator Ted Kennedy drove off the bridge at Chappaquiddick, and his woman passenger and the Kennedy political magic died. The mass rallies against the war in Southeast Asia now involved hundreds of thousands of Americans, both young and old.

Civilians were massacred by American soldiers at MyLai in Vietnam in 1968, though Americans didn't learn of this till after autumn of 1969. In 1970 Kent State students were killed by the National Guard. Four hundred and forty-eight colleges and universities in the United States experienced student strikes, and many higher education institutions were temporarily closed. In 1971 fighting in Indochina spread to Laos and Cambodia and worldwide student protest continued.

In 1972 the Watergate break-in of Democratic National Headquarters took place and the cover-up and the lies in which President Nixon was involved began. Yet he was re-elected in a near landslide. In 1973 Vice-President Spiro T. Agnew resigned and pleaded *nolo contendere* to income tax evasion. The Watergate scandal accelerated, and in a "Saturday night massacre" Attorney General Elliot Richardson resigned and special Watergate prosecutor Archibald Cox was fired by President Nixon. The next year the first presidential resignation in American history took place after tapes revealed Nixon's early involvement in the cover-up and after the House committee recommended impeachment.

Indiana State University felt the impact of those years of international and domestic discord much less than did more cosmopolitan universities in metropolitan areas. The majority of the Indiana State University students were either from Terre Haute, a small city of 70,000, or from the area local TV people call Illiana, the small town and farm area within a fifty-mile radius of Terre Haute, which is near the Illinois border. Most came from homes in which political beliefs were conservative, life-styles conventional, religion traditional, and the work ethic taken for granted. They weren't likely recruits to social dissent. Yet, paradoxically, historians know Terre Haute best for its radical native sons of the early twentieth century: Eugene V. Debs, perennial Socialist candidate for President and jailed conscientious opponent of World War 1, and Theodore Dreiser, author of novels that shocked his times, leftist in politics.

Indiana State University was also attended by a black minority from such northern Indiana industrial communities as Gary and East Chicago. Urban-oriented and black-conscious, their life-styles differed from and sometimes conflicted with those of small town students from farming, railroading, and coal mining backgrounds.

Indiana State University was never closed down by the black and the youth revolts. Yet strikes and demonstrations did occur. A Black Studies program and a Black Student Center were instituted largely in response to the urging of black separatists. Blacks segregated themselves at basketball games and did not rise during the singing of the national anthem. Anti-war whites demonstrated and sometimes clashed with other students, largely over such symbolic acts as flying the flag on high or at half-mast.

I signed anti-war petitions, occasionally attended rallies, and urged more appointments of blacks to the ISU staff. Beyond that I took little part in the campus protests, since I rejected as self-defeating such social strategies as black separatism and anti-war occupation of administration buildings.

The surrounding social ferment affected educational organizations, including the Association for Supervision and Curriculum Development. As an opponent of racial segregation and a proponent of integration in school and society, I had worked on ASCD policies and actions with liberal whites and with both Northern and Southern blacks. At almost every national conference throughout the Fifties and Sixties, we introduced and usually carried resolutions supportive of both desegregation and human relations education. For instance, at the first ASCD conference following the *Brown vs. Board of Education of Topeka* decision, a resolution was adopted pledging "our effort to develop respect for an implementation of this decision." As the desegregation battle continued, the resolution was repeatedly reconfirmed or rephrased to express the ASCD's opposition to the evasions and delaying tactics of state legislatures. A 1959 resolution called for equal educational opportunity for children of migrant workers, deprived children, and all those suffering from social and educational segregation. A 1965 official position paper supported a pluralistic society not bound by narrow racial, religious, social class, or regional attitudes. In 1967 the ASCD called for assessment programs that valued and maintained the diversity of our children.

The coalition of liberal whites and integrationist blacks, which sometimes informally caucused during ASCD conferences, usually prevailed in spirited business meetings and frequently encouraged forward-looking action by the executive committee. For instance, from the late Forties through the early Sixties, steady though gradualistic action by the ASCD leadership eliminated the last vestiges of dual state units in the South from the organization. A commission on intergroup education was established under my leadership, then that of Juliette Bursterman, a vigorous black teacher educator from Connecticut.

We had some setbacks, too. I have described earlier my struggles in the early Sixties to gain financial support from the executive committee for ASCD intercultural education kits after I came to the presidency from the chairmanship of the Commission on Intergroup Education. After my three-year leadership span, the executive committee disbanded the commission, to me a regrettable move, since the commission, which had more black members than any other ASCD body, had important work in prospect.

In 1969, at the Conrad Hilton Hotel in Chicago, a focus of the violence during the Democratic Party Convention the year before, the annual ASCD conference encountered militant protest. No educational historian has yet examined the situation; any account must necessarily have a subjective flavor.

In 1968 fifteen black educators, largely long-time ASCD members, met at the Atlantic City conference of the ASCD and reported to the executive committee that 1,063 people were listed in the program for leadership roles at the conference, yet only twenty-three were black. In the following year the executive committee and President Muriel Crosby responded by attempting to increase black membership, since only a few hundred blacks belonged to the 15,000-member organization. No reliable count existed, because the national ASCD, supportive of color-blindness, didn't ask for racial identification of its members. The convention planners achieved an increase in the number of blacks scheduled for leadership roles at the forthcoming 1969 Chicago conference.

After the Atlantic City conference, the executive committee appointed a commission on social hang-ups chaired by a white educator and made up, like most ASCD commissions, of both whites and blacks. A black-white exchange, to be held after the final luncheon at Chicago, was scheduled by the ASCD Executive Committee for the program. The national ASCD office sent invitations to some Chicago-area teachers who were black to attend the forthcoming conference meetings without paying the customary registration charges and to participate in the black-white exchange in order to achieve greater balance among the participants.

As the Chicago conference opened, a hundred or so non-members, largely militant blacks, joined the Social Hang-ups Commission, which now referred to itself as the "augmented commission." The activist blacks had learned of the conference from commission members and other sources. The commission, unofficially expanded, developed activities and programs not contemplated in the convention program planned by the official ASCD Conference Planning Committee. On the eve of the convention, Saturday night, three members of the Commission on Social Hang-ups, including the chairperson, met with Executive Secretary Fred T. Wilhelms, two associate secretaries, and President Muriel Crosby. The discussion was bitter. President Crosby has recalled that she indicated that she would resign in protest unless the plans for unauthorized activities by the augmented commission were canceled. Wilhelms continued the meeting after President Crosby left for another appointment. A negotiated agreement was reached that the black-white exchange would be extended to Monday and Tuesday evenings in addition to the Wednesday session already scheduled and that non-members could participate actively in conference groups but would not disrupt proceedings.

On Sunday morning President Crosby resigned. Later on Sunday a delegation from the augmented commission met with the executive committee (in the last session that former President Crosby would attend) and asked to read a position paper at the opening session. The delegation also asked for funds for the expenses of non-members who had come to the meeting. The executive committee, now chaired by a past president, Harlan Shores of Illinois, acquiesced on reading of a position paper and appropriated $500 to the Commission on Social Hang-ups.

A militant statement that the ASCD was not a legitimate organization was read by a non-member to the assembled 7,000 members at the opening session. Richard Foster, superintendent of schools at Berkeley, California, closed his scheduled major address to the second session by requesting funds from the audience for the expenses of non-members attending the conference; the conference newspaper reported that $1,377 was collected. Members of the augmented commission, attending subgroup meetings and also the customarily closed meetings of commissions, often succeeded in focusing discussion on their concerns.

At the business meeting, another unscheduled statement by the augmented commission was read prior to consideration of resolutions. Representatives of the Commission on Social Hang-ups recommended from floor microphones that all resolutions be defeated. However, all of the resolutions, save for a weak one on federal aid, were adopted by large majority votes. At the final session of the conference, Executive Secretary Wilhelms read a statement on the events as he had experienced them. In the months that followed, the executive committee took steps to clarify the roles of commissions and the ground rules for conferences. The committee also increased black representation in leadership for the forthcoming 1970 San Francisco conference and on commissions through appointment of long-term members and newcomers to the organization.

So much for the facts on which most observers would agree. As in the Japanese film *Rashomon*, perception of the events varied sharply. Muriel Crosby, the president who resigned, was no newcomer to the field of race relations. She had developed effective intercultural education programs as assistant superintendent in Wilmington, Delaware, and was a long-term liberal and proponent of civil rights, experienced in interracial tactics and strategies. Immediately following the conference, she described the events in a 49-page mimeographed statement as an "attempted immobilization...shameful in the annals of professional educational organizations," condemned "the unwarranted acquiescence of the executive committee to the rape of ASCD," and indicated that she resigned in protest "against intimidation and the violation of the rights of members." Of her meeting with the three representatives of the Commission on Social Hang-ups on Saturday, she wrote that she had been informed that the chairman had lost control to the augmented commission yet still supported their confrontation tactics. Of her last meeting with the executive committee on Sunday, she reported that the executive group discussed demands by the augmented commission, raised now to $10,000 for expenses, the scheduling of Monday and Tuesday night black-white exchanges, continuous use of a room for planning confrontations, facilities and services and materials for production of an underground newspaper, the opportunity to read a statement at the opening meeting, and the right to "have confrontation" at all sessions. She suggested to the executive committee that copies of her one-page letter of resignation be distributed to the ASCD membership. The executive

committee did not distribute her letter and delayed any announcement of her resignation until the final luncheon session
at which she had been scheduled to speak. Former President
Crosby left the conference before it closed and returned home
without addressing the final Wednesday session.

At the final luncheon, ASCD Executive Secretary Fred T.
Wilhelms described his perception of the events. Fred had been
a college professor and a writer, and was then an experienced
administrator of educational organizations, having recently come
to the ASCD from the associate secretaryship of the National
Association of Secondary School Principals. He began with a
tribute to Muriel Crosby, then described his office's attempt to
bring black Chicago teachers to the conference for the scheduled
black-white exchange and how the Commission on Social Hang-
ups supplemented these invitations by inviting community militants to sit in throughout the meeting. He said that as the
conference opened he heard reports that "gave some indication
of an attempt to disrupt the planned ASCD conference and substitute what the small group felt was more appropriate." Of the
delegation's meeting with President Crosby, he reported that the
hang-ups commission members "seem to be confirming and
backing the intention of the group they had recruited to move
into our meeting and create stress and dissonance.... I must
insist that, given the conversation she had had with the three
members of the commission, Dr. Crosby was being rational in
coming to believe that a disruption of our conference was being
planned and that the commissioners approved." He reported
that after Muriel Crosby left the meeting with the commission
members, he negotiated additional black-white exchanges, a
room for the commission, and participation by non-members
without disruption. As to ensuing events, Wilhelms said, "My
own perception is that the group has by and large conducted
themselves in the framework of the rational tradition. In my own
contacts with them, they have pressed their points but not in a
disruptive way, and I suspect that in a variety of ways they have
indeed been helpful to us."

A third perception of events was that of the executive
committee after being instructed by the board of directors to
provide an accounting in the form of a review and assessment. In

April, the new president, Alexander Frazier, an elementary education professor at Ohio State University, reviewed conference events with no mention of disruptive confrontation or unauthorized commission action save for the comment that Muriel Crosby's "resignation came as a protest against what she saw to be an unwarranted attempt by the Commission on Social Hang-ups to alter the conference program." The executive committee report explained that the Crosby resignation was not announced early in hopes that she would reconsider. As to adequate control over the activities of the Commission on Social Hang-ups: "The proposals for additions to the conference came as a surprise to the executive committee.... Requests actually presented seemed moderate enough.... The support given by the executive committee to the achievements of the Commission on Social Hang-ups has been steadfast and whole-hearted." The executive committee report proposed more aggressive recruiting from ethnic minorities, more opportunities for members to learn how to respond to militants in school situations, an increase in commissions on social crisis and change, conferences to provide for more participation, and an entreaty to Ms. Crosby to rejoin the executive committee and association.

Later still in June, the executive committee adopted ground rules for national conferences:

> All appointments to committees, commissions, and councils (except committees of the board of directors) are made by the executive committee and issued by the executive secretary.... No solicitation of funds is permitted.... Unless specifically designated as "open," the meetings of the various committees, commissions, and councils and the board of directors are closed to all but their members, except by official invitation. When appropriate, non-members of these groups may arrange in advance with the chairman to make specific contributions.... Certain sessions are open only to those who are registered for them.... Within the planned framework of purposes and procedures, all conferees are invited to join in the normal give-and-take of discussion—which in the ASCD tradition sometimes includes spirited debate. However, of course, conduct which goes beyond this to disrupt is inadmissable and, if necessary, is to be controlled by the chair.

However, the board did not send Muriel Crosby's letter of resignation or her longer mimeographed statement to the membership.

My own personal diary records that my first intimation of problems came on Saturday evening as the conference was about to open. A member of the Commission on Social Hang-ups said to me agitatedly in the hotel lobby, "Bill, I wish you'd see what you could do with your friends, Fred Wilhelms and Muriel Crosby. They're both up tight simply because we're inviting a hundred blacks to the convention to take part in the program. Your friend, Fred, says that he will even call in the Chicago police if there's any kind of disturbance at the convention. Can you imagine! They're really both up tight. Somebody better talk to them or they'll have the goddamn police in here." I called Fred, my long-time associate dating back to the Consumer Education Study, and told him of the comments, but he was too busy to join me to talk things over. Later, Fred pointed out to me that he had said that there were several thousand ASCD members who had laid out a lot of money to attend a conference of a certain kind, that they had a right to it, and that he'd protect that right. Someone had asked him in a shocked voice, "You mean you'd use force?" He had said, "You're damned right I will if you try to spoil their conference." He had contemplated use of the convention's own security guards rather than the Chicago police.

No longer a member of the executive committee or board of directors, I was serving as a member of the ASCD Resolutions Committee during the events in Chicago. Throughout the preceding year, conference resolutions had been solicited from the membership. Resolutions received from the membership and those developed by the resolutions committee had been agreed upon in weekend meetings during July 1968 and January 1969 and had been published in the ASCD *News Exchange* in February of 1969.

The resolutions to be voted on were forthright. One resolution, endorsed and supported by the resolutions committee and presented to the Chicago conference at the business meeting, stated:

> We recommend that ASCD intensify its efforts to actively seek black and other minority group membership, to identify such leadership, to foster further assignments of such leadership at

all levels of its own ranks, and to utilize more extensively the already existing avenues for all of its members to participate fully and completely.

We recommend that ASCD actively seek out and cooperate with groups and organizations which are working toward the extension of integration by promoting deliberate efforts to support black participation and leadership.

We recommend that ASCD's commission on social hang-ups devote concentrated and extensive attention to this matter of human relations and take immediate steps to implement the above resolutions by:

1. Disseminating to affiliated units suggestions and information about successful practices which have been used to encourage and obtain increased membership of black and other minority groups.
2. Making a survey of the leadership ranks of ASCD and disseminating the findings with specific suggestions and/or guidelines for the total membership.

At the Sunday morning meeting of the resolutions committee, we went over the ground rules for adoption of the resolutions, including the understanding that the open hearing would accept minor changes and refinements of wording but no new resolutions. On Sunday afternoon we were to begin gathering and developing possible resolutions for next year's conference. However, we were unable to proceed, for we had a visitor who was a member of the augmented commission. He talked in vague and general terms, avoided making any particular point, delayed the work of the committee, and constantly sought to provoke committee members by his responses to even the most factual of questions put to him. He pointed out, for instance, that he didn't like or trust white people and that the committee must act on his suggestions right then and there before he went on to a second point, despite repeated explanations that the committee was simply receiving suggestions at that point. He indicated that the committee pretended not to understand him because he was black, that he didn't trust the committee or any of its members, that the committee was trying to get rid of him, and that his responsibility was to report back to the hang-ups commission as to his bad treatment by the committee. After forty-five minutes he left, only to come back with three other blacks and one white. The resolutions committee heard out the visitors and adjourned at four P.M.

The Monday open hearing on resolutions went smoothly, with no confrontation, harassment, or delay. On Tuesday, in a meeting held at the Pick-Congress Hotel down the street and away from the confrontation at the Conrad Hilton, the resolutions committee incorporated minor changes and rewordings in resolutions suggested at the open hearing.

Meanwhile, rumors were sweeping through the membership as to the president's resignation, confrontations at commissions and group meetings, and demands by the augmented commission. After her resignation, I chanced on Muriel Crosby in the Conrad Hilton lobby and asked, "When are us peasants going to find out what is going on here?" She said, "What is happening is that the conference has been taken over by the Commission on Social Hang-ups, and outsiders are using our own funds in the taking over."

Aware that something was going on and uncertain of what it was, the membership attended the business meeting in numbers never before seen in the ASCD's history. Members of the hang-ups commission asked at the microphone for rejection of all resolutions, including the resolution calling for greater participation in the ASCD by black members. By wide majorities, all resolutions, save the inadequate one on federal aid, were accepted.

The conference then turned to statements of concern from any who wanted to speak. I read this statement:

> My name is William Van Til, Indiana State University. I am a past president of the Association for Supervision and Curriculum Development, 1961-62. I speak for no group; I speak for myself alone.
>
> I have the following statement of concern: I urge that in **the days, weeks, and months after the conclusion of this ASCD conference in Chicago**, the events of the past few days at this conference be reviewed by the elected representatives of the ASCD—the officers, the executive committee and the board of directors. I urge them to seriously consider as their **first priority** such matters as these:
>
> 1. The circumstances surrounding the resignation of the presidency offered by the president of the ASCD, Muriel Crosby, the reasons for this resig-

nation, and the handling of this resignation by the ASCD.

2. The proper responsibility and relationship of the elected representatives of the ASCD—the officers, the executive committee, and the board of directors—to the programs, plans, and activities of any appointed commission, committee, or council of the ASCD.

3. The appropriateness or inappropriateness of any commission, committee, or council itself expanding its own membership through the addition of ASCD members or non-members.

4. The appropriateness or inappropriateness of any ASCD conference speaker requesting his listeners to make a financial contribution to any collection for any ASCD commission, committee, or council or for any other purposes at an ASCD conference.

5. The gains and losses to social and educational values, to human relationships among blacks and whites, and especially to the democratic way of life encountered through use of the technique of planned confrontation of committees, councils, and commissions by individuals and groups during this ASCD conference.

6. The implication of the above for the planning, programs, and conduct of the proposed 1970 ASCD meeting in San Francisco.

This statement was greeted by loud and prolonged applause from the membership. It was the first time that anyone at the conference had said publicly that President Crosby had resigned. Supporters of the Commission on Social Hang-ups responded that I was speaking for "the ASCD establishment." I reiterated that I spoke for myself alone. At the board of directors meeting that followed Wilhelms's presentation, the board instructed the executive committee to evaluate the events of the convention and account to the board.

After the conference I sent my statement of concern to all board of directors and executive committee members. When the executive committee adopted rules for the next convention to be held in San Francisco, I wrote them a letter of endorsement as to the new rules but suggested again the desirability of the membership hearing Muriel Crosby's version of the events. Again I sent copies to the board of directors and received in turn many supportive letters and a few dissents. Fred Wilhelms wrote me:

> As to our not publishing a complete statement of Dr. Crosby's position, I guess you will agree with me that this is a matter of tactics, even if you don't agree that we have taken the right one. We have had to face up to the likelihood that if we publish one side we would indeed be obligated to give equal time to the other side, and the prospects would be for a continuing series of rebuttals and rebuttals of rebuttals of rebuttals. The executive committee has taken the position that we had better just go ahead. But I am delighted that you caught the fact that in making that decision we also made some decisions about clearing up procedures and trying to build some guarantees of orderliness which are shorthanded by the ground rules.

The next year, at the San Francisco conference, there were meetings of a group that called itself the Radical Caucus. But no disruption of the 1970 ASCD meeting was planned and no confrontation occurred. As a consequence of both evolutionary processes within the organization and the confrontation of the Chicago conference, participation in ASCD leadership by long-time and recent black members increased markedly over the next several years. In retrospect, the organization appears to have emerged from the Chicago confrontation stronger than before.

Varied perceptions of the affair are still held by participants. This is the way I saw it. Others may remember the conference differently. History has never been a science.

Chapter Forty

INDIANA STATE
UNIVERSITY YEARS

B y definition, professors are people who teach in colleges
or universities; some of us also carry on research and
write books. I was lucky enough to be among the happy
few who, in addition, are allowed opportunities to publish columns and participate in leadership of national organizations. "One Way of Looking at It" was the title of the column I
wrote for Indiana State University's *Contemporary Education*
from 1968 to 1971, then for the much wider audience (1979 circulation 132,000) of *Phi Delta Kappan* from 1971 to 1978.

Some columns had a light touch, such as a blow-by-blow
account of my encounter with a computer attempting to teach me
fifth-grade geography. Others were serious crusades for change,
such as the one in which I drew deadly parallels between Phi
Delta Kappa race barriers of the 1930s and sex barriers of the
1970s. Though the latter column ran directly counter to the
position taken by PDK chapter delegates at their 1971 biennial
council, Stan Elam carried uncensored my criticism of organization policy. (Shortly afterward [1973], Phi Delta Kappa changed
its constitution to sanction the admission of women, after several
chapters led the way by initiating women unconstitutionally.)
Some of my columns stirred disagreement, such as a defense of
busing for desegregation. Others drew plaudits, such as "The Rac-
coon Died," which compared my insensitivity to a dying animal to
society's insensitivity to human cries for help on social problems.[1]

---

[1] "One Way of Looking at It" usually focused on social problems. In the

Interspersed were occasional autobiographical columns, such as "To Walk with Others," a tribute to Emily Curry, the principal of the elementary school I had attended, and a criticism of the changelessness of my high school ("He Went Back"). A column on experiences in breaking into print ("Writing for Educational Publications") elicited an invitation (which I didn't accept at that time) to write a book on the subject. Satire, I found, was still appreciated, for *Educational Horizons* reprinted a column kidding the small-is-beautiful advocates ("The Second Coming of the One-Room Schoolhouse"), though the world ignored a column I liked better, "Horace Mann's Only Appearance on TV," a spoof of TV discussions on education.

I gathered the better of the *Contemporary Education* columns in a pamphlet called *One Way of Looking at It (1971)*, and the early *Kappan* columns I liked in another pamphlet, this one titled (with remarkable originality) *Another Way of Looking at It* (1974), both published by Indiana State University. Temporarily flush with funds as enrollment climbed in the late 1960s, ISU had earlier published and disseminated three of my talks: *Universities and Crises*, an address to our university faculty; *The Year 2000: Teacher Education*, a presidential address to the National Society of College Teachers of Education that had appeared in abbreviated form in a monograph published by that organization; and *The Laboratory School: Its Rise and Fall?*, a talk to the National Association of Laboratory School Administrators. President Rankin got substantial public relations mileage for Indiana State University from the five pamphlets, and I enjoyed supervising the distribution of the free copies. My role and title also help account for invitations from editors for lead

---

stormy years 1968-1973, I wrote of revolts in universities ("Welcome to the Club, Gentlemen"), black separatism ("But There Aren't Enough of You"), attacks on permissiveness ("The New Demonology"), prejudice ("Stereotyping Youth and Negroes"), student demands ("Freedom is Non-Negotiable"), space travel versus human needs ("Let Them Eat Space"), the inanities of school dress codes ("The Hair Decision of 1973"), computer-assisted instruction ("Man vs. the Machine"), the strategy of confrontation ("Confrontation and Consequences"), abuse of the environment ("Story of a Lake"), the TVA ("Environment vs. Technology").

articles or editorials for their journals.[2]

Prior to the Indiana State University years, many anthologists had included "Is Progressive Education Obsolete?" in their books of readings. How many I don't know, since the holder of the copyright, *Saturday Review*, was legally entitled to grant permission to reprint and collect fees without bothering to check with the author. Book publishers sometimes courteously asked my approval of inclusion and sent me copies of the anthology in which my article appeared. Some discourteously didn't, and I would learn of its appearance, if I learned about it at all, from a passing comment by a colleague at a convention. All I know for sure is that I have on my shelves ten copies of anthologies published between 1962 and 1969 that include "Is Progressive Education Obsolete?"

In the late 1960s I began asking for a modest fee of $50 whenever aspiring anthologists approached me for permission to reprint articles in collections intended to enrich themselves and their publishers. Under the old copyright laws, the journals that owned an author's article could cut the writer in or not at their discretion, so my requests were based on shaky ground. However, though few publishers are generous, some are overly optimistic, particularly prior to publication. And, after all, anthologists are aware that people do talk; to include a reluctant contributor would be poor public relations.

Anthologies proliferated during the years of the black and student revolts when relevance to learners and to social realities was demanded by readers and professors. From 1967 through 1974, thirteen more volumes that reprinted my articles or columns came to decorate my shelves. Anthologists favored "The

---

[2] *Today's Education* featured "The Key Word Is Relevance," *Childhood Education* "The Temper of the Times," *New Era* "Education and the Resolution of Conflict," *Educational Leadership* "In a Time of Value Crisis." *Kappan* editors asked me to edit an issue, "Curriculum for the 1970s"; the National Education Association reprinted an article, "Discipline in the Classroom," in a pamphlet; *Contemporary Education* published my views on "Junior High School or Middle School?"; and *Forum*, a J. C. Penney home economics publication, abbreviated my portrayal of "The Relevant Teacher."

Genuine Educational Frontiers" from *Saturday Review*, plus a mixed bag from the *NEA Journal, Woman's Day, Educational Leadership,* and *Contemporary Education* on making assignments, discipline, relevance, high school curriculum, computerized instruction, the junior/middle school. Even the oddball satire, "The Remarkable Culture of the American Educators," one of "The Importance of People" columns for the ASCD, appeared between book covers. By the mid-1970s the anthology boom in publishing was over, for profitability declined with the ebb in social protest and the end of the demand for variety in readings for teacher education.

My first six academic years at Indiana State University were marked by a volume of publications unparalleled since my Bureau for Intercultural Education days. As a writer, I was fecund as the proverbial shad: three textbooks and two revisions, seven pamphlets of my own, four original contributions to books or pamphlets by others, an edited issue of a journal, ten articles, twenty-seven columns, plus reprinting in anthologies and continued editing of the John Dewey Society's *Insights.* The distinguished professorship role had emancipated me from administration and I had voluntarily cut back on the speaking engagements that, in tandem with administration, had worn me down at New York University. My teaching responsibilities were light, though I took them seriously. University and college administrators were supportive of my contribution through writing.

I still worked with national organizations in education, the other distinctive aspect of my fancily titled professorial role. I had always respected the contributions associations made to the profession through journals, yearbooks, newsletters, meetings, etc. Yet would more internal efficiency and more coordination among groups enhance their contributions?

The question was especially germane to the National Society of College Teachers of Education. Initiated in the early years of the twentieth century (and with a roster of well-known past presidents, including my namesake Lotus Delta Coffman, who served in 1917, precisely fifty years before my own presidency), the society had recently fallen on hard times. Professors of education were increasingly affiliating with organizations in their fields of specialization rather than remaining with an umbrella organization. Just before I assumed the presidency, president R. Stewart Jones wrote in the January 1967 *NSCTE Newsletter* that "this new year finds the society emerging from a nadir in membership and perhaps even in morale and clarity of purpose." The same issue carried letters from members suggesting that the organization play a more significant role in teacher education or dissolve. For the past three years, the membership had hovered at 427.

In the role of mother hen, the National Society of College Teachers of Education coordinated the scheduling of February meetings in Chicago of the History of Education Society, the Comparative Education Society, the John Dewey Society, and the Philosophy of Education Society, as well as its own sessions. Our host was the large and influential American Association of Colleges for Teacher Education, attended and supported by the top administrators or their delegates from higher education institutions with teacher education programs. The university and college administrators liked having organizations of professors in attendance; no doubt we reminded the presidents and their cohorts that professors were also part of the teacher education enterprise. Our presence was sometimes convenient for administrators who were shopping for new staff members; conventions often take on the atmosphere of slave markets. Astute and experienced Edward C. Pomeroy, executive secretary of the AACTE, appreciated our distribution of his organization's *Journal of Teacher Education,* one of our services to our NSCTE members. The affiliated organizations brought able speakers to Chicago, including the John Dewey Society lecturers; the professors also increased the attendance at general sessions of the AACTE conference. Consequently, the American Association of Colleges for Teacher Education staff readily provided the professors' organizations with meeting rooms and facilities for registration. Fortunately, Goliath was friendly, for David, with 427 members, had little power.

During my term, some of us who were National Society of College Teachers of Education officers came up with the idea of greater clout and more effective functioning for the several small organizations through greater cooperation and a degree of federation. Neither NSCTE nor the small specialized organizations could afford the salary of a full-time executive secretary to collect dues, put out publications, and expand membership. Maybe our richer administrative brothers could subsidize our worthy endeavors through a delegated AACTE staff member. Perhaps our programs might be listed in the AACTE program at the back of the book, thus luring some AACTE members to our meetings. Perhaps AACTE could be persuaded to value us more if we considered moving elsewhere, possibly to the annual conference held by the American Educational Research Association.

In 1967 and 1968 planning meetings were held in Terre Haute by the National Society of College Teachers of Education. Through the second Terre Haute meeting, representatives of the National Society of College Teachers of Education and the affiliated organizations, having developed greater coordination and now having been joined by an ambitious social foundations society, the American Educational Studies Association, began the quest for AACTE appointment of and support for an executive secretary.

Negotiations under my leadership and that of my successor, philosopher of education Ernest E. Bayles of the University of Kansas, were hampered by the individualism of skeptical organizations and the suspicious nature of college professors. Some representatives feared being co-opted—a negative word inherited from the student revolt—by an AACTE supported by funds from the coffers of teacher education institutions. AACTE Executive Secretary Ed Pomeroy was unready to make a commitment until his own board had ample opportunity to discuss the matter. After much haggling in the months after the Terre Haute meetings, two of the affiliated organizations, the NSCTE and the John Dewey Society, took advantage of AACTE's eventual though belated funding for the services of an executive secretary. My own position was to take the money and do the Lord's work with it.

Indiana State University made a contribution to the expenses of the second Terre Haute meeting and benefited by faculty sessions conducted by such academic luminaries as Freeman Butts of Teachers College, representing the American Educational Studies Association; Joe Burnett of the University of Illinois, representing the Philosophy of Education Society; David Tyack of the University of Illinois, representing the History of Education Society; Glen Hass of the University of Florida, representing the John Dewey Society; and several other national leaders.

Recognized as sympathetic to interorganizational cooperation, I was soon appointed by the NSCTE to another coordinating
body, Associated Organizations for Teacher Education. Could
our 427-member David exert influence on this Goliath too? On
paper, the AOTE appeared to have substantial power, for the
fifteen associated groups represented a membership of 200,000
educators and ranged in size from such giants as the National
Council of Teachers of English to the small John Dewey Society
and National Society of College Teachers of Education. In actuality, the representatives of organizations that made up the
AOTE gathered twice a year to listen to a few speeches and to be
briefed on developments in teacher education as seen by the staff
of the American Association of Colleges for Teacher Education.

I soon allied myself with a wing that wanted the organization
to be more than a channel of AACTE information to member
groups. Associated Organizations for Teacher Education had
been originally sponsored by the American Association of Colleges for Teacher Education (which thoughtfully provided for
heavy representation from the latter group), and AACTE Executive Secretary Edward Pomeroy preferred the information channel role for the AOTE. Yet those who wanted the AOTE to
develop its own program, through speaking collectively in areas
in which teacher education might otherwise be unheard, gained
in influence. So the AOTE developed a task force on teacher
education in inner-city schools and created yardsticks and standards for the development of educational technology by business, along with fostering the AACTE's favorite project, developing guidelines for national accreditation standards. The major
goal of the action-oriented wing was the holding of a national
conference on redesigning teacher education.

I served the AOTE for two three-year terms, from 1967 to
1973. Late in my second term I was requested to develop a document on issues in teacher education for consideration at the
forthcoming national AOTE conferences. The small NSCTE,
with its membership drawn from varied disciplines, proved to be
an ideal sounding board. In 1972 I wrote NSCTE members, asking for the issues they thought most critical, and used the resultant list as pump-priming for AOTE organizations as they

gathered perceptions of issues from their own members. My Committee on Issues in Teacher Education then assembled the issues, reported on them to the Madison, Wisconsin, AOTE meeting in 1972, then provided the major source of input for our National Conference on Teacher Education held in St. Louis in May 1973.

So those who wanted the AOTE to speak as an independent voice in teacher education had their way. David had once again exerted considerable influence on Goliath.

The Association for Supervision and Curriculum Development remained my major organization. When the board of directors of the ASCD convened in San Francisco in 1970, a year after the confrontation at Chicago, the board members had an addition to their agenda. Over the past several years revisions to the constitution had been devised and adopted, among them the creation of a review council "to work toward the improvement of the Association by translating concern and criticism into new information" and "to evaluate the policies adopted and the manner and effectiveness with which such policies are implemented by the Association... to attain its purposes."

To give this body a substantial period of tenure, the revised constitution specified five-year terms for each new member, save for the first appointees, who were to serve terms reflecting in their length the size of the vote they received from the electors, the ASCD board. Elected were Karl Openshaw (1970-71), former associate secretary; Harold Drummond (1970-72), former president; Jack Frymier (1970-73), active in ASCD research programs; William Alexander (1970-74), former president; and myself (1970-75)—the board apparently remembered my Chicago statement. All chosen were ASCD veterans, ideologically and personally compatible.

In our first meeting in May 1970, we elected Harold Drummond as our first chairman, an ideal choice because of his persistence, integrity, tact, and wry sense of humor. After considering how we would work, we turned to building recommendations for the 1971 conference; unlike the U.S. Supreme Court, we were to provide new information and to evaluate rather than to make ultimate judgments.

Our recommendations for consideration by the board and executive committee at the next conference were hard-hitting and tough-minded. At the San Francisco conference, the self-styled Radical Caucus had charged that the Association for Supervision and Curriculum Development helped "to maintain an oppressive public school system." We asked representatives of the caucus to meet with us in our fall meeting and provide information. They did, though reluctantly; the Radical Caucus never could quite decide whether to work within or outside the ASCD structure. The review council agreed that "denying students the rights of citizenship which are guaranteed to them under the U.S. Constitution (*e.g.*, freedom of speech, right to refuse to testify against oneself, etc.) must be recognized as oppressive practices, and these practices cannot be condoned." The council, however, rejected the charge that the ASCD helped to maintain an oppressive public school system. The review council concluded: "The consistency of ASCD's position and opposition to oppressive practices, as judged by its publications and resolutions, is remarkable, in fact." We recommended that the board of directors commission a study on oppressive practices in schools.

Another recommendation dealt with opposition to racism and supported integration in the ASCD. We commented:

> Among the most firmly established traditions and policies of the ASCD are opposition to racism, rejection of all types of segregation and separation, and support for integration and democratic human relationships. Nineteen resolutions since 1947 have supported some aspect of human and civil rights which was critical in the particular conference year. For instance, the annual conference of the ASCD in San Francisco in March 1970 unanimously adopted the following resolutions:
>
> We recommend that:
> 1. ASCD oppose, in every way possible, the use of public funds for the support of private schools organized to maintain racial segregation.
> 2. ASCD voice opposition to black separatism and any other form of separatism as a solution to the problem of racism.
> 3. ASCD, in the extension of integration, support the conscientious utilization of professional competence in leadership positions in education, and

indeed in American life as a whole, regardless of race, creed, or class.

The council also recommended that each commission, committee, and council of the ASCD reflect this resolution through its composition. Specifically, the review council pointed out that the board had elected no minority group members to the review council itself, nor did the council on black concerns include non-blacks.

The review council's good start overcame, in part, suspicion by some that the review council would be a brake upon progress exercised by "five old men." In succeeding years the review council was equally outspoken. For instance, in the year of my own chairmanship, 1973-74, we opened our report with: "The need for ASCD to exert an aggressive, initiatory leadership is the most frequent concern and criticism heard by the review council from ASCD members and through its own deliberations." We recommended that the organization "speak out" to the public and "express the association position on issues and problems affecting education." We called on Gordon Cawelti, the new executive secretary, "to take leadership in fostering the new, the initiatory, and the innovative as a top priority within ASCD activities." The review council report asked for stronger relationships between the state units and the national office through a designated liaison officer. Our report suggested new publications and the revival of institutes and small conferences. We advocated emphasis on study of alternative futures.

As a review council, we had the right to review the work of the executive secretary, staff, executive committee, board, commissions, etc. As I said later in a column on the role of a review council:

> Quite understandably, any review council in any organization will make some people uneasy. For a review council may inquire into the activities and workings of all aspects of an organization, whether executive committee, board of directors, executive secretariat, staff, working groups, committees and commissions, etc. It isn't always comfortable to have a group within an organization which communicates concerns and criticisms and evaluates policies and asks whether adopted policies are being carried out effectively. Thus, some of the

temporarily powerful will be tempted to ignore them, and others will be tempted to abolish any review council.

At first we were discouraged when skillful parliamentarians, like a perennial ASCD influential, Dick Foster, managed to persuade the large board of directors to table some recommendations so that they might be dealt with by members of the executive committee. Yet when we reviewed what had happened to our resolutions, we found that the large majority were implemented, sometimes without formal action taken by the governing boards. When a recommendation was ignored, we brought it back year after year. My own calculation is that of thirty-seven recommendations spelled out between 1971 and 1975, all but six were substantially embodied in activities of the ASCD. Thus I concluded:

> All in all, the provision of a review council seems to me to be a significant development in the effective and reflective operation of an educational association. It reminds the organization that it has a past. It helps keep the organization alive and vital in the present. It helps the organization move flexibly into the future. You may want to consider this structural device in the organizations with which you work.

Not all my activities with organizations were solemn attempts to improve the profession. For instance, Bee and I were regular party-givers at conference after conference at the ASCD. We also frequently gathered my former graduate assistants and doctoral students for drinks and dinner. We continued a tradition, instituted at Las Vegas, of hosting the "permanent" ASCD staff, an able yet often neglected group who contributed to the success of the ASCD's conferences. Bee occasionally joined me for an AOTE session, such as a Florida meeting. Too, there was the Spring Conference, that free-wheeling discussion group. I played the role of factotum for two enjoyable years and rode herd on the members while being shot at by the irreverent brethren.

Another long-time continuing relationship I enjoyed was with United Educators, publishers of *American Education* and *Wonderland of Knowledge*, plus sets of books for children. The earliest meetings of the board of educators, an advisory group, were held in a mansion on an estate in Lake Bluff, Illinois, a meat packing baron's former home now converted into a hive of cells for the publishing company. The sessions seemed to me overly ceremonial, bland, and insufficiently focused on improvement of the company's publications. After the 1957 meeting, in which my first contribution, a vigorous critique of an activity book for children (reviewed largely by Bee, who was more knowledgeable in elementary education than I), was accepted, filed, and then forgotten, I had pushed in 1959 and 1961 for a systematic study of the encyclopedias, hard-hitting advice by the board, and responsible followup action by management.

Rather than continuing to hold sessions in what looked like a throne room where department functionaries put their best feet forward through self-serving reports, management responded with board meetings away from the Tangley Oaks headquarters. Attendance was limited to the board of educators and three top officials, the president, the secretary-treasurer, and the vice president, who was also editor-in-chief. So the board of educators convened in Sarasota (1963), Ste. Adele, Canada (1965), Boca Raton (1966), Scottsdale, Arizona (1970), and Bermuda (1974). Those meetings were interspersed with occasional returns to the Moraine Hotel or Tangley Oaks or Harrison House conference facilities on Chicago's North Shore. The pleasant settings encouraged informal relationships and frank discussions, and the meetings grew more productive of improvements, more relaxed in tone, and less ceremonial in nature.

Over the years, replacements following retirements brought varied orientations to the eight-person board: a woman dean of a Canadian library school, an astronaut, a library dean at Case Western Reserve who was a prolific columnist, curriculum man Glen Hass, and my former colleague Virgil Clift, of NYU. Clift, a black, supplemented white Southerner E. T. McSwain, education dean at Northwestern, in keeping the encyclopedia revisions abreast of current black struggles. Early on, McSwain had discovered in *American Educator* an illustration purporting to represent life in Africa. The picture portrayed a Ubangi woman with a plate inserted in her mouth; he had raised holy hell until it vanished forever from the set.

Our conference arranger was the colorful editor-in-chief, Everett Sentman, whose free spending in resort and local settings made up for the meagerness of the honorariums paid the board members for their days in attendance. The officers saw to it that we and accompanying wives were wined, dined, and entertained in the grand deductible business expenses tradition. Sentman also held United Educators receptions at Association for Supervision and Curriculum Development conferences for ASCD members whom Glen Hass and I invited. On one occasion, just before a Minneapolis conference of the ASCD, the manager of a private club, which Ev had heard was the best in town, loftily turned down a United Educators request for a reception to be held at his club. He soon changed his tune, for Sentman had him bombarded with messages from Senator Hubert H. Humphrey, the superintendents of schools of both St. Paul and Minneapolis, and other assorted governmental officials.

The board of educators enjoyed their advisory role and each other. We studied the encyclopedias in advance of our meetings, and we both praised and heckled the editorial products. In turn, we were both heeded and ignored by company officials.

Everett once told the board that I had been appointed to the continuing chairmanship in 1969 by the officers because I was "an abrasive maverick." Naturally, the "abrasive" chairman belligerently denied the adjective; he was assured by his board colleagues that he was really sweet, mild, and lovable. The chairman softly denied that allegation too.

Time fled by during my first six years at Indiana State University. My teaching was largely in small doctoral seminars with students in guidance and psychological services, in educational administration, and in elementary and secondary school curriculum. As specialists, they often didn't talk each other's languages and had to learn to understand and sometimes counter each other's views. The guidance and psychological services people were gung ho for the individual learner and sympathetic to programs based on the needs of students. The administrators talked buses, bonds, and budgets. The curriculum people thought in terms of relevant content and processes of change. I tried to help them to recognize that the individual, society, and values must all be taken into account, whatever the doctoral student's specialization. In my seminar on foundations of education, they read William Heard Kilpatrick on the needs of learners, George Counts on social realities, and Boyd Bode on values. Then all

374

encountered the reconciling John Dewey, with his emphasis on the interaction of psychological, social, and philosophical foundations. I also conducted curriculum seminars and my writing for educational publication course. In retrospect, my major regret as to teaching is that I didn't offer a high-enrollment course on the master's degree level to reach a wider student audience. Indiana State preferred that I help to develop the doctoral program through seminars and my membership on many doctoral committees, and I went along with the decision.

As always, my graduate assistants were stimulating and indispensable: Marvin Kelly, a rebel against administration who tried college teaching, public school administration, and eventually found his niche as a religious educator; R. Joseph Dixon, a socially sensitive, serious, home-and-family oriented high school administrator, who wrote an excellent dissertation comparing the approaches of intercultural educators of the 1940s and ethnic educators of the 1970s, which culminated in a co-authored pamphlet; Ronald M. Leathers, an assistant professor at Eastern Illinois University whose background in language arts helped in his work on my writing. In 1974 they were followed by Robert C. Morris, former professional football player with the Houston Oilers and New Orleans Saints, who was to work with me for two years, learn to be a prolific writer, and become a professor at Auburn and the University of South Carolina. Four more varied personalities would be hard to find.

We continued our tradition of a social and evaluation session at our home as a final meeting of each class or seminar. Bee's breakfasts for new university wives became an established annual tradition. So we acquired scores of cordial new acquaintances, though we made fewer close new friends—the latter seemed harder to come by as we grew older. Our best friends were our early friends, the Turneys and the Ohlsens. Merle Ohlsen, my former colleague at the University of Illinois, had succeeded Ed Roeber following Ed's death. Merle and I constituted a Union of Distinguished Professors that met just once each year to needle President Rankin into keeping our salaries a notch above that of full professors.

As a community to live in, Terre Haute had more strengths than weaknesses. We followed university athletic events, convocations, symphonies, the community theater, and foreign movies. We watched the incredible performances of ISU's Larry Bird, including his culmination as a college player during the 1979 season when the basketball team won thirty-seven straight games before losing to Michigan State in the NCAA final. I added ineptness in fishing to my skill in foldboating.

The closeness of our family circle persisted. Geographically, we were apart, with Jon in the Philadelphia area; Barbara in Knoxville, Tennessee, where Bob completed doctoral study to become a clinical psychologist later in the Bay City, Michigan, area; Roy in Boston. Yet we traveled to see them and they came to Lake Lure for holidays and special occasions. Jon (whom we falsely accused of believing the United States to be made up of an East Coast and a West Coast separated by a vast desert) inspected our property soon after our settling in, succumbed to its lacustrine charms, and admitted, "I never thought I'd be spending my vacations in Indiana!" Barbara and Bob commuted almost monthly to Lake Lure and, from 1970 forward, brought along our first grandchild, Linda Alison Nichols. After a western trip by motorcycle and Porsche, son Roy and his friend Mike polluted our lake with soapsuds following bathless days of camping. Occasionally Roy would appear in our driveway, frozen rigid from pit stop top-down driving from Boston. Jaunting about Europe in 1972, he telegraphed us from Switzerland to send him his birth certificate. We responded with a document and a message, "Long live love!" In Zermatt, he married Linda, the Long Island girl whom he had pursued abroad.

Each Christmas all or some of our children with their families converged on Terre Haute. We cut and decorated a tree from the property, saw slides of earlier days, and experienced nostalgia thick enough to cut with a knife.

Though summer employment was part of my ISU agreement, Bee and I found vacation time to travel together. Despite our travels, I nursed an incurable itch. I wanted to go around the world. The itch became a rash as 1974, the year of my sabbatical, approached. I scratched experimentally with a trip in the late spring of 1973 through Portugal and Spain to see how Bee and I would take to life abroad, away from our beloved families, home, and work. We liked our jaunts by car from Lisbon to the

Algarve, then a villa at Costa del Sol, then more jaunting to the Alhambra, El Greco's Toledo, and Goya's Madrid. So we took the plunge and letters went out, travel literature arrived, and I happily planned a world trip for January through June 1974.

I put to bed the revisions of *Education: A Beginning* and *Curriculum: Quest for Relevance*, concluded my AOTE work with the national meeting in St. Louis, turned *Insights* over to Rich Stephens, the John Dewey Society meeting at the ASCD over to Harold Turner, and the annual John Dewey discussion at the AACTE back to the JDS officers. I'd be away for a while, and it was time anyhow to cede to a younger generation—in 1974 I would become 63. Of relationships to organizations, I maintained only my ASCD review council connection. Of my writing commitments, I retained only my *Kappan* column, which I planned to write from abroad.

Before we went off to make sure that the world was really round and wide, we wrote a mouth-watering Christmas letter to our friends that concluded:

> Goodbye for a while. We plan to live around the world in:
> Mexico, Tahiti, Samoa during January
> Fiji Islands, New Zealand during February
> Australia, Indonesia, India during March
> Nepal, Iran, Turkey during April
> Greece, Spain, Morocco during May
> Home in June
> To us, the place names sound like distant beckoning bells:
> Puerto Vallarta, Mexico City; Papeete, Moorea-"Bali-hai"; Pago Pago, Apia; Korolevu, Suva; Waitangi to Te Anau; Sydney, Tasmania, Adelaide; Bali; Bangkok; Calcutta, Allahabad, New Delhi; Katmandu; Shiraz, Teheran; Ankara, Izmir, Istanbul; Rhodes, Athens, Delphi; Barcelona, Madrid, Costa del Sol; Casablanca, Marrakech.

Chapter Forty-One

A WIDE
WIDE WORLD

As early as 1971 I knew that I wanted to travel and learn and work abroad during my coming 1974 sabbatical. So I asked advice of internationally oriented government and organization personnel along endless Washington corridors of the United States Department of State; the Department of Health, Education, and Welfare; and the National Education Association; and at the meetings and in off moments on the lively, lovely island of Jamaica during the World Conference of the Teaching Profession and the International Council on Education for Teaching. Informants told me that the approximately two years of "lead time" I had given myself for planning service abroad was about right, neither too long nor too short. They suggested that a first decision was whether a would-be international traveler wanted to earn income abroad or not. Most advised working in a single nation; fewer approved seeking consultation in a dozen or more countries. I embodied what they told in a November 1971 *Kappan* column, "Anyone for International Work?," then tried to apply the advice to myself. To me the matter of compensation was immaterial, thanks to a kitty from royalties; anything offered would be acceptable. Since the goal was to go round the world, working in a single country was automatically ruled out.

I knew what I wanted to do. I wanted to lecture and consult in both developed and underdeveloped countries. I also wanted to be a footloose and fancy-free tourist in exotic climes, unshackled by responsibilities. In other words, I wanted to have my cake

378

and eat it too. Could I do both, reconciling realism as to services rendered and romanticism as to travel enjoyed?

My old friend Doug Ward, formerly of the Consumer Education Study and the University of Illinois and now a veteran international educator, read my *Kappan* column and responded with a practical suggestion worth its weight in gold:

> I do have a recommendation which on first reading may appear to be questionable but which I thoughtfully support. A member of Congress from Indiana could request that ... the Department of State send out a circular airgram carrying a brief biography and specifics on what kind of services you could offer, well in advance of your trip. In fact, arrangements should be initiated now, because State's wheels grind exceeding-slow. This kind of treatment is virtually impossible **unless** it is initiated by a congressman, but with that support, indeed **push**, it is not uncommon. The draft of what is to go out should be prepared by you. When it reaches an embassy, it will go to the cultural affairs officer, who will try to come up with invitations.

When Senator Birch Bayh came to town for a meeting with Democratic committeemen, I asked him to put in a word on my behalf to the Department of State and the United States Information Agency. Graciously and generously he did; Birch represented his constituents well until swept away in the Reagan landslide. The Acting Assistant Secretary for Congressional Relations for State and the General Council and Congressional liaison for USIA responded affirmatively. They sent my vita and proposed itinerary abroad, and soon I was corresponding with and visiting Nelson O. Chipchin, programming officer, Overseas Speakers Division, USIA, in Washington. Never a believer in all eggs in one basket I also solicited help from acquaintances in the New Education Fellowship (an international version of the former Progressive Education Association) and the World Council for Curriculum and Instruction, as well as old reliables in ASCD, AACTE, and NEA. I wrote to individuals throughout the world whom anyone suggested.

Believe it or not, by late 1973 the realist-romantic had his cake and could eat it too. I was booked for 1974 work in Mexico, American Samoa, New Zealand, Australia, Thailand, India,

Nepal, Turkey, Greece, and Spain. Bee and I were to be completely do-as-we-please tourists in Tahiti, Western Samoa, Fiji, Bali, Iran, and Morocco. I read tourist literature, planned the details of an independent trip, and nailed down hotel reservations.

To provide a contrast with the coming tropical days, nature thoughtfully provided a snowy December, so Lake Lure looked like a New England Christmas card as we left. But the Mexican resort of Puerto Vallarta, our first opportunity for sun-tanning, provided a surprise. No bags! After all of Bee's meticulous packing for five months abroad, somewhere along the American-Texas International-Aeromexico route our bags were lost. We bought bathing suits in town and lived in them and in our travel clothes for two days until the next Aeromexico flew in. From the Puerto Vallarta airport windows our red bags were a welcome sight; that night there was no better dressed couple sipping margaritas and listening to the mariachis in the garden of the Playa de Oro.

Mexico City supplied a different surprise. We were met and adopted at the airport by Dr. Fernando Palacios of the Ministry of Education's *Direccion General de Mejoramiento Profesional del Magisterio Comision para la Aplicacion de Medios y Procedimientos Modernos al Majoramiento Profesional*, economically translated as the office of inservice education. Our preliminary correspondence had dealt in general with possible lectures; he immediately whirled me into five talks in five days (including one on Saturday and one on the eve of our midnight departure) to many Mexican teachers in splendid auditoriums equipped with United Nations type translation technology. He told us he was at our beck and call, and, as good as his word, he and his associate Rodrigo Fuentes took us through the magnificent anthropological museum and the light-and-sound show at the pyramids as well as provided us the ministry box at the dramatic dance program *Folklorico*, along with introducing us to Mexican food that tourists never encounter. Though compensation had not been discussed, he provided a substantial "gift" that neatly sidestepped Mexican tax formalities as to a foreigner's earnings, and waved us off at the airport for the longest flight we had ever taken, Mexico to Tahiti. Mexican *hospitalidad!*

Everything the artists and writers claim about Tahiti is true.

The island is aflame with flowers, the people are relaxed and beautiful, and the seas are a fantasy of colors. We even lived on the beach in a grass shack (with modern conveniences) opposite Bora Bora, one of the many islands reputed to be James A. Michener's Bali Hai of *South Pacific* fame. Bora Bora shifted hues in every changing light, and I was content to watch and photograph. We made friends with two American couples, one of whom, the Arthurs, we were to meet again on other South Seas islands, in Bangkok, and back home. A five-day expert, I wrote on Mexican education for my *Kappan* column, combining impressions with statistics supplied me by Palacios. For my own enjoyment, I began a series of not-for-publication travel sketches: "Lost, Ah Lost" about the missing red bags, "The Man Who Knew Hemingway" about an encounter in Puerto Vallarta, and "The Brave Gambler" about Palacios, who had set up elaborate plans for my lectures after only fragmentary indications that I would actually be available. For a week, we bathed and soaked in Tahiti's ambience.

Surely other South Seas islands could not be as enchanting as Tahiti. Yet they almost were. After down-at-the-heels Pago Pago on the shabby island of American Samoa, where I observed and reported through the *Kappan* an overdependence on teaching via TV, we vacationed in authentic native Samoa, the independent nation of Western Samoa. Homes in Western Samoa are open to soft breezes and without walls, and thus life goes on as though people were on stage. Aggie Grey's Hotel in Apia is managed by Aggie herself, a Samoan woman whose graceful dance movements in the Fia Fia (the happy) made you forget that she was 76 and envision only the beauty she must have been. In what other hotel in the world are guests greeted with walls garlanded with *tapa* decorations and shell loops, fresh pineapple in room refrigerators, eternally hot pots for tea or coffee, bananas available for the plucking just beside the bar? In whatever other hotel are dinners announced by beating on a hollowed-out tree trunk, after which boys playing waiter move among the common tables seating twelve to serve chicken cooked in coconut milk, shrimp salad in avocados, breadfruit, banana fritters with lime, sukiyaki, suckling pig, sweet and sour, tara root, papaya? Where else is the swimming pool surrounded by hand-carved wooden figures that look like idols? Where else would the innkeeper, completing her dance, drape me with a lei and kiss me on both cheeks? I have sometimes been asked about the finest hotels in which I ever stayed. To which I now reply, "The Waldorf-Astoria, the Boca Raton Club, perhaps the Flamingo and the Fontainebleau—and of course Aggie Grey's." They say incredulously, "Aggie Grey's?" So I tell them.

Bee was welcome on Fiji, for her cousin, a nun, had once lived there for many years; the cousin had in the early days worked on a nearby island to which lepers had previously been confined. The sisters asked me to write some words of wisdom in their convent guest book; I responded with Adlai Stevenson's words at Eleanor Roosevelt's funeral, "It is better to light one candle than to curse the darkness." A Chinese priest, Father Hsu, showed us housing projects and took us through a modern leprosarium, a shivery experience.

A week in New Zealand persuaded us it was the one country of the world we would live in if we should ever be driven from America by political insanities in the form of fascism. Not only does New Zealand live up to its advertising as having "the unspoiled wilderness of an Alaska, breathtakingly beautiful fiords like Norway, majestic Alps like Switzerland, villages like England, and lush green meadows like Ireland." New Zealand also has a sensible, highly equalitarian social system, sound health insurance programs for the citizenry, clean air, and cordial people. I lectured on both islands, centering at teacher education colleges at Wellington on North Island and Dunedin on South Island. Included in my program were talks to citizens whom the Educational Development Conference, despite the nation's educational centralization, hoped to involve in policy making. Wherever we went, my preliminary correspondence with the inspector general of the Department of Education, A. N. V. Dobbs, assured entree and a welcome.

As tourists, we bused north to the tropics at Bay of Islands, hydroplaned back to Auckland, then on to New Zealand's Yellowstone called Rotorua. We flew to South Island, then used New Zealand's splendid bus system to Te Anau's glowworm caves, Queenstown on Lake Wakitipu, alpine Mount Cook. We nostalgically foldboated on the Avon River in Christchurch, which might well have been in Great Britain, and flew on reluctantly to metropolitan Wellington and departure.

It was work time again in Australia at Sydney, Melbourne, Adelaide—talks at Maquarie University, to the Council of Adult Education, and five teachers colleges. We sold Australia short, for I worked too long and we played too little. So our main recollections of a week in Australia were agreeable Australian educators who relaxed with drinks even at lunch before their lectures; the Australian passion for sports; the impressive Sydney Harbor through which we sailed past spidery bridges, the fabulous opera house, and gaily hued sails on our ferry trips to our hotel in Manley, a resort in the Sydney area. I reflected that this was the way it would have been, intensive work and superficial social observation, if I had chosen to earn rather than learn. I came away impressed with Australia's attempt to focus education on urgent social realities and learned still more through correspondence with Bill Stringer of Australian teacher education, whom I was later to host at Indiana State University.

Now I was ready to relax. Where? Where else than Bali?

Bali is another of the American dreams of unattainable exotic lands. Forget, though, the naked breasts, which now are dangled only by scofflaw senior citizens recalcitrantly objecting to twentieth-century local legislation. Visualize instead a more appealing sight, men and women dressed like walking rainbows, constantly bearing flowers, fruits, and foods to innumerable humble shrines, crafting wood carvings, sitting under banyan trees, even celebrating death with cremation ceremonies as the soul goes back to becoming part of the universe and available for entry into a new living body. Visualize pyramids of fruit and flowers borne gracefully atop heads, a monkey dance that persuades you the actors are not human, the outriggers running in the wind. But never forget the daily lives of the Balinese people who work in the rice paddies and live in the hovels.

Bangkok in Thailand introduces itself as opera *bouffe*, a wild melange of three-wheeled cabs, ornately decorated trucks, both venerable and spanking new buses, toy-like old Toyotas and impressive new limousines, scooters and motor bikes, all competing madly in the incredible traffic. Bangkok is a floating market, a tourist incursion into the lives of people as *farangs* (foreigners) peer from their boats into shanties, houseboats, stores, and observe clothes-washing, toothbrushing, trading, swimming, and defecation in the brown-gray of the *klongs* (canals). Yet Bangkok is also the Americanized academic and sports program of the International School where I spoke, the shiny green Buick that brought me to a talk at regal UNESCO offices, the former assistant superintendent from Pennsylvania with his white Mercedes Benz and handsome bachelor apartment, the American curriculum director with her *objets d'art*, the American principal and his teacher wife living it up in a long, lively wind-swept apartment complete with a maid who found that teaching didn't pay enough, the cautious Thai educators who gave me minimal information about their schools and dodged questions about any local educational problems. In Thailand one ends in puzzlement, to steal a word from *The King and I*. We ended our across-the-world meetings with our new friends, the Arthurs—Grace who owned a tobacco enterprise in North Carolina and Jim, a lawyer from the Northwest—at a fabulous dinner hosted by Grace's Oriental business associates.

So we came to Calcutta. The Indian metropolis was our first stop for a series of talks scheduled by USIA. The Calcutta visit was to be followed by United States Information Services sponsorship in Katmandu, Istanbul, Ankara, Izmir, Athens, and Madrid. (Since the word "Agency" was reminiscent of the CIA, "Services" was the term used abroad.)

The ides of March had passed and now the end of the month was near. We were more than halfway around the world; ahead lay Nepal, Iran, Turkey, Greece, Morocco, Spain, and home. As a speaker-consultant and an observer, I had learned and, I hoped, had contributed. As tourists, we had journeyed and made friends and lived and loved in some of the most delightful locales on the face of the globe. Bee and I were healthier and tanner than when we left wintry Lake Lure. I looked older; realizing a secret dream, I had grown a shaggy white beard, accidentally initiated at Puerto Vallarta when the bags failed to arrive and I was temporarily razorless. We could imagine no better travel experience than our trip so far. And the joys of April and May were still ahead.

Yet as we trudged a concrete spiral, caged with wire, from the airfield to the airport terminal above and toward the dull roar of the Calcutta night, I had a fleeting premonition that we should turn back, reboard the plane, and fly anywhere else. Apprehension vanished when we were met by an Indian chauffeur for USIS and brought to one of Calcutta's best hotels for three days of lectures and tours.

What happened next I described in my last *Kappan* column from abroad, "Calcutta: A Vision of the End of the World."

> To paraphrase T. S. Eliot's *The Hollow Men*,
> This is the way the world ends,
> Not with a bang but a cheeseburger.

Concerning India, I have encountered two persuasions. There is a boastful type who pays no attention to health precautions, apparently drinking out of any nearby fountains and eating "whatever the people eat," or the more credible type who uses boiled and bottled water solely, shuns the uncredentialed vegetables, generally behaves as though Pasteur hadn't made it all up after a bad night. As science-respecting people, we accept the latter interpretation of the universe and hence ate carefully in Calcutta, India, in March 1974. But naturally, because the world is a place of shades and shadows, and life is a set of floating hazards and unpredictabilities, I got a contaminated cheeseburger at one of Calcutta's best hotels. After four good intercommunicating speeches to educators, many of whom really cared about humanity, at the University of Calcutta, Birla College, American University Center, and Ramakrishna Institute, I dropped like a stunned ox in my own bloody vomit.

If you're going to be sick in Asia, better be sick in a city where you are working for the United States Information Services. I realize it is not fashionable to say anything good today of the government of the United States and totally *de trop* to say anything kindly of the bureaucracy. But you haven't been sick—I hope—in Asia. Put the ugliest face on it and point out that it isn't good publicity for the Foreign Service boys to have somebody die on their hands while practicing his specialty abroad. Point out that their houses abroad allow them to live beyond the style to which they would be accustomed at home. But when you're struck down you're glad that the USIS and the American Embassy are there with their characteristic foreign service names like Holbrook Bradley. Their loyalty to you is total. They have a magnificent Indian USIS staff doctor, Dr. Wats, who comes to your hotel where you're vomiting away your life blood in the middle of the night. They have access to a small hospital, handicapped technologically yet suffused with kindness and caring. They have a compound in which they live, guarded by constantly patrolling Indian soldiers, with an apartment where your wife can wait it out and where you, too, if you manage to survive, can contemplate recuperation. However, we took a three-plane, thirty-hour sleepless journey back to the United States for diagnosis and treatment.

All this takes place in Hell—my only descriptive word that comes close to describing Calcutta. Yes, I've seen the Victoria Memorial and the art galleries and mansions too, but my pervading memory of Calcutta is the unimaginably dense-packed streets. Incredible numbers of human beings are born, live, and die on the squalid streets. Naked babies lie in the dust and the sacred white cows drop their loads beside the little heads. The old sit and wait for death. Outside the Department of Education of the University of Calcutta is a vast garbage dump in which the ravaged bodies of what once were human beings compete with the sacred cows for a morsel of food.

If you want to change an intelligent and sensitive man's attitudes on a problem, I suggest you send him to Calcutta. Don't give him any temporary shelter, such as my bureaucracy with its little glass-box cars. Let the Roman Catholic hierarchy in their white robes spend a week on the sidewalks in a population that's too thick, thick. And then let them go home and see if they can make up more of those prissy little essays against proponents, in and out of the church, of population control. Send some of the living-room liberals from America who worry over a currently fashionable problem which always, strangely enough, has some mild impact on their own physical comfort. Worldlings that they are, they will be acquainted with culture shock, could in fact deliver lectures on it. But see if the massive uncaringness, part of the armor, the self-imposed blindness of many of the Indian and American intellectuals, doesn't just for a moment grab their hearts so that they cry in the streets like crazy prophets, "Someone must see! Someone must do something! Someone must care!" before they go back to explaining to themselves that India has tried all faiths, all philosophies, all reforms, all revolutions, and that none of them work. So the armor and blindness are restored and culture shock is neatly filed and categorized, and they can go their way again, caring not about these hordes of people but only about selected problems which will affect their own comfort and convenience.

What I experienced in my Calcutta illness was culture shock perhaps—yet different too. It may have been a version of future shock, but not the kind that Toffler writes about. My version of future shock was a prophetic one. Under doctor-administered drugs, it came to me that Calcutta represents what the cities of our world may sometime die of. Not the bright plastic world of some of the futurists, such as Herman Kahn. Not the world of silent abandonment and desolation in Rachel Carson's *Silent Spring* or Nevil Shute's *On the Beach*. The apocalypse coming for the human race may be a slow, noisy death of the big cities.

I felt it in 1974 in Calcutta as the poor publicly foraged and died while the rich drove sightlessly and unheeding through the streets. I felt it when the "low shedding," a severe shading down and brownout of power any time of the day or night, began unanticipated at any moment. In huge areas of the city all power would go off. Cars continued to move tensely and dangerously through the streets, flashing their lights momen-tarily as required by law, then roaring head-on toward each other in the darkness. The telephone system flickered and died, then briefly roused. Transportation stopped and re-sumed. The city was noisily dying.

My vision was that Calcutta today presaged a likely future after energy use-up, environmental breakdown, widening gaps between rich and poor, the collapse of old religious caring, and the incapacity to achieve new social caring. The poor would die first, after desperate attempts at rebellion, sometimes suc-ceeding, more often failing. Hanging on to the end would be the patricians in the native population who had their own built-in enclaves. They would buy what they could. The poor would go first when they used up their edible garbage; some would hang on longer than others. The rich would go last when they used up their lifelines. The silence would come over the clamoring, sweltering, exuding, contrasting city. Life would no longer pulse in the garbage eaten by the poor. The last air conditioner would go off, the last bulb hidden in the last refrigerator would shed no more light for the patricians.

So in Calcutta I witnessed in future shock through my drugged visions the end of the world of the cities. When? Some day. Don't ask me what my horror vision means to educators.

Because if you don't know that it means that there must be a colossal gathering of forces for **caring and survival**, then my journey to the end of the night and my witness to the end of the world will have no meaning to you.

In my vision of Hell, the last emaciated patrician came out of his house. He saw no poor people. But since he had never seen the poor people throughout his life, this was not unusual. But now he looked for the poor to teach him where to dig in the garbage. But the poor people were all dead. He fell on his face on the garbage and began clawing. After a while there was no movement at all on the vast garbage dump as the world ended in Calcutta and maybe in your city. So went my vision.

Why? Because not enough people CARE. Some do. But not enough by far. And that is why humankind today is in deep, deep trouble.

I dictated much of this account to Bee when I was under the sedation of Valium in my hospital bed in Calcutta. Afterwards Bee told me that I would speak, then often relapse into coma, then rouse and say "period, new paragraph," and take up again. I thought the column would be my last publication. It wasn't death I minded so much as the process of dying.

After ten days in a small Indian hospital with tender loving help but little technology, they flew me to a New York hospital, which had little tender loving help but lots of technology. Bee, with USIS help, gallantly struggled with the bureaucracy of the Indian customs service and banks and airlines as she made arrangements for our departure. Incredible as it sounds to the ears of Americans who live in a land in which doctors no longer even make house calls, Indian Dr. Wats accompanied us all the way to New York.

Despite careful preplanning, Indian Airlines, the carrier for Swissair at Calcutta, hadn't gotten the message that I was a stretcher case, so, after delay accepted patiently by amazingly tolerant Indian passengers, my body was shoved onto a narrow shelf in the cockpit sometimes used for naps by a flight crew member on long trips. At Bombay across the subcontinent, little Indian men carried my hulk precariously down the steps of the plane and up the long stairway of a hotel in the airport for a brief rest. Swissair hadn't gotten the word there either. Aboard a Switzerland-bound plane, Bee addressed a plea to the passengers and some willingly changed seats so that my body could stretch across six seats of the last row of the plane. The first aid station at Zurich was efficient and hygienic. The exhausted wife, doctor, and patient caught a nap.

By then Swissair had gotten the word and had a curtained space for my dangling medical equipment and me. So we flew the Atlantic to a waiting ambulance, another aspect of the tremendous compassion and helpfulness that everyone related to USIS, whether abroad or at home, extended. I spent eleven days in New York Hospital-Cornell Medical Center for treatment of a reactivated ulcer, dormant since World War II but retriggered by the food poisoning and accompanying systemic revolt. Then Joe Dixon met us at Indianapolis, and Roy and Barbara came to Terre Haute to help. Now they had two patients, for Bee picked up bronchial pneumonia during her exhausting ordeal, whether in Calcutta or on the nearly continuous thirty hours of flying home to the States. She got me back to Lake Lure and collapsed.

We lived. We had gone around the world.

Chapter Forty-Two

SOME
SWAN SONGS

When you emerge from the shadow of death and enter again into the light of life, you look at the world anew. From a beach chair on the lawn overlooking Lake Lure, I sensed as I never had before the coming of spring. First bloomed the massed yellow of forsythias and daffodils; then my mother's favorite, the magnolia. The dogwood and crab apple flourished briefly; the lilacs lingered longer. The cottonwoods, sycamores, and maples limned light green leaves against the unchanging dark greens of the pine brothers, black and white and red, disdainful of any change of season. The grass grew under my feet as I tapered off valium. Nature's miracles that spring of 1974 included my regaining of health.

Established patterns soon reasserted themselves. As Bee recovered, Roy and Barbara returned home. The kindly ministrations of Betty Dixon, who had lived with Joe and their children at Lake Lure while we wandered, and of Susie Carter of Indiana State University's nursing faculty, were succeeded by Joe Dixon with his dissertation problems and my writing projects. I no longer wept uncontrollably as I had under the sway of valium, a drug purported to tranquilize, yet for me an enhancer of depression. The World War II ulcer, reactivated by my illness in Calcutta, subsided. I could resume my normal life. I even taught in summer session.

Joe Dixon had shepherded through my *Kappan* columns on Mexican education and TV instruction in American Samoa; now I revised and amplified the Calcutta experience for the June

1974 issue. After it appeared, a letter to the editor from an all-knowing zealot not only condemned my support for limitation of population growth in India and implied that I was a racist, but also presumed to diagnose my illness as just another "bellyache." Long recognizing that any reference by a columnist to birth control policies opposed by some religionists draws fire, I made no response. Other letters refuted the racism charge and indicated appreciation of the emotion-packed column; an existential philosopher of education told me that he thought that it was the most powerful column I had ever written. "Calcutta: A Vision of the End of the World" soon found its way into anthologies.

Before I left on the world trip, the National Society for the Study of Education had invited me to edit a yearbook on secondary education. With the committee, I had selected possible authors, and while I was abroad and during my recuperation Joe had carried on correspondence for authors' acceptances of assignments to write chapters. Now I took over the editing of *Issues in Secondary Education.*

On coming to ISU, I had intended to work on no more yearbooks. By then I had edited or written for eleven yearbooks and had decided that my dues were paid. But the National Society for the Study of Education invitation was especially tempting. Since 1902, the NSSE, an organization of 4,500 members, had published two yearbooks each year on questions of high concern to the educational profession. Educators whom I respected such as Robert J. Havighurst, Ralph W. Tyler, and John I. Goodlad were active in leadership of the organization, and I had an acquaintance dating back to National Council for the Social Studies days with Kenneth J. Rehage, the secretary-treasurer. So when my fellow doctoral student at Ohio State University and my long-time friend Harold Shane persuasively argued that the 1976 yearbook would be a fitting culmination of my attempts to communicate ideas on education, I came around.

There were some advantages to editing a yearbook destined to be published in 1976, when the editor would reach age 65. No more nine rewrites as with Hilda Taba in 1945. No more leg work as with senior editor William Heard Kilpatrick in 1946. No more contribution of lonely minority voice chapters as to the National Council for the Social Studies yearbooks of 1946 and 1951. No more repudiation by a committee member as in the *Forces Affecting American Education* experience in 1953. The editor of *Issues in Secondary Education*, now himself a veteran, had a strong say as to the constitution of the committee, the chapter structure, and the choice of chapter authors. While he respected the authors' freedom to write as they pleased and while he shunned the over-editing that publishers had sometimes inflicted on him, he came out with a book that, on the whole, represented the viewpoint on secondary education at which he himself had arrived.[1] The editor and a sampling of authors presented the book early in 1976 at conventions of the National Association of Secondary School Principals in Washington, the American Association of School Administrators in Atlantic City, and the ASCD in Miami Beach. Nine thousand copies were printed, half for the membership and the other half for libraries and individual buyers, and by 1978 secretary-treasurer Rehage was considering a second printing in paperback. Almost all of the reviews were favorable. As an editor, I felt good about the structure, quality, and reception of *Issues in Secondary Education*.

Yet I prized even more another book, though only one copy of it exists. The summer of 1975, a year after my Calcutta debacle and recovery, had a special significance to Bee and me. Our wedding anniversary arrived August 24, one day after Bee's birthday, as it was in the habit of doing. But this time it was our fortieth. What might make 1975 a very special summer celebration? I had noted that eminent people were sometimes presented on notable occasions with a book of letters of reminiscence from their associates. But I had never heard of such a presentation to

---

[1] After an introductory chapter by the editor on the contemporary scene and a history chapter by Robert H. Beck, foundational chapters dealt with the individual (Arthur W. Combs), values (Lawrence E. Metcalf), social realities (Willis W. Harman), and curricular experiences (Arthur Wells Foshay). Then Vernon H. Smith and Robert D. Barr on alternative schools and action learning; the editor on clusters of content appropriate for modern secondary education; J. Lloyd Trump and Gordon E Vars on staff organization and the core curriculum; Ronald T. Hyman on teaching strategies; and Ronald C. Doll on administration and supervision. Shane and Virgil Clift closed with projections as to the secondary education of the future.

a woman whose career was her home and family, however distinguished her additional contributions may have been. No mean hand at adapting the ideas of others, I wrote to scores of Bee's friends. Would each write her a letter of recollection but send it surreptitiously to me at my office?

Miraculously, they kept the secret. To make sure, I intercepted and opened Bee's mail at home—and on the flimsiest excuses and to her astonishment. Then in August at an outdoor party at our neighbor Turney's home on Lake Lure, I presented her with *Dear Bee*, a bound book made up of 184 letters to her. Before the assembled multitude gathered on the lawn below Dave's porch, I said, "It is almost impossible to surprise Bee. But this time I think she really will be surprised." And I began to tug the heavy bound book of typed and longhand letters from my briefcase. But I should have known from forty years of marriage that Bee was untoppable. She said, "What are you going to do— divorce me?" Aware of my total dependence upon Bee and conscious that I wouldn't be worth a damn without her, the audience broke up with laughter. The book was presented and a new decade of life and love got underway.

Throughout my career, Bee had been my editor, supplying explanations of grammatical constructions that baffled me, catching typographical errors with twenty-twenty vision, improving on style yet never censoring. Her help was never more needed than when I decided to write a last textbook on education.

In 1976 I inquired of Houghton Mifflin about a third edition of *Education: A Beginning* and *Curriculum: Quest for Relevance*. The distribution of each had far outstripped any of the books I had initiated or chaperoned through publication as a member of the editorial committee in education. Bill MacDonald had been promoted into inaccessibility somewhere in the stratosphere of the company and yet another editor in a long succession occupied the College Department throne. She told me that new editions were not currently contemplated. However, she did want me to write a book on secondary education. The ways of publishers invariably mystify me; neither then nor later did Houghton Mifflin want third editions of two demonstrated commercial successes. So I went to work on *Secondary Education: School and Community*.

After two years as my good right-hand man, Bob Morris,

clutching an excellent dissertation on McCarthyism in education, left in mid-book for an assistant professorship at Auburn
University. My new graduate assistant, Mary Ross, who combined charm and hard work, wrought wonders in checking
footnotes and helping us keep the copy clean of typographical
bobbles. Ruan Fougerousse, who had come to work with me while
she was an apprehensive freshman and was to continue on as my
secretary while a mature teacher, typed and retyped 1976 and
1977 drafts from my incredibly crabbed handwriting. The book
went to Houghton Mifflin on schedule.

This time I drew a copy editor who was out to eliminate every
vestige of sexism from the company's products. A version of
Thurber's war between the men and the women was raging in
the editorial offices at the time and obviously affecting Houghton
Mifflin's personnel. I too dislike sexism, so l painstakingly, albeit
sometimes awkwardly, had used the plural form in place of the
singular ("they" rather than "he" or even "she"), used "he or she"
rather than the taboo "he" when the singular was inescapable,
and willingly had substituted "humankind" for "mankind" and
"chairperson" for "chairman." (I did draw the line at "chair," for
chairs are to be sat upon rather than entrusted the responsibilities of administering programs.) I must admit that I gulped when,
in copy-editing, "the creature from Mars" replaced the traditional "man from Mars" in a gimmick that opened one chapter;
when " founding fathers" was deleted from a discussion of the
American Revolution; when "businessperson" replaced "businessman" in a discussion of early nineteenth-century industrial-
ism, *et cetera ad infinitum.* I was a supporter of the women's movement even before it and my editors were born, and I dislike a good
movement being made to appear ludicrous through zealotry.

However, the editing was careful though pedantic, changes
were checked with me though they usually went the company
way, and the production pace was deliberate though the editors
were firmer on my meeting agreed-upon deadlines than on their
meeting their own schedule of editing and production dates. My
pregnancy with this book wasn't easy. Once in a while I wondered
whatever had happened in publishing since I had stumbled on that
breed of warm, supportive editors typified by Maxwell Perkins and
Wallace Meyer of Scribner's and Fred Wilhelms of the Consumer

Education Study. Yet I was pleased with the issue when born.

Like my writing, my closing years of teaching had a swan song quality about them. After I returned to teaching in June of 1974, my colleagues, reminded of my mortality and coming retirement, flooded my seminars with their doctoral candidates and themselves enrolled in my writing course. By the time I had committed the geriatric sin of reaching age 66-1/2, for which the sentence imposed by ISU was mandatory retirement, almost half of the School of Education faculty had enrolled in Education 617 during the ten years I had taught my course on writing for educational publications. For my final offering of the course in the intersession of 1977, I recruited far afield and registrants came from Alabama and Georgia, as well as from nearer home.

Accompanied by crossed fingers and admonitions to be careful about cheeseburgers, I went abroad twice during the three years preceding my retirement. A letter from Paul Regan, the A.I.D. man with whom I had jolted by jeep in the Tabriz area of Iran, invited me to go to Switzerland as the American representative to a June 1975 UNESCO conference on aims and goals for education, to meet with nine philosophers and educators from Western industrialized countries, the Eastern European socialist bloc, and the Third World nations. Though taken aback by this miscasting, I readily participated and found to my surprise that despite the wide cultural and experiential differences among a Brazilian education official, a Togoese ambassador, an Indian institute director, a Senegalese chairman of a philosophy department, an international scholar-activist (Paolo Freire, author of *Pedagogy of the Oppressed*), a Polish philosopher, a British comparative educator, a French editor, and a Lebanese philosopher on leave with UNESCO, we could make a beginning on agreements on education. For instance, we agreed on an increasingly active role for learners, lifelong education, eliminating outdated knowledge, developing interdisciplinary programs, deschooling the schools (*i.e.*, improving schools, making them serve mankind, not discarding them *a la* Ivan Illich), the importance of social structures and of the distribution of power, and the need for educating individuals, improving society, developing values, and using relevant knowledge. We disagreed on the value of memorization, the nature of authority, and the relation of ideas to action.

At the Geneva conference my stereotypes were frequently shattered. Paolo Freire, despite the fiery tone of his books, was pleasant in social relationships and tolerant in discussion. The professor from Communist Poland surprisingly spoke up for education of the individual in curiosity, creativity, and appreciation of a variety of values and for widening of intellectual and emotional horizons. This was Marxism?

Yet a funny thing happened to me on my way to better understanding. I came away with the uneasy yet distinct impression that wherever I went during the conference in Geneva a UNESCO man who was a Soviet Union national showed up. Even when I sat alone after lunch in a broad meadow to recharge my psychological batteries following the group's animated conversations, he sat under a nearby tree. I can only conclude that I was a new boy in town and therefore subject to casing by Soviet surveillance. Or is this a case of American oversensitivity? I'll never know. After a week of conferencing, I vacationed through traveling to Chamonix, took the cable car across the awesome frozen slopes of Mont Blanc, Europe's highest peak, and forgot about my shadow.

A year later, on another European trip, more of my stereotypes were denied. With Bee, I went to the Black Forest in 1976, where I talked to 400 school principals of the European Region of the Defense Department Dependents Schools. When I had found that most of the principals had been with the dependents schools for many years and had little intention of returning to America to work in school administration, I had thought that they might be out of touch with developments in American education and that possibly they couldn't cut the mustard any more in school systems back in the United States. I learned that I was wrong on both counts: The principals of the dependents schools were remarkably up-to-date on educational trends. Reluctance to return to the States stemmed from involvement in their present work with American youngsters from military-related families, not from any inability to cope with Stateside education. Like educators back home they struggled with questions of how much unity and similarity and how much diversity and differences were desirable in their school system, an unknown giant that served 112,000 children and youth in a tri-continental area over three times the size of the United States of America.

Following the conference, Bee and I revisited the Munich area so that I might see for myself some dependents schools in action. Also, we wanted to stop over with Bee's niece Jeri, whose children were attending such schools. We made a sentimental journey to Garmisch-Partenkirchen, where we once had left Paul and Janet Weinandy before our first foldboat trip down the Danube River. Never skiers or climbers, yet confirmed lovers of mountaintops, we rode the cog-and-pinion railway to the crest of Zugspitze, 9,721 feet high, comparing it with earlier technology-assisted conquests of Mont Blanc, 15,771 feet, Jungfrau, 13,461, and Grossglockner, 12,460, to say nothing of more modest cable car ascents of Sandia Mountain near Albuquerque and the Grand Tetons at Jackson Hole, Wyoming.

We traveled in America to see old friends, among them the Weinandys on Cape Cod and Peg of the Pal O Mine Club with husband Howard Safarik on North Carolina's outer banks, and to gather annually with Bee's brothers and her club members and with my long-time friend Ben Sanders in the New York area. We visited Roy's family at Sugarbush in Vermont, where Roy was teaching tennis and playing off-hours with tennis luminaries in a summer program. (Back home we boasted, "Our son, the tennis player, while teamed in doubles with Ken Rosewall...") Visits to newly arrived grandchildren increased, Barbara and Bob's Laura, Roy and Linda's Justin and Desiree. At a Christmas 1976 family reunion at Roy's in Amherst, Jon, divorced, announced his marriage to Trudy Heller; soon there were two more grandchildren, Ross and Claire, for proud grandparents to visit in Philadelphia. Meanwhile, Bob Nichols often burned the roads between Michigan and Indiana while Barbara and their daughters watched warily for stern state troopers.

By 1977 my mandatory retirement from employment by ISU was imminent. My recent columns continued to deal with educational and social issues, such as "Going the Second Mile," which advocated moving beyond desegregation to achieve true integration; "Reform of the High School in the Mid-Seventies," which called for more work experience and action learning; "Tricentennial Speech, 2076: Two Versions," which described one

397

desirable and one horrible future scenario; and "Education and Jimmy Carter," a projection of Carter's probable education policies. Some columns reported and generalized on personal experiences, such as "Start Your Own Spring Conference," "Toward Some Agreements at Geneva," "The Role of a Review Council," "The Unknown Giant," and "Can Educators Trust Representatives of Government?"

Now, for the May 1977 *Kappan*, I wrote "Whose Retirement?," a light-hearted column about divergent responses to retirement by the Not-a-Damn-Thing retirees who propose to head for rocking chairs and after a year or two begin rocking; the Pellet Pursuers, who opt for golf; the Better Homes and Garden retirees, who putter and garden; and the Caped Crusaders, who, emancipated from economic thralldom, now join the ranks of reformers. I closed the column with:

> Listening with my third ear, did I hear some reader ask **me** "What are **you** going to do?" Shucks, you don't want to hear about li'l' ol' me. Well, what I'm going to do is to keep right on with my writing, and after my 1978 book I'm going to do an anthology on.... I'll continue consulting and speaking too, and let me tell you my idea about taking my Writing for Educational Publications course on the road.... As to working with education and community organizations, I think I'll.... And I never visited the Grecian islands of the Aegean Sea or cruised to Alaska, so I'll...

Books about aging often report ambiguities of retirees—acceptance of being set out to pasture yet fears, enjoyment yet boredom, etc. I experienced no such ambiguities. I simply decided not to retire. Not now. If possible, not ever.

I don't mean that I fought the mandatory retirement system that ended my teaching career though I was hale and hearty, able and willing to continue. I considered briefly the possibility of resisting and rejected it. Retirement at the end of the semester in which a professor became 66 was an established and entrenched policy of Indiana State University, and the university administration was delaying, as long as it legally could, full compliance with the congressional mandate to extend the age of mandatory retirement to 70. Indeed, nervous at declining enrollment and population projections, ISU was soon to encourage early retirement through offering an additional semester's pay to professors who quit work prematurely. When young, indiscriminately and in the manner of Don Quixote, I fought all battles for just causes that happened along. With advancing age, I had learned to choose my wars with an eye to some chance of winning. Yet I did appreciate the lone voice I heard raised on behalf of my staying on, that of my black colleague in the School of Education, Wesley Lyda. Thanks, Wes—good try.

So I decided to enjoy the rituals and ceremonies that accompany retirement from teaching and to reach into my quiver for arrows that defied the mandatory retirement rules of bureaucracy. Additional arrows in the quiver were consultation, talks, writing and work with national organizations. The university might retire me but I refused to retire myself.

When a Hemingway character likes something very much, he sometimes says inarticulately, "It was good." I concur—my retirement celebrations were good. Because education is one of "the impossible professions" in that a teacher's contribution is necessarily intangible and self-doubts as to making a difference come with the territory, some degree of feedback at the road's end is good. Though Henry Adams assures us that a teacher affects eternity, more immediate evidence is always appreciated.

In March in Chicago the John Dewey Society under the chairmanship of Mary Anne Raywid devoted a half day of the annual meeting to my efforts. Under a generous title, "The Educational Thought of William Van Til," W. Richard Stephens, now president of Greenville College, Illinois, and Harold Turner, professor-administrator at the University of Missouri at St. Louis, described the views I had put forth in forty-four years as an educator. Discussants included former graduate assistants, colleagues from several universities, and co-workers in the John Dewey Society. In a grateful response acknowledging the society's plaque for long service, I quoted Shakespeare's Henry IV address to a little group of adherents on the eve of the forthcoming Saint Crispin's day battle and pointed out its appropriateness to the work of the John Dewey Society:

> We few, we happy few, we band of brothers...
> And gentlemen in England now a-bed
> Shall think themselves accurs'd they were not here

And hold their manhoods cheap whiles any speaks
That fought with us upon Saint Crispin's day.

The retirement celebration at the ASCD conference in Houston was less decorous; it took the form of a party for Bee and me at the Sheraton with Dave and Miriam Turney as hosts. An assortment of my ASCD friends and acquaintances were in attendance in the Indiana State University suite. Festivities and the flowing of the bowl ceased only for a surprise announcement from my former graduate students that a collection of my writings was in press. Gleefully, they informed me that this would be the first of my publications on which I wouldn't have a chance to read proofs. In years past, some of them had become nearsighted from working with me on this chore. So now I threatened bodily violence if they had introduced any typos. They assured me that any errors would be of my own doing, since the printer was photographing pages from my already published works.

The retirement season culminated in the summer of 1977 through a Lake Lure celebration that brought together former graduate assistants for a breakfast at our home and ISU friends and colleagues for an afternoon party at Turney's home just down the lake. All of our children plus son-in-law Bob and three of our grandchildren, Barbara's daughters Linda and Laura and Roy's son Justin, were in attendance. Unveiled was *Van Til on Education*, a labor of love by a committee of five: Harold E. Turner, Jack E. Blackburn, Charlyn Fox, John H. Lounsbury, and Robert C. Morris, bankrolled by fund donors and contributors. The indefatigable Bob Morris had seen the publication through the Auburn University printing services.

The book was a large paperback showing the author, complete with pipe, on the front cover; a montage of family photographs, including pictures of me from college graduation into senility, constituted the back cover. The selections had been made by many of my former graduate students, including the committee, and represented their favorites from among my writing. Their choices ranged from a chapter of *The Danube Flows Through Fascism* (1937) to one of my journal articles, "Crucial Issues in Secondary Education" (1976), and the author readily admitted that he couldn't have made a more representative selection had he labored a year on the project. I joyously autographed copies for the creators and financial supporters throughout that memorable July 15 afternoon.

The university—more precisely, Dean Dave Turney and his successor Dean Richard Willey—said thanks through providing me an office in the new School of Education building with all the familiar accoutrements of jammed bookshelves, overflowing file cabinets, desks, and typewriter. Tangible expressions of appreciation garlanded the office walls and decorated my desk. Phi Delta Kappa and Kappa Delta Pi contributed various certificates of recognition; the ASCD, the John Dewey Society, and Associated Organizations for Teacher Education earlier had provided plaques recognizing services. They joined earlier awards for *The Making of a Modern Educator* and the Centennial Achievement Award of Ohio State University, a 1970 trophy.

An issue of the *Junior High Middle School Journal* was dedicated to me. Editor Max Bough had gathered essays from my former students, including collaborators Gordon F. Vars and John H. Lounsbury and first doctoral student Vernon Replogle and even two of my former University School students, Peg Morris and Bob Tucker. Editor Robert Leeper revived "The Importance of People" in *Educational Leadership* for a column by Bob Morris, subtitled "Some Reflections by His Last Doctoral Student," and Bob also wrote about his work with me for an issue of Indiana State's *Contemporary Education*. Phi Delta Kappa made me a life member in a campus meeting at which I talked on experiences in professional publication.

Even more appreciated than plaques and publications was recognition by my colleagues that I hadn't vanished from the planet. Throughout my supposed retirement, my campus colleagues kept dropping into my office for conversation and advice about their writing. Almost four years after I laid down the chalk, they came to the retrospective that Bee planned to celebrate my seventieth birthday, and a half dozen of them gave dramatic readings of some of my columns.

At journey's end, who among us doesn't welcome whatever tributes and trophies may come our way? "It was good." Include me among the grateful.

Chapter Forty-Three

RETIREMENT?

O ld man, what now?

Like many retirees, at first I caught my breath. While Barbara and Bob took a vacation trip through the West in August 1977, we baby-sat two of our grandchildren, Laura, one and a half, for almost a month, and Linda, seven, for a Lake Lure week after her stay with her New Jersey grandparents. In September Bee and I traveled to the Grecian Islands in the Aegean Sea and drove around the Peloponnesian peninsula, thus restoring one segment of the world trip interrupted by the Calcutta calamity. As travel writers have reported for centuries, Rhodes, Crete, Mykonos, and the antiquities of the peninsula are jewels and Athens is wondrous; we added Greece to our short list of lands to which we must someday return. Just to remind us that we were home again, a New York taxi driver charged us an incredibly exorbitant amount to transfer us a few hundred yards within Kennedy Airport from the TWA terminal to the nearby Allegheny terminal for our return to Indiana.

There were loose ends left from my incarnation as a textbook writer. The galleys of *Secondary Education: School and Community* were waiting for us on our return from Greece in October; by working day and night Bee and I got them back with record speed, within one week. With Barbara, Linda, and Laura, we made a journey at the end of October to Long Island to deliver to son Roy, daughter-in-law Linda, and grandchildren Justin and Desiree a gift, our faithful red Chrysler Newport (successor to the 1967 blue beauty), which had logged 100,000 miles for us and was now to run the roads between Bayville on Long Island Sound and Hofstra University in Hempstead where Roy taught economics. On our return, the first of the page proofs of *Secondary Education* were awaiting us. We worked on them at Lake Lure in dreary November and in Florida during December and sent them back on time.

One blessing of retirement was escape from snow and frozen roads; Florida seemed the natural choice. We rented a house for the winter south of Tampa on the shores of Little Cockroach Bay just past Goat Island and Tropical Island and near Whisky Key. Despite such titillating names and the state's high-pressure publicity campaign for tourism, Florida let us down. December through February was too cold a period for swimming, fishing, and boating, our preferred recreational activities; we settled for biking and walking. Christmas without children or grandchildren was empty.

Even cold Florida seemed better than snowbound Terre Haute on our return. We fled to San Francisco for the ASCD conference, where I served as parliamentarian at the business meeting (and enjoyed a delicious opportunity to rule longtime friendly antagonist Dick Foster out of order). On our return March 10, we got bogged down in our Lake Lure driveway by the persistent snow. We resolved that next time we would go to the authentic tropics and stay through March.

By winter's end I had caught my breath. Since I rejected as retirement models Doing Not a Damn Thing, Pellet Pursuit, Better Homes and Gardening, and Caped Crusading, I needed some other late-life pattern. For me, practitioner of the work ethic that I was, the decision was not difficult. My only perplexity was determining which of the possible work projects would best use whatever competencies I had, yet be reconcilable with my newly acquired mobility.

Perhaps a visiting professorship? Yet I liked spring, summer, and fall at Lake Lure with our water-oriented recreation and our new sun deck that jutted toward the lake, and I liked the idea of wintering in the tropics. And I remembered too well the loneliness of visiting professors I had encountered, such as V. T. Thayer, the distinguished progressive educator, who had retired from his Ethical Culture Schools directorship and had come to

403

Fisk University in Nashville for a season of teaching. (I remembered too that, when I tried to employ Thayer for summer session teaching at Peabody, the administrative bureaucracy had told me that John Dewey himself, though productive into his nineties, couldn't be employed at Peabody after age 65.)

Perhaps the book on curriculum I had long promised myself to write? In November I had explored the possibility briefly with editor Steve Mathews of Allyn and Bacon, who was willing to proceed. But I didn't look forward to the long hours of library research that would be necessary, and I had a sneaking suspicion that I had waited too long to bring forth the definitive book that would replace Hilda Taba and Ralph W. Tyler in the curriculum hagiarchy.

Perhaps developing a string of back-to-back engagements to speak to teachers at inservice meetings of school systems, or delivering lectures to universities or to ASCD state units? In the fall I had talked at the dedication of a William Heard Kilpatrick building at Georgia College and had addressed ASCD groups in Virginia and Missouri. Yet I remembered the grueling trips of the NYU period, attended by disillusionment as to the likelihood of making a difference in education through one-shot appearances. And, in a lifetime, how many identical plastic Holiday Inns and slippery wet back roads should a man be asked to bear?

Perhaps a wide-ranging anthology under some such title as *Education for the Eighties?* But in the late 1970s anthologies were anathema to publishers, who now insisted on the best-selling Textbook for the Course. I queried publishers and in response got invitations to do a curriculum book rather than an anthology.

So I decided to do what I really wanted to do—help educators and other professionals to write for professional publication. Two channels seemed open: workshops, each of several days' duration, or a book. I took both routes.

Evidence accumulated that workshops on writing were viable. Robert Leeper, editor of *Educational Leadership,* had tentatively experimented with a special session on writing for publication at the 1976 Association for Supervision and Curriculum Development annual conference. He had anticipated a small audience, yet so many ASCDers attended that his 1977 and 1978 special sessions were held in rooms that accommodated several hundred. I was a panelist at each session; at the 1978 conference a videotape in which Bob Morris interviewed me on writing was also presented. At a national conference on writing at Wichita State University, interest in writing for educational publication was high; participants came from both coasts and the midsection of the country, not simply from Kansas as I had falsely prophesied.

Because of such programs and some letters I wrote to deans, the word went out of my interest in helping writers. So in the spring of 1978 I was invited to talk on writing at Jackson State University in Mississippi, conduct a workshop at St. Cloud State University in Minnesota, and return to Jackson State for a regional workshop attended by black educators and partially financed by the Association of Teacher Educators. In the fall, invitations to conduct workshops came from the University of Northern Iowa, North Texas State University, and the University of Northern Colorado. (I can't account for the coincidence of three successive "Northerns.")

Through trial and error, a pattern of workshop organization emerged—talks open to campus and community; workshop sessions limited to twenty participants; individual conferences with writers. The talks dealt primarily with breaking into print through journals and books; the workshop forced each participant to clarify a proposal for writing through developing a journal query or book proposal that all participants then commented upon; the individual conferences helped those who wanted advice on outlets for manuscripts prepared prior to the workshops.

Encouraged by responses to the spring workshops and talks, I decided to shelve the curriculum book, at least temporarily, and to develop a book on writing for professional publication. I didn't go to Houghton Mifflin with a proposal as I had earlier because, sadly enough, promotion of my *Secondary Education: School and Community* seemed to me to have been handled ineptly during the crucial prepublication and first weeks after release. Once again my careful responses to the author's questionnaire had been largely ignored; advertising in the ASCD convention program didn't appear until 1980 when any possibility of a strong initial impact was past.

Apparently, too, the times were out of joint for any textbook on secondary education; in the late 1970s enrollment in education courses in secondary education fell sharply. However, the reviewers were generous. I wryly classified *Secondary Education: School and Community* as "a critical, not commercial, success," that ancient auctorial rationalization. My editors, I feel sure, more economically termed it "a dog," for it was to sell only 4,500 copies between 1978 and 1981, far less than my two earlier Houghton Mifflin textbooks, which totalled 87,800 through 1981.

Yet I thought my book on secondary education was the best of the three. My three textbooks for teachers didn't change the world, as you and I well know. Still, I hope they may have helped some people to be better educators and motivated some to work for a society in which education will not be undervalued.

The lack of early promotion, joined with what seemed to me to be a degree of current editorial staff didacticism and rigidity, convinced me that I should turn elsewhere if I wrote future books during retirement years. I terminated the Houghton Mifflin relationship with regret because I appreciated the ability of Bill MacDonald and his early editorial successors to produce fine textbooks.

Allyn and Bacon had a demonstrated ability to market individual copies of books through sales by mail, my best hope, since courses in writing for professional publication were as rare as unicorns' teeth. Steve Mathews of Allyn and Bacon was direct and honest, a man who knew the book trade. On a summer trip East in 1978 to see Roy, I met Steve at the Parker House in Boston and told him that, though books of advice for free-lance writers were legion, no one had ever done a book on writing for professional publication. Steve remarked that this argument always made him wonder why nobody ever had—perhaps they knew something he didn't know. But he'd check some sample populations as to sales potential. After a few weeks of consulting his computer and possibly cooking toads and frogs in search of auguries, Steve responded enthusiastically and we agreed to proceed.

Because Steve was the kind of editor who thought in terms of sales and left content to authors, I was given a free hand for any radical departures. So I cast the entire book of thirty chapters in dialogue form. In Part One, "Publishing Opportunities," my characters included Bill, who bore a remarkable resemblance to me; Charlie, a hybrid of skeptical graduate assistants

I had employed; and Mary, who sounded like the ISU assistant professors who often sought my advice on articles or books. For Part Two, "The Writer at Work," I put Bill into interaction with Andy, an alter ego bequeathed my middle name who was representative of the English professor I might have become. Part Three, "In the Editorial Offices," put Bill into conversations with Pam, a crusty veteran book editor; Jack, an experienced professor-editor of a journal; and Keyne, a publishing functionary who rivaled a computer in his ability to spout the economic facts of publishing life. The book closed with answers to a variety of miscellaneous questions asked of me in workshops, an approach I privately referred to as my "Dear Abby" device. Each of the thirty chapters save the last carried an illustrative appendix, such as actual journal queries and book proposals by workshoppers, comments by professionals on why they wrote, a bibliography of publishing opportunities in various academic disciplines, etc.

I hadn't had such fun in the preparation of a manuscript since I had written *The Danube Flows Through Fascism* forty-two years earlier. The dialogue approach allowed me to write creatively, a yen inherited from my youth. My characters Bill and Andy allowed me to be autobiographical yet, as Harold Benjamin said of his mirror image J. Abner Peddiwell, let me "lie a little." Allyn and Bacon opened the doors of their shop and their files to me; Roy and I taped long interviews with many staff members as grist for the section on editorial practices and procedures. Both Bee and Roy helped with research drudgery and contributed insights.

Workshops in the field kept me in touch with the questions writers actually ask and the tough problems they face. I conducted workshops in 1979 at Northeast Missouri State University, Alabama A & M University, the University of Southern Mississippi, Southeast Missouri State University, the University of Montevallo, and the University of Northern Iowa. In 1980 workshops were held at the Florida Atlantic University, the University of Arkansas at Pine Bluff, the University of South Dakota, Temple University, and Corpus Christi State University. Not Harvard or Columbia or Chicago or Stanford, you will note; they didn't need my help. The higher education insititutions I could best serve were the emerging universities, with locations like Northeastern or Southern implanted in their titles, with faculty members who wanted to publish but needed help as to know-how, and with administrators who recognized that professors shouldn't be asked to make bricks without straw. Though—possibly because—we worked day into night in intensive two- to four-day workshops, consultation was a joy, not a chore. I didn't even resent my occasional excess optimism as to scheduling, which once rushed me from a Maryland speech to Arkansas and South Dakota writing workshops, all jammed into five successive days.

I could work on *Writing for Professional Publication* wherever I found myself—on planes, at workshops, in the office at ISU that I happily maintained in the School of Education or my carrel at the Cunningham Memorial Library, at the Allyn and Bacon offices, at home at Lake Lure, or while wintering in sunny climes. On the road in workshops I tapped the ideas and questions of my potential readers. In Terre Haute I had the help of the reference division of the library, Bee's digging, Roy's research on appendices, and frequent correspondence with authors and editors. Yet since the book was based primarily on my own experiences as a contributor to professional publications, I often wrote my drafts comfortably on my sun deck or in my study at home, or on balconies in the tropics, and then mailed off cassettes for transcription.

Hours of writing could be fitted into days with my wife and our increasing number of grandchildren at home beside Lake Lure or in our new winter milieu, Puerto Rico along the Atlantic Ocean coast. After the Florida disillusionment, we had explored winter living arrangements in Puerto Rico and the Virgin Islands and had settled on rental of a condominium in Luquillo, a small Puerto Rican community. Each winter morning I wrote, then we sunned and swam and beach-walked each afternoon, and made new friends at cocktail hour. In writing the book I came close to living the life of the novelist I had aspired to be in my salad days.

My enjoyment of preparing *Writing for Professional Publication* extended even to editorial relationships, for though Steve Mathews was promoted upstairs and ceded editorial responsibility to a new editor—throughout my writing experiences editors constantly materialized and dematerialized—Dave Pallai proved helpful and reliable. As editor, he even answered questions promptly, a new experience for me. My good luck extended to splendid copy-editing of manuscript, galleys, and page proofs in Williamsport, Pennsylvania, by Sally Lifland, bookmaker. When I first learned of Sally's calling from her stationery I was inclined to phone in a bet, but soon learned to appreciate that her enterprise was a cluster of publishing services, thoughtfully and scrupulously rendered.

The readers of my manuscript were all that any writer could ask for. Stan Elam, who edited the *Kappan*, Robert Leeper of the ASCD's publication program, John F. Ohles of Kent State University, Richard D. Kimpston of the University of Minnesota, Jean Grambs of the University of Maryland, and Virgil A. Clift, emeritus of New York University, were fertile in suggestions and constructive in criticisms. Contrary to the usual publishing procedure, the reviewers knew whose book this was and the author knew who was writing the reviews. The result was a much better book than a foolish masquerade of anonymity would have produced. Mutual respect gets better results than secrecy, though I am sure devotees of refereeing articles and masking identities of book authors and manuscript reviewers will never be persuaded of the validity of this observation.

The book was published in October 1980 with a handsome jacket representing a page containing title, description, and author's name about to be lifted from a typewriter. The publisher sent out thousands of flyers and was rewarded by respectable sales of more than 5,000 in the first six months, more than the total sales of *Secondary Education: School and Community*. Understandably, one of my favorite reviews was the one that appeared in the *Kappan* headlined by the editor, "A **Savory** Book, Would You Believe, About Writing for Publication," and a review in *Educational Leadership* that concluded, "This reviewer's verdict: *Writing for Professional Publication* will be on my desk as a reference for years to come."

My last *Kappan* columns, published in 1977-78, were "Wanted: Effective Communication," which renewed my plea to educators to use fully the mass media; "Scenarios for Education: Year 2000," which sketched a pessimistic, optimistic, and "most likely" future; "Editorial Roulette," which needled publishers' manuscript reviewing procedures; "What to Expect If Your

Legislature Orders Literacy Testing," which criticized Florida's clumsy accountability procedures; and "Convention Sites and the ERA," which examined the boycotting of convention cities by the women's movement. They brought "One Way of Looking at It," initiated ten years before in *Contemporary Education*, to a close.

The education honorary, Kappa Delta Pi, awarded me membership in the Laureate Chapter, composed of sixty veteran educators. In 1980 Bee and I traveled to Nashville for the induction. Save for an invitation from the black university, Fisk, I hadn't been back to Nashville since the hectic curriculum change and integration conflicts of the 1950s. At the banquet, national president O. L. Davis said friendly things about my contribution to desegregation in the South. In my response I had the opportunity to tell members of a young generation what working for better race relations was like in the early Fifties in the city in which, as blacks and whites, they now dined without impediment.

In 1981 I talked at the University of Central Florida, Indiana University, and Miami University and served for a week as Distinguished Visiting Professor at New Mexico State University. Speaking engagements in 1982 brought me to Indiana University of Pennsylvania, Greenville in South Carolina, and Minneapolis. Because a stupid national policy loaded the dice to encourage retirees to sit passively on their rumps till the funeral bells tolled, I took on no other speaking engagements than these, since royalties on the new book were arriving. (Though Congress joyously taxed all earnings from post-retirement publications and consultation, congressional legislation limited the earnings of retirees under age 72 on pain of losing a dollar of Social Security for every two dollars earned beyond a prescribed low amount.) Since the First Amendment guarantees freedom of speech, Congress fortunately had no way of limiting speeches without honorarium delivered to national organizations. So I talked to a John Dewey Society meeting on the eve of the ASCD conference of 1979, gave what the ASCD titled the Distinguished Lecture to the 1980 Atlanta conference, addressed a Kappa Delta Pi regional meeting in 1981, and spoke to the ASCD and the biennial convocation of Kappa Delta Pi on writing for professional publication in 1982.

Freedom of speech also applies to writing without pay for

journals, so, at the invitation of the editor of *Educational Leadership*, I did an editorial on the *Bakke* decision that advocated finding new and better ways of achieving affirmative action programs. An article for the ASCD on ways of building confidence in schools in an age of disbelief was picked up and reprinted by *The Education Digest.* "Alternative Reagans: Four Possible Futures" appeared in the *Kappan* shortly after the new national administration came into power and began realizing the worst of my expectations.

I salved my uneasy conscience concerning the unwritten curriculum book with an article, "What Should Be the Content of the Curriculum?," a hard look at Taba and Tyler's curriculum rationale that urged the new generation to do the same. An *Educational Forum* article will never replace the book I might have written, but at least it attempted to point out a curriculum road for the Eighties.

Chapter Forty-Four

LOOKING

BACKWARD

No autobiography is complete without answering, at least to the subject's satisfaction if not always to the reader's, an inescapable question: If you had to live your life over again, what would you repeat and what would you do differently?

Let me sidle up to the question by beginning with what I would do again, given a reincarnation of a recognizable me. (Note that the qualification rules out the evasive answer, "I would choose not to be me at all, but instead would be a completely different person who would combine Superman's strength, Albert Einstein's intellect, Jesus's compassion, Franklin D. Roosevelt's political skills, Clark Gable's looks, Leo Tolstoy's writing ability..., etc.") Here's what I'm glad I did and presumably would do again.

I'm glad that I wrote, given Principal Emily Curry's encouragement, and went to college, given my mother's difficult decision. I'm glad I finally found the admissions office at Columbia. The college opened the door for me to a liberal education and to a dual career, and I walked through with the guidance of professors like Mark Van Doren and Verna Carley.

I'm glad I married Bee. Different though we were, we belonged together. Call it chemical affinity, cosmic attunement, magnetic attraction, or whatever other hybrid of science and poetry you prefer. Or, simply/complexly call it love.

I'm glad we traveled widely when we were young. No old man's *Queen Elizabeth* cruise could surpass a young couple's foldboat voyage by Long Island Duck. The wine tasted better then. The unexpected around the bend was more welcome. The legs climbed less protestingly. The world even smelled better.

I'm glad I engaged in social action. Though risks are always present, a satisfaction grows deep inside that is otherwise unattainable. When I worked for peace or established youth hostels or strove for school desegregation or campaigned for Adlai Stevenson and for Lyndon Johnson, I felt that I was contributing to the achievement of the democratic dream.

I'm glad that I lived the professor's life, which in my day provided many options. I'd teach again. I'd work again with organizations, take on leadership responsibilities, and remain active in selected groups throughout my life span. I'd again be a writing professor.

I'm glad that I drifted into the dual career of educator and writer. Freedom and economic security are concomitants of having vocational alternatives: you can write what you please when you have a reliable source of income other than your publications. Yet I must admit to occasional self-doubts about the desirability of dual careers when I think about James A. Michener, like myself a former laboratory school teacher. Once when Jim was editing for Macmillan and I was editing the Bureau for Intercultural Education series for Harper, he suggested we lunch together so that he might benefit from my experience in publishing my *Danube Flows Through Fascism* through Scribner's. Other commitments caused cancellation. Else, with consummate idiocy, I might have advised him concerning his manuscript then under way, "Jim, the war is over. Nobody will want to read tales about obscure naval officers and minor events in the South Pacific. Better stay with editing."

I have no doubts whatever that Bee was right in wanting children, and I was wrong in my hesitation born of fear that they would replace me in her affection and deny us opportunities to travel. Her capacity to love proved encompassing enough to embrace dogs and friends as well as husband and children. Our children lit up our lives; they join my glad list. They traveled with us to summer workshops, to Europe, and on vacation jaunts; I'd do it again despite Robert Benchley's memorable quip that traveling with children is like traveling third class in Bulgaria.

By 1983 when the first edition of *My Way of Looking at It* was just published, Barbara in Bay City, Michigan, skillfully combined teaching of East Asian refugees and remedial work for native Michiganders with mothering Linda and Laura and homemaking in a big white house on a broad avenue in a small city. With Bob Nichols, who became as close to us as any son by birth, she launched Academy Psychological and Educational Associates in 1981, a local service for which she provided educational help and for which Bob contributed psychological therapy. In Medfield, Massachusetts, Roy, now a teacher of economics at Bentley College, lived in a delightful rambling, brown-shingled, eagle-topped, low ceilinged house begun in 1702 in a rural area on the outskirts of Boston. With homemaker Linda (differentiated from Bay City grandchild Linda A. as Linda B.), his labor of love was constant renovation of the house and grounds, along with the rearing of children Justin and Desiree. His proposal for helping solve our national transportation problems through sharing rides is a gem. As befits a chairperson of a department of sociology and urban studies, Jon lived in his book-crammed and document-overflowing three-story house in the inner city of Philadelphia and crossed the Delaware River (by bike in good weather) to his office on the Camden campus of Rutgers University. He and Trudy, each of whom had emerged with mutual love and trust from the trauma of earlier divorces, combine parenting with teaching and writing careers. Miraculously, they produced two children, Ross in 1977 and Clare in 1979, along with two 1982 books, Jon's *Living with Energy Shortfall* and Trudy's *Women and Men as Leaders*.

I'm glad that old age, a vastly overrated time of life, is redeemed by the pleasure of being a grandparent. I had dedicated *Secondary Education: School and Community* to "the youngest of the Van Til family—Linda, Justin, Laura, Desiree, Ross—for whom secondary education is still ahead." Then Claire made it a sextet. We have great days with our grandchildren at Lake Lure, especially Barbara's Linda and Laura, who have always lived nearer to us than the rest, and we regularly make the rounds to their homes in the East and Midwest. When we venture on such pilgrimages, the hospitality of our children is boundless and the love of our grandchildren is abundant.

By 1983 emphases were emerging: Linda, people-oriented

and a good conversationalist; Laura, an adventurous taker of risks; Justin, active, keen, and a longball hitter; Desi, creative and penetrating; Ross, already a music and mathematics lover; and Claire, still so young as to defy such facile and feeble categorizations as these. As grandparents are wont to do, I speculate about their future. What athletes and scholars, artists and teachers, builders and writers, homemakers and career people, revolutionaries and conservatives, celebrities and just folks are in the making? What kind of adult human beings will they be in the twenty-first century? It's too bad that grandparents aren't allowed to stay around to find out.

What would I do differently if I had the chance? I'd expand my education beyond literature, the humanities, and the social sciences to embrace science and mathematics, my _terra incognita_. I'd acquire more tools, ranging from typing skills to statistics to music appreciation, and those newcomers, the computer and the word processor. I'd get a faster start on my education and purge it of much of the irrelevant clutter that hampered it. I'd be more of a scholar.

I wouldn't be a chairperson or division head. Too much of one's life gets spent on administrivia. I'd think not twice but seven times before taking any administrative post. Administration is useful and essential and somebody has to do it. But for me I'd substitute more community action and organizational leadership.

Somehow I would learn to be comfortable with conflict and would enter into the fray with less agony. I wouldn't demand error-free written products and suffer when this will-o-the-wisp inevitably proved unattainable. I'd adopt toward both deserved and undeserved criticism the to-hell-with-them attitude of the anonymous vulgarian who wrote, "I am sitting in the smallest room of my house. Your criticism is before me. Soon it will be behind me." But now I am coming too close to wishing myself a different person than I am.

If I were living my professional life again, I would give more of my time and resources to collaboration of educators and the general public through community action and state and national legislation. If citizens believed that good education was too expensive, I would urge them to consider the costs of ignorance. I would insist that education is much more than schooling and would foster social travel, work experiences, and community participation by the young. I would oppose even more strongly than I have authoritarian education marked by rote recitation, absorption of inert knowledge, and imposition of fixed answers to controversial questions.

I'd try still harder for wide acceptance of the kind of education I practiced and advocated. I would work for schools in which every child and youth is seen and treated as an individual, each with a unique personality, each with personal and social needs. I would try to persuade educators to teach about the pressing social problems of their day so that human beings might survive in a world at peace, with better human relations in an environment conducive to personal growth. I would ask my colleagues to help children and youth to understand and experience a democratic way of life through application of the method of intelligence in their studies, respect for individuals in their relationships with others, and concern for the common welfare in their social thought and action.

I would recognize that massive common effort would be needed to put even a fraction of these educational aspirations into effect. But I would refuse to believe that the individual doesn't count and can play no role in making a better world. I would still try to make some difference through having lived.

Chapter Forty-Five

A SELF-PUBLICATION
EXPERIENCE

S o the first edition of *My Way of Looking at It* was published in 1983. By that date my list of published books was respectably long and my experience with book publication substantial. But my autobiography was to be a new experience for me—self-publishing.

The publishers of my earlier books had included Scribner's, Greystone, McGraw-Hill, Harper and Brothers, Bobbs-Merrill, Houghton Mifflin, and Allyn and Bacon. Some of my books were trade publications; most were produced by the educational divisions of publishing houses. Since I couldn't expect publication of an autobiography by publishers' educational arms or by the educational organizations for which I had edited yearbooks, should I turn to the trade divisions of commercial publishers for consideration of my autobiography?

Two factors contributed to my making only perfunctory inquiries to a small number of commercial publishers. First, I was convinced that if I myself were a trade editor, I wouldn't publish *My Way of Looking at It*. The manuscript simply didn't have the essential ingredient needed for commercial success in the competitive publishing world of the 1980s—it lacked lurid antisocial exploits conveyed largely through obscenity and profanity. Admittedly I do have a few pens obtained informally from Holiday Inns and Ramadas. However, I have never learned to communicate through multiple repetitive variations on the f-word. And I doubted that the pens alone, trophies of speaking engagements, would sufficiently qualify me for entry into the steamy world of contemporary confessions.

So I sent a few half-hearted inquiries to major publishing houses and got back a couple of friendly letters, including one invitation to consider writing another education textbook. Only Knopf showed any interest in my autobiography; then cooler heads in the firm prevailed.

There was another reason for the lukewarmness of my approaches to the familiar publishing houses. This time I wanted to produce a book without the ministrations of editorial angels. I wanted to say what I had to say without consideration of the omnipresent "market" and without catering to editors who wanted to write my books themselves. Walter Duranty of the *New York Times* had spoken for me many years earlier when he titled his autobiography *I Write as I Please*. So had the greatest of editors, Maxwell E. Perkins of Scribner's, my first editor, when he said simply, "The book belongs to the author."

So, aware of probable bumps but hoping for some pleasant turns, I took the self-publishing road. My autobiography would be written, edited, printed, marketed, and mailed as a Van Til enterprise. The publishing house would be Bee and me.

What title? Titling a book is often the last decision in the editorial process. Thumbing my nose at the conventional wisdom, I had decided upon a title before I had written the book. *My Way of Looking at It* was a variation of the head that had been used for my *Contemporary Education* and *Phi Delta Kappan* columns, "One Way of Looking at It".

What to call our new publishing house? That was easy. We looked out the window at our sun-dancing lake and came up with Lake Lure Press. Officers and employees? Bee as President, me as Secretary-Treasurer and factotum.

Lake Lure Press didn't have to search out manuscripts. It already had one, its pages scarcely ruffled by mid-Manhattan publishers, a tidy bunch. Only an index was lacking. In the past, the preparation of the index had been the publisher's chore; now it became mine. I put in some happy and nostalgic days preparing the index and thinking about people whose trails had crossed mine. I learned of another advantage of the author preparing the index—you discover (and presumably eliminate) inconsistencies on many matters such as middle initials. Sometimes you encounter the Great Beast, gross errors. I commend index compilation to all authors who are serious about their work.

Stan Elam was relaxing after a long and successful career of editing *Kappan*. He had edited all of my columns for a decade and was on my short list of "good editors." Who else is on the good list? Robert Leeper of *Educational Leadership*, Bill MacDonald of Houghton Mifflin, Bill Hackett of Bobbs Merrill, Steve Mathews of Allyn and Bacon (and of course Maxwell Perkins and Fred Wilhelms). Who's on the black list? Mostly copy editors of my textbooks such as Susie (whose editorial sins I have enumerated earlier) and a few other zealots who, striving for political correctness, have over-edited my efforts to communicate.

As a freelance consultant, Stan gave my manuscript the benefit of his editorial eye, suggested type sizes (a matter on which I was and remain abysmally ignorant) and added his friendly comments to those of other pre-publication readers. The back cover carried appraisals from Stan and from Mary Anne Raywid of Hofstra University, Fred T. Wilhelms education organization executive, Virgil A. Clift of New York University, and Glen Hass of the University of Florida.

Off went the manuscript to Sally Lifland, the able and helpful mistress of a typesetting company in the mountains of Pennsylvania. A Michigan company produced a handsome paperback with blue cover. Back came cartons packed with books. They were greeted with euphoria and stored in our garage.

We tapped the first box for freebies for my children and grandchildren and an assortment of people who had helped in the book's making. I performed one of the rites of publishing and reaped one of its rewards by inscribing each copy with words appropriate to my relationship to the recipient. Writing the inscriptions for our six grandchildren, who were too young at the time to read the autobiography with understanding, I thought back to my comment in the last chapter that it's too bad grandparents aren't allowed to stay around to see how their grandchildren turn out.

Now we had to enter unexplored territory—selling the book. The maps of early mariners often warned as to *terra incognita*, "beyond here be monsters." The heavy boxes of books brooded in the garage and waited for disposal.

We completed a flyer which put the best foot forward through description, pre-publication readers' comments, and order form. After consulting Delphic oracles and stewing up a witches' brew of hog entrails and newts' eyes to help our prophesying, we priced the book at $14.95 plus postage and handling. An ancient Ouija board was used in the decision to print a thousand copies.

The flyers went to all members of several small educational organizations in which I had held top office, such as the John Dewey Society, the Society of Professors of Education (titled during my presidency the National Society of College Teachers of Education), and the Spring Conference. We wrote to the leadership and a sampling of the membership of a large organization of which I was a past president, the Association for Supervision and Curriculum Development.

We bought mailing lists such as listings of libraries and lists purporting to name people addicted to buying trade books. Our Seelyville post office near Lake Lure got used to our occasional bulk mailings of leaflets. A few wholesalers laid in small stocks. Bookstores in University communities in which I had taught gingerly purchased some copies after making sure we agreed to accept returns. Nor did we overlook relatives and friends and former students with whom I had continued relationships. We were amazed and amused when the massive catalogs of publishers included Lake Lure Press along with the giants of the industry.

As the orders came in, we promptly responded with copies complete with inscriptions for identifiable purchasers. Back came welcome checks, sometimes accompanied by even more welcome comments by recipients, "We last met you at," "I read you in college," etc. One of the joys of self-publishing is the intensely personal relationships between the author and many readers.

Weeks after the autobiography's receipt still more letters came in from readers who shared their experience, emotions, agreements, and disagreements. Often they were appreciative of my personal inscriptions. They felt themselves kin to the author through friendship ties, organizations, books, or common interests. By contrast, the relationships between authors and readers of conventionally marketed books are absent or tenuous.

We also discovered a dark side of book selling, familiar to all publishers who market by mail. A few deadbeats who ordered books didn't pay their bills. They varied in background. One who ordered two copies was a prisoner; this we later deduced from his address. We wished him success in selling the copies. Another phony ordered on the stationery of a Catholic college. This particularly irked our president, Bee, who wrote personalized follow-up letters to her crooked co-religionist. Though the letters were unanswered, they served as good therapy for their writer.

As orders slowed to a trickle, we had sold about 900 copies. The boxes in the garage had almost vanished. So we sent the remaining copies to those university libraries which were not sufficiently enlightened to buy the book. We hoarded about 50 copies to give to future friends or hosts of future speaking engagements.

We will not bore you with details of our financial transactions, amateurishly accounted for in two wire-ringed notebooks. Sufficient to say we ended by just about breaking even. In the world of self-publishing, breaking even is scored as an overwhelming victory.

Yes, our labor was unpaid. No royalty checks came in the mail. But the dour warnings that we would lose our shirts (and probably underpants) were wrong. I wrote as I pleased. Thank you, Walter Duranty. The book belonged to its author. Thank you, Maxwell E. Perkins. It was a good experience.

Chapter Forty-Six

PUERTO RICO, OUR SECOND HOME

P uerto Rico is our second home. We are not married to Puerto Rico; our relationship is better described as a longtime unsanctioned love affair.

Columbus discovered the *"isla encantada"* in 1493. Bee and I discovered it somewhat later, the 1950s. We owe our discovery to the conservatism of the University of Puerto Rico and the enterprise of Walter A. Anderson of New York University. UPR, motivated by academic snobbery and reluctance to be tarred with the vocational brush, was refraining from developing a sorely needed graduate program for the island's educators. "Andy," dean of the School of Education of New York University, an innovative administrator, saw an opportunity and leaped at it.

So the NYU School of Education offered a Master's degree open to Puerto Rican teachers and administrators. The degree was achievable through two summers of study under NYU faculty members in Puerto Rico plus one summer of study in New York City at the Washington Square campus. Puerto Rican educators flocked gratefully into the new classes.

For a decade (1957-1967) I spent most Junes teaching curriculum and social foundations courses at "NYU under the palms." The Puerto Ricans were a joy to teach. No matter how early the faculty arrived at the public school which housed our program, many of the Puerto Rican educators were there before us: eager, friendly, questioning, thirsty to improve their schools. After classes they stayed around a long time, unlike our New York City teachers conditioned to flee to the subway at the first clang of a bell.

Our life style in Puerto Rico was delightful too. The faculty migrant workers lived in the Condado Beach Hotel, a comfortable dowager among hotels along San Juan's Condado tourist strip. Back home in the New York area we led widely separated private lives "up in Westchester, over in Jersey, out the island," as well as in Manhattan. Entertaining one's colleagues necessitated planning of logistics and facilitating expeditions. But in Puerto Rico all faculty members and wives had taken to the hotel's beach by mid-afternoon. A cocktail hour in somebody's room and dinner at eight somewhere on the island followed. Bee and I made more faculty friends each Puerto Rican June than during the remaining eleven months of the year.

Most faculty members and their spouses acculturated fast. We learned that there were two times: Puerto Rican and mainland. When invited to dinner at a Puerto Rican educator's home (and there were many such invitations), we learned to arrive by Puerto Rican time, one to two hours later than the time indicated by the host. Even so, dinner would be a long time coming.

We encountered early one of the best traditional virtues of the islanders—"*hospitalidad.*" Each session ended with class parties at which the faculty received presents from the student body; many charming cups, wooden bowls, platters, and other native crafts ornament our shelves at home. After a year or two of present-giving, Walter Anderson, in his role as dean, grew uneasy. "It just doesn't look right," he told the faculty. So he assembled the classes and explained that there would be no presents at the session's close since the faculty, though highly appreciative, should not be favored in this way. The students listened carefully and respected his words, if not his message. Consequently, at the final parties that year everyone—faculty and students alike—received a present. The present for each student was an inexpensive gadget from a local variety store. But the presents for the faculty were handsomer than ever. Andy, the great white father (a politically incorrect faculty usage), surrendered to the power of the culture. Next year the gift-giving to faculty members resumed. But presents to students were omitted. "*Hospitalidad*" had triumphed over academic respectability...

Time passed and for a dozen years Puerto Rico baked in the sun without us. I left NYU in 1967 for a role at Indiana State

University that President Rankin titled the Coffman Distinguished Professorship. After a decade with ISU, I retired from university teaching but retained my office for my work as a consultant and a writer. Home continued to be our house on Lake Lure in the boondocks, ideal living for three seasons of the year but susceptible to Midwestern snowdrifts and icy roads. So we cast about for a wintry retreat, tried Florida and the Virgin Islands, then settled upon Puerto Rico. Throughout the 1980s and to the present writing in the 1990s we lived (and still live) from December through March at the eastern end of Puerto Rico.

We found that Puerto Rico had changed since our NYU decade yet largely remained the same. Some changes were highly visible. For instance, wooden shacks had been largely replaced by houses of masonry. In place of the battered traveling junkyards that had dominated earlier roads, there now ran sleek Japanese compacts. Rather than the serpentine two-lane road between San Juan and Ponce, where horns blared at every twist, drivers now took a superhighway comparable with any in the world. Roadside stands hawking *coco frio* or roast pig persisted but MacDonalds and kin fast foods establishments were clearly inheriting the earth. The mom and pop *colmados* were yielding to acres of shopping malls populated by Wal-Marts, Walgreens, and K Marts. *Supermercados* abounded, identical with mainland markets save for higher prices and names like Amigo and Pueblo and Gigante. High rises and one family housing had proliferated everywhere; along the beaches, in the hills, in the capital, in the smaller cities, in the suburbs.

Yet the more things changed the more they stayed alike. Behind the facades of Burger Kings and condominiums and sprawling middle class residence communities, there was an underlying reality reminiscent of earlier decades. Unemployment stayed high, for instance 14.6 percent in 1994. Forty-five percent of children lived below the poverty level. Long lines still gathered at banks when the relief and entitlement checks came in. Rising middle class tides had not lifted all boats.

Pessimists point out that the Puerto Rican standard of living is lower than the poorest of the fifty states of the United States. Optimists point out that Puerto Rico has the highest standard of living in the entire Caribbean area. Both pessimists and opti-

424

mists are right. They agree that Puerto Rico has come a long way from the New Deal era when Puerto Rico was termed the "poorhouse of the Caribbean."

Established customs stubbornly resisted change. Drivers, whether in jalopies or Mitsubishis, still raced through the yellow lights, ignored stop signs, and ran red lights. Letters to the editor continued to complain of trash along the roads, dogs running at large, slow telephone repair and installation. When repairmen in their relaxed and unhurried ways said "*manana*," they still meant "some one of these days." The newspaper columnists still wrestled with the status problem of whether Puerto Rico should retain its present Commonwealth status (about half of Puerto Ricans said yes) or become a state within the United States (almost another half said yes) or become independent (very few said yes).

Puerto Rico still had a profusion of holidays, by one count 11 U.S. holidays and nine Puerto Rican holidays. Soon after we arrive in December we celebrate not only Christmas and New Years but also Three Kings Day, Eugenio Maria de Hostos Day, and Martin Luther King's Birthday. We are gone when the island celebrates Emancipation Day, Commonwealth Day, Puerto Rico Discovery Day, and days dedicated to the memory of José de Diego and José Celso Barbosa and Luis Muñoz Rivera (don't confuse the latter with Luis Muñoz Marin for whom the San Juan Airport is named).

Pleasant eternals persist. The island remains incredibly lovely—pristine beaches along every shore, the mountain spine of the Cordillera, the lofty rain forest atop El Yunque, the luxuriant vegetation of hibiscus, oleanders, bougainvillea, flamboyant, the enduring charm of Old San Juan with its massive fortresses, city walls, balconied streets, convents and churches. In Puerto Rico the weather forecasts are changeless; during winters the meteorologists, now as during the 1950s, predict monotonously, "mostly sunny, high around 85, low in the 70s, 20 percent possibility of showers, wind ten miles an hour east." No wonder the "*isla del encantado*" has become a tourist mecca.

Puerto Rican tourism had begun with the Condado strip (which was home to the migrant NYU professors), expanded to Isla Verde near the airport, flirted with the Dorado area west of San Juan, and is now concentrating on development of luxury resorts on the eastern end of the island, such as El Conquistador, a shangri-la where prices for a room begin at $325 a day and soar to a stratospheric $1,610.

Need I say that, though we live at the eastern end of the island, we do not reside at El Conquistador? We live comfortably and within our means at Playa Azul, one of the two condominiums an hour away from San Juan in Luquillo on the Atlantic shore.

We happened on Playa Azul in 1979 through a sentence Eugene Fodor had inserted in his guide to the Caribbean, a throwaway sentence which he probably forgot soon after he had set it down. Fodor wrote that, if the tourist wished to live in a condominium outside the capital area, the prospective renter should write to Neggie Maldonado. So we wrote to Neggie, who turned out to be a vivacious Puerto Rican woman with a flirtatious eye and a variety of condominium apartments to rent. We rented one, sight unseen, for a month. The tryout of Playa Azul was part of our exploration of Caribbean winter refuges which also brought us to a Virgin Islands hideaway near Secret Harbor and to a motel-like apartment on Water Isle off Charlotte Amalie. (Incidentally on Water Isle we met the amiable low-keyed Eugene Fodor himself, along with his ebullient Hungarian wife. They were staying, as we were, in a housekeeping unit in a pleasant but far from luxurious place. The author of a famous series of guide books to the world's best hotels preferred his wife's cooking to that of five star hotel restaurants.)

Playa Azul had it all. The condominium consisted of three towers, each twenty-two stories high, with a recreation area which included a social building, a pool, a tennis court, a hand-ball area, two basketball courts, and a children's playground. Just outside the compound wall the Atlantic pounded restlessly and a broad beach stretched a half mile in each direction. From our balcony fronting on the ocean we could see the predecessor of today's El Conquistador ranging along a hill to the east and the red roofs of Rio Mar, a residence resort, snug in the hillside to the west. One mile away from us stretched quiet waters of Luquillo Beach, acclaimed in the Caribbean. Out at sea the cruise ships glittered by. Inland El Yunque brooded darkly.

But it wasn't the sun on the Luquillo beaches or the charm of old San Juan that kept us coming to Puerto Rico every winter from 1980 on. It was the people. I once told my former neighbor on Lake Lure, Birch Brooks, that when I retired I planned to spend each winter in a different area such as in the Southwestern desert country, along the Gulf of Mexico, on the Mexican border or beside the Mediterranean. Birch said, "You probably won't," I asked why not. "Because you will find a place that you will like and people whom you look forward to seeing each winter." He was right.

The mainlanders begin to trek into Playa Azul in December, save for a few six-monthers who arrive in early November and stay through April. Independent though the mainlanders are, they are also highly interdependent people. They live on an island, Puerto Rico, while also living on an island within Puerto Rico, the condominium called Playa Azul. Though none that I know of are Marxists, they contribute according to their abilities and help others according to their needs. For instance, Wilbur who is recognized as the Mayor of Playa Azul (unofficial and without portfolio) and nurse Mary, his wife, are available for advice and action any hour of the day or night. (In an inadequate response, I counsel Wilbur on the articles he should be writing about his fascinating experiences as a veterinarian.)

When our electricity went dead, we called on Karl's technological background to resuscitate it. When a newcomer arrived at the portals with a mountain of groceries from the first day's shopping, Bee brought him up to our apartment to borrow her shopping cart. A few days later he and Ed jump-started our car after our headlights had been left on overnight. Helen knows Spanish from her years in Argentina with Julian so each year she teaches a class for Playa Azul mainlanders. A young Canadian couple introduced line dancing and at the every-Friday-afternoon picnic at the beach line dancing persisted long after their departure. Lee teaches decorating T-shirts and consequently designs sparkle on the beaches and in the lobby. Forrest and Eleanor, political activists back home, work with townspeople on humane approaches to the problem of stray animals. At long last Al and others, managed to persuade the "junta" (the condominium's governing body) to install steps into the pool for the use of "*impedidos*." Helene regularly hosts a Xmas party in her penthouse shortly after Myra has hosted a seasonal gathering that overflows next-door into our apartment. When I needed hospitalization, Lloyd and John carted me down the hall to the elevator and to the ambulance; Steve donated blood. And that's just a sample.

Bee has compiled a special address book which lists the apartments and phones of 194 people in Puerto Rico (I counted them) who range from acquaintenceship to close friendship. People sometimes call her for a needed phone number or when they forget where a party is going to be held.

I suspect our interdependence contributes to our mutual acceptance of each other. Our friendship groups often cross religious, racial, and political lines. Locales for lowering barriers include beaches, bridge games, folk dancing, Sunday brunch at Roosevelt Roads Navy base, and even occasionally unreliable elevators, "Would you believe it! The door opened and I was facing a blank brick wall." We are aided in acceptance by people like Father Bill, an annual vacationer in Luquillo before his recent lamented death and a powerful ecumenical force, whose message during masses in the Playa Azul social building were heard by some of the Protestants, Jews, and unaffiliated as well as by faithful and once in a while Roman Catholics.

Yet we keep our distinctive identities. We go (or we don't go) to our respective churches and synagogues; prefer to discuss politics with people sensible enough to agree with us; sit on the beach with our best friends, whether the clusters be black or white or biracial.

Our common denominator is that we are all mainland Americans. Son Jon quips that we live in a ghetto—a Yankee ghetto rather than a Jewish or black enclave. We try to refute this by citing our guest lists for parties and pointing to our all-condominium suppers prepared both by Puerto Rican residents and the mainland owners/renters. Yet we have to admit the partial validity of Jon's observation for it's hard for the twain to meet during Playa Azul winters when the Puerto Ricans are at work and the mainlanders at play.

We enjoy our second home where our friends include teachers, story tellers, anesthesiologists, community activists, professors, dentists, florists, researchers, authors, nurses, entrepreneurs, and even one candidate for governor. Our conversations range from cerebral (deconstructionism, the environment, John Dewey's little known interest in mathematics, the pros and cons of volunteering) to utilitarian (the best restaurants, the decline in Puerto Rican fishing, the virtues of Playa Azul III as compared to I and II, the preferable *supermercados*, the best bets for air travel back to the States).

Puerto Rico, we are glad that we followed Christopher Columbus to your shores for we are happy with our season in the sun. Why not all year round? As everybody except New Yorkers says about living in New York City, "It's a nice place to visit, but I wouldn't want to live there." Despite the unraveling of American society, we still prefer spring, summer and fall on the American mainland beside our Indiana lake. However, if the reactionary religious and economic right-wingers grow too virulent there's always.... New Zealand maybe?

Chapter Forty-Seven

ON THE ROAD—
THEN SHIFTING GEARS

With the marketing of *My Way of Looking at It* well under-way, in 1983 I renewed activities related to encouraging educators to write. Whenever higher education institu-tions—whether in the boondocks or the metropolitan areas—invited me to work with their faculties, I went. In 1978, shortly after my supposed retirement, I had first taken my writing for professional publication workshops on the road and by now I had established a pattern.

Weekend workshops usually began with a Friday night dinner for faculty participants, courtesy of the college/university administration which thus beneficently bestowed institutional blessing upon the undertaking. I then talked in general on writing for professional publication. The evening closed with my request for preparation by each participant of a one or two page query to journal editors. A query is a letter intended to accom-plish three things: inform the editor of the essential idea struc-ture and conclusions of the prospective article; persuade the editor that what the writer had to say was worth reading; tell the editor who the writer is and why he or she is qualified to write. I stressed directing article queries to specific magazines and journals with which the writer was well acquainted. As to books, queries should be supplemented with a prospectus and compari-sons with kin books. Each person was asked to prepare and reproduce a query by midmorning Saturday.

The Friday night session adjourned with my picking up cards carrying any questions participants wanted to raise as to writing. I took the written questions with me to my hotel for grouping and study.

On Saturday, each participant in turn distributed and read aloud his/her query. I contributed reference materials descriptive of the particular journal or magazine or book publisher targeted. Each listener then played the role of the editor addressed by the query. Animated discussion and critiques followed. After all the "editors" were heard, the author was allowed a response. Each consideration of a query culminated in individual and group recommendations as to whether to reject or to encourage the writer to proceed with the proposal. In addition to playing a role as senior editor, I would often inject relevant mini-lectures or commentaries based on the questions received earlier.

By Sunday afternoon the swifter revisers among the professors would have second (and much improved) drafts ready for another round of editorial consideration and advice. At the close of the session each participant had thought through the nature and content of his/her proposed article or book, the possible outlets, and what to expect from editors. Evenings and between sessions, I was available for individual conferences on already completed writing or work in progress.

On Monday morning, the professors, presumably tired but stimulated, would return to their teaching, having missed no classes. They would promise themselves to send off one or more queries that week. I would fly home and look forward to receiving reprints months later from successful writers. The questions raised by the group would be tucked away for future reference.

Some workshops were longer than weekends. The most sustained were the two week institutes on writing for professional publication sponsored each summer from 1984 through 1990 by Phi Delta Kappa and Indiana University. Stanley Elam, the superlative *Kappan* editor who was appointed as the first institute director, invited me to join the staff and to prepare a pattern for the first of the institutes. The structure was used throughout all seven institutes. Because scores were in attendance from throughout the nation, subgroups for neophyte article writers, experienced writers, and book authors were established. My favorite assignment was to the beginning writers group in which I used the writing of queries approach, supplemented by preparation of articles for consideration and discussion by the group members.

At the institutes we made use of the rich resources available on the Bloomington campus for presentations whether by participants themselves, staff members of *Kappan* (edited on campus), experienced authors on the Indiana University faculty, and the staff members of the institute along with invited specialists. Planning of presentations, the creation of groups, and scheduling as a whole was the responsibility of a planning committee chosen early by the participants.

A typical day would open in an auditorium with presentations to the entire institute, then shift to subgroups. By midafternoon participants were on their own to write where and when they wished. Conferences with individual staff members could readily be scheduled. Since participants were in residence at dormitories during the two week session, a social committee sponsored activities ranging from theater parties to picnics in Brown County's state parks.

Much that I learned from the interaction with participants in the weekend workshops and from both staff and students in the early institute years found its way into the second edition of *Writing for Professional Publication*. The massive card file of questions asked by participants prior to the opening of sessions was an especially influential source of additions and deletions. I updated the content of the chapters and reserved major changes for the illustrative material that supplemented the 29 chapters. Here sources and statistics were added and changed, obsolete materials eliminated, and short pieces which had been tested in the workshops added.

Professor Jon Van Til of Rutgers University, who is both my son and a scholarly colleague whom I respect, made a significant contribution to the second edition through a brand new chapter on word processing. Like the rest of the book, this chapter took the form of a dialogue. In this case the discussants were "Bill," an innocent in the brave new world of technology; "Andy," the professor of English literature whom Bill might have become; and "Jon," a sophisticated user of word processors, computer technology, and other marvels.

In preparing my second edition of *Writing for Professional*

Publication I was highly fortunate in being able to build upon competent editing of the first version. Nor did I have criticism of the royalties, which were respectable. Admittedly though, I was not happy with Allyn and Bacon's policy of steadily increasing the price of the books. I wished someone would tell publishers about Henry Ford's history-making discovery that mass production and low prices are better bets for profit-making than limited production and high prices. As the price of the second edition soared, I embarrassedly advised my students to find used copies of the first edition.

Then in the later 1980s I changed some of my living and working styles. Maybe it was because in 1985 I had a second dress rehearsal for death. This time it happened in Puerto Rico; my earlier rehearsal had taken place in Calcutta in 1974. On a beautiful winter day at Playa Azul, I had come down with a combination of prostate and ulcer problems; Bee and my friends had wheeled me down the hall on a dining room chair with casters to a waiting ambulance and several weeks of hospitalization. On hearing the news our children conferred; then the two with the most open schedules flew down to help Bee and me in multiple ways.

Or maybe it was because I began to feel that I had enough of staying at Holiday Inns (they rightly advertise "no small surprises"). Or accumulating Delta Frequent Flier miles on the road. Maybe it was because my term on the Resolutions Committee of the Association for Supervision and Curriculum Development terminated in 1985 and I refused the ASCD president's invitation to become chairperson for a new term. Maybe it was because in 1986 I had completed a couple of years as laureate leader of Kappa Delta Pi's Book of the Year Committee. Perhaps it was because the second and final edition of *Writing for Professional Publication* appeared in 1986 and I was temporarily feeling that's enough writing of books for awhile.

Or maybe it was none of the above. Probably it was the reluctant realization that I was old. Satchell Paige said, "Never look back. Somethin' might be gainin' on you." I didn't have to look back to be aware that somethin' had been gainin' on me. I could get into the flat sitting position in my foldboat but I would have needed a derrick or the help of many hands to get me out.

When I dropped things I found that floors had grown more distant from my hands than they used to be. My legs refused even my most profane demands. Fortunately, upstairs in the attic things seemed to stay as they always had been. Except of course for declining hearing. (Just the other night Bee commented to me that the wide-ranging Bill Geist of CBS had written whimsically about "pig racing." I said "pink braces?" She repeated, "pig racing." "Oh," I said, "big Graces? About the British Royal family?")

So at first subconsciously (and later with full realization) I began to shift gears. I no longer accepted any and all invitations to speak and, in turn, the invitations grew fewer. Now increasingly Bee accompanied me on speaking engagements. As to conferences, formerly we had both regularly attended the annual meetings of ASCD (at which the luncheons for past presidents and their spouses had become our high points), as well as the Spring Conference for free trade in ideas and for good fellowship, and the Kappa Delta Pi biannual conferences where the laureates spoke to the breakfast meetings. Now we began to pick and chose—"How far? Who'll be there?"

We expanded our recreational pursuits. For years now we have lived at Lake Lure with its readily available opportunities for swimming, fishing, gardening and what we like to call "property walks." Now we added two new toys, a VCR to bring movies of our choice into our family room and a spa with pounding jets to bring the California lifestyle to our Indiana patio. Since the foldboating days with the Weinandys on the Mosel River, we had traveled far afield, culminating in our round the world trip. Now we poked into corners with which we were relatively unfamiliar. Our trips took us to the Pacific Northwest, to Hawaii, to the South's Georgia coast and to Chapel Hill, to the Canadian Rockies, to Maine and Nova Scotia. Late in our lives we discovered the joys and comforts of cruising and in the years between 1986 and 1991 we voyaged to Caribbean islands and South American shores via the *Carla Costa, Daphne, Amerikanis*, and *Regent Sea*. In the 1990s we graduated in the cruise world to the best on the high seas, Holland American's *New Amsterdam* to Alaska and Princess Line's *Star Princess* to tropical islands.

We have been a close family and have tried to keep that closeness despite geographical separation. So now we visited our children even more frequently in their homes in Pennsylvania, Michigan, and Massachusetts/Maine. Barbara and Bob and family live a day's drive from us in Bay City, Michigan, and continued to be regular holiday visitors and our companions on trips to the Carolinas and Eastern Canada. Jon stops in frequently on his way to speeches and consultations somewhere else. Roy is too far away for more than infrequent visits to Maine but our calls contribute to the profits of proliferating long distance telephone carriers and our letters are long. Sometimes we have the delightful opportunity of enjoying life with our grandchildren on their visits to us without their parents. Anniversary celebrations for our aging relatives and friends, permanently and provincially settled in New York City and its environs, bring us east, especially to Long Island. Our own annual summer celebrations of Bee's birthday followed next day by our wedding anniversary bring most members of our families to occasional reunions.

So life on the road sputtered out as we shifted gears toward a more personal kind of travel and a more relaxed lifestyle.

Chapter Forty-Eight

MEMOIRS

OF EDUCATIONAL

ASSOCIATIONS

A s to writing, two possible roads stretched ahead of me in the years in which I would be in my latter seventies. I could try my pen (but it was a computer age) at breaking new ground (if I could) with a book on curriculum which was long awaited (long awaited only by me). Or I could use whatever years of productive writing might remain to summarize. Two roads diverged and, unlike Robert Frost, I took the one most traveled by, the less adventuresome road of looking back. It was a road I had traveled in part through *My Way of Looking at It: An Autobiography* and which I enjoyed taking.

The Association for Supervision for Curriculum Development clinched my decision by inviting me in the mid-eighties to write a history of ASCD. The organization had grown phenomenally in recent years and was in danger of losing track of its past. As the snake sheds its skin, ASCD had shed many of its records and documents as it grew. It had outgrown headquarters after headquarters and thrown away file after file.

Writing a history of ASCD from fragmentary archives would be difficult enough for a professional historian and, as I saw it, quite impossible for me, a generalist in education and in the social sciences. So I proposed an alternative. How about asking some past presidents to look back on aspects of the ASCD program with which they were especially identified? The ASCD leadership liked the idea. As President Jerry Firth wrote in his foreword to what became *ASCD in Retrospect*:

The decision by the Executive Council to bring together into a single volume the development of our Association was significant. The invitation to the incomparable William Van Til to serve as editor and to gather other former presidents and leaders has resulted in a product far more powerful than anyone had anticipated.

(I told Jerry that I particularly enjoyed that "incomparable" because I was reminded of the old vaudeville routine which goes, "How's your wife?" followed by the response "Compared to what?")

So as editor of this prospective pamphlet, I determined a chapter structure and specified contributions from nine past presidents and the current executive director. All accepted my invitations and all delivered their manuscripts on time. I wasn't surprised. There is a tremendous loyalty and commitment to ASCD among long-time leaders. No better impression of ASCD in the days that I knew it most intimately has ever been written than Fred T. Wilhelms's words in a 1960 column in *Educational Leadership*. Writing on "The Importance of ASCD," he commented:

> Two characteristics: caring tremendously about children and teachers and what happens when they get together; the ability to involve almost everybody; these, to me, make ASCD stand out above all other organizations. Of course, these two root down to something deeper—I don't exactly know what— a vision of what society could be, perhaps, so goading a vision that it never lets compromise be comfortable; a faith in the human person so deep-rooted it cannot be shaken.

Galen Saylor, familiar with the beginnings, described the origin of ASCD in the early 1930s. Denver supervisor Prudence Bostwick wrote of the earliest years of ASCD when supervisors constituted the largest professional category in the membership. Alice Miel, protagonist of group process and group dynamics, wrote on the years when active participation by every conference attendant was the hallmark of ASCD, 1946-1969. William M. Alexander described the multiple curriculum activities of ASCD during its first two decades.

I wrote on "Social Forces and ASCD." My essay stressed ASCD's role in international affairs, its opposition to McCarthyism and censorship, its advocacy of human and civil rights, its support of separation of church and state:

> ASCD, over a period of more than 40 years, has taken positions on controversial issues on society and schools. It has **supported** social forces that foster the historic American democratic values and support democratic education. It has also **opposed** social forces—those that would lead to war; institute censorship and stifle the use of intelligence; deny human and civil rights; impede government doing for its people collectively what they cannot do for themselves individually; discriminate against women, blacks, and minority ethnic groups; break down walls of separation of church and state; and penalize children and youth for the failure of adults.

One of ASCD's black presidents, Phil C. Robinson, described the commitment of ASCD to the inclusion of all racial and ethnic groups and the elimination of segregation within state units (national was never segregated). Jack Frymier, a long-time supporter of more research in the ASCD program, reported on the research committees and institutes and resultant publications. Educator and psychologist Arthur W. Combs emphasized the relationship of ASCD to the humanist tradition as illustrated by his widely read yearbook *Perceiving Behaving Becoming*, published during my presidency. The limited supervision activities of ASCD from the 1960s to the mid-1980s were chronicled by the incoming president, Jerry Firth, who called for much more stress on the "S" (for supervision) in ASCD.

To me, one of the most perceptive chapters was by O. L. Davis. In his chapter on recent curriculum developments he included an insightful analysis of changes in the constituency of ASCD from a few hundred central office curriculum workers and supervisors plus some college professors of curriculum and instruction to an organization in 1986 of almost 70,000 with school principals and classroom teachers as its largest membership groups and with professors, supervisors, and curriculum directors shrunk to a small proportion. By its 50th anniversary in 1993, ASCD enrolled more than half of its membership as principals (36 percent) or teachers (19 percent). With a changed constituency, the program of ASCD changed markedly.

The last chapter was by Gordon Cawelti, who was largely

responsible for the growth of ASCD from an organization which numbered 12,000 in 1973 when he became executive secretary to one which totalled 164,282 in 1991 when he resigned as executive director. In his chapter he looked ahead to areas of future focus.

To ASCDers who prefer Santayana's "Those who cannot remember the past are doomed to repeat it" to Henry Ford's "History is more or less bunk," *ASCD in Retrospect* is an essential source.

ASCD in Retrospect was published in 1986 as a handsome 104 page pamphlet with the names of the authors listed alphabetically on the cover. Copies went to the comprehensive membership. All past presidents and past executive secretaries were invited to Alexandria, Virginia, for a luncheon celebration at which the book was presented by all authors in attendance. Their fellow presidents were generous in their appreciation of the publication. (As far as I know, only one chose to badmouth me in later years for the unforgivable oversight of not including him in the authorship.) A year later I summarized the *ASCD in Retrospect* findings at a talk at the 1987 ASCD conference to an audience composed mostly of the long-time ASCD members— history grows more important to us as we grow older.

Shortly afterward an invitation from Craig Kridel of the University of South Carolina resulted in a memoir on William Heard Kilpatrick. In a 1988 issue of *Teaching Education* which assembled profiles of teaching educators, I included my favorite anecdotes about Kilpatrick. For instance, I told how at 35 I served as Bureau for Intercultural Education legman to the 75 year old philosopher in developing a John Dewey Society Yearbook, *Intercultural Attitudes in the Making*, and how he amazed me by adding my name to his as co-editor of the book. I am happy that the memoir has been selected for reprinting with minor additions in a 1996 Garland publication called *Teachers and Mentors* edited by Kridel and others.

However, rather than recollections of individuals, the memoir I really wanted to write was a report on my experiences with the John Dewey Society. My memoir of the middle years of the John Dewey Society began as a short piece and years later ended up as an *Educational Theory* essay of more than eight thousand words with forty footnotes. First contemplated by me in the mid-1980s, the writing was frequently postponed. I was spurred into action in 1991 by the publication of Daniel Tanner's highly useful *Crusade for Democracy*, a history of the early years of the John Dewey Society. Tanner's quest for survivors among the sixty-seven educational leaders who founded the John Dewey Society in 1935 had turned up only three. "If not now, when?" Reminded of my own mortality, I worked intermittently on a memoir based on more than a quarter of a century of continuous and close relationship with the Society, 1946 to 1973, a period when I had served as an elected board member, as president, and as chair-person of commissions which carried board membership. My hope was that the essay might be helpful primarily to future historians. Most useful for current members may be the conclud-ing overview of the two major types of society activities:

> The John Dewey Society currently maintains activities related to theoretical considerations in order to broaden the base of knowledge. It also explores vital social and curricular issues and problems in order to help individuals reach conclu-sions and follow through with social action. Both emphases have their proponents; dependent on the board's predilections, sometimes the pendulum swings one way and sometimes the other. Both in interrelationship are approaches worthy of support in the unending struggle for democratic education.

Essentially the memoir described the inception and develop-ment of a variety of Society activities, some "extension of knowl-edge" and some "activist."

> "Extension of knowledge" activities included *Educational Theory,* the Ohio State University Press *Studies in Educa-tional Theory,* and the Lecture Series. The "activist" activities included the original Yearbook series, *Insights,* local and regional meetings, awards, and the open discussions at the Dewey Conference. Extension of knowledge activities were of primary interest to philosophers, historians, sociologists, cur-riculum theorists, and comparative educators. Activist activi-ties were of primary interest to practitioners in curriculum, supervision, and administration, whether in school systems or universities.

Several of my friends urged me to publish the memoir in *Educational Theory,* the University of Illinois journal created by the John Dewey Society. *Educational Theory* is a refereed journal so I had an experience unusual for me, utilizing criticism by two anonymous readers, each representing the concerns and sensitivities of the co-sponsors of the journal, currently the John Dewey Society and the Philosophy of Education Society. After decades of invitations from editors to write, I had almost forgotten through personal disuse the process of referring unsolicited submissions to readers before acceptance and modifying manuscripts in response to anonymous referees.

To a writer there is a kind of satisfying closure that comes with the publication of a book. As a worker within educational associations I found something of the same kind of satisfying closure in trying my hand at supplying memoirs for the use of future historians of educational organizations. I was there, historians. This is how it looked to me, this ASCD, this JDS in the twentieth century.

Chapter Forty-Nine

WHAT
I HAVE LEARNED

O ne of the things no elder can resist is giving advice to the younger generation which, of course, pays no attention whatsoever. So I no longer even tried to resist opportunities to speak out as a septuagenarian nearing octogenarianism on what I have learned and what I believe. Better now than after Alzheimer's catches up with us.

Editor Craig Kridel gave me a first opportunity to look back by asking, "What is your advice to today's younger generation of teacher educators?" My response appeared in 1987 as the first article in the first issue of his *Teaching Education*, one of the handsomest journals ever published by the education profession. Here it is:

> *Acquire somehow a broad liberal education.* Venture into both worlds, the humanistic world of literature, the arts, the social sciences, history, philosophy, *et al*, and the scientific world of mathematics and the several physical and natural sciences. Wrestle with the tough interdisciplinary problems of humankind that cut across the arbitrary boundaries of the separate subjects. Experience widely. Travel. Grow.

> *Obtain a solid professional education.* Know your specialty but don't let it imprison you. Stress the foundations of education—philosophical, psychological, historical and social. Master needed technical skills, such as the uses of the computer, statistics, language. Explore and recognize the realities of school and society, yet keep your faith in your hopes and goals.

As early as possible, learn who you are. A teacher? A researcher? A generalist or a specialist? Are you a writer? A counselor? A community activist? An administrative facilitator? A leader of organizations? Some combination of several such elements? Do what you do best, most naturally, most joyously, whatever is most you. Welcome the rewards and avoid complaints about whatever penalties accompany being yourself. And if in midstream you decide to change roles, since that now feels right to you, do so wholeheartedly, without trepidation or reservation.

Avoid oversimplification. Two quips are helpful reminders. "Things are more complicated than most people think." "Educators have difficulty bearing more than one thing in mind simultaneously." People often pounce on aspects of the elusive truth and proclaim them to be the whole truth. In education we have been known to hop on bandwagons, adopt panaceas, obey ephemeral national reports, rediscover the wheel. Avoid oversimplifications—among them my own.

Try to make a difference. A quotation from Edmund Burke says it well: "The only thing necessary for the triumph of evil is for good men to do nothing." (Women too.) I closed *My Way of Looking At It* with "I refuse to believe that the individual doesn't count and can play no role in making a better world." Try to make a difference through having lived.

To the special issue of *The Educational Forum* commemorating the 75th anniversary of Kappa Delta Pi (the organization and I were born in the same year) I contributed along with other laureates an essay in a section which editor Yamamoto very generously titled "Counsels of the Wise." Under the title "What I Have Learned" I wrote:

As to the world, that this is the only planet that we have got. That we are all members of one family, the human family, and all members of one race, the human race. That more than science and high technology will be needed to make a livable world. That there must be a colossal gathering of forces for caring and survival.

From living I have learned something about human society, that democracy, however imperfect and beset by problems, is far preferable to any form of authoritarianism...

I have learned from personal experiences also. That the

443

family is one of humanity's most rewarding inventions and that I have been lucky in mine. That traveling while young widens horizons. That social action, though risky, can be deeply satisfying. That hard work in fields to which one is devoted can be as joyful as play. That perfectionism is an unattainable and neurosis-creating goal...

...As an educator, my specialty is curriculum, particularly the question of what knowledge is of most worth. I learned early that significant educational programs must meet the needs of learners, throw light on social realities, and foster humane values. From these curricular sources, relevant knowledge should be derived and utilized. John Dewey knew this; alas, some of his disciples and all of his opponents do not.

At the invitation of the National Association of Laboratory Schools I ventured a follow-up to my earlier pamphlet *The Laboratory School: Its Rise and Fall?* This time I tried my hand at a piece of advice to the education reform movement of the 1980s and the imperiled laboratory schools of the nation. *Laboratory Schools and the National Reports (1987)* was in essence a proposal:

> By now these proponents of national reports are aware that the curriculum of American schools is not fundamentally changed by publication of a report, however attractively packaged and highly publicized. Nor is the curriculum basically changed by legislative alignments of required credits...
>
> So there may be a new opportunity for some laboratory schools to be among the centers for implementation, research and evaluation needed for the implementation of some aspects of the national reports. Laboratory Schools are our institutions where research and experimentation can take place despite resistance from politicians, the public, and timid officialdom.

So far as I could tell my proposal had all the impact of the proverbial rose leaf falling in the Grand Canyon. The national reform reports continued to equate publication with educational change. The reformers scolded the education profession, wrote reports, and enjoyed brief moments of publicity. They provided for no trials or demonstrations of their proposals, which usually expired quietly. The Laboratory Schools continued to follow their self-defeating policies of expecting faculty members to be all things to all men—innovators, teachers, researchers, writers, disseminators, and all without help from grants or relationship to reform movements.

Perhaps my best opportunity to put into play what I had learned came through an editorial request from Kappa Delta Pi. So I joined fellow laureates Ernest L. Boyer, Theodore M. Hesburgh, John Hope Franklin, Ralph W. Tyler, and others in a collection of essays. My contribution was subtitled *A Call for Action* in the resultant 1990 pamphlet *Honor in Teaching: Reflections*. I argued:

> Major changes on four fronts must occur if the teaching profession is to be held in honor in American life. (1) We will need to put our own house in order. (2) We will need to reeducate the public as to the true curriculum fundamentals. (3) We will need to dedicate ourselves to a wider conception of the well-being of children and youth. (4) We will need to work with like-minded citizens to achieve a better society.
>
> Spelling out these four directions:
>
> [1] If we are to achieve improvements within our own house, we teachers need as a profession to have a greater say in our own affairs. More say as to materials and curriculum; more say too as to administration and management....
>
> [2] If education is to be honored, it is time for educators to be heard on curriculum. Too long the debate on education has been dominated by policy makers outside the educational community.... The time has come to turn away from quack remedies and to speak up for authentic fundamentals of curriculum development. Put most plainly, American educators should meet the needs of children and youth, help them to understand and act on imperative social realities of their time, and teach them to live a democratic way of life....
>
> [3] If education is to be honored as a profession, we must dedicate ourselves to a wider conception of the well-being of children and youth. Who else is there who can better represent children and youth? Children and youth are our constituency....
>
> [4] While being advocates who **lead** in the struggle for better lives for children and youth, educators also can continue to work as citizens for a better society for Americans of all ages and a better world for all inhabitants of this planet.

My essay also summarized the criticisms of the reform

reports of the 80s which I had been making throughout the decade:

> Though both excellence and equality should characterize American schools, many of the reform reports of the 1980s focused on achieving excellence and rendered only lip service to achieving equal educational opportunity in American life for Blacks, Hispanics and children of the poor. Proposals for improving the learning of the 3 Rs often did not recognize the central importance of meaningful content and the power of the family environment. Reports such as *A Nation at Risk* singled out, from among the many possible goals for American education, economic competition against societies such as Japan's; other goals for education were minimized.
>
> Reform reports have often recommended more of the same —more of the content and methods that haven't worked well before, more required courses, more credits for graduation, more remedial work to teach what hasn't been learned because of its meaninglessness. Legislators have responded by joining the numbers game—more graduation requirements, longer school years, more time on task. (The use of the word "task" is a characteristic misconception of the proper relationship of teachers and students in the educational enterprise.) The Eighties were the decade in which more of what wasn't succeeding was mistaken for improvement.

In summarizing I risked repeating myself. But I know no other way of affirming my basic beliefs than through setting forth what I have learned.

Chapter Fifty

MILESTONES

I 'd like to think that the good things that began to happen to me professionally on the eve of the 1990s were the result of my having written on what I had experienced and learned and now believe. But I don't think this is the way it really happened. The good things were longer in the making.

For instance, election to Ohio State University's Hall of Fame. The University began the recognition program in the mid-1980s by honoring the giants who had lived their long careers at Ohio State. Named in 1986 were Boyd H. Bode, philosophy; Edgar Dale, cinema; H. Gordon Hullfish, philosophy; Delbert Oberteuffer, physical education; John Ramseyer, administration; and Laura Zirbes, elementary education. All were my colleagues during my decade at Ohio State. Harold B. Alberty, curriculum, my advisor, and Keith Tyler, audio-visual, followed in 1987. Of the long-timers, Harold P. Fawcett, University School mathematics, and Louis E. Raths, evaluation, were among those named in 1988 and 1989.

Having honored those who had stayed with Ohio State and built an education program which had earned national recognition, the awards began going to a second tier, those who had left Ohio State University for careers elsewhere. Ralph W. Tyler, curriculum theorist, and I were among the four 1989 selections.

The Hall of Fame ceremony in 1989 was a pleasant reception and banquet at the Faculty Club. Ohio State University faculty members presented biographical encomiums while the recipients so honored tried to assume facial expressions appropriate to the occasion and to decide on the proper balance of humor and seriousness to employ in their responses.

Despite our geographical separation, all of our children, Jon, Barbara, Roy, and son-in-law Bob, attended this command ceremony. In our free time we six took a sentimental journey to the many places Bee and I had lived during our eight years in Columbus neighborhoods during the 1930s and early 1940s. Our residences were motley. Our first, 464-1/2 Vermont Place (the one-half meant the second floor), called back memories of parties with new found faculty friends at which we all hunted for ghosts in the cupola above our circular bedroom. East Duncan Street's second floor was where my Danube book was written and where Jon came home after his birth. California Avenue promoted us to whole house renting. We have many memories of East Cleft Road out in the county (near the dam that James Thurber immortalized in *The Day the Dam Broke*). They include adding a girl baby and a dog to the family. Barbara was born the year of summer teaching at Northwestern University. The dog was named Doc, so called because we thought we should have at least one doctor in the family and it didn't look as though it was going to be me. Leaving the rural area we went back to the city to Midgard Road which was cheek and jowl with a railroad track.

Our Columbus residences culminated in the purchase of a little house on Beechwold Boulevard. It was topped by an attic-like second floor which we converted into a study. When we bought this house for $4,300 in 1942 the mortgage people had only one question: "Your credit rating seems very good. But why did you move so often?" We explained that we traveled during summers in Europe or on the East Coast and avoided paying unnecessary rent. Appeased, they nodded.

All these shrines we toured with much taking of pictures while the present occupants viewed us with puzzlement from behind twitching curtains. "Why would they want to take pictures of our house?"

On my home campus of Indian State University there were rumblings throughout the 1980s concerning what to do about a man who, though long retired, still showed up at this office fairly regularly, left his office door open for faculty members who might want advice on their writing, and continued to write and publish his books and articles—and all this while not on the payroll. Each winter he went away to Puerto Rico and each spring he came back for the annual ASCD Conference held somewhere in America. Eventually the faculty made a decision to institutionalize him.

So the College of Education's Willey Colloquium Committee, organized to perpetuate the memory of the good but short-lived Dean Richard Willey, was authorized to create and develop an annual Van Til Lecture as part of their responsibility. Simultaneously, the Department of Secondary Education considered establishing a scholarship fund, then had the better idea that an annual writing award might be more appropriate. So a Van Til Writing Award was established to go to a graduate student in the School of Education whose writing was judged the most meritorious of the year. The award was to take the form of a plaque and certificate and, more materially, a check for $400. The Lectures began in 1989; the Writing Award began in 1990.

The program distributed at the lectures often reads: "The Annual Van Til Lecture at Indiana State University was initiated by the faculty of the School of Education in the late 1980s in order to honor William Van Til, Coffman Distinguished Professor Emeritus of Education, by presenting lectures relating to and extending his professional interests and contributions." This concept of extending my interests and contributions differentiates the lecture series from the other lectures sponsored by the Willey Committee.

I was invited to give the first lecture in the spring of 1989. Since my essay, *Restoring Honor to the Teaching Profession: A Call for Action,* was still a year away from publication within a Kappa Delta Pi pamphlet by laureates and since the content represented exactly what I wanted to say to the profession right then, I chose this subject for the opening lecture of the series. I hoped to set a precedent that would encourage lectures that would be calls for action on educational problems. ISU's president emeritus Alan C. Rankin contributed a generous introduction to the Coffman Distinguished Professor whom he had employed in 1967. We had a full house for the talk and the reception.

Lecturers during ensuing years were Asa Hilliard III on abuses of intelligence testing; Mary Anne Raywid on alternative schools; John H. Lounsbury on middle school curriculum; William H. Schubert on teacher lore; and Carl D. Glickman on school renewal. Each reflected and extended some emphasis from my professional past: Hilliard racial and intercultural relations; Raywid my Ohio State University School teaching; Lounsbury our book on the junior high school years; Schubert my autobiography; and Glickman the Illinois Secondary School Curriculum Program field work.

The lecture for 1995 was by Jon Van Til, a respected researcher and writer on voluntary action and nonprofit organizations. I had long been committed to voluntarism and activism and I had suggested him to the committee as a possible lecturer for the year following my death. Committee member Greg Ulm had responded in effect, "How about now?" Jon titled his lecture "Education in the Farewell State: The Challenge of Voluntary Action." He described both opportunities and limitations for voluntary action in an America where anti-government ideologues were replacing the "welfare state" with the "farewell state."

Most of the seven lectures have appeared in Indiana State University's journal *Contemporary Education*. At this writing, plans are underway for a pamphlet which would bring them together with a transcript of Ulm's audio-visual interview with me on the lectureship taped for use in classes and by the lecture committee when I am no longer "available," as Greg delicately puts it.

The annual lecture is scheduled for a spring day following our return from Puerto Rico and is usually followed by a reception or lunch at the university or at Lake Lure. It is always preceded by presentation of the annual writing award, the creation of the Department of Secondary Education. In 1989, the Department raised through a single appeal more than $7,000, and has since used the interest to present its annual monetary award of $400 to the chosen writer. A departmental committee studies the dozen or so entries, unidentified as to their author or department, and selects the best three to five, asks for my appraisal of these as a non-voting reader, then makes its choice independently. Miraculously, the committee and the non-voting reader so far have been in total agreement on the winners. The titles of best writing of the year reflect education's multiplicity as well as the committee's objectivity as to the winners' departments. Topics have included "Are They Teaching Grammar in the Junior High? (Do they Want To?)"; "Children and Race"; "Buberian Thought, Education, and the Impact Teacher"; "HIV/ Aids, Confidentiality and Duty to Warn"; "The Marginality of African-American Adolescents"; "Democracy in a Prison Setting: Success Behind Bars."

One of the reasons for establishing the writing award was that writing on education usually generates little feedback to its author. So I was grateful as the world neared the 1990s to find that some of my own past efforts were still remembered. John A. Beineke took time out from his writing of a definitive biography of William Heard Kilpatrick to interview me in 1989 for *Social Education*, the journal of the National Council for the Social Studies. The interview compared past and present reform movements, the resurgence of interest in John Dewey's ideas, and the directions in which education should go. A few years later, Beineke decided to do a reconsideration of a 1962 article on progressive education which I had written for the *Saturday Review*, a magazine then widely read by the thoughtful lay public. The article had evoked controversy in the form of letters to the editor and had been widely reprinted in more than a dozen education anthologies.

"Is Progressive Education Obsolete?" had contended:

As the inescapable queries reassert themselves and the tentative proposals of the varied interpretations of progressive education are considered, educators will find it necessary to utilize the insights of Dewey, Bode, Counts, and Kilpatrick. An education which takes into account the individual, society, and values—an education which builds upon the soundest possible scholarship derivative from psychological, social, and philosophical foundations—is imperative in developing a curriculum appropriate for twentieth-century man.

The central questions posed and the relevant contributions toward workable answers to our times made by such interpreters of the progressive movement in education are not obsolete. They must and will persist. In time, they will be embodied in the form of new proposals for modern education, new syntheses which build upon our predecessors, as is common in the world of ideas. The over-anxious grave diggers, and those who currently give them comfort, will discover as this twentieth-century moves along that what they have mistaken for a corpse is very much alive.

In his 1993 "Reconsideration" article for *Teaching Education* Beineke concluded that "a prognostication similar to Van Til's could be ventured today that another period of progressivism is inevitable." He cited substantial evidence in support of his thesis.

Despite the political war cry of the 1992 presidential campaign—"It's the economy, stupid"—evidence continues to mount that humankind does not live by bread alone. Plaques and cups and certificates festoon the residences of golfers, tennis players, and other assorted awards winners. My trophies take the form of recognitions from fellow educators. The one I am proudest to have received reads, "The John Dewey Society presents to William Van Til the Outstanding Achievement Award in Education 1991 in recognition of your contributions to education and culture that reflect the spirit and vision of John Dewey."

When I was 80, Bee and I traveled to San Francisco and Chicago for the 1991 meetings of the John Dewey Society at which the award was presented. Lawrence A. Cremin, the historian and a Teachers College president, posthumously received a similar award that year from the Society.

The large handsome Dewey plaque has survived the great office purge of 1994 when Bee and I sent off the bulk of my archives to Stanford University's Paul Hanna Collection on the Role of Education in the Twentieth Century at the Hoover Institution, and to the University of South Carolina's Museum of Education. The plaque dominates my small study at home, grudgingly sharing its space with diplomas, certificates from the OSU Hall of Fame and the Kappa Delta Pi Laureate chapter, plaques from presidencies, and cherished letters from Adlai E. Stevenson and Boyd H. Bode.

Another reminder that all writing on education is not necessarily destined to fade away fast came in 1994 when a book that John H. Lounsbury, Gordon F. Vars, and I had written, first published in 1961, was spotlighted at the National Middle Schools Association convention. The co-authors of *Modern Education for the Junior High School Years* participated in a panel, billed by the NMSA as "a historical event," to discuss the ideas proposed in the book and its role as a predecessor of the middle school movement. Questions raised by the large and friendly audience ranged from our opinions of the just published *The Bell Curve* (we were highly critical) to our predictions as to the future of the middle school movement which John hailed as a renaissance of progressive education. John and Gordon were much at home at the convention; I was a newcomer. John is generally acknowledged to be one of the three initiators of the middle school movement and Gordon has been faithful to the development of the core curriculum for the middle years through the National Association for Core Curriculum which he fathered. As for me, during the panel I claimed that if they were the fathers then I was the grandfather of the middle school movement since both men were my former doctoral students and close professional associates. The audience enjoyed the genealogy.

These are some of the pleasant milestones passed along the way as I moved into my eighties. Yet inevitably some milestones are reached which, rather than carrying kudos, indicate the reality of mortality. Such was a milestone I reached in 1994. I closed my office at the university. For the seventeen years since my 1977 supposed retirement I had maintained an office at Indiana State University, though my visits became progressively fewer. Bee and I described the milestone this way in 1994 in our annual Christmas letter to our friends:

> Closing his office at the University was a mixed emotions experience for Bill. In his sixty-one year career as an educator and a writer he taught thousands of students, worked with hundreds of colleagues, wrote tens of thousands of communications, talked to hundreds of audiences, and wrote almost three hundred publications. Now, by his own free choice, it was time to discard many files and ship off to future researchers more than 20 massive cartons for the archives of two universities and two educational organizations. The Indiana State University library acquired 1,065 education books from his shelves; a few books were brought home. He turned in his keys. And no birds sang.

Chapter Fifty-One

THE GUINNESS BOOK
OF WORLD RECORDS

las, the statistics on my teaching and writing cited in our
1994 Xmas letter will never qualify me for the *Guinness
Book of World Records*. I am sure a legion of people have
taught more students over a longer period of years and
until later in life. As to writing on education, many educator/
authors surpass my feeble numbers. For instance, *Guinness*
might consider among my own friends Louise Rosenblatt whose
Literature as Exploration, written in the 1930s, is still in print in
a new edition in the 1990s, or Harold Shane whose publications
must have totaled about 600.

But *Guinness* might consider me in a quite different category—marital records. No, I cannot compete in number of wives
with Eastern potentates or early Mormon polygamists or even
with old Tommy Manville or the Gabor sisters. Yet I challenge
the world to find another man who carries in his wallet a card
which lists sixty years of celebration of his wedding anniversary
with his one and only wife. *Guinness* editors, please take note.

The card—to tell the truth it has grown to two cards, both
sides—originated after the earliest wedding anniversaries Bee
and I celebrated. The first, in 1936, occurred in the luxurious
atmosphere of the Grand Hotel Steiner in Prague just after visits
to Bee's Czechoslovakian relatives and before our foldboat cruise
on the Elbe River. The second, in 1937, was in Yugoslavia in a
delightful pension perched on a cliff overlooking the translucent
Adriatic which stretched to the city walls of red-roofed Dubrovnik.
The third was in Ottawa after we foldboated the rustic Rideau

Canal from the St. Lawrence River to the Canadian capital. And the fourth, in 1939, was a joyous reuniting in a handsome Manhattan hotel after Bee's summer spent with infant Jon at her parents' Long Island bungalow at Lake Ronkonkoma and after my return from youth hosteling by train and bike across Canada and the United States. (I carried with me the first draft of a prospective travel book, *Rolling Youth Hostel*, intended as a successor to *The Danube Flows Through Fascism*, but never published.)

So our anniversary card began in four different settings and led to our resolve that an annual Summer Celebration be held on or near August 23rd and 24th, Bee's birthday and our wedding anniversary respectively. Whenever possible, the Summer Celebration was to take place in some exotic locale.

So when our fifth wedding anniversary rolled around, in what intriguingly unusual place did we find ourselves? In Athens! But it was not Athens, Greece. It was Athens, Ohio, where we went to the movies and saw *Blondie Has Servant Trouble*. A literary friend described this fifth year debacle as symbolic of the decline of American marriage. We denied the canard.

Yet it is true that for a long while our Summer Celebrations were limited to locales seldom deemed exotic. For we had three war babies, Jon born in 1939 when World War II began, Barbara in 1941 when the United States entered, and Roy in 1945 when Germany and Japan surrendered. Our Summer Celebrations became baby showings at our parents' homes on Long Island. The farthest afield we traveled was to Springfield and Kansas City in Missouri for my Northwestern University-sponsored workshops to which our growing family journeyed despite gas rationing and packed trains. Indeed, the only notation on the anniversary card for 1945 reads starkly: "Car broke down."

In the postwar years the card listed Broadway shows and restaurants interspersed with such offbeat places as Central City, Colorado (where we saw Mae West in a play); San Diego and Tijuana (after my summer teaching at USC); and an anniversary aboard the S.S. Ryndam (we were enroute to a European sabbatical along with Jon 15, Barbara 13, and Roy 9).

During my NYU decade we limited our anniversary range largely to inns in the Poconos, for NYU expected me to teach summers in Puerto Rico and at Washington Square. In 1960 we were the guests at a gala 25th wedding anniversary party with friends and relatives at the home of Bee's brother and sister-in-law in the rolling hills of the Connecticut countryside. We topped off the event with a stay in Atlantic City with Roy.

But after the last of our children left home as Barbara married, 1967, and Roy graduated from Swarthmore, 1966, our Summer Celebration card went out of control. Bereft of reason, it chronicled—hold on to your hats at the curves—San Antonio fair, Monterey, Denmark/Scandinavia, Gatlinburg/Smokies, Mackinac, Williamsburg/Outer Banks, St. Louis, Sugarbush, Greece, Boston/Cape Cod, Cincinnati. Pause for a breath and a forty-fifth anniversary in 1980 at friend Turney's at Lake Lure where Bee was completely surprised with a book of letters titled *Dear Bee* solicited from friends by me. Then—here we go again—New Harmony, St. Louis second appearance (in a rut?), Knoxville fair, Colorado Rockies, Canadian Rockies, Hawaii, Mississippi River, Pacific Northwest, Chapel Hill, Alaska, Lake Weld in Maine. Punctuate the second list with family parties in Terre Haute and on Long Island celebrating the fiftieth anniversary and accompanied by a book of letters Barbara gathered largely from my professional friends.

But not all of our Summer Celebrations were happy occasions. Darker days were also observed as in 1990 when my dizziness related to an inner ear problem caused the card to report succinctly "sick in the head," and in 1993 when a knee operation took place precisely on Bee's birthday and the card reported "knee replaced, not Bee."

Season the trips and parties with quieter observations at home with our adult children, our grandchildren, and my mother whom we had finally persuaded to give up the Corona house to which she had tenaciously clung for 57 years. She was 82 when she came with us in Mountain Lakes and then to Terre Haute and 89 when she fell. Unable to walk, she was cared for in a local nursing home where one or the other of us visited her daily until her death at 93.

We decided to celebrate Bee's birthday and our sixtieth anniversary in 1995 with Jon's, Barbara's, and Roy's families at Lake Lure. As early as possible a date was set; it was for a summer weekend representing a consensus among all individual family members. Happily the weekend of July 28-30 stretched beyond its intended boundaries. The Maine delegation made up of son Roy and granddaughter Desi prepared for Thursday night a Greek dinner with feta cheese. The next night the Michiganders led by daughter Barbara and son-in-law Bob offered a typical outdoor American barbecue of hamburgers, hot dogs, *et al.* On Saturday the Pennsylvania branch led by daughter-in-law Trudy and son Jon created grilled chicken breasts with herbs and basmati rice, an Indian dish. Sunday was a day of dispersal so Bee's well stocked refrigerator came into play. Roy stayed on awhile after his daughter Desi flew home.

Sleeping presented few problems, even though Timmy Schell, Roy's best friend from Mountain Lakes High School days, joined us with his wife and three children for a night on their way west. For everybody from 50 to 84 slept in our house and everybody 25 and under slept in the screened summer house on the hill a short walk from a vintage outhouse. At two AM on the first night of occupancy a thunderstorm threatened ominously and all residents of the summer house, including the Schell children, decamped and cluttered our living room and family room on couches and in their sleeping bags.

Recreation was in the tradition of doing your own thing and was pursued singly or in groups. Water sports included fishing, diving, swimming, floating in aquatic armchairs, setting records for standing on floating mats, pedal boating, sailing, and voyaging on Lake Lure in Long Island Duck V. On dry land some chose tennis at nearby Rose-Hulman Institute courts or golf on an improvised course on our lawn or all-girl trips to the Honey Creek mall to shop and look over the local boys. Bob in his role as Paul Bunyan and Roy as Jungle Jim chose as their recreation fighting back the encroaching wilderness; they succeeded in virtually defoliating our property. Some—and we won't try to identify anyone here—took afternoon naps. There was much talking and sharing and picture taking and very little TV.

We convened for ceremonials thrice. Friday night we presented to collegians our annual checks to help with education costs. This year they went toward Laura's sophomore year at Lake Superior State, Desi's freshman year at Princeton, and in recognition for Ross' having become 18 and being about to embark on a year of travel and work before entering Penn State. (Linda A. had already completed programs at Michigan State and Western Michigan and was now a school social worker; Claire was still in high school; Justin, in absentia from our celebration, had just found his first job after graduation from Colby.) All three honorees signed in ceremoniously on a chart which runs from Linda A's first year in college in 1988 to Claire's graduate school year which is projected to be 2001. Then we all played a sport invented by the Van Til family, living room bocci. Try it sometime; it's not patented. Your equipment is two lines of yarn at each end of your living room carpet and three tennis balls (differentiated by color or markings) for each competing doubles team. Your goal is getting closest to the yarn line without crossing it.

The Saturday afternoon gathering was audio-visual. Slides featured five of our grandchildren during their visits this past winter to us in Puerto Rico. All had spent long hours on the beaches and walked the rain forest trail atop El Yunque. But their choices of options selected from a list of possibilities were quite different. Ross and Claire chose a nature preserve trip through mangrove swamps near El Faro lighthouse; Desi and friend Nina a hike to the fort El Morro and through Old San Juan; and Linda A and Laura a day at the races at El Commandante.

After slides we gambled that cousinly supportiveness would be stronger than cousinly rivalry by showing a video of Desi's masterly performance as Emily in the graveyard scene of Thornton Wilder's *Our Town* produced by her local community theater. I have seen *Our Town* at least four or five times but the tears came anyway.

Then we ran Jon's lighthearted introduction to his Van Til lecture in the spring of 1995. After suggesting that Kato Kaelin would have made a better lecturer, Jon said:

> In all candor I must confess to a fear that it may have made a mistake in selecting me as the second member of my family to deliver the Van Til Lecture. To be sure I do not fault your selection, seven years ago, of William Van Til as the inaugural lecturer for this series. But surely you would have gotten a livelier speech today from his other son, Roy Van Til, Associate Professor of Economics at the University of Maine. The best speaker in the family, Roy has also inherited my father's gift

of packaging institutions pithily: you would have heard much today about life at Ghettoblast High School, Suburban Comfort Middle School, and Polyglot Prep. Or if a knowledgeable talk about the realities of special education were in order, Barbara Van Til Nichols, M.A., could have delighted you with tales of her many years of successful teaching in the public schools of Bay City, Michigan. The most experienced classroom teacher in the family, Barbara's innovative and imaginative approach to her special students would have given you a variety of ideas for enlivening even the most challenging classrooms. And, as most of you know, you really missed out not asking Beatrice B. Van Til to give her long-awaited lecture on "An Insider's View of the Private Side of Progressive Education." The most sophisticated observer of educational politics in the family, my mother would have drawn upon her own experience as a classroom teacher, a school board member, and education's hostess with the mostest. Her speech would have delighted and enlightened you with its sections on "What William Kilpatrick heard," "Why John changed his name from Huey to Dewey (instead of Louis)," "The day they caught an H. Gordon Hull-fish in Lake Lure."

The afternoon showing concluded with a world premiere, Greg Ulm's interview with me on the Indiana State University lectureship. It had been brought to the house the day before and I had not seen it. So I feared the worst from this discriminating and potentially derisive audience. But the technician who produced the film, shot on our sundeck with the lake in the background, was highly skilled. He had cut my occasional fluffs and stumbles as well as excised the roar of the National Guard planes that occasionally thundered by. The jackets and covers of books I had written were nicely dispersed and he had firmly edited out whatever he judged to be extraneous to my career or to the lecture series. In deference to our audience, we confined the showing to the autobiographical section rather than continued into the description of past lectures. We held the whole program of presentation via audio-visuals to one hour and fifteen minutes and managed not to lose any members of our audience to the inviting lake.

Whether *Guinness* includes me or not, I'll keep right on carrying my anniversary card(s) in my wallet. But the Summer Celebration of 1995 will be a hard one to summarize in one line.

Chapter Fifty-Two

MEMORIES

T he final convening on Saturday night was the apex of the sixtieth Summer Celebration. It was a Jon, Barbara, Roy production. After Bee and I had been smothered with gifts and love, each of our trio took over.

Jon is currently adding genealogy to his many interests. He talked directly to the younger generation. Through words and charts he traced back to the 18th century Bee's Czech antecedents and the Scotch forebears of my Dutch, Irish, English and Scotch mix. He made the ancestors of the young ones come alive, as he talked about people like their great-great grandmother Susannah Rex MacLean, widowed and wandering with her brood of children, including my mother aged five, from Canada toward New York City.

Barbara and Roy each read excerpts from letters which Bee and I had written over the past many years. Some were informative; many just fun. Some we remembered; others Bee and I had completely forgotten. Here is a sampling from Barbara's "Mom and Dad" file of cards and letters. Some she read aloud; others she marked for later perusal by us:

From Dad in 1982, an except from letters to the three families: Sometime in the 21st century, when your children read about the winter of 1982 they will say, "Why did our crazy parents choose to live in the Northeast and Midwest and endure that winter in the years before good king Ronald Reagan renamed that area American Siberia and made it a penal colony for criminals, food stamp recipients, and liberals?" Their sun belt spouses will then shrug and say in their native tongue *"quien sabe?"* and roll over on the beach to leisure their *farnientes*.

From Mom to me in May 1973:
I was thinking of our three young ones the other day and was feeling so pleased at the way each developed—different yet very much alike in terms of their depth of character, seriousness of purpose, really great human beings. Later Dad and I agreed that indeed we were very fortunate and very happy.

From Dad in 1977 before he and Mom spent the first winter of their retirement in Florida:
Santa Claus dropped into my office the other day for a visit and told me that he had decided to place under the palm tree in Florida an envelope containing $125 for each of the three families to help with transportation to Florida. I tried to explain to him that one family was coming by dog sled pulled by two giant handsome boxers, that another planned to make no restroom stops between the Canadian border and the tropics, and that a third contemplated a drawing room on a parlor car. Thus their needs would be different. However Santa Claus explained that he was a capitalist institution and found the Marxist pattern of "from each according to his abilities; to each according to his needs" too confusing. So count on finding the envelope under the tree.

To Laura and Linda A from Mom after a 1988 cruise:
We are now back in San Juan waiting to disembark. I won a prize for being the *oldest* grandma. Many looked older but they just wouldn't tell.

From Dad in a January 1990 letter to the three families after the hurricane Hugo hit Puerto Rico:
Hugo's handiwork is still evident in eyeless boarded-up Playa Azul apartments, fences down, trees down along the beach, pool drained, shelters for homeless, great slabs of sidewalk torn up, and stories, stories, stories, stories.

From my indomitable Mom in 1993, a short time after her knee operation:
Suddenly I see the light at the end of the tunnel. No arthritic pain at all—just quite a bit of hurt as I struggle to regain the strength in the musculature surrounding the knee. It has been a truly remarkable experience. In a sense a very rewarding experience—top surgeon, wonderful caring nurses, therapists,

lab technicians, volunteer workers, a priest who visited me—
the list goes on and on.

A 1989 postcard from Dad from La Quinta in Indianapolis where Mom and Dad regularly stay before flying to Puerto Rico. Bob and I happened to be staying that weekend at Marriott Suites in Downers Grove, Illinois:
Dear Bar & Bob,
So here you are at a luxury hotel waited on hand and foot while your poor old parents are living on welfare checks from the government and staying once a year in small motels with Spanish names and free post cards. A sad situation. But enjoy.
—Love, Pere

A card from Mom in 1992:
The thought that just struck me—what a wonderful family I have and whatever would I do without them.

Now Roy follows with a sampling from his "Mere and Pere" collection of cards and letters (our nicknames date back to his junior high years):

From Pere in a postcard from Arizona to 10-year old Justin in 1983:
Justin, if you were an Indian instead of a German-Italian-Czech-British Isles-Dutch kid, you'd be playing ball in a small nearby arena that I visited which is even older than Fenway Park—unless the home of the Red Sox is more than 900 years old, which it appears to be.

From Mere in 1989, a sample of her amazing ability to seize upon the positive and spread her caring touch to the family:
This anniversary should be an especially happy day for all of you. You have come through a very difficult time so far this year. Now you can look at Desiree, completely well, and Justin, a great sixteen-year-old. Roy has become an important member of the faculty and is happy with his work. Linda B has a job in which she has made a great contribution.

From Pere in 1986, in a letter to Desi as she prepared for her trip to the national finals in the Odyssey of the Mind competition:
Enjoy. It's spring and you're young and there's a wonderful world west of Vienna, Maine, for you to experience. When you lose, cry a little and get over it fast. If through a miracle you win, don't sign a contract for starring in Hollywood without consulting your family!

An early Puerto Rico stay in 1979. First, from Mere:
A light shower is falling. From our balcony we can see for miles and miles, following the isolated, widely scattered showers that move quickly along, moved by the prevailing easterlies. The ocean today is like a serene lake. Sunday in bright, hot sunshine, the waves were over ten feet high and the surf was so strong only the very young and very foolhardy ventured in...

Second, from Pere—as if you couldn't guess:
It is time for the small picture of life at Playa Azul: For instance, today I was studying the varied highly tropical bikinis on the beach and crying out, as is my custom, "Shameless hussies! Fie!" Mere contributed one of her one-sentence gem-like summaries, "Bob would lose his eyeballs." We now have made enduring lifelong friendships with people whose names we will forget by March. Mere of course takes the lead by going up to people on the beach or the elevators and saying, "Spik Englesa?" (She thinks this is Spanish and I don't have the heart to disillusion her) to which the person responds, "Yes, most people in New Hampshire do."

From Mere in 1980, after a rare visit to Puerto Rico from the New England branch of the family:
We miss you! I think of how Roy and Linda B dove through the big waves and how Justin rode in with the surf, and how Desi laughed and wanted to go out deeper. Let's look forward to another time in the future.

From Pere, responding to a not infrequent letter of self-doubt from his younger son in 1979:
I notice that you deprecate yourself in your letters. You shouldn't. As Thoreau says, you march to a different drummer. There is nothing superior or inferior about choosing a different drummer.... Hang in there, we love you and respect your chosen drumbeat.

From Mere in same letter:
I just want to underline what Dad has said above—you are a truly beautiful human being and I love you very much.

From Pere to the grandchildren January 2, 1993, urging them to become the next generation of tireless communicators:
I am writing to you from the Enchanted Island on a beautiful sunny day on the first weekend of 1993. No, I am NOT writing to remind you that January 8 is my 82nd birthday for I realize

you have already mailed me an Expensive Present (like a Mercedes-Benz) or a lovely one dollar card or at least some lousy scrap of paper, torn from an old notebook and with doodling on it without any signature. No, I've never given any thought to my coming birthday which is January 8 when there will be a full moon and Elvis who shares my birthday will return as a spirit. By the way, I had a nice birthday card from him.

From Pere, a comment on aircraft:
We came to the Virgin Islands on Prinair, an airline maintained with Scotch tape and paper clips. I told Mere the plane was reliable for it behaved well throughout the Spanish-American War.

From Mere in 1993, a few lines that show her optimism and her resolve to Carpe every Diem that comes her way:
There are many changes here at Playa Azul—signs of aging all around, and illness. But thank heavens some things stay the same like the glorious expanse of ocean I am looking at right this moment and the beach and the warm water and good friends.

From Mere in 1981:
We rode out into the dark Caribbean, between islands, glimpsing views into isolated tiny islands well out from the land. I only saw one life preserver on the boat and sure hoped that we wouldn't overturn. The Phosphorescent Bay was an interesting phenomenon—when you dipped into the water and let the water run through your fingers it was like the stars. And when one looked overhead, the stars were brilliant. I sure wished Roy was along to give me his wonderful lecture on the stars.

From Mere and Pere in the 1986 Christmas letter:
Let us continue, each in his or her own way, to work toward peace on earth and good will toward all fellow human beings— the shining goals we all reaffirm in greetings during the Christmas season. For us, this means opposition to the suicidal arms race, to abuses of power by leaders, to indifference to poverty and racial injustice. We still think it is better to light a candle than to curse the darkness.

The last convening of our sixtieth Summer Celebration then closed with a joint letter to us from Roy, Barbara and Jon, obviously drawn up by Roy:

Dear Mere and Pere,

You have used words for most of this century to convey lovingly to others your great wisdom, extraordinary kindness, infectious humor, inspiring love, activist spirit, boundless optimism, insatiable curiosity about the splendor of this planet, and your infinite decency and sense of fair play. Those hundreds of thousands of words have brought unmatched joy and love and laughter to us for so many decades. Thank you for the countless letters, phone calls, and conversations. Our three humble words are all we can offer in return: We love you!

Happy Anniversary, and keep those elegant and outrageous words coming for many years to come.

With love and gratitude,

—Roy, Barbara, and Jon

The cars and planes carrying our loved ones left on Sunday, except for Roy who kept on pushing back the jungle. He left on Wednesday. We were quiet for a long time afterward with our memories.

Today is the first day of the rest of my life.

INDEX

Frasier, George Willard, 112-119
Frazier, Alexander, 355-356
Freire, Paolo, 395-396
Frymier, Jack, 369, 438
Furness, Betty, 322

G

Gage, Nathaniel, 207
Garland, 439
George Peabody College (*see* Peabody College)
Gibboney, Richard, 230
Gilchrist, Robert S., 122, 180
Giles, Harry Herman (Mike), 133-134, 143, 160, 190, 201
Giles, Mary, 127-128, 133-134
Gill, Margaret, 289, 291
Glickman, Carl D., 450
Goodlad, John I., 391
Goslin, Willard E., 227-229, 232, 235, 239-242, 260
Grambs, Jean, 409
"Great Human Issues of Our Times" series, 259, 269
Greece, 402
Greystone Press, 164, 417
Griffiths, Daniel E., 330-331, 334
Grobman, Hulda, 277
Groebli, John, 230
Guinness Book of World Records, 454-463

H

Hackett, William, 292-293, 320-321, 342, 419
Hall of Fame, Ohio State University, 447-448, 452
members, 447
Hand, Harold, 103, 199, 203-205, 207-209, 215, 321-322, 328
Hanna, Paul, 452

Harap, Henry, 199, 202, 209
Harper, 190, 193-194, 417
Hartshorn, Merrill, 282
Haskew, L.D., 315
Hass, Glen, 284, 367, 419
Havighurst, Robert J., 391
Hawaii ASCD, 292-293, 294, 317
Hedges, William D., 230, 323
Heller, Trudy, 397, 414, *especially chapters 51, 52*
Henderson, Kenneth, 208-210
Herring, John, 104, 108, 112, 117
High school teaching, farewell to, 171-180 (*see also* University School, Ohio State)
Highlander Folk School, 219-220, 222-224, 272, 287
Hill, Henry H., 226-229, 232-235, 260, 262, 271
Hilliard III, Asa, 450
History of Education Society (HES), 366-367
Hitler, Adolf, 149-150, 161, 163, 167-168, 237
Hobbs, Mary, 268
Hobbs, Nicholas, 228-229, 232-233, 235, 268
Holt, 320-321
Honor in Teaching: Reflections, 444-445, 449
laureate contributors, 445
Hook, Sidney, 332
Hoover Institution (California), 452
Horton, Myles, 272, 287
Houghton Mifflin, 341-348, 393-394, 405
editorial committee, 341
authors, 341-342, 417, 419
Houses, 11-17, 133-134, 181-182, 186, 187-191, 207, 267, 338-339, 375-376, 448, 456-459
Hudson River, 155-156, 162
Hullfish, H. Gordon, 178, 200, 238

P

Palacios, Fernando, 380
Pallai, David, 408
Pal O Mine Club, 91, 93, 132
Paris in the Spring, 138-147
Parker, Francis W., 331
Payne, John, 295, 297, 300, 330, 334
Peabody College, 226-235, 247, 258-260, 266-272
    faculty, 231-235, 259, 267-269, 404
Peace Action, 160-162, 170, 287
Peckham, Earl, 276
Perceiving Behaving Becoming, 438
Perkins, Maxwell, 152, 342, 394, 418-419, 421
Persepolis, 298, 307
Persia, (*see* Iran)
Phenix, Phil, 326
Phi Delta Kappa, 362, 401, 431-432
Phi Delta Kappan, 134, 343-344, 362, 378, 381, 390-391, 397-398, 409-410, 418-419 (*see also* "One Way of Looking at It")
Philosophy of Education Society (PES), 366-367, 441
Platte, DeGroff, 230
Polynesia (Tahiti, Samoa, Fiji), 380-382
Pomeroy, Edward C., 366-367
Pop, a story, 69-72
Prejudiced—How Do People Get That Way? (pamphlet), 322
Professor, the young, 203-217
Professors of Curriculum, 287
Progressive education, *especially chapters 13, 14, 15, 16, 17, 21, 24, 25, 28, 32*
Progressive Education Association (PEA), 176, 199, 208, 237, 280-281, 285-287, 379
Puerto Rico, 274, 345, 408, 422-429, 433, 458
    friends and helpers, 427-429, 433
    Playa Azul, 427-429, 433
    our second home, 422-429, 433, 458
    University of, 422

R

Radical Caucus, 370 (*see also* Association for Supervision and Curriculum Development)
Rankin, Alan C., 334-335, 363, 424, 449
Raths, Louis, 160, 176
Raywid, Mary Anne, 399-400, 419, 449
Reactionary forces, against, 236-246
Reading
    childhood, 33-36, 41, 76
    Columbia College, 78-79, 80, 82-83, 95, 101
    high school, 40-41, 76
    short story course, 72
Regan, Paul, 295, 304, 395
Rehage, Kenneth, 391
Replogle, Vernon, 212, 401
Retirement, 395, 397-401, 402-441
Revolts, 1967-1973,
    black, 349-351
    student, 349-351
Rickover, Hyman, 289, 338
Rideau Canal, 158-160, 162, 164
Rinehart, 320-321
Robertson, Jack, 276
Robinson, Phil C., 438
Roeber, Edward, 335, 375
Rolling Youth Hostel, 162-163, 164-165, 455
Roosevelt, Eleanor, 108, 173
Rosenblatt, Louise (Ratner), 454

Index

48, 50-55, 61-62, 64-65, 72, 168, 247, 275, 278, 343-344, 348, 456, 560

Van Til, Florence Josephine (Shean), 12-13, 16, 19, 26, 43-44, 48, 50-51, 54, 61, 106, 247, 344

Van Til, Jacob, 3-6, 13-15, 51

van Til, Jacqueline, 45-47

Van Til, Jon, 160 forward, 162-163, 168, 181-182, 188, 189, 191, 229, 247-257, 266-267, 269-270, 278, 318, 332, 338, 376, 397, 413-414, 428, 432, 435, 448, 450, especially chapters 51, 52

Van Til, Justin, 397 forward, 402, 414-415, especially chapters 51, 52

Van Til Lecture Series, 449-450, 458-459

Van Til, Linda (Bautz), 376, 397, 402, 414

Van Til, Maria (Mitchell), 5-6, 13, 51-53

Van Til on Education, 400-401

Van Til, Ross Heller, 397 forward, 414-415, especially chapters 51-52

Van Til, Roy, 189 forward, 191, 229, 247-257, 267, 270, 277-278, 294, 318, 338, 376, 390, 397, 402-403, 406-408, 413-414, 435, 448, especially chapters 51, 52

Van Til, William Joseph, 5-6, 12-17, 19, 26, 28-31, 37, 43, 46-47, 48, 50-54, 68, 75

Van Til Writing Award (ISU), 450-451

Vars, Gordon E, 230, 319-321, 343, 452-453

Vietnam War, 333, 349

W

War years, 163, 164-170, 171-192 (*see also* World War 11)

Ward, Douglas, 181-186, 213, 379

Warren, Paul, 276, 323

Wars over religion, 4-6, 8, 31, 50-53, 75, 131, 270, 277

Warwick (New York) (*see* New York State Training School for Boys)

Wats, Dr., 388-389

Watson, Goodwin, 287

Wedding anniversaries, 145, 151, 160, 163, 454-465

Weddings, 131-132, 338-339

Weinandy, Janet, 133-134, 140-142, 397

Weinandy, Paul, 133-134, 136-137, 140-142, 153, 164, 397, 434

Weir, Edward, 212

Westfall, Byron, 336, 340

What I Have Learned, 442-446

What Popular Magazines Say About Education (pamphlet), 211

White, Charles S., 212-213

White, Ellis, 277

Wilhelms, Fred T., 183, 185-186, 192, 211, 319-320, 351-355, 357, 360, 394, 419, 437

Willey, Richard, 401
  colloquium committee 449

Willis, Margaret, 121

Wirth, Fremont, 269

Woodring, Paul, 325

Workshops,
  Columbia, 199, 204
  Kansas City (Missouri), 188-189, 204
  Langston University (Oklahoma), 316
  Ohio University (Ohio), 166-167, 204

477